Fighting the French Revolution

To Jackie with love
(and appreciation for your patience)

Fighting the French Revolution

Revolution

The Great Vendée Rising of 1793

by Rob Harper

Pen & Sword
MILITARY

First published in Great Britain in 2019 by
Pen & Sword Military
An imprint of
Pen & Sword Books Ltd
Yorkshire – Philadelphia

ISBN 978 1 47386 896 0

A CIP catalogue record for this book is
available from the British Library.

Printed and bound in the UK by TJ International Ltd, Padstow, Cornwall.

Pen & Sword Books Limited incorporates the imprints of Atlas, Archaeology,
Aviation, Discovery, Family History, Fiction, History, Maritime, Military, Military
Classics, Politics, Select, Transport, True Crime, Air World, Frontline Publishing,
Leo Cooper, Remember When, Seaforth Publishing, The Praetorian Press,
Wharncliffe Local History, Wharncliffe Transport, Wharncliffe True Crime and
White Owl.

For a complete list of Pen & Sword titles please contact

PEN & SWORD BOOKS LIMITED
47 Church Street, Barnsley, South Yorkshire, S70 2AS, England
E-mail: enquiries@pen-and-sword.co.uk
Website: www.pen-and-sword.co.uk

Or

PEN AND SWORD BOOKS
1950 Lawrence Rd, Havertown, PA 19083, USA
E-mail: Uspen-and-sword@casematepublishers.com
Website: www.penandswordbooks.com

Contents

Glossary of Political Factions and Terms

Ancien Régime: The regime in place before the French Revolution.

Ci-devant: 'Former': A term derisively used in reference to officers who could claim noble descent.

Committee of Public Safety (CPS): Created in April 1793 following the treason of Dumouriez and the outbreak of the Vendée Rising. It was formed of nine (later twelve) members, appointed for a month at a time, from Deputies of the National Convention. It was effectively the executive government of France responsible for internal and external security and in time came to direct the Convention. Danton controlled it in the early months but it was firmly under Robespierre's influence from late July 1793. The conduct of the war and appointment of generals was a key function of the CPS.

Enragés: Literally the 'madmen' or 'enraged'. The most extreme of Revolutionary movements who assisted in the violent overthrow of the Girondists. Their core leadership would be crushed by the Montagnards in September 1793. Many were absorbed into the Hébértist faction.

Girondists: A loosely organised group of Jacobins formed around Jacques–Pierre Brissot and other Deputies from the Gironde. They were in effective control from 1792 until 2 June 1793 and sought to weaken the grip on power held in Paris and backed by the Paris Commune, by promoting a less centralised and more federal form of government. Their attempts to stem the power of the Paris Commune led to their downfall. Supporters were sometimes called Federalists.

Hébértists: Followers of policies espoused by Jacques Hébért, considered more radical than the Montagnards, notoriously anti-Christian, and determined to destroy the Girondists, they manipulated the National Convention through their power within the Paris Commune. They endured a fierce power struggle with the Montagnards in late 1793 and were brought down in March 1794. Leading figures included Bourbotte, Ronsin, Momoro and Carrier.

Montagnards: Known as 'the Mountain' from their habit of sitting in the upper tier of the Assembly. A Jacobin group led by Maximilien Robespierre, more extreme than the Girondists (their ideological opponents), who believed in a centralised form of government. Strongly influenced by the Jacobin Club and its links to the *sans-culottes*. They were instrumental in implementing the Terror and were effectively in power from mid-1793 until July 1794. Key figures included St-Just and Marat. Many Montagnard Representatives served in the Vendée.

National Convention: The elected assembly of deputies who formed the first republican government of France. Created September 1792.

Paris Commune: The elected governing authority for Paris, centred on the Hotel-de-Ville. It frequently refused to follow orders issued from the National Convention and exerted great influence and power during the critical days of 1793. For most of the year it was firmly under the control of the Hébértists.

Representatives on Mission: Deputies sent on mission to the Departments to apply the law and maintain order. Those sent on mission to the armies would help raise troops, maintain morale, ensure supplies, and keep an eye on the generals. During the Terror they were vested with extensive power.

Sans-culottes: Literally 'without breeches'; used to define the lower class revolutionaries who would have worn loose fitting trousers not the knee breeches associated with wealthier classes. It came to be a name proudly adopted by militant revolutionaries.

The Terror: The name given to the period between June 1793 and July 1794 when the law allowed for swift and brutal punishment through Revolutionary Tribunals, often with little formal trial. More people were executed in the region affected by the Vendée Rising than anywhere else in France. Representative Carrier was especially notorious for the implementation of the Terror and the mass execution of Vendéen rebels and refugees. The extent of his brutality resulted in his own recall and execution.

Unit of Distance Measurement

League: A distance frequently used in contemporary sources. Although, theoretically, a standard eighteenth century French league was equivalent to between 6 and 7km (depending on which league was being used), measuring the known distance referred to in several accounts indicates that the term was applied loosely. Where contemporaries do not pinpoint locations, enabling a metric distance to be inserted in the text, I have retained the use of the term 'league'.

Key to maps

D'ELBEE	Vendeen leaders or armies
	Vendee movement
KLEBER	Republican leaders or armies
	Republican movement
✕	Engagements (Republican victory has date in italics)
	Roads
⬤	Woodland
	Rivers
	Hills
	Salt marsh/wetland/flood plain
	Towns/villages (varies with scale of map)
✕	Windmills

Timeline for 1793

Date	France	Battles of the Vendée Rising Republican Victory (R), Vendéen Victory (V). Major/ strategically-significant engagements in CAPITALS.
January		
21	Execution of Louis XVI	
February		
1	France declares war on Britain and Holland.	
13	The First Coalition formed against France by Britain, Prussia, Austria, Holland, Spain and Sardinia.	
24	The National Convention decrees conscription of 300,000 men to be raised by lottery.	
March		
1	France annexes Belgium.	
4		Armed rioters force national guards out of Cholet.
7	France declares war on Spain.	
9	82 Representatives sent out to raise the 300,000.	

10	Creation of the Revolutionary Tribunal to address counter-revolutionary offences.	Machecoul (V)
10-18		Hundreds of parishes take up arms in the Vendée and large parts of surrounding Departments to resist the Lottery. Numerous settlements fall under their control.
11		Clisson (R)
12		St Florent-le-Vieil (V); St-Mesmin(V); Paimboeuf (R)
13		Jallais (V); Chemillé (V); Les Herbiers (V)
14		CHOLET (V)
15		Chantonnay (V)
16		Coron (V)
18	Dumouriez defeated at Neerwinden.	
19	Death penalty declared for rebels found bearing arms.	LA GUÉRINIÈRE (V); The Rising now refered to as the 'War in the Vendée'.
21	Revolutionary Committees of Surveillance established.	
23		Pornic, twice (V/R)
24		1st LES SABLES D'OLONNE (R)
27		Pornic (V)
29		2nd LES SABLES D'OLONNE (R)
April		
1	France evacuate Rhineland (except for Mayence (Mainz)).	St-Lambert-de-Lattay (inconclusive).

5	Dumouriez deserts to Austrians.	
6	Committee of Public Safety (CPS) established.	
8	Seige of Condé begins.	La Grassière (R)
9	Austrian army invades France. Deputies sent on mission to the armies.	
10	Seige of Mayence begins.	Roc-de-Cheffois (R)
11		ST-PIERRE-DE-CHEMILLÉ (V)
12	Marat arrested for inciting violence and murder.	La Châtaigneraie.(R)
13		LES AUBIERS (V); Challans (R); St-Gervais(R)
19		PAGANNES (V); Port-St-Père(R)
21		Machecoul (R)
22		BEAUPRÉAU (V)
24	Marat's acquittal celebrated by the *sans-culottes*.	
28		Noirmoutier (R)
30		Legé (V)
May		
2		Palluau (R)
3		Mareuil-sur-Lay (R)
4	'Maximum' price of grain fixed by law.	
5		THOUARS (V)

12	Girondist 'Commission of Twelve' established to investigate actions of the Paris Commune and Sections leads to serious disturbances.	
13		LA CHÂTAIGNERAIE (V)
15		Palluau (R)
16		1st FONTENAY-LA-COMTE (R)
23	French defeated at Famars.	
24	The Committee of Twelve orders arrest of Hébért, leading to widespread unrest in Paris instigated by the Commune. Enragés leaders arrested.	
25		2nd FONTENAY-LA-COMTE (V)
26	Robespierre and Marat call for insurrection against the Convention.	
29	Lyons revolts against Jacobin authorities.	
31	'Journée de 31 Mai': Paris Commune provokes mass demonstrations calling for expulsion of Girondist Deputies from the Convention.	

June

2	'Journée de 2 Juin': Leading Girondists ousted from Convention and twenty-nine arrested.	

6-7	Federalists take control in Caen, Bordeaux, Toulouse, Nîmes and Marseille, along with widespread national protest at the expulsion of Girondists.	
7		DOUÉ-LA-FONTAINE (V)
8		MONTREUIL-BELLAY (V)
9-10		SAUMUR (V)
10		MACHECOUL (V)
17-25		Vendéens occupy Angers
24	Democratic constitution approved by the Convention, but events cause it not to be put into effect.	
25		Parthenay (R)
29-30		NANTES (R)
30		1st Luçon (R)
July		
3		BOIS-AUX-CHÈVRES (R)
5		1st CHÂTILLON-SUR-SÈVRE (V). Nantes declares for Federalist cause.
10	Condé falls to the Allies.	
12	The Jacobins overthrown in Toulon.	
13	Charlotte Corday, a Girondist supporter, murders Marat.	
14		Château d'Aux (R)
15		MARTIGNE-BRIAND (R). Nantes authorities retract declaration of 5th.

18		VIHIERS (V).
23	Fall of Mayence.	
25		Pont Charron and Pont Charrault (R)
26		LES PONTS-DE-CÉ (V)
27	Robespierre elected to the CPS which uses Terror to maintain its position.	
28	Fall of Valenciennes.	LES PONTS-DE-CÉ (R)
30		2nd LUÇON (R)

August

1	A policy of destruction of the Vendée agreed by the Convention.	
5		Doué-la-Fontaine (R)
9	Seige of Lyons begins.	
14	Carnot elected to CPS.	3rd LUÇON (R)
23	Levée-en-Masse ordered.	
24	The Duke of York beseiges Dunkirk.	
25	The Republic recaptures Marseilles.	
26		La Roche-sur-Yon (R)
26–31		Assaults on NAUDIÈRES and SORINIÈRES (R)
27	The Allies occupy Toulon.	

September

5	*Sans-culotte* invasion of the Convention. Terror becomes 'the order of the day'.	CHANTONNAY (V); assaults on NAUDIÈRES and SORINIÈRES (R)
7		Érigné (R)

8	French victory at Hondschoote raises Seige of Dunkirk.	
11		Martigné-Briand (V)
12	Le Quesnoy falls to the allies.	ÉRIGNÉ and LES PONTS-DE CÉ (inconclusive)
14		THOUARS (R); DOUÉ-LA-FONTAINE (R)
16		1st MONTAIGU (R)
17	'Law of Suspects' embraces all opposed to the Republic.	
18	Seige of Toulon begins. Bordeaux recaptured by the Republic.	VIHIERS (V)
19		PONT-BARRÉ (V); TORFOU (V)
21		2nd MONTAIGU (V)
22	The Spanish Army breaks through the Pyrenees.	Pursuit of Canclaux (V); ST-FULGENT (V)
29	The 'General Maximum' decreed to control food prices and wages.	Noirmoutier (R)
28	The allies beseige Maubeuge.	
30		Réaumur (inconclusive)

October

1	Barère calls once again for the destruction of the Vendée.	
2	Policy of de-Christianisation accelerates under extreme factions.	
6		TREIZE-SEPTIERS (R)
9	Lyons surrenders.	Bois-aux-Chèvres (R)

10	The French government declared 'revolutionary until the peace' handing absolute power to the CPS and suspending the constitution.	
11		CHÂTILLON-SUR-SÈVRES twice (V/R)
12		NOIRMOUTIER (V)
13	French defeated at Weissenberg Lines, Landau beseiged. Danton leaves Paris for his home town of Arcis-sur-Aube exhausted and sickened by developments in Paris.	
15		LA TREMBLAYE (R)
16	Marie-Antoinette guillotined. French victory at Wattignies raises Seige of Maubeuge.	
17		CHOLET (R)
23		LAVAL (V)
Night of 24-25		La Croix-Bataille (V)
26		ENTRAMMES (V)
28		Craon (V)
31	Leading Girondists executed in Paris.	Saint-Gilles (R)

November

2		Ernée (V)
3		FOUGÈRES (V)
6	Philippe Égalité (former Duke of Orléans) guillotined.	

10	Festival of 'Liberty and Reason' celebrated.	
14-15		SIEGE OF GRANVILLE (R)
17	Robespierre orders arrest of Danton's supporters.	
18		PONTORSON (V)
20	Danton returns to Paris and calls for restraint and 'indulgence' towards opponents.	
20-23		DOL-ANTRAIN (V)
		La Garnache (inconclusive)
28-30	Hoche defeated at Kaiserslautern.	

December

3-4		SIEGE OF ANGERS (R)
4	The Law of Revolutionary Government increases power of CPS.	
5		Beauvoir (R)
6		Bouin (R)
7		Lége (R)
7-8		LA FLÈCHE (V)
9		Clermont (V)
10		Pontlieue (V)
11		Les Quatre-Chemins (V)
12		Pontlieue (twice) (V/R); Arnage (R)
12 -13		LE MANS (R)
13		Boupère (V)

19	Fall of Toulon.	Ancenis (R)
20		Réaumur and Pouzages (R)
21		Cerizay (V)
22–23		SAVENAY (R), the end of the 'Great War of the Vendée'.
26	Austro–Prussian defeat at Geisberg liberates Alsace.	Pont-James (V)
31	General Biron guillotined.	Machecoul (V)

Introduction

On 1 October 1793, with republican armies massing on the borders of the Vendée, Bertrand de Barère, member of the Committee of Public Safety, called on the armies to strike hard and put an end to 'this inexplicable war'.[1] In August he had used similar language, believing it a duty of the new Republic to cut out this running sore, symbolic of all that the Revolution despised. His fresh call for the destruction of the Vendée was enthusiastically supported by the National Convention, and once again armies were on the march.

The year 1793 witnessed the near destruction of the new French Republic by external and internal enemies. The year had barely begun when Louis XVI was publicly executed and as the year progressed decrees poured out of the National Convention vying in their eloquence, ruthlessness and passionate appeals to *La Patrie* as the early victories of 1792 turned to a succession of defeats.

The Paris Commune dominated the brutal politics of 1793 and during this tumultuous year Maximilien Robespierre would rise to prominence and take control of the National Convention. But while life and death political struggles were underway in Paris, the west of France, centred on the Vendée, rose up en masse against the same revolution that had supposedly brought *liberté, égalité and fraternité* to the people.

The war was sparked when the National Convention introduced enforced conscription by lottery, as France had been haemorrhaging men and volunteer numbers had dwindled. Yet the Vendée region chose to fight against the Revolution and all that it represented rather than fight the nation's enemies on the country's frontiers.

The Vendée Rising is a complex war and contemporary accounts, written in the heat of the moment, are often couched in politicised and extreme language. Napoleon called it a 'War of Giants' and in this ferocious conflict some of his future elite began their rise to fame, including men such as Grouchy, Cambronne, Kléber, Berthier and Marulaz. Yet this war also led many to an appointment with the 'national razor'.

The largely rural population of the region was faced with a brutal policy of repression and some would argue even one of genocide. The Revolutionary Tribunal, declaration of death to rebels without mercy, and Terror becoming the order of the day were all, in part, a direct response to the Vendée Rising. The near anarchy in government led to the suspension of the constitution 'until the peace as the Committee of Public Safety slowly and ruthlessly sought to save the French Revolution. In this titanic struggle both sides fought with armies that grew to tens of thousands of men, of all arms, and of remarkable resilience. Yet few battles are mentioned in military histories and, inexplicably, the conflict is generally overlooked or sidelined in books on the French Revolutionary Wars. I hope this book helps to redress the

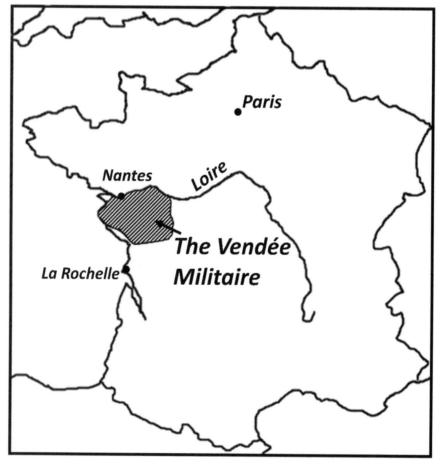

Area affected by the Vendée Rising.

balance and introduce an English-speaking audience to a largely forgotten yet pivotal struggle.

I have endeavoured to take the reader chronologically through the period known as the 'Great War' that continued relentlessly from March to December 1793, and have set out to combine into the narrative a clear appreciation of the fighting capabilities of the republican and royalist armies that appeared and disappeared through that tumultuous period.

I have retained French spellings for all place names and officer ranks which do not have direct English counterparts. As many army and unit titles are long, I have felt it necessary to abbreviate them to save on space. So, for example, the *Grande Armée Catholique et Royale* has largely been abbreviated to the Grand Army, and battalions (notably the Departmental Volunteers) have been shortened from titles such *as 9th Bataillon de la Gironde* to 9th Gironde.

Commonly known as the Vendée Rising, the area of the troubles also embraced large parts of Maine-et-Loire, Deux-Sevrès and Loire-Inférieure, and the area controlled by the rebels became known as the *Vendée Militaire*. For simplicity, and following common contemporary practice, the people of the region that rose up against the Republic are generally referred to as royalist, rebels or Vendéens (using the French spelling).

Only a few years before 1793 the region had largely fallen within Poitou and Anjou and the Vendéen armies often identified themselves with these older names. Many also used more localised names, examples being: the *Maraichains* (for those from the coastal marshland called the *Marais*) or the *Paydraits* (for the area south-west of Nantes known as the *Pays-de-Retz*). Where relevant, such titles are occasionally used.

It is important to be clear that the Vendée Rising is completely different to, and mostly separate from, the Chouan Risings north of the Loire. In essence the Vendée Rising was much more effective at inspiring a wide area to rise up en masse and was far more of a threat to the Republic as a result.

Chapter 1

Fighting the Revolution, a Brief Background to the Vendée Rising

On 21 January 1793 Louis XVI was led by tumbrel to the Place de la Révolution in Paris. As he attempted to address the crowd his voice was drowned out by a drum roll ordered by General Berruyer. With a swift drop of the blade the King of France was dead. This single act pushed several European powers to war with France. Indeed France, in a heightening of tension, declared war on Britain and the Low Countries in February, and Spain in March.

The Girondist faction within the National Assembly had enthusiastically led France into war in 1792 and the early victories secured their power base. Following a series of defeats their more extreme opponents, the Montagnards, gained significant influence and gradually pushed the country towards a period of dictatorship led by the Committee of Public Safety (hereafter referred to as the CPS).

The vast majority of people in the Vendée region, indeed in much of France, were deeply shocked by the attacks on the monarchy and also by attacks on the Catholic Church. As early as July 1790 all parish priests were ordered to swear an oath of loyalty to the nation and the constitution. That same November those failing to take the oath were considered to have resigned their posts. With the Pope speaking out against the Revolution and this Civil Constitution, priests were placed in an unenviable position: choose between loyalty to the Republic or loyalty to the Church. The Republic stigmatised the Pope as a foreigner and had decided that *they* would appoint the bishops and the clergy, *not* the Pope.

By November 1791 'non-juring' priests, as those refusing to sign the Civil Constitution were known, were put under surveillance and placed under threat of imprisonment or exile if they attempted to hold services. By August 1792 many priests were emigrating and numerous religious houses closing and in September of that year the infamous massacres in the Paris prisons included over 200 priests and 3 ex-bishops. From expulsion of priests, the Revolution now appeared to be sanctioning their murder.

A sizeable minority of priests decided to defy the government and remain. The Vendée region retained many non-juring priests who held services in secret, while the state-sponsored priests faced endless problems and even direct threats.

The anti-Catholic policy, a product of the more extreme influences within the Convention, was undoubtedly a fundamental factor in provoking the Vendée Rising, and the emblem of the *Sacre-Coeur*, 'the Sacred Heart of Christ', became the universal badge under which the rebels fought.

Across the region, as priests were being imprisoned or thrown out of their parishes, so the initial murmuring began to spill into localised troubles. These took on a much more serious form in August 1792 when the civil authorities sought to recruit volunteers to fight for the Republic. On 22 August, in the Bressuire area towards the east of the region, Baudry d'Asson, a former army officer, gathered 6,000 peasants. The vast majority were armed with pitchforks or clubs and they marched on and seized Châtillon-sur-Sèvre, the focus of the recruitment. On the following day they headed for Bressuire, but national guards and local detachments reached the town first and frustrated attempts by the rebels to seize the town. On 24 August the rebels were routed at a place called Moulin-Cornet and a period of repression followed.

While attacks on the Church were a focus of anger there were other contributory factors. This overwhelmingly rural region was witnessing a new, largely urban, *bourgeoisie* exploiting the nationalisation of church property. These 'outsiders' were seen to be benefitting from the Revolution while the more isolated communities, tied to the land, experienced incessant interference and increasing attacks on their traditional way of life.

Perhaps unusually, the area seems to have retained a strong bond between a paternalistic local gentry closely engaged and identified with their local communities in the rhythms of seasonal and religious life. As a consequence there seemed to be little open animosity between the rural communities and the gentry often associated with the French Revolution.

Attacks on the church, monarchy and gentry were seen in this region as attacks on the community as a whole. Fundamentally, however, the rebels fought under the dual banner of Church and King and for their own liberty and freedom of conscience. It would be wrong to assume, however, that the area was entirely antagonistic to the Republic, as it had furnished volunteers in 1791 and 1792, and there were 'patriots' in evidence across the area.

The Conscription of 300,000 men

The opportunity to challenge the regime presented itself in March 1793 when the Convention, in desperate need of troops, resorted to the conscription of 300,000 men. These were to be gathered by drawing lots from all eligible males (i.e. healthy single men aged between 18 and 40). Replacements could be purchased and national guards were excluded.

The Vendée was ordered to raise 4,197; the Loire-Inférieure 7,372, and Maine-et-Loire 6,202.

Officials immediately set about organising the lottery and instructions trickled down from the Department to the local administrators, with notice given to each area as to when and where the lottery would be enacted. General Verteuil, in command of the 12th Military District, was ordered to send fifty national guards to Fontenay, La Châtaigneraie and Montaigu, and one hundred to Les Sables d'Olonne and Challans. 'to maintain the peace and assist with the recruitment'.[1] Ominously, however, the region had been stripped of line regiments and in the Vendée Department there were only 1,300 thinly spread troops.[2]

In February 1793 efforts had been underway to recruit to the National Guard in anticipation of a repeat of the previous year's troubles. This met with a violent reaction in the coastal area and the administrators of the district of Challans were expressing concern that the region seemed to be on the verge of rising up en masse.[3]

With news that enforced conscription was coming, many young men from a wide area, focused on the Vendée, were determined to oppose the lottery and, if deemed necessary, were quite prepared to take up arms against the French Republic.

Many areas across France would react to the increasing extremism of the Republic but, while numerous disturbances were quickly suppressed, the Vendée Rising spiralled out of control.

The Region and its People

Royalists idealise the Vendée rebels as noble and devout peasants fighting for God and the imprisoned boy-king Louis XVII, while republicans prejudge them as ignorant, misguided fanatics, led by priests and aristocrats.

It is true to say that the majority of the people were tied to their region and very much influenced by their traditional rural way of life. There were very few towns of note. The largest, Cholet, had a population of only 8,500 and a handful of towns were over 5,000 strong.[4] The population of the entire region of the *Vendée Militaire* totalled around 755,000, including patriotic towns and villages in its fringes.[5]

Economically this fertile and relatively isolated region focused mainly on small scale cattle or crop farming, with vineyards towards the Loire, salt marshes towards the sea, and few local industries of note. The region had few well-maintained roads, with only that from Nantes to La Rochelle, through Montaigu and Luçon, considered good. The main route connecting Saumur to Cholet, La Roche-sur-Yon and La Mothe-Achard (where it joined the Nantes to Les Sables d'Olonne road) was only good for short stretches.[6] Many other roads were little better than tracks and, for those unfamiliar with the area, could become an impenetrable maze.

Many rivers also cut across the area. The most strategically significant were the Loire, Sèvre-Nantaise, Layon, Grand Lay and Petit Lay. The Sèvre-Nantaise cut across the region in a south-easterly direction from Nantes and for long stretches was a formidable and well-wooded barrier. Bridges, such as Pont-Charron and Pont-Charrault on the Lay, Pont-Barré on the Layon, and Les Ponts-de-Cé on the Loire, all became hotly contested.

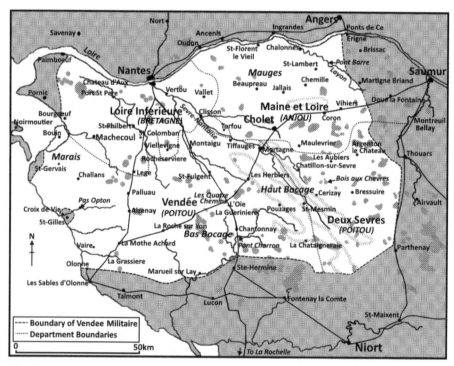

The Vendée-Militaire.

The largely flat coastal plain was known as the Marais and was distinguished by vast salt marshes towards Les Sables d'Olonne and Noirmoutier, with distinctive raised causeways cut up by man-made waterways that were difficult to negotiate at all times of the year. Bouin, a town on the mainland east of Noirmoutier, formed an island within these marshes.

The Bocage (often distinguished between the Haut-Bocage, the more elevated eastern half, and the Bas-Bocage to the west) was characterised by high-hedged small fields and deep holloways in an area of rolling hills and wooded river valleys. The Mauges, although less hilly, was otherwise not dissimilar.

The farms and town houses were generally modest in size and built in a dull sandy-brown stone, with low-pitched roofs topped with red clay pantiles (except in the Marais where single-storey thatched cottages were common). The many isolated farms formed small fortresses surrounded by high-hedged fields, each a challenging obstacle for republican troops. There were few large châteaux and the influence of Catholicism was evident in the many churches, chapels and wayside crosses.

Chapter 2

'Patriots, Robbers and Cowards': The Republican Armies in the Vendée Rising

To appreciate the nature of the War it is important to understand the organisation and quality of the opposing forces.

The War in the Vendée became the responsibility of the Army of the La Rochelle Coast and part of the Army of the Brest Coast. These armies were formed from the Army of the Reserve in April 1793. In October they were merged, with the Army of Mayence, into a new Army of the West. North of the Loire, contingents from the Army of the Cherbourg Coast also became involved.

For most of the period these armies operated in independent columns, often as divisions of a few thousand men. At least until the summer these divisions had an ad-hoc structure and included a handful of cavalry and some cannon.

The part of the Army of the Brest Coast involved in the War managed to retain a stable command structure until October, while the generals of the Army of the La Rochelle Coast went through a succession of appointments, dismissals and executions. The arrival of the Army of Mayence was meant to help end the war quickly but only heightened political tension.

Before the Revolution the French army was essentially one of volunteers, but the rank and file were generally from the worst elements of society. By late 1790 they lacked 30,000 men and, in time of war, if recruits were not volunteering in sufficient numbers, the government would resort to the use of the unpopular *milice*: forced recruitment through the drawing of lots.[1]

The Creation of a National Guard

At the beginning of the Revolution there was a rush to establish a National Guard to combat fears of an aristocratic backlash. Enlistment was voluntary but was not open to the poorer classes. On paper the National Guard seemed a formidable body of troops and in mid-1790 totalled 2,571,700 across France.[2] Most of the national guards in and around the Vendée-Militaire became embroiled in the conflict.

The Volunteers of 1791

There were numerous calls for volunteers between June 1791 and August 1793, broadly categorised as the Volunteers of 1791, 1792 and 1793. The following is a brief overview.

In January 1791, with the regular army lacking over 50,000 men, a reserve force of 300,000 volunteers was created from the existing National Guard, to be enlisted for one campaign only in time of war. They were activated in June 1791, after the royal family attempted to flee France, and were better paid than their regular counterparts. They were considered to be of good quality and patriotic.

Meanwhile, over sixty per cent of the officer corps in the regular army left France during 1791-2, heightening suspicion over the loyalty of the regulars.

The Volunteers of 1792

There were many recruitment drives in 1792:

- In January a levy of voluntary enlistment into existing line regiments was ordered.
- On the declaration of war in April all existing volunteer battalions were increased from 571 to 800 men and a further thirty-one battalions were raised: still only from tax paying citizens.
- On 31 May fifty-four 'Free Companies' (*compagnies-franches*) were levied.
- In June every canton in France was ordered to send five national guardsmen to a camp near Paris to take part in the annual celebration of the 14th of July and protect the area while troops were rushed to the frontiers. Known as *fédérés* they were formed into eighteen battalions and some later fought in the Vendée.
- Also in June an auxiliary reserve of 100,000 men was levied (75,000 for the army, 25,000 for the navy). These had been recruited in June 1791, paid a retainer and remained at home, but could be called out for up to a six month period if required.[3]
- In July, with the country 'in danger', a further levy brought existing volunteer and regular battalions up to strength and created forty-two new volunteer battalions. Any citizen could now join up. These troops would only have to serve for one campaign (although 50,000 sent to line regiments signed on for three years).

- In July a levy of chasseurs and grenadiers was taken from existing national guards battalions for the Army of the Centre.
- In August a further levy of 30,000 from the Departments around Paris was instigated.

The 'Volunteers of 1792', as many of these became known, were in general considered poorer in quality than those of 1791, although evidence from Seine-et-Marne shows little demographic difference between the recruits of 1791 and 1792.[4]

By the end of 1792 the regulars and volunteers were at last paid the same.

The Levies of 1793

With the onset of 1793 vast numbers of volunteers completed their service and left the army, but the Republic needed troops quickly:

- In February 1793 the National Convention ordered the conscription of 300,000 men by drawing lots, sparking the Vendée Rising.
- On 27 April, Departments were asked to carry out a further levy of troops to fight in the Vendée. This helped raise the Orléans battalions.
- On 24 June an urgent voluntary levy to race to the defence of Nantes was instigated.
- In August 1793, mass conscription was ordered. All single able-bodied men aged between 18 and 25 were immediately called up. Many became embroiled in battles in the Vendée.

The Republic Troops in the Vendée Rising

The scale of the Vendée Rising took the Republic completely by surprise and by late March they were frantically organising divisions in attempts to suppress the revolt.

The year 1793 was one of experimentation, as demonstrated in the many unit types. These troops needed to be equipped, clothed and fed, all of which was an immense challenge and none of which was necessarily successful.

In the Vendée there were frequent appeals for shoes, claims that troops were half-starved, nearly naked and poorly armed, and troops were being armed with short pikes due to a lack of muskets, particularly amongst the levy battalions. On 30 March, Generals Berruyer and La Bourdonnaye reported that of their 18,500 men, 7–8,000 lacked *fusils*.[5]

As a further example, on 25 August the 2,404 men of General Joly's 1st Brigade of the Army of the La Rochelle Coast lacked 800 chemises (shirts), 343 pairs of gaiters, 363 pairs of shoes, 500 bonnets-de-police (cloth caps) and 386 pantalons. The lack of reference to bicornes in any of his returns may imply that his men were wearing bonnets-de-police in their place.[6]

In June the representatives characterised the republican troops in Niort as follows: old soldiers of the line who were well-armed but badly clothed; volunteers who were badly armed, badly clothed and undisciplined; and requisitioned national guards who were badly armed, badly dressed, undisciplined and with many deserting.[7] Five hundred of these latter had been imprisoned.[8]

Having made an inspection of the Army of the La Rochelle Coast in late May, Ronsin reported only 10,000 of 28,000 men in a state to fight, and Biron told the Ministry of War that the Paris battalions in Niort were refusing to fight without their cannon.[9] In September, General Tuncq remarked that the often-defeated army had only been created 'to furnish the rebels with cannon, arms, supplies and munitions'.[10] Representative Carrier's report of 12 November follows the same theme:[11]

'I found in the Saumur column a crowd of robbers and cowards, who furnished every kind of communication to the brigands of the Vendée to such a degree that when the latter were in any need they said "Let us march on Saumur and we shall get what we want"…There are few patriots and few brave men among them…The Luçon column is composed of some good battalions, but there are some who do not hear the sound of battle without alarm. There are brave soldiers in the Châtillon column but many are also cowards!'

Insubordination was rife among many volunteer battalions, notably those from the Paris Sections. Add to that the interference from the representatives of the people and commissaires and you begin to appreciate why the revolt spiralled out of control. It was only after the capture of Saumur in June that the Convention really started to take the Rising seriously. However, in the summer, *sans-culotte* generals such as Rossignol, L'Échélle, Santerre and Muller were promoted beyond their ability and veteran officers such as Kléber or Canclaux treated with suspicion.

The troops would be trained according to the Regulations of 1791 and would become familiar with deploying in line, echelon, square and column of attack. When deploying in defence the infantry would generally try to form up in two parallel lines, one behind the other, with a reserve of infantry, and cavalry on the flanks or also in reserve. Artillery was generally split up along the front line, with some retained in an artillery park or reserve.

Patriotic civilians were also involved in defending their towns and villages and small numbers of customs officials, naval and river personnel also became involved.

The National Guard

Many towns in the region had units of national guards ranging from a few dozen to thousands for a city like Nantes. In turbulent regions like the *Vendée Militaire* there was difficulty recruiting to the National Guard, particularly in the rural areas. If Nantes followed the normal pattern, their national guard would have been organised into battalions of 500 men (including a pair of 4pdr guns).[12]

The national guard wore what became the standard regulation uniform for the later revolutionary period, although there was some variation between units and many were in reality poorly armed and in civilian dress so on occasion were mistaken for rebels. Their primary role was to defend their locality or quell localised troubles and the War forced many into battle.

Numerous small cavalry units also frequently appear in army returns.

Gendarme Divisions

Two mixed units known as the 35th and 36th Divisions Gendarmerie, of around 500 and 800 men respectively, performed well in several battles, and elements of other Gendarmerie 'Divisions' were also involved. The 36th Division, famously commanded by Rossignol, was formed from men who had stormed the Bastille and proudly bore the name *Vanqueurs de la Bastille*. Two companies from the Grenadiers of the Convention linked with them before marching to the Vendée, which accounts for their greater strength.

Gendarme Cavalry

Local mounted units of gendarmes formed improvised bodies of cavalry and regularly feature in battles in the Vendée. They generally performed very badly and often refused to charge.

The Regular Infantry

The small numbers of regulars deployed in this War were supposedly the best trained troops, although their depleted ranks were filled with raw recruits just like any volunteer battalion. They were divided into line regiments and light (chasseur) battalions.

Most line regiments wore the regulation white uniform (although a few wore *habits* (jackets) of sky blue or red) and were formed into battalions of eight fusilier companies and one of grenadiers; the grenadiers often detached into ad-hoc columns of mixed arms. 'Tirailleurs' were formed by extracting small numbers of men from each company specifically trained in sharpshooting and skirmishing. Most regular battalions in the Vendée were chronically understrength.

According to Bittard-de-Portes, rumours spread in republican ranks that the rebels would spare line troops and only targeted national guards. The republicans in Nantes, therefore, dressed the 34th Line like national guards.[13]

Chasseur battalions were formed into eight chasseur companies and one of carabiniers, although in the Vendée the regular chasseur units largely operated as detached companies.

The Convention was defended by a battalion formed in 1792 commonly known as the Grenadiers of the Convention. They were formed into a battalion of four companies totalling 400 men and were recruited from across the army. Highly regarded, they were in the Vendée from April 1793.

Line Cavalry

Line regiments in the Vendée, several formed by merging volunteer cavalry units, included the 7th, 8th, 9th and 11th Hussars,[14] several understrength regiments of chasseurs (7th, 12th, 13th, 13th bis, 14th, 24th and small detachments of the 2nd, 8th and 10th), and the 16th and 19th Dragoon. Barely any heavy cavalry fought in the region.

Volunteers

The vast majority of troops were volunteer battalions named after their Department of origin. They generally wore a uniform based on that of the national guards and were formed into eight companies: seven of fusiliers and one of grenadiers. As with the line regiments the grenadiers were often detached.

Volunteer Chasseurs

These units were dressed in a wide array of uniforms, mostly with green or blue coats but varying coloured facings, and often only one or two companies strong. They bore titles such as Chasseurs-du-Midi and many such units fought in the region.

Beysser's Volunteer Cavalry

Formed by Beysser on 7 March 1793 as the 21st Chasseurs, on 20 April they totalled 200 cavalry, including part of his former regiment the 'Dragons de Lorient'. Both units were dressed in scarlet jackets with black lapels, collar and turnbacks (all piped-red); they were in Nantes on 25 June and were later redesignated the 15th Chasseurs.[15] They totalled 225 men in September.

The Légions

A number of volunteer units were formed into Légions: a mixture of light infantry, cavalry and artillery.[16] Those involved in the Vendée were:

Légion-de-la-Fraternité

Formerly the Légion-Germanique they were renamed the Légion-de-la-Fraternité in May 1793 after a purge of 'suspect' officers.

When formed in 1792 it comprised four squadrons of light-cuirassiers (cuirassiers-legérs) totalling 500 men; four squadrons of pikemen (piconniers) and dragoons, totalling 150 pikemen and 350 dragoons; two battalions of chasseurs-à-pied, each of four companies of 120 men; one battalion of arquebusiers totalling 480 men (200 armed with arquebuses); and a company of artillery totalling 158 men. About 1,000 served in the Vendée under Colonel Beffroy, including 122 cuirassiers, and on their arrival only 600 were considered fit for immediate action, the rest being without arms or uniforms.[17]

It was commonly believed that a number of the Swiss Guard, who had escaped the massacre at the storming of the Tuileries Palace, ended up in this Légion, only to desert to the rebels and form the famous Swiss Company.[18]

The light-cuirassiers wore buff jackets and highly unusual armour, comprising a helmet that protected the head and neck, metal scales protecting the throat, and iron armour covering the arms, thighs, chest and back. The horses may have had chainmail coats.[19]

The pikemen and dragoons were dressed in green jackets with tarleton helmets and tricolor plumes; red lapels; red or white turnbacks; white collar and shoulder straps (the latter piped-red); and sky blue cuffs with red cuff-flaps. The saddle cloth was dark-green edged red. The chasseurs are shown in a similar uniform but with short light-infantry gaiters. The arquebusiers seem to have been differentiated by black lapels and collar and the artillery are shown in a dark blue uniform with red epaulettes and white-piped black collar.

On 26 June the cavalry became the 24th Chasseurs and, in August, the 11th Hussars (at which point the infantry became the 22nd Chasseurs-à-Pied).[20] General Tuncq remarked that the 11th Hussars were dressed in 'colours confused with those of the brigands', implying they were very badly clothed.[21]

Légion-du-Nord

Created in May 1792, this légion fought on the northern frontier. They arrived in the Vendée in mid-June 1793 when they comprised two battalions of chasseurs-à-pied (1,130 men); four squadrons of chasseurs-à-cheval (365 men); and two 8pdr cannon and four caissons (although soon increased to eight cannon described as horse artillery).[22] The infantry were down to 267 men on 27 September.[23]

Both the infantry and cavalry wore sky blue uniforms with the collar, fringeless epaulettes, pointed cuffs and piping to their boots all in green. They wore a white-over-green plume on an unusual Henry IV style hat. The infantry wore a sword hung from a waist belt. The cavalry are shown on a sheepskin saddlecloth with a sky blue dog's-tooth fringe.

Légion-de-Rosenthal

Formed in September 1792, this légion comprised 237 chasseurs-à-pied formed into three companies and 75 horse in two companies, later increased to 300 foot and 400 horse.[24] They arrived in April and their 'deplorable indiscipline' was noted by Representative Carra.[25] In June the cavalry became the 19th Chasseurs-à-Cheval. Their uniform was green with straight-cut facings, white breeches and a tarleton helmet.

Légion-des-Ardennes

Fifty chasseurs-à-pied from this légion accompanied Westermann in late June.[26]

Légion-Nantaise

This légion was created by the Girondist Deputy, Coustard-de-Massy, on 7 June 1793. It comprised two battalions, each roughly 1,000 strong, and some cavalry and artillery. They first went into action on 20 June.[27]

Légion-des-Alpes

Sent to the region in April, the cavalry are shown in bicornes and a sky blue long-tailed jacket with red piping, collar and pointed cuffs; their trousers are variously shown as buff or sky blue, piped yellow. [28]

Légion-des-Francs

This légion was formed by merging several volunteer companies during the Siege of Mayence, to which was added a squadron of chasseurs-à-cheval. On arrival in the Vendée they totalled 120 horse and 399 foot. They are shown wearing a green jacket with white lapels (piped-red) and red collar, cuffs and turnbacks, although were probably quite varied in appearance.

Compagnies-Franches

The many independent free companies generally dressed in green or blue light infantry-style uniforms and many appear in army returns. The Toulouse Company was praised for its contribution during the First Battle at Fontenay, whereas the Volunteers of Barbézieux were troublesome to General Boulard.

Paris Battalions

Twelve battalions were raised to fight in the Vendée in May and June, comprising the Second Formation of Paris Battalions numbered 1st to 7th, 7-bis, 8th, 8-bis, 9th and 10th and often known by title and not number (for example the 5th being the Batallion-de-l'Unité). Many were over 800 strong, supported by battalion guns. They had a reputation for indiscipline, although Boulard did manage to turn some into good soldiers.

'The heroes of 500 Livres'

The infamous 'heroes of 500 livres' (the bounty paid on signing up) were raised by the *sans-culotte* General Santerre specifically to fight in the Vendée.

They were (at least in part) distinguishable by their unusual uniform which comprised a brown jacket and Breton style double-breasted buff *veste*, red lapels, pointed cuffs and turnbacks, and buff breeches and collar.

Although the battalions were strong their reputation was dreadful. Among them were the 9th Paris 'Réunion'; 4th Paris '2nd des Gauvilliers'; 8-bis Paris 'Faubourg St-Antoine'; and 7th Paris 'Mont Conseil'; all forming Santerre's Brigade in June. They are easily confused with battalions from the Second Formation due to the repetition of battalion numbers and titles.

In addition to these two levies, Paris furnished several other battalions, three companies of chasseurs-à-pied, and fifteen companies of gunners.

The Orléans Battalions

Fourteen battalions were formed at Orléans in June, specifically to fight in the Vendée, by mixing new recruits with line troops and experienced volunteer companies; including fifty-four men for each battalion sent from the Army of the North. Formed of five companies from line and four companies from volunteer regiments they would have worn a mixture of white and blue jackets.

The Fédérés-Nationaux

A few fédérés battalions are mentioned in the Vendée, notably the Half-Battalion Finistère with Leygonier in April.

Pioneer Companies

In July the Army of the Brest Coast formed nine pioneer companies, each fifty-four strong, who helped construct defences and made moving through the difficult terrain easier.[29]

The Conscripts of the 'Levée-en-Masse'

Carnot's 'Levée-en-Masse' resulted in tens of thousands of largely unarmed, untrained and poorly clothed peasants gathering in towns on the periphery of the Vendée. They were dressed as civilians and most were armed with pikes or farmyard implements. They were universally considered a liability and were gradually merged into existing units.

Volunteer Cavalry

A diverse array of volunteer cavalry units featured, rarely over squadron strength, and referred to as chasseurs, hussars or dragoons. Excluding those connected to the Légions, two of the more famous were:

Hussards-Américains

This unit was raised from freed black slaves and was officially known as the 13-bis Chasseurs. Totalling eighty-four men they were deployed in the Vendée by order of 13 May and later became a familiar sight as an escort to Representative Carrier. They wore a sky blue chasseur-style uniform with white lace, red collar, pointed-cuffs, shoulder straps and turnbacks (all piped-white), and sky blue saddlecloth piped red, white and blue. They also wore a hussar style busby.

Hussards-de-la-Mort

Only a handful of these hussars appeared in the Vendée, merged with other units, and their contribution is often exaggerated in histories of the War. They had once formed part of the famous black-uniformed hussars who fought on the northern front.[30]

Volunteer cavalry were gradually absorbed into regular regiments. For example, the Hussards-de-la-Mort, Hussards-de-l'Égalité, Chasseurs-de-Rosenthal and Hussards-de-la-Légion-des-Alpes became the 14th Chasseurs-à-Cheval.

The Artillery

The great majority of artillery comprised 4pdr battalion guns, officially two to each battalion. There were a few small artillery parks with heavier guns, although rarely a howitzer. Plenty of ordnance of widely varying calibre and age was pressed into service.

The 'artillery-volante' (a trial form of horse artillery) was utilised to good effect, but only a few such batteries are mentioned in the War.

Heavy artillery in fixed positions defended key bases such as Les Sables d'Olonne, Granville or Nantes.

Artillery trains were managed by civilian contractors who, as will be seen, frequently fled when under threat.

Gunboats

On 2 May General Menou asked for gunboats to keep the Loire under Republican control.[31] Some prevented rebels recrossing the Loire in December.

The Navy

Naval vessels supplied republican garrisons along the coast, and on at least two occasions became embroiled in combat. Naval gunners helped man Les Sables d'Olonne's cannon.

Representatives of the People and Political Commissaires

In addition to the elected representatives sent by the National Convention and attached to the armies fighting in the Vendée, there were many others who appeared in the region for whole or part of the war: inspecting the coastal defences; ensuring ports were secure; checking on the political situation in key towns; watching 'suspect' generals, representatives and troops; raising recruits; reporting on the War's progress, or in their Departments where they would become embroiled in events and remain to stiffen resolve.

While some representatives were a hindrance, others developed effective working relationships with the generals. Some were even in the forefront of battle; Merlin de Thionville was noted for his bravery.

In June a Central Commission was established in Saumur through which a group of representatives was tasked with ending the war and 'assisting' the generals in directing operations, ensuring supplies, and helping to reorganise the Army of the La Rochelle Coast. This was renewed when that army was forced back to Tours and became particularly unpleasant when the Hébértists effectively took over its functions.

Representative Carrier made interesting observations on some of the generals which indicate that some were respected, even by this notorious Hébértist (some of their biographies can be seen in Appendix 1):

'General Chalbos is a brave patriot; he has military talent but I find in him a prudence that is too sluggish for the Vendéen War… Marceau, Canuel, Muller, are ardent revolutionaries, pronounced and principled republicans, courageous, talented soldiers. What a pity that these Children of the Revolution should not have a thorough knowledge of military tactics and plans of campaign!'

Of Kléber he wrote:

> 'In battle he shows unequalled coolness and courage. He is the general who has the greatest military knowledge in the Army of the West, of Brest, and perhaps of all the republican armies. Plans of campaign, arrangements of an army, orders of march, he knows everything perfectly. He has the frankness, the speech, the habits, the *sans-culottism* of a true republican; the only defect that I can see in him is that he is a little too severe on fighting days.'

Taking a selection of others he wrote:

Vimeux 'is an old soldier who deserves the greatest esteem, an excellent patriot without Kléber's knowledge.'

Haxo 'has the coolness and bravery of Kléber without his military knowledge.'

'Beaupuy is a *ci-devant*; but what a good and brave general! He has always led the vanguard.'

Marigny 'is a brave bastard often in the thick of action. Speaking seldom, always on duty, he executed his orders punctually and precisely.'

'The brave Rossignol…can carry out movements very well in a given plan of attack or defence, but it must be acknowledged that he has no talent or initiative.'

'L'Échélle had no military talent, but what a fine republican he was! What an excellent *sans-culotte*!'

Of the Army of Mayence he noted that 'those who slander it are great scoundrels and conspirators…our successes are due to them…they profess the most pronounced and burning republicanism.'[32]

Commissaires were appointed directly by the Convention (some being representatives) and were often agents of either the CPS or the Paris Commune (which effectively ran the War Ministry for much of 1793). They were spying on everyone.

Perhaps the most infamous of these commissaires were the group who arrived in June, grandly entitled 'National Commissaires of the Executive Council'. Ronsin, 'Assistant to the Minister of War', was at their head, assisted by other unsavoury characters such as Momoro and Grammont. As the summer progressed some were appointed to senior military commands and assisted with the purge of *ci-devant* officers.

Military Depots

The war drew in tens of thousands of men and to train, arm, and equip them the Republic established a number of military depots of which the principal were La Rochelle, Niort, Tours, Orléans and Rennes. Troops and supplies were constantly moving to and from these depots and many thousands of wounded were evacuated to their hospitals.

The Treatment of Prisoners

The frequent references to the use of the guillotine is a reminder that rebels were to be shown no mercy and the infamous drownings in the Loire, primarily instigated by Representative Carrier, were to begin later in the year. There are instances of some women and children who escaped butchery, but on the whole to be captured as a rebel resulted in death.

The 'Amalgame'

Decrees of 26 February and 12 August ordered line and volunteer regiments to be merged at a ratio of one line to two volunteer battalions, renamed demi-brigades (theoretically designed to strengthen the resilience of the volunteers by adding a line unit). The 'Amalgame' only commenced in the Vendée in the late summer and the above ratio was not always applied.

Chapter 3

'For God and the King':
The Catholic and Royal Armies

During the Spring two principal armies developed, with a third group of smaller armies towards the coast: By far the largest army, formed in the north and east of the region, was soon referred to as the Army of Anjou and Haut-Poitou *(Armée-d'Anjou et Haut-Poitou)* and subsequently the Grand Army Catholic and Royal *(Grande-Armée Catholique-et-Royale)*. The Army of the Centre *(Armée-du-Centre)* recruited from the central and southern part of the region, and the many smaller armies near the coast and towards Nantes, would loosely be entitled the Army of the Pays-de-Retz and Bas-Poitou *(Armée du Pays-de-Retz et Bas-Poitou)* but as they often fought independently they commonly used more localised names.

Calling the Men to Arms

As peasant armies, the organisation was largely determined by the requirements of the peasants themselves: this meant that they would be called on to meet an immediate threat, or attain an agreed objective, then disperse back to their farms or trades until the next crisis threatened. With the exception of the winter campaign north of the Loire, when their retreat was cut off, the rebels could rarely be held together for more than a week at a time and were reluctant to go far from home, primarily regarding this as a war of defence.

Among the many ways of calling the men to arms the rebels used messengers, sounded the tocsin, and even set the sails of windmills as specific angles to alert locals to the proximity of a threat. When called to arms the peasants would gather in companies under parish captains at prearranged locations (often the parish church or town square). The companies would then merge to form divisions at larger muster points. Each peasant would take a few days' provisions, often carried in a canvas bag thrown over the shoulder.

Some women (most famously Renée Bordereau) and young teenagers fought in the Vendéen ranks and occasionally acted as spies or messengers.

Normally only half of a parish quota would gather so that the rest could continue farming. Only in dire emergences, such as during September and October, would all be summoned.

The officers were selected from all ranks of society and (with a few exceptions) their personal bravery and leadership qualities determined whether their appointment would be sustained. The most senior leaders included the peasant trader, Cathelineau; the retired colonel, Royrand; former junior army officers, D'Élbée and Bonchamps; the naval lieutenant, Charette, and the gamekeeper, Stofflet. Henri de la Rochejaquelein and the Prince de Talmont are representative of the small number from the higher nobility.

The Organisation of the Armies

There were, as noted above, only two principal units of organisation for the infantry: the parish companies and the divisions. No intermediate level of organisation existed, although varying numbers of companies might be grouped together for specific tasks before each engagement.

The Parish Companies

These companies varied in strength (although 50-100 seems average) and were led by elected parish captains supported by lieutenants, sergeants and corporals. Drummers or men with hunting horns were often attached. Populous parishes might raise several companies, and responsibility for assembling them rested with local committees led by a person of note, but never a noble.[1]

There is evidence for a degree of coercion with regard to less-than-willing locals, although occasional indiscriminate killing by republican troops left many with no option but to join the Vendéens. The armed troops would generally rely on stolen republican ammunition, but did manufacture some cartridges.

The Divisions

There was some variation in the structure of the twenty or so divisions, but they would be commanded by a general, supported by majors, ADCs, and officers with ranks such as lieutenant-general, adjudant-de-division, aide-major, and major-assistant. Other titles mentioned included commanders of outposts and parish messengers.[2]

A single division could muster anything from 1,000 to 10,000 men. Bonchamps' division was generally considered to be the most well organised and disciplined and benefitted from additional recruits from north of the Loire which may have added as many as 3-4,000 to his base of 7-8,000 men.[3]

Each division formed small bodies of permanent or elite companies from their best marksmen (generally called chasseurs or tirailleurs). In battle these companies often merged together to form the elite of the army.

The rebels also formed bodies of sappers and even had engineers in their ranks.[4]

Regular Companies

Sources generally agree that there were three 'regular' companies: the Compagnie-Francaise, the Compagnie-Suisse, and the Compagnie-Allemandes: each of about 120 to 200 troops (although their strength fluctuated). They were kept on a permanent footing and D'Élbée formalised their organisation in July.

The Compagnie-Francaise (French Company) was formed from non-Vendéen French under Joseph de Fay, formerly captain in the Régiment-de-Picardie, who joined the rebels after Saumur. He was ill for most of August and September but fought at Châtillon, Cholet and throughout the campaign north of the Loire, escaping after the battle of Savenay to join the Chouans.[5]

The Compagnie-Suisse (Swiss Company) was formed from Swiss and German deserters under Baron Keller and included a number of former Swiss Guards.

The Compagnie-Allemands (German Company) was formed mainly from German speaking deserters. Like the Compagnie-Suisse many may have come from the Légion-de-la-Fraternité. When not on campaign they often served as guards to the rebel arsenal. They were commanded by either Pivickeuham or Verdraz.[6]

By late summer the Swiss and German Companies numbered around 600 men. They had no distinctive uniform and dressed like the peasants.[7]

Compagnies-Bretonnes (Breton Companies)

The strength of these companies varied over time, but they provided a reasonably disciplined body of troops under Bonchamps' command and often fought in the front ranks. Bonchamps also led men called

'Hommes-des-Bonchamps' from within the Vendée. Both seem to have formed a semi-permanent army, paid in kind through the provision of food, clothing and weapons.

Charette's Grenadiers and Stofflet's Chasseurs-de-Roi

Towards the end of August Charette ordered each of his parishes to form their most robust men into a company of grenadiers. When necessary these could be combined into a single body of troops.[8]

Stofflet had an elite company called the Chasseurs-de-Roi which included German deserters; being from Alsace Stofflet could communicate with them in their own language.

In early September command of the Vendée-Militaire was placed under four main generals: Bonchamps, La Rochejaquelein, Charette and Lescure. Each was ordered to establish a permanent body of their bravest 1,200 men, to be drilled like line troops, and Charette's grenadiers may have been his contribution.[9] At best this can only have been partially achieved.

Republican Deserters

An unidentified number of national guards, volunteers and regulars joined the rebels, including some from the 4th, 31st and 84th Line.

The Bande-Noire

A band of scouts formed at Dol in November, called the 'bande-noire', were distinguished by a black armband on their left arm. Formed from German speaking deserters, they had a brief existence.[10]

Cavalry

By early June some German deserters were formed into a body of forty-five cavalry to form a cadre of four squadrons each of ten men; some were from the 8th Hussars.[11]

The cavalry formed slowly and comprised a minority of well-mounted men and a majority of men on farm horses, often with rope for horse gear and incapable of regular drill or deployment. They were, however, useful for gathering supplies, scouting and pursuing the enemy.

Small bodies of cavalry were attached to each division and at its peak the Grand Army mustered a few thousand, but not many could be used on the field of battle. The German deserters gained a reputation for pillaging and brutality.

According to Béjarry, Charette's cavalry was composed of gentlemen and others who had arrived with horses but held no command in the parishes. This cavalry doubled as scouts and ADCs and could form up as a body of horse to exploit victory or cover a retreat.[12]

Each division's headquarters included a small mounted escort for the most senior officers.

Artillery

In the first weeks of the war the rebels captured a range of ordnance of widely varying age and calibre. As the months passed they formed an artillery park at Mortagne-sur-Sèvre, and an arsenal in Cholet, formed from over 200 captured cannon. On campaign they rarely deployed more than forty cannon.

On the field of battle the artillery was normally split among the divisions in small units: most generally being with the centre. The vast majority of cannon served the Grand Army and many guns were harnessed to cattle.

The artillery became well organised, with caissons, supply wagons and even mobile forges. Although often poorly handled, there are instances of their use being effective. In December, D'Obenheim noted that they always had difficulty forming horse teams, lacked horseshoes, and that they did not manufacture grapeshot. They largely relied on captured munitions, although saltpetre was quarried in Chalonnes.

The Army of the Centre

There were genuine attempts to provide a more formal structure within the armies, but this was only ever partially achieved as the rebels rarely had the time they needed to develop the organisation and drill the men.

The Army of the Centre offers a good example of the level of organisation attempted by the rebels.[13]

Its Regulations were set out on 4 April. At its top was a Military Council, composed of two generals and four general officers. They planned to form four divisions from an undefined number of parish companies, these divisions taking the name of the main town in an area.

Each division was to form its own staff, consisting of a general, lieutenant general, major, two adjutants, standard bearer, surgeon, chaplain, secretary and treasurer. They were also ordered to organise a permanent company of fifty chasseurs. A fifth company, entitled the First Chasseurs, was to accompany the commander-in-chief and be 120 strong (plus nineteen officers and NCOs, a standard bearer and two drummers). White, yellow, green and red woollen plumes were planned for the four chasseur companies.

Each division was also instructed to organise twenty-five 'brave and well mounted' cavalry entitled dragoons, and a further body of sixty cavalry, with green plumes, was to be placed under a colonel to provide the guard of honour for the headquarters.

Guarding the Frontiers

Small permanent guards were established on the frontier of the Vendée Militaire, particularly along key river lines.

Prisoners

With the rapid influx of prisoners, prisons were established: notably in Montaigu, Cholet and Mortagne. Many captured republicans, however, would have their heads shaved and were then released on the promise they would not serve against the royalists for a year. If recaptured they faced execution.

La Championnière wrote that Charette rarely executed prisoners, whereas La Cathelinière took the view 'kill or be killed' and his prisoners were executed by a small man with a red beard who showed no emotion when carrying out this task.[14]

Care of the wounded

The rebels evacuated the wounded as best they could, utilising wagons and horses. They established a rudimentary system of hospitals in key towns, religious houses and deep in some forests.

Uniforms of the Vendéen Armies

The most common distinguishing mark of the Vendéen rebel was the 'Sacre-Coeur': a small patch of white cloth with a red heart, surmounted by a cross, sewn onto their jackets. White paper or cloth cockades were often seen attached to their hats.

At the second battle of Les Sables d'Olonne the rebels could be distinguished by 'little rosaries and small red strands of silk and wool'.[15]

Except for the small number of republican deserters (who must have adapted the clothing they deserted in) and a sprinkling of ex-royal army officers who chose to wear their old uniforms, the vast majority of the troops wore civilian or peasant costume.

One of the most readily distinguishable items of peasant dress was the broad-brimmed felt hat, although bicornes and woollen hats were also in evidence. A short form of top-hat, which widened at its base, was also in evidence (note the cover image of Henri de la Rochejaquelein). The chequered red-and-white scarves manufactured in Cholet had a degree of popularity in the Grand Army and the peasants generally wore their hair long.

Other common distinctions were short waist or hip-length jackets (with or without collars); loose fitting shirts; baggy breeches or trousers; and canvas gaiters and clogs (sabots), although bare feet were equally common. Most peasants clothing was made from canvas or wool and natural dyes enabled them to produce clothing of mid-blue, grey, beige, various browns, dark green and red. The jackets were often adorned with rows of buttons, as were the sides of their breeches, and wide waistbands were common.

The Marais seem to have had some specific distinctions (highlighted in Crosefinte's detailed work).[16] These included a tight-fitting jacket, cotton belt, broad-brimmed felt hat with velvet trim, and especially loose-fitting trousers. Their jackets were generally dark brown and were too narrow to button up over the chest. Crosefinte also mentions evidence for wide red or green transverse-striped waistbands; dark blue or brown raw-wool stockings protecting their lower legs and feet; and large sabots. Wool or iron-grey coats of ample size and with large hoods were commonly seen in winter. Some of Charette's men, known as the 'moutons-noire' (black sheep) wore black sheepskins in place of jackets and came from the wilder parts of the region.

Thigh length blouses, not unlike a shepherd's smock, were also common amongst the rebels; as indeed were captured items of republican clothing.

White, black and green plumes were noted among the cavalry, as was their habit of attaching captured tricolour-cockades and epaulettes to their horses' tails as a mark of derision. They also had a fashion for sporting waist belts in chequered or striped coloured fabric.[17]

Bonchamps was said to have dressed his elite companies in red and in April Stofflet formed a small body of gamekeepers dressed in green (probably the core of his elite company) and a company of elite under Sapinaud also dressed in green.[18]

In July Stofflet formed a body of dragoons, and horse and foot chasseurs (500 attached to each division) dressed in green uniforms, with white facings, and given rank distinctions. The dragoons are said to have worn helmets.[19]

In the period from March to September there was little to formally distinguish rank, although senior officers began to adopt broad white waist sashes and varying coloured headscarves beneath their hats. White, or black and white, plumes, and white scarves or black armbands tied above the left elbow, were common, black being a symbol of mourning for the executed King.

In September Bonchamps, La Rochejaquelein, Lescure and Charette were ordered to wear green jackets with white, black or green collars and, although neither La Rochejaquelein nor Charette followed the rule, green jackets became popular for officers in general.[20]

At Fougères in November, distinguishing features were made for the most senior generals:

- La Rochejaquelein, white waist sash with a black knot
- Stofflet, white waist sash with a red knot
- Marigny, white waist sash with a blue knot
- Talmont, white waist sash with a blue and gold knot

The tails to each of these sashes hung loose, while other generals simply wore the white waistband without the knot or tails. Junior officers simply wore a scarf or band on their arm, and some identification within the armbands may have distinguished their role or grade.[21]

Joly made a point of wearing peasant costume, his one concession being a white headband around his broad brimmed hat.[22]

Charette wore a variety of flamboyant uniforms, including a sash with a gold fringe and a Henry IV style hat with white plumes and gold piping.[23]

La Rochejaquelein wore a dark-blue frock coat and was soon distinguished by his headbands and scarves, such that several officers imitated him to lessen the risk that he became too easily targeted. Commissaire Benaben proudly reported that they captured his hat in the rout at Le Mans, describing it as 'surmounted with six white plumes'.[24]

Cathelineau was noted for his modest dress and is described on one occasion as wearing a large hat with a ribbon attached by a silver buckle, and a grey jacket and trousers with lead buttons.[25]

Flags, Guidons and Standards

Crosefinte provides numerous images and comprehensive details on the flags and standards of the royalist armies which limited space does not permit describing here.[26]

Flags, guidons and standards were numerous in the royalist armies and included the Army Guidon carried with the headquarters, divisional standards, personal standards of senior officers, parish company flags and banners, and cavalry guidons.

From the outbreak of the Rising there are numerous references to rebels carrying white flags and parish or religious banners. White was the obvious colour for the background to their flags, being the colour symbolising royalist France. Flags soon appeared bearing fleurs-des-lys.

There were at least twenty divisional standards, generally bearing fleurs-des-lys and the royal coat of arms on a white background. The Guidon-General of the Grand Army was white with a gold fringe, bearing the shield with the arms of France surmounted by a crown in the centre, and a crossed épée and crucifix below the shield (in gold). It had gold fleur-des-lys to each corner.

Parish flags were diverse in appearance, although many contained a religious reference or image, or references to the King and name of the parish. Many were rectangular in design and borne hanging down from a horizontal pole fixed to a pike. Some parishes adopted the same design used for divisional standards but with the parish name added.

To indicate how similar many flags became, when the Prince de Talmont was seen with his own family flag at the head of the cavalry he was ordered to remove it, La Rochejaquelein making it clear that 'we only recognise the fleurs-des-lys'.[27]

Weapons

As time went by, growing numbers of troops were armed with an array of captured muskets, swords, carbines and pistols. However, being a rural based army the majority were inevitably armed with various forms of scythes, pitchforks, pikes and clubs. There are surviving examples of some of these fearsome weapons, including bayonets strapped to poles and improvised weapons not dissimilar to medieval halberds. A common weapon was an adapted scythe, where the blade was removed and then refixed to a shaft.

Tactics

A small minority of the Vendéens would have been familiar with French army regulations: most probably those of 1779, perhaps less so those of 1791. Both sides recognised the Vendée was not cavalry country, so cavalry were generally deployed in modest numbers.

From the outset the Vendéens used irregular tactics, learning from each encounter how best to tackle the republicans. The peasant-soldiers should not be thought of as entirely undisciplined, as while they may have adopted unorthodox ways of fighting, they frequently showed remarkable resilience.

The peasants of the Marais would use the banks of the water-filled ditches to remain hidden, ready to ambush republican columns. If battle turned against them they were known to use long poles, typical to the area, to leap the ditches and escape.

The rebels knew their terrain intimately and General Kléber remarked that the nature of the countryside demanded the utmost vigilance.

Once assembled, the divisions would be given their orders, which were invariably brief and to the point. On approaching the field of combat they frequently split into three main columns and a reserve, with the centre column typically grouped around a stronger artillery contingent.

If the terrain allowed, the rebels approached as close as they could undetected, aiming to infiltrate the terrain to the front and flanks of the republicans. On a given signal their marksmen and tirailleurs would open up a withering fire from the flanks, taking particular care to target officers and gunners. This sudden discharge would be followed by a headlong charge accompanied by terrifying screams, one notable cry being 'Rambarre! Rambarre!' a call traditionally used to round up cattle and signifying that the enemy had been outflanked.

General Turreau indicated that a republican column might find itself under sudden and fierce assault from all sides at once, adding that officers used to conventional warfare said they would prefer a year campaigning on the frontier to a month in the Vendée.[28]

They often deployed in a crescent, with their best tirailleurs and marksmen on the flanks. Turreau recalled that the rebels could be seen loading their muskets as they advanced, even at the run, and while they were untrained in methods of battalion firing they could maintain a firefight just as well and just as effectively as the republicans.

D'Obenheim, who marched with the rebels in November and early December, reported that their infantry could be placed in one of three classes:[29]

First Class (4–5,000 men): These formed the key combat force composed of experienced peasant-soldiers and some deserters, including the Swiss, French and German Companies, the Breton Companies of the Anjou Division and troops from 'Chouan' territory. He added that 'you never saw better tirailleurs'.[30] They were drawn from all the divisions and nearly all the principal leaders would fight with them.

Second Class (3–4,000 men): These were held in reserve ready to move quickly into battle to support the First Class by adding weight of numbers, or thrown in to threaten the enemy's flanks. They were variously armed and of average quality.

Third Class (The bulk of army): These poorly armed troops would generally only join in combat if they were sure of victory, but could be inspired in extreme situations.

The First Class troops were regarded as the 'shield for the army and the refugees', consequently if they were in any way shaken everyone else was prone to panic. However, as D'Obenheim noted, each battle caused them to progressively diminish in strength. He noted the army's reluctance to fight without La Rochejaquelein leading and Stofflet at the head of the infantry with the standards.[31]

The leaders, invariably in the front line, would be looking for weaknesses in the enemy's ranks to exploit any opportunity, and although victory might often depend on their first assault, if the element of surprise was lost, the rebels were known to continue a prolonged firefight from cover.

When faced by artillery the Vendéens adopted an unorthodox but successful tactic. The officers would fix their eyes on the enemy cannon and as the matches were lit would cry out 'ventre a terre' on which order the men would throw themselves flat on the ground, then on the call 'portez vos armes' they would leap up and with the shout 'en avant' would charge the guns. By racing forwards and throwing themselves flat between rounds they would eventually attack and overpower the gunners.

The rebels were uncomfortable when attempts were made to deploy them in regular formation although they did on occasion deploy in rudimentary closed columns.

If threatened by counter-attack the rebels could simply disappear into the countryside, covered by their cavalry, or allow the pursuit to develop and lure detached units into ambushes.

Republicans often complained that their fanaticism meant that they were not afraid to die. Berruyer reported that they seemed willing to abandon everything held dear in the world to follow 'villainous priests who, with a crucifix in one hand and pistol in the other, give them benediction and threaten to kill them if they show weakness in battles'.[32]

The representatives, reporting on the defeats in September, claimed that the rebels had around 100,000 men, 'half are well armed and the rest are composed of enraged fanatics all determined to die'.[33]

On 4 November 1793 Kléber made clear observations on rebel tactics, with advice on how to face them in battle.[34]

He observed that their plan of attack and defence was nearly always the same: 'They constantly expand their line so as to envelop us and throw disorder in our troops.'

He advised that the republicans needed to adopt different tactics depending on whether the rebels were attacking, deployed waiting to be attacked, or when the opposing armies were marching to attack each other. In these scenarios he wrote that the Rebels used little artillery, even less baggage, and engaged in only one way of fighting:

> 'When they march to attack us they usually deploy in three columns, irrespective of the terrain; but...their right hand column is nearly always more numerous and formed of their best troops. Their centre column is supported by some cannon fire while the others extend themselves *en tirailleurs* along the hedges, but the right will always make the main attack.'

When the republicans were marching towards them in a single column, which was often the case, the rebels normally positioned their central column on a height while their flanks occupied advanced positions along the hedges, in ditches, and out of sight. 'The battle starts in the centre and while we are deploying on our flanks, the enemy line takes us in the flank aiming to cut us.'

When the two armies were approaching each other he indicated that this was more unpredictable, although they always tried to adopt one of the above tactics:

'Everything depends on the immediacy of the orders of our generals, but always mindful that the enemy will be looking to extend beyond our lines, and will slide along the hedges and through the thickets.'

He also noted that they tended to march in open order, unlike their own closed ranks, which caused the republicans more casualties.

Kléber recognised that fighting the rebels demanded cool officers and disciplined troops.

'Remember that the enemy's centre is normally formed from their worst troops, that pikes...are nearly the only defence for their cannons, that all their frightened men are gathered there behind them.'

If marching in a single column, and anticipating that the enemy were near, he advised that the army's advance guard should be preceded by three to four hundred tirailleurs. These tirailleurs would march on a wide front to spot the enemy, estimate the space they occupied, and report their positions to a dozen or so chasseurs-à-cheval who should be to their rear. On contact with the enemy these scouts were to take hold of a strong position, which could then be secured by the advance guard. The main body of the army would then occupy the advance guard's previous position and the reserve that previously occupied by the army. 'In marching thus from position to position you will be able to ensure rallying points and prevent routs.'

The advance guard should be at least 4–5,000 strong, with a 4pdr or 8pdr cannon and a howitzer, and the reserve should be composed of 50 brave cavalry and 4-600 good troops.

In attacking the enemy Kléber proposed two options:

'When the position of the enemy is known...then the left of our advance-guard will take up a good position before the enemy and hold itself in defence, while our right will forcibly attack the enemy's left, cut his line and turn him, to take him in the flank and rear. Meanwhile, the reserve...will vigorously charge the enemy's central column on the road...through which they will then be able to fall on the flanks and rear of the enemy line. This movement, if well executed, will promptly silence the rebel artillery and rout them.'

He added that if the enemy right flank was seen sending men to support their centre, the republican left could press forwards (this manoeuvre could also be applied in reverse). However he stressed it was preferable to force their right flank back, as if it was driven in, the centre and left would soon break.

If engaged in mêlée he indicated that speed was essential, and if possible the rebels should be vigorously charged to cut their lines and cause them to rout.

> 'To achieve this, as soon as the battle is engaged with our advance-guard it will be desirable to march…two or three battalions from the main body of the army to their support, who will promptly move to the extremes of our line…if possible to take the enemy in their flank.'

Kléber concluded by noting that if these measures appeared impractical, it would be important to form a square at the extreme of each flank to prevent the risk that a rout might spread among the troops.

The Vendéens did not always consider themselves duty-bound to their officers, rather it was the peasants themselves that chose to fight behind leaders they respected or trusted. The leaders were always expected to set an example and lead from the front. Consequently they were frequently wounded and many were killed.

Ultimately the Vendéens remained a disparate group of armies, without a clear political or strategic plan other than responding to threats to their territory.

Kléber's tactics for fighting the rebels.

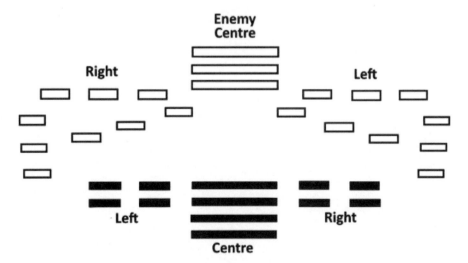

a) The Rebels' preferred deployment in attack.

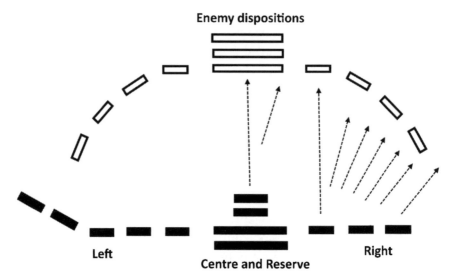

b) Kléber's advice to defend with the left wing and attack in the centre and right.

Chapter 4

'Running like a Trail of Gunpowder':
The Rising Takes Hold

At the beginning of March disturbances broke out between Les Sables d'Olonne and La Roche-sur-Yon, between Cholet and Angers and in settlements near Vihiers on the Cholet to Doué-la-Fontaine road.[1]

On Sunday, 3 March, large numbers of youths gathered in Cholet determined to resist the lottery planned for the following day. True to form rioting broke out on 4 March but was suppressed by a battalion of national guards. However, the rioters gathered in greater strength and, although poorly armed, rushed and routed the national guards. Although suffering around a dozen casualties, they had won and marched triumphantly north to link up with others.[2]

This success was soon emulated across the Mauges with small numbers of republican troops rushing to quell one disturbance only to find others igniting elsewhere.

Uncoordinated pockets of trouble were spreading like wildfire throughout the region. The obvious targets were the main local towns where lists of those eligible for conscription were held and where the lottery was to be carried out. Patriots were reporting gangs actively operating across the countryside and Nantes was being inundated with urgent appeals for help but had to prioritise its own safety when its communications were cut off both north and south of the Loire.

Day by day and hour by hour rebel numbers grew. Most were armed with farmyard weapons but small numbers of muskets provided some firepower.

On 10 March the District of Clisson, between Nantes and Cholet, was in complete turmoil as rebels were gaining the upper hand. Around 1,000 men gathered in communities 12km south-east of Nantes and disarmed and expelled patriots.[3] Recruitment was abandoned in communities near Machecoul as local rebels threatened to 'smash in the heads' of anyone attempting to carry out the lottery.[4]

Machecoul, defended by only 100 national guards and some gendarmes, vainly tried to resist an attack by 3,000 rebels. On its capture, Souchu, one of the rebel leaders, systematically executed around 542 republicans.[5]

Troubles now escalated significantly in Loire-Inférieure as many towns fell into rebel hands, including Legé and Loroux-Bottereau, and thousands assembled to oppose the authorities in Vallet, 20km east of Nantes.[6]

By 11 March a small garrison had reoccupied Cholet and reported the tocsin ringing across a wide area.[7] On the following day the authorities in Tiffauges, 18km west of Cholet, indicated that the whole district was in open revolt, and Chemillé, a similar distance to its north-east, was urgently appealing for help.[8]

During the night of 12 to 13 March Challans was evacuated by the local republican authorities.

The Comte de la Boutetière wrote, 'If you cast your eyes on a map you would see that the insurrection was running like a trail of gunpowder along the parishes bordering the Departments of the Loire-Inférieure and the Vendée'.[9]

The Recruitment of Leaders

The authorities were losing control within hundreds of parishes and as the open defiance spread the rebels knew the Republic would retaliate. The countless uncoordinated risings led to the creation of numerous small bands of men and if they were going to resist the Republic they recognised the need to be led by experienced military men, or men with clear leadership qualities.

A number of former officers were therefore approached to take command. Many of course were gentry, one of the prerequisites of officer status before the Revolution. They included Couëtus and La Cathelinière, Guerry, Charette and Louise-Marie Roche-Saint-André in the Pays-de-Retz and coastal area; the Royrand brothers, Sapinaud-de-la-Verrie, Sapinaud-de-la-Rairie and Gabriel Baudry d'Asson in the Bocage; Bulkeley near La Roche-sur-Yon; Bonchamps, D'Élbée, La Bouëre, Nicolas and Jacques-Nicolas Fleuriot in the Mauges; and in the Loroux area, Lyrot and D'Esigny. Former NCOs included Joly, towards La Mothe-Achard; Stofflet and Perdriau in the Mauges; and the former musketeer, Laugrenière, in Poitou.

Some had no military experience but were men of high standing or natural leaders, several peasants among them. In the Mauges this included Cady, Cathelineau, Tonnelet and Forestier; in the Pays-de-Retz, Guérin and Lucas Championnière; in the Bocage, Auguste Béjarry, Amédée-Béjarry and Verteuil; towards the coast, L'Abbaye and Guerry-du-Cloudy;

and in the south-west, Du Chouppes, Savin and St-Pal. More details on some of these individuals can be found in Appendix 1.

Some of the most influential leaders were of humble origin, completely at odds with republican propaganda. Others joined the Rising later in the spring and summer and their stories will be picked up in due course.

The Escalation of the Rising: Mid-late March

The widespread troubles reported in early March now took a much more serious turn as rebel numbers grew dramatically and they began to show a degree of coordination in their actions. The character of the Rising quickly developed into a series of strategically considered localised campaigns and is best described by each area in turn.

The Mauges

St-Florent-la-Vieil 12 March

Located on high ground on the south bank of the Loire, roughly equidistant between Nantes and Angers, St-Florent-la-Vieil is dominated by its large abbey, from where the town radiates along winding streets of close-packed houses into the surrounding countryside.

On 12 March, 150 national guards with two cannon, moved to St-Florent-la-Vieil to oversee the lottery. They assembled in the town square and covered its approach roads when news that thousands of young men wearing white cockades were marching on the town.[10] Some of these young men were armed but most only carried farmyard implements and ahead of them marched a delegation calling for a suspension of the lottery and for the national guards to hand over their weapons.

An initial fracas led to four peasants being killed and many wounded. The furious mob charged, overpowered the national guards, and captured both cannon.

This brief engagement marked the official beginning of the Rising and is celebrated by a plaque in the town square. On the following day Bonchamps agreed to lead these rebels and headed for St-Florent to put some order in their ranks.

Jallais 13 March

Early on 13 March, in the small village of Pin-en-Mauges between Cholet and St-Florent, Jacques Cathelineau heard news of the preceding day's events. A highly respected local figure he was approached by a group of men and immediately accepted their request to become their leader. The tocsin rang in surrounding parishes and they were soon marching on the republican post at Jallais. Perdriau, who had been present at St-Florent, joined him on route and between them they mustered 500 men.[11]

Jallais was occupied by some local patriots and thirty-four national guards, supported by a single cannon.[12] They were on high alert and had deployed on the banks of the River Evre, 2km south of Jallais.[13] Perdriau and Cathelineau marched from Jallais in two columns, and after an initial hour-long firefight some rebels were sent across fords to threaten the republican flanks, forcing them to withdraw. A third rebel column from Le May cut their line of retreat and forced them to disperse.[14]

After a brief rest to eat and retrieve abandoned weapons the rebels headed for Chemillé, 10km to the east. Their numbers soon reached 2,000 men.[15]

Chemillé 13 March

Chemillé was defended by 100 national guards, some gendarmes and one cannon, who knew that peasants were approaching on the Jallais road.[16]

Cathelineau and Perdriau dispersed their men along the banks of the Hirôme before crossing the river and marching uphill towards the enemy.[17] Some rebels marched via the town of St-Pierre-de-Chemillé to attack the republican flank.

After a brief cannonade Perdriau and Cathelineau led a charge, captured the cannon and turned it on the Republicans. The peasants continued a fusillade that lasted around an hour, slowly thinning the enemy ranks, while 2-300 men marched into Chemillé from the south.[18] Caught on two flanks nearly all the republicans surrendered.

Cholet 14 March

Their next target was Cholet which was now defended by around 1,000 Republicans.[19] On the way they were joined by a column under Stofflet who was moving north from Maulévrier and had occupied Vezins on 13 March.

By 14 March the rebels were several thousand strong and supported by two cannon.[20] Around mid-morning Cholet received a summons to surrender but rejected it and the troops marched out to face the rebels on the Pagannes Heath, 2km east of the town. As they deployed it began to pour with rain.[21]

On approaching Pagannes the armed rebels dispersed behind hedges and trees while most of the men and the cannon continued along the main road. They hesitated when they saw that the enemy were in position. Cathelineau soon rushed forwards followed by some of his men, but while republican fire failed to hit them a shot from the rebel guns mortally wounded the Republican commander, the Marquis de Beauvau, and the Vendéens surged forwards and around the republican flanks.[22] Some dragoons were ordered to charge but turned and fled from the battlefield and the republican infantry were jostled back into the streets of the town where they in turn were routed.

The château held out for several hours only to surrender when combustible material, gathered and lit on Stofflet's instruction, spread fire within its walls. The republicans lost 300 killed, 100 capture, and several cannon.[23]

Coron 16 March

The rebels established a strong garrison in Cholet and on 15 March headed for Vihiers in response to reports that a republican column was approaching from Doué-la-Fontaine. The ever increasing numbers of rebels camped that night in Vezins.

This new republican column, commanded by a Citizen Avril and Chef de Brigade Grignon, was about 2,000 strong and reached Vihiers on 14 March.[24] On the morning of 16 March they were spotted east of Coron.

According to Deniau, the rebel gunner Six-Sous deployed cannon on the main road at the eastern edge of Coron loaded with scraps of metal, and Cathelineau, Stofflet and Perdriau spread their men out behind hedges to either side of the guns to await the enemy attack.[25]

As they advanced the Republicans were preceded by a seventeenth century bastard-culverin. They deployed in line 1km east of Coron and their cannon fired on the Vendéen guns. When Six-Sous responded, thirty-two national guards fell, throwing disorder in their ranks.[26] The republicans were in the process of pulling back to reform when rebel tirailleurs leapt the hedges and charged their flanks and the subsequent republican rout only stopped at Doué-la-Fontaine.

Casualties were light but more weapons were captured, including the bastard-culverin which was renamed the *Marie-Jeanne*. This gun, capable of firing 10 pound shot, became an iconic weapon venerated by the rebels and often seen adorned with flowers. It was frequently used to signal the beginning of battle.

On the following morning the rebels entered Vihiers, then marched north-west to Chemillé, aiming for the 3,500 strong republican post at Chalonnes.[27] On route columns under D'Élbée and Bonchamps swelled their numbers to around 20,000 men, now supported by several guns. On their approach the Chalonnes garrison fled north of the Loire.[28]

Clisson 11 March

While all this fighting had been underway in the north-east, to the west around eighty national guards in Clisson successfully repulsed three rebel columns, with a combined strength of 3-4,000 men, that approached in succession from the north-west, the north and the south-east.[29] Patriots from Pallet, Clisson and Vallet however, retreated to Nantes on 15 March under the protection of national guards.[30]

The Bocage

12 to 14 March

Near St-Mesmin, around 30km south of Cholet, 2,000 armed patriots marched to confront a similar number of badly-armed rebels led by Baudry d'Asson. The rebels managed to engage in hand-to-hand combat with their farmyard weapons and the republicans fled in a south-westerly direction abandoning their weapons on route.[31]

Verteuil and the Béjarry brothers overpowered the republican post at L'Oie on 12 March and on the following day Baudry d'Asson routed the garrison at Pont-Charron, seizing this highly strategic river crossing a short distance south of Chantonnay.[32]

On 13 March parishes around La Roche-sur-Yon rose up under Bulkeley and Du Chouppes, and St-Pal became leader of rebels further south still. La Roche-sur-Yon fell to the rebels three days later.

Further north-east 2,000 peasants marched on Les Herbiers under their newly appointed leader Sapinaud-de-la-Verrie.[33] The republicans withdrew early in the afternoon, conceding three guns to the rebels, and Sapinaud went on to seize both Mortagne and Tiffauges.

Around 11am on 13 March a large band of peasants appeared near the eastern edge of Montaigu. Some 200 national guards with two cannon blocked their path and opened fire, forcing them to pull back. A little later 4-5,000 men approached from the north, charged the national guards, and routed them.[34]

Marcé verses Royrand 15 to 19 March

On taking command Royrand went straight into action and on 15 March he attacked 1,200 republicans in Chantonnay who withdrew south after an obstinate fight.[35] Royrand and Sapinaud-de-la-Verrie then gathered the rebels at L'Oie and attempted to put some order in their ranks.

The republicans were determined to re-establish communications between La Rochelle and Nantes and General Marcé set out from La Rochelle on 15 March instructing republican detachments to gather at Ste-Hermine, 15km south of Chantonnay. He anticipated that his march north would be supported by troops sent south from Nantes. By 16 March Marcé had assembled 4,500 men grandly entitled the Army of the Vendée.[36] His senior officers were Boulard and Baudry, and representatives Niou and Trullard accompanied them.

Marcé left 1,600 men to guard Ste-Hermine while he marched north to Pont-Charrault on the River Lay. He left more men to cover this post and continued to Chantonnay where his advance guard repulsed 2,000 rebels led by Sapinaud-de-la-Verrie.

Marcé announced that he would march on St Fulgent on 19 March having assumed that Sapinaud's men had dispersed when in fact they had fallen back to L'Oie to rally to several other leaders. Their combined strength totalled 5-6,000 men, of whom only 3-400 carried muskets or fusils, with limited ammunition.[37] They were supported by two 4pdr guns, a 12pdr, and 100 cavalry formed almost entirely from peasants mounted on farmyard horses.

Setting out from Chantonnay in the morning Marcé left 300 men to guard his line of communications and arrived at the Gravereau Bridge towards midday. Royrand had cut this bridge and republican workmen had been endeavouring to rebuild it since 7am.

Marcé's force now comprised a volunteer battalion, about six weak national guards' battalions, and a detachment from the 60th Line. His infantry totalled around 2,200, to which he could add 200 horse and nine guns.

By 3pm they were descending towards the Moulin-de-la-Basse-Rivière, only to discover the next bridge broken and the river swollen by the incessant rainfall. Although Marcé ordered its repair the republicans were now between two rivers in countryside that offered plenty of cover to the north and on their flanks.

Allowing for a degree of caution from the many post-action reports the following rough chronology can be pieced together, largely thanks to Chassin's collection of documents.[38] At about 4pm large numbers of men were spotted around 1km to the north whom the representatives believed might be friendly troops coming from Nantes as they could hear them singing the *Marseillaise* (the rebels had in fact put their own words to this famous tune).[39]

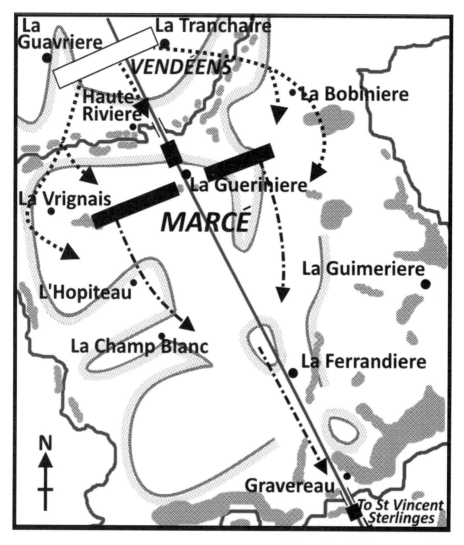

The Battle of La Guérinière.

At about 6pm an officer, ADC and trumpeter were sent on ahead but had difficulty identifying them due to the weather and failing light. This delay in scouting enabled the Vendéens to spread out, screened by the trees and high hedges. Royrand's column moved east on La Tranchaire and Sapinaud's moved west, both aiming to outflank the republicans and take advantage of crossing points unlikely to have been known to their enemy.[40] While these columns were deploying, their armed troops were moving under cover towards the republicans. When the action commenced, the Vendéens formed a crescent which stretched beyond the republican flanks.

Marcé decided to protect the two bridges and placed 100 cavalry at the Gravereau Bridge and a further detachment in St-Vincent-Sterlinges. Most of his troops were in two congested columns leading down to the bridge, so he sent some tirailleurs into the wooded country along the riverbank and then began to deploy the troops. Having selected a place for a battalion to his left he was returning to deploy more troops when an enemy fusillade opened up across the river to the west of the bridge. The direction of the river at that point enabled the rebels to spread out along the front and left flank of his column.

With a full scale attack now underway Marcé endeavoured to deploy more battalions on his left flank aiming to align them along hedges on a small plateau dominating the river. Two battalions were also deployed on his right. It was soon apparent that some republican artillery had been deployed on the slope of the hill and not its crest and could not fire at that angle. Leaving two cannon near the bridge to contain the enemy Marcé withdrew his other guns to higher ground, but while doing so his horse was shot and he fell wounded.

One of the battalions on his west flank broke and after the battle Marcé said the army would have held if this battalion had not fired on their own chasseurs and grenadiers before retiring in disorder, spreading confusion in the ranks.[41]

Niou urged Marcé to retire forthwith, but rather than retreat in the face of the enemy he attempted to re-establish some order amongst his troops. The two cannon at the bridge were ordered to fire grapeshot to gain Marcé time to rally the army, but no grapeshot could be found and round shot had to be used instead.[42] Royrand's brother was killed as he attempted to lead some rebels forward and the peasants near the bridge now sought cover and ducked as each shot rang out.

Sapinaud is credited with the tactic used many times by the Vendéens. He instructed his men to throw themselves to the ground when the cannon flashed, then jump to their feet and rush the guns before the republicans had time to reload. Leading the column in person he soon overpowered the guns and captured the bridge.[43]

It was probably around this time that Marcé ordered forward 100 cavalry to cover the republican left flank and hopefully spread panic amongst the rebels in the darkness, but a confused fight in broom-covered fields led to them being overwhelmed and retreating to the Gravereau Bridge.

Boulard recalled that in the dark his men were seeing the enemy everywhere and had completely lost their nerve. Marcé now conceded to Niou's demands and issued orders to retire. He personally remained with the rearguard while Boulard raced to the Gravereau Bridge hoping to rally troops to its south.

A frantic and confused fight developed on the La Guérinière plateau, with small pockets of republicans holding out behind the high-hedged fields but being submerged under overwhelming numbers of rebels. Marcé succeeded in rallying some men to the north-west of Gravereau and carried out an orderly withdrawal overnight.[44]

Returning to the battlefield on the following day the Vendéens noted 500 republican dead to 250 of their own. They had captured two cannon and sixteen wagons containing plenty of fusils and ammunition.

The republicans retreated on Marans and the unfortunate General Marcé was arrested the day after the battle and would be guillotined in January 1794.

The battle at La Guérinière had repercussions far beyond its scale and the Rising was now referred to as the War of the Vendée. The shock of this defeat was to lead the Republic to organise a new and much more sizeable assault.

Nantes: A City Besieged

Nantes had been cut off and was unable to communicate with Paris. On 17 March a column was sent to disperse rebels threatening to assault the city from the north and rudimentary earthworks were thrown up along the approaches to the city. Although some of the Nantes National Guard had been dispatched south of the Loire, priority had to be given to protecting the city at the cost of a number of outlying towns. Communication with Paris was eventually re-established with a republican victory at Ancenis, but Nantes would be in a high state of anxiety for months to come.

The Coastal Vendée

The Republic managed to retain pockets of land along the coast: notably St-Gilles, Croix-de-Vie, Paimboeuf and Pornic. On 12 March a column led by Danguy and Cadou marched on Paimboeuf hoping to destroy the list of those eligible for the lottery.[45] Some cannon fire, a cavalry charge, and support from gunners and sailors from the frigate *La Capricieuse* and the corvette *L'Impatient* moored nearby soon dispersed them. Danguy was captured and would be executed in Nantes on 6 April.[46] Paimboeuf was to remain firmly in republican hands.

On 17 March the small garrison of national guards on the strategically important island of Noirmoutier surrendered to rebels under Guerry de la Fortinière, Des Abbayes and Guerry-du-Cloudy.

Pornic 23 March

The newly formed royalist committee in Machecoul was keen to attack Pornic which was being used as a base for republicans harassing the area. Under the Marquis de La Roche-Sainte-André a column set out on 23 March and at Bourgneuf he was joined by Guérin and La Cathelinière with rebels from the Pays-de-Retz. They soon seized Pornic but failed to prevent its small garrison from slipping away.

With this republican town in their control the peasants went on a drunken rampage and failed to deploy outposts. As a consequence they were routed that same evening by a republican detachment less than one hundred strong and in the ensuing panic 266 rebels were killed.[47] Soon after this debacle La Roche-Saint-André left to join Royrand.

Pornic 27 March

Charette now arrived in Machecoul, having recently joined the Rising, and endeavoured to put the 3-5,000 rebels into some order and introduce rudimentary military drill. He agreed to lead a second attack on Pornic and Guérin and La Cathelinière, offering their support, united with him at Bourgneuf on 26 March.

Thousands of badly armed rebels were now moving on Pornic in four columns, defended by only 200 national guards and two small guns.[48] Columns were seen approaching the town along two roads from the east and most of the republicans deployed in the town's square ready to confront them.

The republicans were able to concentrate their fire on the exits from these two roads and forced the front of the rebel columns to halt and commence weak retaliatory fire from cover. With little progress being made Charette issued instructions to set light to the town, which had the desired effect and forced the republicans to evacuate. The republicans managed to escape to Paimboeuf when the two rebel columns sent around the northern outskirts failed to cut them off.[49] The rebels were to hold the town for a month and Charette carried out an orderly withdrawal that evening, taking with him the two captured cannon.

Les Sables d'Olonne 24 March

The republican town of Les Sables d'Olonne was a key port on a network of roads that led east to Luçon and Niort, south to La Rochelle, and north to Nantes. Securing the town might enable the rebels to communicate with the English and would be a significant blow to the Republic.

Les Sables d'Olonne is on a peninsula of land with the sea to the south, harbour and estuary looping around to the west, and salt marshes to the north. The eastern approach to the town was protected by stone walls.

By 23 March the republican garrison totalled 3,500 troops supported by eight guns.[50] Except for 250 men from the 110th Line the infantry were national guards and the cavalry were a mixture of gendarmes and national guards.[51] Lieutenant Colonel Foucard was nominally in command although Representative Gaudin was the real authority.

The town's outposts were on high alert and patriots from miles around sought refuge within its walls. On 20 March news of Marcé's defeat reached them and 22 March was spent fortifying the town and raising batteries.[52]

Around 1pm on 23 March troops rushed to arms when the enemy was spotted to the north and sailors manned the batteries at the town gates.[53]

Joly, self-proclaimed general of the 'Royal Army of Sables', in command of a vast swathe of land centred on La Mothe-Achard, planned a coordinated assault on Les Sables supported by rebels under Guerry-du-Cloudy, Du Chaffault, St-Pal, Rorthays, Bulkeley and De Chouppes.

He issued orders to gather at 10am on 24 March on the Pierre-Levée heights, 4km north of the town. His and Rorthays' column was the largest and two other columns were to be led by Guerry-du-Cloudy, Du Chaffault and St-Pal. Guerry-du-Cloudy, marching from Vairé, only arrived at midday and Du Chaffault failed to appear at all.

'The brigands were badly armed, badly led and badly disciplined,' wrote Collinet, but he noted that they had 7-8,000 infantry and 400 cavalry.[54] To oppose them the republicans deployed an advance party at La Vannerie formed of 600 national guards, 120 line troops, 200 cavalry and 2 guns.[55]

As a diversionary move Joly sent 300 men to seize Olonne and its small garrison soon fled to Les Sables.[56] Encouraged by this victory the rebels advanced on a wide front towards La Vannerie. The republicans began firing their cannon and the rebels panicked when Joly was thrown to the ground as his horse was struck. Joly managed to rally them and form three columns, with their front and flanks protected by the cavalry and each bearing a white flag inscribed with the words 'Victoire ou Mort'.[57]

The republicans dropped back from La Vannerie between 3 and 4pm to deploy behind a stream nearer the town.[58] Joly now directed the bulk of his troops towards the eastern approaches to Les Sables.

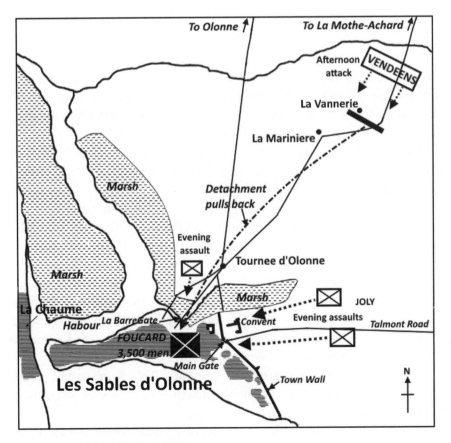

First Battle of Les Sables d'Olonne.

Around 4pm he sent a proclamation to the town calling for its surrender and setting out that the Rising had taken place because of attacks on their liberties, religion and king. They were given three hours to surrender or face the consequences of an assault.

As no response was forthcoming Joly sent 2,000 men towards the gateway on the Talmont road, 3,000 towards the abandoned Convent of Saint-Croix, and 3,500 towards the La Barre Gate.[59] He also deployed two 18pdrs to fire on the defences.

The royalists were being urged forwards by their leaders and directed to climb the walls of the convent and assault the nearby gate. Thanks in large part to the republican artillery at least two assaults were beaten back.[60] The badly handled royalist cannon were of insufficient calibre to breach the walls, so with night falling Joly ordered the army's withdrawal. The republicans admitted to about eight casualties.[61]

Les Sables d'Olonne 29 March.

From 25 to 28 March more fortifications were constructed, an armed vessel was anchored in the harbour, and some 36pdrs were deployed.[62] Olonne was reoccupied and reinforcements increased the republican forces to 3,000 national guards and volunteer infantry, 320 line troops, 236 cavalry and 360 naval gunners. The town could also call on 1,500 unarmed men.[63]

The second rebel advance was spotted on 28 March and by 7pm all the troops in Les Sables were at their posts, including 600 men deployed in La Chaume and over 300 in the St-Nicholas Fort.[64]

The rebels had set out from La Mothe-Achard at 3pm accompanied by sixteen cannon. On reaching La Tournée d'Olonne, north of the town, they raised an entrenchment for their guns while some of their infantry advanced along surrounding sunken roads.[65] This time Du Chaffault arrived from Avrillé with 3,000 men and brought Joly's numbers up to 6,000.

At dawn the artillery on both sides opened up, but over time the heavy calibre republican cannon wore down rebel morale and from as early as 6am some were seen retreating northwards. By 7am only those near La Tournée d'Olonne and behind the entrenchments remained.

A Vendéen column expected from Talmont failed to appear and making no headway Joly changed tactics and began firing red-hot shot on the town, but to little effect.

The Republicans succeeded in dismounting many Vendéen cannon and demolished part of their entrenchments, leaving them with only two 18pdrs still in action.[66] At about 8.15am a chance republican shot struck ammunition near the rebel battery and killed a number of gunners. The rebels could take no more and were seen fleeing 'like a flock of sheep' through the fields, abandoning their weapons in their haste to get away.[67]

The republican losses were light as opposed to 366 rebel dead, more killed in the pursuit, and 100 captured. They also captured fourteen cannon and eleven supply wagons.[68] By 30 March a further 1,700 troops arrived in Les Sables, ruling out further attacks for the time being.[69]

Chapter 5

'In less than a month the troubles in the Vendée will be at an end'

Representatives Carra and Auguis to the National Convention, 24th March 1793

The Advance of the Army of the Reserve and the April Campaign

The first priority for the Republic was to contain the Rising and all available troops were concentrated in towns around the edge of rebel territory. Towards the end of March Leygonier and Ladouce were in Angers with 4,500 men; 4,000 were in Doué-le-Fontaine; Quétineau moved to Thouars with 3-4,000 men; Gauvilliers covered the north bank of the Loire with 1,500 men; and Chalbos and D'Ayat were gathering thousands of men from Niort to Les Sables d'Olonne. By the end of March Canclaux was also able to give time to plan a strike south from Nantes.

On 25 March republican columns set out from Angers, Doué and Thouars. Ladouce was ordered to march on the River Layon and St-Lambert-de-Lattay with 2,500 men; Quétineau had orders to head for Bressuire; and Leygonier, who had taken command of the troops in Doué, marched on Vihiers. A half-battalion of Finistère Fédérés, forming Leygonier's advance guard, were ambushed near Coron and forced to fall back on his main column at Vihiers. The resulting panic temporarily halted Leygonier's advance. Quétineau had more grief from his insubordinate troops than from the enemy in an uneventful march on Bressuire, but Ladouce was soon under attack.

St-Lambert-de-Lattay 29 March to 1 April

Ladouce was in St-Lambert-de-Lattay on 29 March, dug in behind earthworks and abattis. His troops were formed from battalions of national guards from north-east of rebel territory and totalled 1,985 infantry, 106 horse, 52 gunners and 152 pioneers. A further 716 men were posted in Beaulieu 3km to the east.[1] In addition to his own men there were 300 national guards in Chanzeaux, 5km to the south, and a further 1,200–1,500 garrisoned at Gonnard.[2] All these troops directly threatened Chemillé and it was towards this town that Ladouce advanced on 30 March. Stofflet was aware of Ladouce's moves and had alerted the Vendéen leaders in Mortagne, Cholet and Vihiers, who all came to his support and gathered in Chemillé on 29 March.

The local rebel leader, Cady, moved on the republican right flank while Stofflet marched direct from Chemillé. Impatient to move into combat Stofflet raced ahead with his best equipped men, giving orders for the rest to follow on behind. Ladouce's response was to pull back to his entrenchments in St-Lambert. Stopping short of the town Stofflet spread his men out deployed as skirmishers, but neither side seemed willing to strike first. Eventually Stofflet managed to deploy his artillery but the firing was so dreadful that he soon gave up any hope of making progress and withdrew.

Fighting now paused as many Vendéens went home to celebrate Easter. The republicans, meanwhile, were busy preparing the next stage of the offensive planned for early April.

Berruyer's Offensive

General Berruyer was given command of all forces south of the Loire while Labourdonnaye commanded those to its north from Ingrandes to the sea, including both Nantes and Paimboeuf. Berruyer set up his headquarters in Angers and aimed to launch several columns simultaneously into rebel territory as follows:

1. A column of the Army of the Brest Coast was to march from Nantes, sweep through the coastal area, and seize Noirmoutier, while Canclaux remained in Nantes with 3,000 men;
2. D'Ayat was sent to Niort to take command of a division formed from newly raised battalions (6,000 men of which about 300 were line troops). He was ordered to establish a defensive line stretching to Les Sables d'Olonne and St-Gilles. Once in position D'Ayat would march on Fontenay and Chantonnay, retaining a chain of posts up to Les Sables;
3. Quétineau was to occupy Bressuire and cover the area to Parthenay on D'Ayat's right flank. He would then march on Mortagne and Tiffauges.
4. Leygonier was to occupy Vihiers before marching on Cholet and St-Florent.

5. Ladouce, occupying St-Lambert, would march via Chemillé on St-Florent.
6. Gauvilliers was ordered to protect the Loire crossings, notably those at Ancenis, Varades and Ingrandes. The posts of Ancenis and Varades were ordered to remain static until replaced by troops from the Army of the Brest Coast.

His ultimate aim was to force the rebels back against the sea or the Loire.

By April the royalists had established three camps south of Nantes: at Sorinières, La Louée and in the Touffou Forest. Around 6 April the first hint of a republican offensive began when both Sorinières and La Louée were attacked and captured.[4]

Berruyer's plans were far too ambitious based on the resources available to him as he had a mobile force of only 15-16,000 men, dispersed across a vast front, and formed largely from raw or reluctant troops. On 2 April Berruyer wrote that he had expected to find the troops at least passably organised and equipped but nothing of the kind existed: they were badly armed, some not armed at all, and nearly all wanted to go home.[3] He appealed for line troops, fusils, cannonballs and two experienced brigade generals.

However, as these plans were being finalised the representatives in Les Sables ordered Boulard to form a column and move into the Vendée along the coast – without any consultation with Berruyer and contrary to his plan.

As the republican columns were set in motion it was soon clear that their main assault would be from the north-east so the Vendéens quickly gathered 10,000 men in Cholet under D'Élbée, Cathelineau and Perdriau. Stofflet was in Coron with 6,000 men and 7,000 remained with Bonchamps to cover the south bank of the Loire. Some rebels were left in Cholet and Maulévrier with orders to keep an eye on Quétineau's moves to the east. Deniau suggests that the Vendéens were outnumbered, with around 23,000 peasants faced by 30-35,000 republicans.[5]

Berruyer began his offensive on 8 April as Leygonier moved from Vihiers to camp near Coudray-Montbault. Stofflet covered the area of Coron and by skirmishing on the Cholet road he successfully slowed the republican advance throughout 9 and 10 April (no doubt helped by Leygonier's gunners refusing to march without first being paid).

During 10 April, while Berruyer crossed the Layon and recaptured St-Lambert, the Vendéens in Cholet raced to defend the natural strongpoint of St-Pierre-de-Chemillé.

'The Shock of Chemillé': St-Pierre-de-Chemillé 11 April

Thanks to Deniau, the battle can be pieced together reasonably well. He indicated that once in St-Pierre-de-Chemillé the Royalists set up some cannon, three redoubts (two covering the Hirôme crossings and one east of the village) and dug a deep trench near the bridge facing Le Bas Bourg. They also dug a ditch stretching between the redoubts. Within the village the church was converted into a small fortress and the churchyard defences were strengthened by earthworks. A strong battery was deployed in the redoubt facing the St-Lambert road; three cannon within that near the Pont de Berge; two or three in the redoubt to the north-east, and others in the square covering the approaches to the church.

Berruyer was in command of 4,000 troops and although most were volunteers and national guards his army did include Rossignol's 800 strong 35th Division-Gendarmerie, a few cavalry, and sixteen guns. While he headed for St-Pierre-de-Chemillé on 11 April, Duhoux (who had replaced

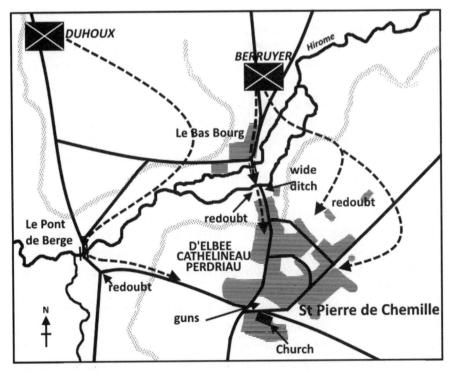

St Pierre-de-Chemillé.

Ladouce) led half of his command towards La Jumellière, from where he would later turn south to re-join Berruyer.

Around 12.30pm Berruyer took up position on high ground 4km north-east of St-Pierre-de-Chemillé to the north of the Hirôme. With warning of their approach the armed rebels deployed in ambush north of the village behind hedges, walls and within buildings. Those armed with farmyard weapons assembled in the village square and its surrounding roads.

After an opening exchange of artillery fire the battle soon developed into a drawn-out fusillade across the Hirôme. D'Élbée may have led some men across the river to fire on the republicans at close range, causing the national guards to lie flat and refuse to move.[6]

Berruyer decided to split his 2,000 men into two columns with the left under Menou and the right under Adjudant General Mengin. Although most of the 35th Division-Gendarmerie had marched with Duhoux, two companies were placed at the head of these columns. The gendarmes now led an advance and forced the rebels back over the river. A rebel counter-attack, supported by the battery on the main road and a cannon placed near a laundry, was forced back to its entrenchments. At one point the gendarmes succeeded in capturing several cannon, until Cathelineau and D'Élbée counter-attacked and pushed the republicans back north of the river as far as the junction of the St-Lambert and La Jumellière roads. The republican artillery then recommenced a bombardment of the rebel entrenchments.

Duhoux's men arrived towards 5pm, enabling Berruyer to form two new columns for a fresh assault. He led the gendarmes in one column and Duhoux led the other. Rossignol, who commanded the gendarmes, claimed his two guns dismounted some enemy artillery as they advanced. Once again the gendarmes broke into the Vendéen entrenchments and then fought their way into the village. Duhoux received a serious leg wound but Rossignol had more success as he led two companies around the east side of the settlement. He aimed to outflank the church but a party of his men were pinned down in the village when they came face to face with three cannon and rebels aligned in platoons. A fierce struggle soon raged with the best of the royalist fighters clinging to the church and surrounding houses and inspired by the personal example of D'Élbée and Cathelineau.[7]

While Rossignol had been advancing from the east, Berruyer pushed the rebels back in the centre and Talot succeeded in crossing the Pont de Berge, seized a cannon, and began to climb towards the village from the north-west. The fight in the square was ferocious and desperate and Perdriau fell mortally wounded. As the gendarmes could make no headway Rossignol dropped back to find reinforcements and came across a battalion to his rear. Although he managed to get their first platoon to advance they would not press home an attack on the enemy gunners and soon fled, forcing him to withdraw his gendarmes.

The light was failing and Berruyer's men were taking significant losses. With the Vendéens distracted by the ongoing melee 133 republican prisoners, tied together to hamper their movements, made for their own lines. In the poor light Berruyer mistook this for a rebel assault and withdrew from the battlefield.

The battle lasted about nine hours and the republicans almost certainly sustained higher casualties. They also lost fifteen cannon.

The 'Shock of Chemillé' is remembered as a legendary feat of arms in the region today, but in reality it only gave the rebels a brief respite. Gauvilliers had been strengthening his position in and around St-Florent and began his move south on 13 April. His men were systematically burning and looting the countryside over the following week and Leygonier was threatening the rebel's right flank as he moved on Vezins and scouted as far as Nuaillé on 12 April.

The Catholic and Royal Army knew that Berruyer could turn on them at any moment and as they had exhausted their ammunition they pulled back on all fronts. Bonchamps withdrew to Beaupréau, where he was joined by Cathelineau and D'Élbée's exhausted men. On Bonchamps' advice they dropped back through Cholet to Mortagne and Tiffauges, followed by large numbers of refugees fearful of republican reprisals.

Demoralised, short of ammunition, and aware that much of their territory was now under republican control, the Vendéens prayed for a miracle. It was to arrive in the shape of 20-year-old Henri de la Rochejaquelein.

Henri de la Rochejaquelein joins the Rising

We left Quétineau marching on Bressuire with 4,000 men towards the end of March. After a clash in Châtillon he placed garrisons in St-Mesmin, Le Forêt and reinforced Argenton-Château. At St-Mesmin 1,000 of his men clashed with 2,000 rebels and around 10 April he rested his column in La Châtaigneraie, only to race back to Bressuire to quell trouble stirred up by the Cher Battalion.

On 11 April he received orders to march overnight to break up rebels gathering in the area of Nueil, Échaubrognes and Les Aubiers. He successfully assaulted Nueil at dawn on 12 April but an hour later, as he was marching towards Échaubrognes, he came under attack. After three hours of combat he retired on Les Aubiers and at 2pm on 13 April he was attacked again by what he later claimed were 10-12,000 rebels, against which he could only deploy 2,500 men and 5 cannon.[8]

Les Aubiers 13 April

Hearing that the Vendéens had retired on Tiffauges, Henri de la Rochejaquelein, from one of the foremost families of the region, feared that the Rising would soon be over. He was heading home when news reached him that a column under Quétineau had left Bressuire and broken up a small gathering of rebels at Les Aubiers. According to Madame de la Rochejaquelein, that part of Poitou had yet to appoint a leader or formally organise themselves, so hearing that La Rochejaquelein had arrived home he was approached by a large crowd of peasants and asked if he would take command. If he agreed they promised to raise the whole area behind him. Delighted by this turn of events he accepted. By the following day he was at the head of several thousand men but with less than 200 fusils between them and little powder. Standing before these men La Rochejaquelein made what became a legendary appeal:

> 'My friends, if my father was here he would inspire more confidence in you, but you barely know me and I am only a child; I hope that I will at least be able to prove by my conduct that I am worthy to be at your head. If I advance, follow me; if I retreat, kill me; if I am killed, avenge me.'

This was greeted with a rapturous response and although most had never experienced combat they marched with La Rochejaquelein on Les Aubiers. When approaching the western side of Les Aubiers he split his men into two columns, with one then marching via Nueil and the other on the Maulévrier road.[9] They were surrounding the republicans camped in the Champs-des-Justice, just outside Les Aubiers, concealed by the high-hedged fields.

Taken by surprise and unnerved by enemy numbers the republicans pulled back to reorganise behind the cemetery walls near the church and covered its main approaches with cannon.[10] Sympathetic locals guided the rebels to houses overlooking the cemetery and the republicans were soon forced to evacuate the town.[11] As they attempted to deploy towards Caphar, south-east of Les Aubiers, two caissons exploded and threw their ranks into disorder. Faced by a furious charge they fled in disorder on Bressuire, abandoning cannon and caissons and suffering an estimated 160 casualties.[12]

Madame de la Rochejaquelein wrote that the tactics used at this battle were to be used repeatedly by the Vendéens. She described how they would silently surround the republicans, appear unexpectedly at pistol range, hurl themselves forwards with loud cries, rush the cannons to seize them and 'fire rarely but aim accurately'.[13]

La Rochejaquelein did not follow up with a march on Bressuire but instead marched overnight to unite with D'Élbée, Bonchamps, Cathelineau and Stofflet, taking them the powder and cannon he had seized. His appearance was a significant boost to the main rebel army.

Pagannes and Bois-Grolleau 19 to 20 April

As Leygonier advanced so Berruyer moved from St-Lambert-de-Lattay to Chemillé on 14 April. On the following day he reported that Quétineau's check at Les Aubiers had slowed his own advance but on 16 April he was in touch with Leygonier's troops at Nuaillé.

With perhaps 10,000 men between them, Berruyer and Leygonier were moving forwards on Jallais and Cholet respectively and Gauvilliers was moving on Beaupréau. However the initiative now swung back to the rebels who by 18 April had concentrated 25,000 men in Cholet, including contingents from both Anjou and the Army of the Centre.

On the morning of 19 April the republican front extended through Beaupréau, Jallais, Le May, Nuaillé and Toutlemonde, and that of the Vendéens through Montfaucon, St-Macaire, Cholet and Maulévrier.[14]

The moated Château of Bois-Grolleau, immediately east of Cholet, was occupied by 200 grenadiers detached from Leygonier's advance guard dug in behind loopholed walls. These posed no immediate threat to the rebels who targeted Leygonier's 2,000 strong advance guard on the Pagannes Heights. The Vendéens deployed in three main bodies with Cathelineau to the left, La Rochejaquelein to the right and D'Élbée and Stofflet in the centre. They soon pressed the republican advance guard back on Leygonier's main body.

Although not specifically recorded, Leygonier's force probably numbered around 6,500, including 200 horse and 12 guns, and he deployed in fields centred on La Simonnière, roughly half-way between Nuaillé and Cholet. The Vendéens surged forwards and onto the flanks of Leygonier's army, and using the same tactics employed at La Guérinière the rebels charged and captured republican cannon deployed on the main road.

With his flanks compromised Leygonier had no option but to pull back, but this only emboldened the rebels to rush forwards and the republicans were soon in rout. The Finistère troops, acting as rearguard, vainly tried to put up some resistance, but to no avail and that night the debris of Leygonier's army gathered in Doué-la-Fontaine.

Several cannon, abundant munitions, and hundreds of prisoners were rounded up. On the following morning the beleaguered grenadiers in the Château of Bois-Grolleau were also forced to surrender.

Concerned that Berruyer might attack their rear the Vendéens did not pursue Leygonier too far but instead pulled back. They need not have feared as over 19 to 20 April Berruyer had struggled forward to Jallais before withdrawing to Chemillé on news of Leygonier's defeat. Gauvilliers, however, was isolated in Beaupréau and was about to face the rebel army alone.

The Battle of Beaupréau 22 April

Led by Bonchamps, D'Élbée, Cathelineau, Stofflet and La Rochejaquelein the peasants were estimated to be 30,000 strong.[15] As they neared Beaupréau, Cathelineau sent 1,500 men to outflank the town via the Château Park to its east. This detachment crossed the River Evre at La Gobinière, around 1km to the east of this parkland.[16]

Once again Deniau provides most detail on this engagement. Around 2pm D'Élbée, Stofflet, La Rochejaquelein and the rest of Cathelineau's column appeared on the Cholet road in sight of Beaupréau. They swept into nearby roads and behind hedges bordering the large meadow south of the town and deployed ten guns.

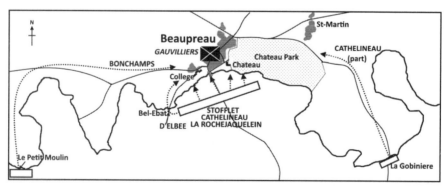

The assault on Beaupréau.

The republicans were in strong positions in Beaupréau which is set high on the north bank of the Evre, but Gauvilliers only had 1,500 men including battalions from Angers, Eure-et-Loire and Indre-et-Loire, and some dragoons.[17] They covered all the approaches and deployed their artillery in batteries facing the narrow bridge across the Evre and in the Place-du-Château. A small bastion had been thrown up on high ground in the Château Park and it was from there that the republicans spotted Cathelineau's men in La Gobinière. Cannon fired on them but overshot and a response from the *Marie-Jeanne* soon dismounted a republican gun.

Deniau recorded that Stofflet galloped to the banks of the Evre crying out to the Republicans, 'Can you hear, it's the *Marie-Jeanne*, can you hear?'. Then he returned, without being hit by the enemy. This act of bravado inspired the peasants. Their left flank approached the river and Cathelineau used planks to cross into the meadows bordering the college. D'Élbée's men crossed at Bel-Ébat and Bonchamps at the Petit Moulin. Once over the river Bonchamps attacked the republican right flank.

Meanwhile La Rochejaquelein and Stofflet's men, from the cover of woodland, opened up on those defending the Château Park and 500 more men were sent eastwards to reinforce those attempting to turn this park.

Gauvilliers men initially held well but became disordered when they attempted to pull back on news that they were being outflanked. Stofflet and La Rochejaquelein used this opportunity to advance towards the bridge. Seeing his men hesitate La Rochejaquelein seized a fusil, fired on the enemy, then galloped to the bridge, followed by Stofflet and some mounted men. Their troops now moved forwards infiltrating the streets and uniting with other rebels in a general advance.

In the town a company of national guards is said to have died under arms rather than surrender, the gunners of the Eure-et-Loire battalion were cut down at their pieces, and it is claimed by Muret that a squadron of dragoons was surrounded and forced to surrender.[18] The republican defence completely fell apart as they fled north, pursued all the way to the Loire.

Gauvilliers had not been present at this battle as he had been in St-Florent when the rebels attacked. His men lost five cannon and many weapons and the republicans admitted to 300 captured and 5-600 killed or wounded. The remaining troops pulled back to Ingrandes.

On hearing news of this further defeat Berruyer withdrew to St-Lambert as both his flanks were now exposed and his supply line to Les Pont-de-Cé at risk. He blamed the setbacks on the indiscipline and cowardice of the men and said the cavalry were useless in this heavily covered country where, he wrote, the enemy fought like those he had faced in Corsica.[19]

By 26 April Berruyer had withdrawn to Les Ponts-de-Cé and indicated that he would remain there until he received reinforcements. Writing to the interim minister of war he said he needed 15-20,000 experienced troops as the enemy had at least 25,000 men who were led by 'audacious leaders'.[20]

As Berruyer retreated, so Leygonier prepared to drop back towards Saumur, concerned that rebels in Vihiers were about to attack him. The patriot women of Doué, however, are reputed to have firmly held the town gates shut, forcing him to reconsider.[21]

Between 11 and 22 April the Vendéen rebels had held, defeated and routed four republican columns and seized abundant military supplies and numerous cannon. They had also gained valuable time to pause, regroup, and plan their next move.

Three commissaires were sent to find out just how serious the situation had become. They reported that the Vendéens were guided by a religious fury whereas the national guards were formed of fathers of families engaged for only fifteen days or a month at a time who persistently asked to go home. 'If this horde of fanatics cross the Loire it will be impossible to stop the torrent that will move to the heart of the Republic...or the seat of the National Convention.'[22]

Berruyer's plan had completely failed. In reality he had insufficient troops advancing in widely separated columns that were targeted in turn by the Vendéens, each time in overwhelming numbers.

After Beaupréau the Vendéens dispersed, seizing the opportunity to head home to their farms and villages and await the next summons to assemble. Now, for a few days, both sides paused.

Roc-de-Cheffois and La Châtaigneraie 10 and 12 April

While the republicans advanced in the north-east, in the south Chalbos moved up to La Châtaigneraie early in April where there was a post of 800 men, and 1,200 men occupied Ste-Hermine. On 10 April he launched an attack against rebels on the prominent position of Roc-de-Cheffois, 2km north-west of La Châtaigneraie. He had hoped for support from Quétineau but discovered he was marching north in accordance with Berruyer's orders.

Chalbos' small force probably exceeded 1,000 men and was supported by five guns. They advanced unnoticed and deployed in three columns near to the rebel positions and when he launched the attack many rebels simply fled, covered by a minority that put up a fight.

Two days later the rebels launched a sudden counter-attack and 3,000 were seen descending from the Cheffois area under Verteuil, one of Royrand's commanders.

To avoid being cut off the republican post at Roc-de-Cheffois pulled back and the rebels used that position to deploy their artillery and bombard the town. Chalbos managed to deploy his men in the roads of La Châtaigneraie as 'the brigands advanced in two columns with astonishing speed'.[23] As they advanced they were firing on the republicans and according to Chalbos this created clouds of dust and bullets 'whistled about their heads', but there were few casualties.[24] However, although the rebel artillery was badly aimed, Chalbos was forced to steady his left flank.

When he felt the time was right Chalbos ordered his cavalry to mount up and he led them in an outflanking manoeuvre to the left of the enemy-held high ground, and with this move the rebels soon withdrew. Chalbos claimed over 200 rebels were killed and two guns captured.

In spite of these small victories D'Ayat's chief of staff expressed concern about the quality of the troops in La Châtaigneraie, Ste-Hermine and Fontenay. The volunteers, he said, did not know how to load their weapons and were visibly shocked when gunfire first began. 'Without line troops this war will not end,' he said, and Chalbos had to take the precaution of deploying his gendarmes behind his volunteers to prevent them from fleeing.[25]

For the rest of the month the republicans on this front simply held their ground and took no further aggressive action.

Boulard's offensive in the Coastal Vendée 8 to 22 April

Completely independent of the activity to the east and north-east, Boulard, who had replaced Marcé, launched an assault northwards against the rebels in the coastal Vendée. By 3 April he had gathered an active field army of around 4,000 men in Les Sables d'Olonne, ably assisted by Representatives Niou and Gaudin.

Boulard reviewed 4,151 troops and sent 320 to St-Cyr-en-Talmondais, 50 to Avrillé, 300 to Olonne, 420 to Port-la-Claye, and left only 500 naval personnel and national guards in Les Sables.[26]

He divided his troops into two columns: one under his personal command and the other under Adjudant General Esprit Baudry (brother of the rebel leader Baudry d'Asson) and began his offensive at 10am on 8 April as news arrived of a further rebel move from La Mothe-Achard.[27] Both columns were led by 100 cavalry as they separately headed for La Grève and La Grassière. They were followed by seventy-two supply wagons, caissons, and carts for the wounded.[28]

Boulard's orders were to march through the Marais, recapture Noirmoutier, and pursue the royalists. His first step would be to march on La Mothe-Achard while Baudry headed for Vairé.

La Grassière 8 April

Boulard brushed aside 600 rebels at Pont Chartran and his advance guard halted before La Grassière where they found the bridge had been cut. The soldiers settled down to eat while workmen began its repair covered by the 9th Gironde and thirty mounted gendarmes who had crossed at a ford and deployed north of the river on a height beyond La Petite Grassière.[29] At around 2pm rebels under Joly's command were seen approaching.[30]

Boulard's men formed up in column on the main road south of the bridge but the troops north of the river, in spite of being protected by earthworks, fled across the partially repaired bridge as the rebels advanced which prevented their own artillery from being able to fire.[31] Joly's men managed to destroy the repairs to the bridge and was also looking for a way to turn the republican position but Boulard countered this threat and moved the 1st Bordeaux, with cavalry support, to successfully turn Joly's left flank. Simultaneously a company of grenadiers and four companies of the 2nd Bordeaux marched on the enemy entrenchments and recaptured the position originally held north of the river.[32]

Boulard occupied La Mothe-Achard that night as Joly retreated north to link up with Charette. Royrand, meanwhile, instructed the rebels in La Roche-sur-Yon to keep an eye on the enemy's march.[33]

Baudry's column, marching on Vairé, clashed with rebels led by Guerry-du-Cloudy dug in near La Grève on the far bank of the Auzance River.[34] Baudry was unable to build a bridge without exposing his workers and the conflict degenerated into a long and fruitless firefight.[35] Overnight the rebels slipped away and at 8am on the following morning Baudry crossed the river and marched to L'Aiguillon. He subsequently destroyed rebel entrenchments at both Vairé and La Gachère.[36]

Aware that the rebels were retiring on Challans, Boulard and Baudry moved up to St-Gilles and Croix-de-Vie respectively.[37] The tocsin was sounding in the Beaulieu area and Boulard soon realised that he had no hope of securing his landward line of communications back towards

Les Sables with the small army at his disposal and found few supplies in St-Gilles. Nevertheless on 10 April he received instructions from Niou to hasten his march on Noirmoutier, while being separately informed that Apremont was in enemy hands and several thousand rebels were near St-Hilaire.[38]

Guerry-du-Cloudy had abandoned St-Gilles to the republicans and retired on St-Hilaire-de Riez during 9 April. On the follow day, having heard that three frigates and two sloops had been sighted and mistakenly believing them to be English, he gathered 3–4,000 rebels and marched towards the coast.[39]

Boulard also feared that the rebels might be about to receive supplies from the English when they spotted three columns of rebels marching to the north of the River Vie.[40] He ordered Baudry to march from Croix-de-Vie on St-Hilaire-de-Riez to cut their retreat, and although the rebels withdrew before he was in position they did sustain some losses.[41]

Boulard left the 9th Gironde in St-Gilles and around midday on 11 April took the Challans road. His column moved along the left bank of the River Vie aiming to cross at Le Pas-Opton. Around 3pm he encountered 'a great number of brigands' forming part of Joly's command, entrenched near some houses at Le Pas-Opton with an 18pdr mounted on braced beams at the crossing.[42] Boulard moved his men to the left of this crossing and the fire from his battalion guns forced the rebels to abandon most of their entrenchments. High tide prevented him crossing the river so he resorted to using grapeshot to force the remaining rebels to withdraw, abandoning the 18pdr and two small guns as they did so.[43]

Baudry had been marching in three columns on the St-Hilaire-de-Riez road, aiming to attack the rear of these same rebels. He was delayed by rebels at St-Hilarie-de-Riez but dispersed them with cannon fire. Marching via La Jettière he rejoined Boulard in time to catch Joly in retreat that night.[44] The Republicans claimed more than 300 rebels killed.[45]

On 12 April Boulard and Baudry entered Challans and made preparations to march on Noirmouitier over the following days.

Challans 13 April

In addition to facing Boulard, Charette, based in Machecoul, was warned on 8 April that a column of 3,000 republicans was marching south from Nantes. On the following day he called for help from rebels in Bouin, announcing that he intended to defend the approach to Challans, where he arrived early on 13 April.[46] Joined by rebels under Joly, Cloudy, Savin and Du Chaffault between them they mustered 3-4,000 men.[47]

Boulard and Baudry's men, however, had pre-empted Charette and deployed in two echelons before Challans as the rebels approached: the 1st Division towards the north-east, the 2nd Division towards the north-west and their artillery in the centre.[48]

The rebels formed up in a semi-circle and attacked the north-eastern part of the town, with Charette on the right. Their armed troops formed a first wave of attack and advanced with loud cries, but when their army was in the process of deploying some cannon they noticed this first wave flooding back onto their second line. Boulard had stopped the initial assault in its tracks when he opened up with his cannon at very close range.[49]

Baudry followed up this success by launching a bayonet attack on Charette's men, who soon fled, abandoning their cannon as they did so. Joly and Cloudy now withdrew and Charette was nearly captured in the pursuit that followed. To negligible losses Boulard claimed 400-600 killed and three small guns.[50]

On 14 April Boulard and Baudry were approaching Noirmoutier, heading for Beauvoir-sur-Mer and St-Gervais respectively, when Boulard received a letter from Les Sables, dated 11 April, reporting a large rebel gathering at La Roche-sur-Yon and that rebels had reoccupied La Mothe-Achard. Representatives Carra and Auguis ordered him to send part of his column to La Mothe-Achard, explaining that D'Ayat's 4,000 troops were covering most of the southern front and they could not risk it being broken. They were also concerned that Berruyer's plan compromised Boulard's advance, believing that the march on Coron had not been carried out in coordination with D'Ayat and might push large numbers of rebels in Boulard's direction. Boulard was therefore instructed to await new orders from D'Ayat.[51]

While in this vulnerable predicament Boulard sought advice from Niou in Les Sables, whose response simply indicated that their own ships had been prevented from sailing by ten English ships sighted off the coast and that he should send some troops to protect Les Sables.[52]

Nevertheless by the evening of 14 April Boulard was at Beauvoir and Baudry at St-Gervais, moving ever closer to Noirmoutier. Boulard was still eager to achieve his first objective in spite of the diverse instructions and on 15 April he inspected the long causeway connecting Noirmoutier to the mainland, normally accessible at low tide, but was forced to concede that it was impractical in the current season.[53]

St-Gervais 15 April

The royalists seized the opportunity to attack Baudry's isolated column and with 7-8,000 rebels they headed for St-Gervais. Charette marched from Machecoul with 3,000 men and one cannon;[54] Du Chaffault and Gaston marched on the Palluau road from the south-east, and Guerry-du-Cloudy approached on the Challans road.[55] Baudry deployed in three bodies to face them. He was attacked by Charette towards 2pm near La Salle, east of St-Gervais, an hour before the other columns arrived. His artillery initially held the rebels back, but when Boulard joined Baudry in person he ordered the troops to pull back to the village while the Chasseurs-du-Midi, 1st Bordeaux and two 8pdrs were ordered to force-march to their support.

Guerry became embroiled in obstinate fighting and Du Chaffault, who reached the edge of St-Gervais, was repulsed in a counter-attack.

Charette led a strong column through unoccupied woodland near St-Gervais and successfully entered the village, forcing the republicans to abandon most of it and redeploy near their cannon on the Beauvoir road. At the western edge of St-Gervais, Charette's men were repulsed by the Volunteers of Barbézieux and these same cannon, and a counter-attack by the 1st Bordeaux forced him to give up the fight and retreat on the Challans road.[56]

According to Boulard the cavalry worked wonders that day and the rebels lost sixty killed, in addition to a cannon, a white flag, and a guidon.[57] The republicans admitted to a dozen casualties.[58] Among the dead was Gaston, who for a considerable time was mistakenly thought by the British government to be the main royalist leader.

After the battle Boulard withdrew to Challans and remained there until 20 April. He not only faced growing numbers of rebels but also mutiny by the Volunteers of the Charente (called the battalion *de la Liberté* formed on 26 March) and the Volunteers of Barbézieux (a *Compagnie-Franche* of around 120 men also from the Charente).[59] Men from these units left the ranks without permission and some may have joined Joly's rebels.[60]

Boulard was unable to continue his advance as supplies had effectively dried up. A further appeal by Niou to pull troops back at last won him over and on 20 April he set out towards Les Sables.[61] He left detachments to cover St-Gilles and on 22 April he was back in La Mothe-Achard. Baudry, meanwhile, re-established a post at Vairé.[62]

Although Boulard had secured Les Sables, the Vendéens had completely thwarted his plans.

Beysser's Advance from Nantes

On 20 April, while Boulard was retiring south, so Adjudant General Beysser set out from Nantes at the head of 2,000 infantry, 200 horse and 8 guns.[63] He headed straight for Port-Saint-Père which was being held by 200 rebels supported by an 8pdr, a 24pdr, and a few small guns.

The 600 strong republican advance guard was accompanied by two 12pdrs.[64] Capturing entrenchments near the River Achenau they discovered that the bridge had been cut and the far bank was defended by rebels. Once counter-battery fire commenced, the republicans soon gained the upper hand, helped by their grenadiers firing on the rebel gunners.[65] Meanwhile the bridge was repaired.

The Vendéens were commanded by a peasant named Pajot (not to be confused with the rebel leader of Bouin with the same name), who hoped to stall the republicans and give time for Charette to march to the sound of the guns. To conserve his ammunition he alternated between periods of musketry and cannon fire and held his ground for over three hours. Unfortunately Pajot was struck and fell seriously wounded, causing his men to take flight. Beysser seized the position and on the following day advanced on Machecoul.

Machecoul 21 April

Hearing of the defeat at Port-Saint-Père, Charette vainly appealed for help from Bouin, St-Philbert and Bourgneuf.[66] His force totalled around 3,000 men and included 80 cavalry and 5 cannon, but Machecoul was only protected by some crudely constructed entrenchments.[67]

Vendéen scouts spotted enemy dragoons 4km north of Machecoul and in response Charette deployed his men in a crude line at the junction of the Bourgneuf and Port-Saint-Père roads, just north of the town.[68]

Towards 6am the republican advance guard appeared and an exchange of cannon fire commenced. According to Savary the battle was something of a farce.[69] Beysser, he wrote, had given orders that when they arrived on the field of battle they should fire their cannon and watch how the enemy reacted. When the army arrived, two 12pdrs unlimbered and began to fire while the cavalry deployed and the infantry formed up in four columns. All at once the firing ceased and the Vendéens were seen to break up and flee, allowing the republicans to enter Machecoul unopposed.

While the rebel flanks did indeed flee Charette and his cavalry, gunners, and some of his infantry remained. Charette attempted to charge the enemy in the vain hope his other troops might return, but his horse was killed beneath him just as the republican infantry were forming up in column of attack. The few troops left to him now fled and Charette was only saved by riding pillion behind one of his cavalrymen.[70]

Beysser claimed he suffered no casualties, rounded up a great number of prisoners in his pursuit, and captured the rebel cannon.[71] One of the prisoners was Souchu, the man responsible for the massacre of republicans in Machecoul. He was swiftly beheaded by a sapper.[72]

Charette rushed to Legé hoping to gather men to slow the republican advance but discovered that many had left to join Joly in pursuit of Boulard. He then headed east with his few remaining cavalry, hoping for support from the Army of the Centre. Some accounts suggest that he received a humiliating reception from Royrand who publicly reproached him for abandoning Machecoul.[73] As men had started to drift back to him Charette decided to return to Legé.

On the day after the battle Beysser sent out two detachments of 300 men to sweep the country for rebels.[74] On 26 April he informed Boulard of his dispositions but was unaware just how reduced in numbers this general was, or of the difficulties he was facing. Beysser's easy march to Machecoul led him to believe the troubles were nearly over. He soon had 100 men in both Port-Saint-Père and Bourgneuf, and 850 at St-Philbert, while the rest remained with him in Machecoul. He now asked Boulard to move north to Legé.

'By marching thus, your column will be able to leave a detachment in each of these posts, send 300 men to St-Étienne-de-Corcoué [8km north of Legé], and you can fall back on me with at least 1,200 men. Once united ... we will be able to undertake the great expedition of Noirmoutier'.[75]

Boulard was astonished by this letter and even more surprised when he received another from Boisguyon (then in Challans) advising him that Beysser believed it was only a question of 'pushing at an open door'.[76]

On 27 April Representative Goupilleau arrived at Boulard's headquarters in La Mothe-Achard and two days later, in spite of all his difficulties, his small column set out for Beaulieu in torrential rain.[77] He repulsed Joly at Palluau but then received a letter from Gaudin in Les Sables, reporting large numbers of rebels gathered around La Roche-sur-Yon, Clouzeaux and Aubigny. With only 500 men in Les Sables, the risk to the port was great.

The Recapture of Noirmoutier 28 April

Beysser, however, was still intent on seizing Noirmoutier, but when he reached Bourgneuf he heard that the island had in fact been captured by the navy.

The assault had been planned by Admiral Villaret-Joyeuse who was responsible for the coast of Morbihan and the Vendée. He deployed the frigates *Achille* and *Superbe* near the island and Captain Boisauveur of the *Achille* launched a surprise landing with 200 men at 1.30am on 28 April. The rebel response was to flee to the mainland and Beysser subsequently garrisoned the island with 700 men.[78]

Legé 30 April

On his return to Legé, Charette managed to assemble 5-600 men and Vrignault brought a further 1,000 from Vieillevigne.[79] Beysser, hearing of this assembly from his base in Machecoul, dispatched Adjudant General Boisguyon with 600 infantry, 40 cavalry and two guns to seize the town. Beysser, however, failed to coordinate this attack with Boulard who was then in Palluau with 1,500 men.

Vrignault seemed happy to defer command to Charette, and the rebels deployed behind trees and bushes on high ground west of the River Logne.

Around 2pm, having marched 20km in terrible weather, the republican advance guard came up against well sustained fire from the royalists.[80] Boisguyon had not expected to meet many rebels so continued his advance, jostling Charette's troops back on Legé. Boisguyon's artillery, cavalry and a company of infantry remained in column on the tortuous and muddy road while a half-battalion deployed facing Richebonne Château and wood (believed to be in enemy occupation).[81] With his other battalion he bypassed the area where Charette had deployed and marched towards the right of the Vendéens. This move obliged the rebels to pull back across the river before rallying on high ground near a small chapel.

The Vendéen left flank covered their retreat and Boisguyon, without waiting for the rest of his column, continued his advance. Charette urged his men to defend the chapel and encouraged them to charge the Republicans, pouring down fire and threatening their flanks. Boisguyon's battalion was unable to deploy under this fusillade so he now attempted to use his remaining forces to cover his withdrawal. He was forced to back-track along the steep road down to the ford, but his artillery had deployed and blocked

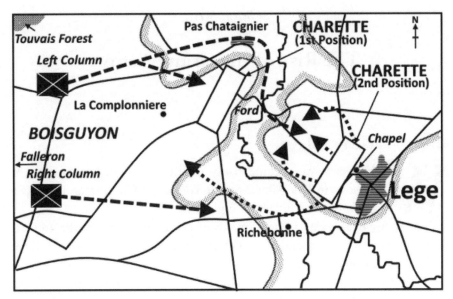

The Battle of Legé.

the way, and the rest of his infantry were hampered from deploying by his cavalry who were trying to escape enemy fire coming from the direction of the Richebonne road.

Boisguyon wrote that his infantry, in complete panic, 'fired when nothing was before them and used up their ammunition'.[82] His artillery, caissons, supplies and many fusils fell into enemy hands and, finding themselves being enveloped by 'a dense swarm of rebels', his column fled towards Falleron. The Vendéens raced behind hedgerows to either side of the road, firing at their enemy and rounding up prisoners. Some of the 4th Line deserted to join Charette's ranks.

Boisguyon claimed that if his men had shown more skill in deploying they could have beaten the Vendéens, but lamented that many in his ranks had never previously seen action.[83]

By the end of April the republicans had seized Noirmoutier, Machecoul, La Mothe-Achard and Palluau and had demoralised many of the rebels. Yet Charette's victory at Legé offered them a glimmer of hope and news was coming in of the complete defeat of republican columns beyond Cholet.

Chapter 6

The Rise of the Grand Army

Mareuil-sur-Lay 3 May

While events were going badly in the north and north-east the garrisons in Les Sables, Ste-Hermine, La Châtaigneraie, Luçon and Fontenay were all on high alert.

The Army of the Centre had limited involvement in the battles to their north. A Vendéen post under St-Pal and De Chouppes, perhaps 1,200 strong, was using the strategically located town of Mareuil-sur-Lay, 9km north of Luçon, as a base from which to harass the republicans.[1] D'Ayat retaliated on 3 May by dispatching columns from Luçon and Ste-Hermine in a surprise attack.

St-Pal had set up tree trunks to appear like cannon served by dummy gunners and fooled the republicans into thinking the post was more powerful than it actually was.[2]

D'Ayat's orders, if carried out correctly, would result in three columns simultaneously attacking around 3am. Two columns set out from Luçon. The first, under his personal command, headed for the Beaulieu heights south of Mareuil and would signal their attack by firing a cannon. The second column, under Lieutenant Colonel Ramond, made a long detour to the west then north to appear at St André, west of Mareuil, and then split into three parts.

The third column, under Canier, comprised the Ste-Hermine garrison and eighty cavalry and marched via the Moutiers Bridge to the woods of La Nicolière, north-east of Marueil. Around ninety men from the second column would be sent into these same woods and the officer in charge was ordered to keep in communication with the third column when it arrived in position. Canier's column would announce its presence by firing its 4pdr cannon.[3] Pioneers were attached to all three columns.

D'Ayat's column deployed on the heights of Beaulieu and could see rebels in front of the church and château and in an observation post on top of a hill.

The rebels immediately started to flee, fired on by cannon as they did so, and Canier's column killed some attempting to escape to the north-east.

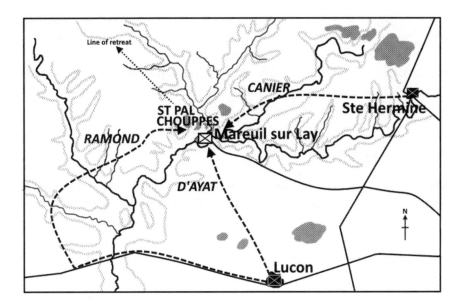

Mareuil-sur-Lay.

Due to the swollen river and the rebel precaution of felling trees to block the roads the second column was delayed and many Vendéens escaped on the La Roche-sur-Yon road to the north-west. In his flight St-Pal left behind his valise and a number of pewter balls, and interrogated prisoners indicated that they had virtually no ammunition.[4]

The March of the Grand Army

While the republicans were desperately trying to contain the revolt and gather troops, Bonchamps, D'Élbée, Sapinaud-de-la-Verrie, Stofflet and Cathelineau had been considering how to expand the Rising.[5] A council of war in Cholet, influenced by La Rochejaquelein, concluded with a plan to march south-east against Quétineau and raise recruits in that area.

On Sunday, 28 April, the tocsin could be heard across the region and within two days 25-27,000 men had gathered in Cholet accompanied by 750 horse and about fourteen guns of varying calibre.[6] Heading for Bressuire they camped at Vihiers that same evening and reinforcements raised their strength to around 30,000.[7] On 1 May they launched an assault on the 800 national guards defending Argenton-Château and captured this post after a short combat, securing more munitions.[8]

From his headquarters in Bressuire, Quétineau was relatively inactive in late April and was busy trying to control insubordination in his ranks. On 1 May he was informed by Leygonier of the attack on Argenton-Château and at 8am on the following day he abandoned Bressuire and retreated to Thouars. On route around 500 troops left his ranks, refusing to serve under a general they considered 'suspect'.

Thouars 5 May 1793

Thouars is a medieval walled town perched high above a loop in the River Thouet. Although the old stone walls were in poor condition it was

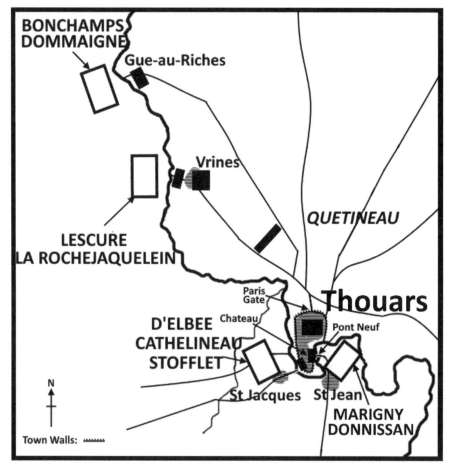

The assault on Thouars.

nevertheless a strong position. To the south, east and west of the town were steep slopes leading down to the river and the royalist army could only attack across a handful of crossings.

The Vendéens had been joined at Bressuire by more former officers: Lescure, his father-in-law Donnissan, Marigny and Des Essarts. They had been imprisoned in the town and, in their haste to evacuate, the republicans simply left them behind. Along with La Rochejaquelein, Lescure immediately set about raising peasants from parishes in the Bressuire area where they were both notable local figures.

The rebel army set out from Bressuire on 4 May and camped that evening at Coulanges-Thouarsis. Although Leygonier recognised the difficulties faced by Quétineau, his own troops in Doué were in no state to help and he dared not move.[9]

General Quétineau lamented his lack of staff and ongoing desertions that probably cost him around a third of his strength. Further raw and untrained volunteers had been hastily summoned from the surrounding area but these 2–3,000 men were to prove of little use.[10]

What armed troops the Vendéens had were probably split among the columns and formed the key fighting force, but ammunition for both the infantry and artillery was limited. The Vendéens had yet to appoint a commander-in-chief so strategy was determined by the elected divisional generals and a handful of other experienced former officers.

In the lead up to the battle most of the royalist army formed into columns as follows:

- Cathelineau, d'Élbée and Stofflet: perhaps 7,000 and a few cannon.
- Marigny and Donnissan: 2,000 infantry and around half the cannon.
- Lescure and La Rochejaquelein: with an advance guard of around 1,500 with a few cannon, followed at some distance by perhaps 5,000 more.
- Bonchamps: probably in excess of 5,000 men supported by Dommaigné with 750 cavalry.

Quétineau chose to fight a defensive battle with most of his troops in fixed position, almost certainly due to the dubious quality of his forces. He deployed 300 national guards at the Gué-au-Riche and his few cavalry were spread out in open land between the Gué-au-Riches and Vrines. The Pont de Vrines was defended by three cannon and 150 men using an upturned wagon filled with dung to block the crossing (all but a small section in the middle of this bridge had been dismantled). A further 900 troops were in defensive positions in Vrines and adjacent vineyards, formed from a company of the 8th Var and two battalions of national guards.

The Pont St-Jean (also known as the Pont-Neuf) was guarded by a detachment and one cannon, with a similar detachment covering the Pont St-Jacques. Quétineau considered these bridges impracticable to attack as they were barely four metres wide.

The Thouars National Guard deployed at the Pont de Praillon, some distance to the south-east, to secure a line of retreat if that proved necessary. Deployed near some mills between Vrines and Thouars were troops under Quétineau's personal command ready to act as a mobile reserve.[11]

Around 1,000 men were in Thouars with at least one cannon deployed in the château. Dispersed along the river and north of Thouars were small detachments deployed to slow any enemy advance and report on their approach.

The first gunfire was heard between 5 and 6am from 1,200 rebels under Lescure and La Rochejaquelein's command gathered on high ground facing the Pont de Vrines. During the morning the rest of their army slowly moved into position. Facing the Pont St-Jacques was the contingent under D'Élbée, Cathelineau and Stofflet; Donnissan and Marigny headed for the Pont St-Jean, and Dommaigné and Bonchamps moved towards the Gué-au-Riche. The Vendéens bombarded the defenders at the bridges at Vrines and St-Jacques for several hours. They may have been trying to lure the republicans into believing these where the principal points of attack.

Towards 10am, and with powder running low, La Rochejaquelein set out to find more and speed up the march of the rest of their column which had yet to appear. The republicans in Vrines also appealed for reinforcements.

While La Rochejaquelein was away Lescure thought the republican defenders were starting to pull back, so he took up a fusil, shouted to the men to advance and descended to the bridge. He was met by a discharge of musketry and grapeshot that peppered his clothes but left him unharmed. No peasants had followed him. He climbed back onto nearby rocks, appealed to them once more, and again descended to the bridge to be met by a new discharge of musketry and grapeshot; again he was unharmed, but still alone. It is quite possible that although known to many of the peasants Lescure had yet to win their confidence.

During the morning Quétineau had been observing the combat at St-Jacques when he became aware that the Vendéens were reinforcing their troops west of Vrines (almost certainly La Rochejaquelein returning with the bulk of his and Lescure's troops). He quickly sent notice to the Vrines defenders to retire on Thouars if their position was forced.

Towards 11am Lescure descended to the bridge for a third time, this time followed by a single soldier. Fortunately La Rochejaquelein and Forest now appeared and the four of them rushed the republican defences. Arriving at the entrenchments Lescure rested his fusil on the parapet and began firing at point-blank range. At last the peasants came to their support, overwhelmed their opponents, and captured around 200 men.

Quétineau immediately sent warning to the troops at Gué-au-Riches to pull back to Thouars, but was unaware that this post had also fallen having put up stiff resistance until overwhelmed by numbers. Bonchamps and Dommaigné were now moving south to support La Rochejaquelein and Lescure while the handful of republican cavalry in their way retreated on the Loudun road.

Two columns were now threatening both Quétineau's flanks: Marigny and Donnissan marching to attack Pont St-Jean and Bonchamps and Dommaigné moving down through Vrines.

The republicans who were retreating from Vrines were tracked nearly all the way to Thouars by around thirty Vendéen horse, including a number of officers. This detachment then dropped back to hasten the army forwards.

Noticing that the rebels seemed to pause near a mill between Vrines and Thouars, Daniaud-Dupeyrat, a Republican soldier and eye-witness, wrote:

'We immediately had all the battalions deployed in line the Deux-Sèvres in the centre, the Marseillais with their two campaign guns and the Thouars National Guard on the left ... and the Volunteers of Poitiers and Châtellerault...on the right.'

They were supported by some mounted gendarmes. The republican officers had spread rumours that the rebels facing them had no cannon, and the troops had convinced themselves that their enemy only knew how to fight sheltered by woodland. Quétineau therefore headed towards this mill. The rebels, however, had been biding their time while more troops and cannon were brought up, and the republicans were allowed to draw near before they opened fire with both musketry and artillery. The shock of cannon fire seems to have broken republican resolve and as panic set in they raced towards Thouars and ignored Quetineau's pleas to deploy in front of the walls and not enter the cramped medieval streets.[12]

On the St-Jean front Marigny had eventually cleared Porte Maillot with his cannon which gave him access to the St-Jean Bridge, and on the St-Jacques front a Vendéen column had forced the bridge and deployed at the foot of the town. Nevertheless both columns still faced some opposition from troops defending the southern approaches to Thouars.

When the rebels reached the town's walls they looked for a way to form a breach. Up against the walls near the Paris Gate La Rochejaquelein climbed onto the shoulders of one of his men to fire on the defenders as a succession of loaded fusils were handed up to him. He also joined in attempts to dislodge stones from the dilapidated walls while coming under fire. Republican morale had largely collapsed when troops under La Rochejaquelein, Lescure, Bonchamps, D'Élbée and Cathelineau poured into Thouars from several directions and they faced little resistance. The town was not pillaged and there was little bloodshed when the republicans surrendered en masse around 5pm.

The immediate consequence of this astounding victory was a wealth of military supplies. Sources generally agree that 5-600 republicans were killed and 3-5,000 taken prisoner. They also seized 3-4,000 fusils, 6,000 pairs of pistols, 2,000 sabres, 8-10 cannon, ample munitions and a large treasury.

An old associate of Lescure, Quétineau was offered a rank in the royalist army, but loyal to the republic he refused. He was released on parole and given safe conduct to Saumur, but was subsequently imprisoned and faced a harrowing trial before the Revolutionary Tribunal, ultimately ending at the guillotine. As a friend of the 'traitor' Dumouriez his fate was perhaps inevitable.

All but 200 of the republican prisoners were disarmed and released on the promise they would not serve against the Vendéens again. Some republicans willingly changed sides and one notable addition to their army was the so-called Bishop of Agra, a certain Guyot de Folleville, one-time curé of Dol. Having left the priesthood he had settled in Poitiers where he joined the National Guard. From there he was dispatched to Thouars with Quétineau's column. The rebel leaders were delighted to have a bishop in their ranks and recognised the army's need for such authoritative spiritual oversight. When he was exposed as a fraud in the autumn this was kept quiet and he continued in his influential role, ultimately dying bravely for their cause.

For the Vendéens the victory at Thouars was proof once more that they could take the fight to the enemy and achieve an overwhelming victory. With the supplies from Bressuire and Thouars they now set about giving their army a more formal structure before considering their next move.

The Army of Anjou and Poitou, also known as the Catholic and Royal Army, was soon commonly referred to as the Grand Army. It was now officially formed into divisions under Lescure, Cathelineau, Bonchamps, D'Élbée, Stofflet, La Rochejaquelein and Laugrénière (see Appendix 3).

Bonchamps was back in Cholet on 11 May escorting the wounded and a large share of the captured supplies. His men had an important role guarding the Loire.

In a council of war it was agreed that the rest of the army would attack the republicans in La Châtaigneraie, over 50km to the south-west. This would also enable them to link up with rebels in that region and expand the Rising.

When they marched on 9 May their forces had diminished to 12-14,000 foot and 6-700 horse, although these numbers would increase as they advanced on La Châtaigneraie.[13] A republican detachment under Sandoz evacuated Parthenay as the rebels approached, reoccupying the town three days later.

La Châtaigneraie 13 May

The Vendéens held a council of war on 11 May to plan the assault on La Châtaigneraie and on Lescure's advice they agreed to attack the town from three directions at once.

Chalbos was holding La Châtaigneraie with a force of 3,000 men supported by two 12pdrs and a 4pdr (although Chalbos claimed he faced 12,000 rebels with only 2,000 men).[14]

Large numbers of rebels were reported to be gathering in Réaumur, St-Pierre-du-Chemin and Moncoutant, north and north-east of La Châtaigneraie, but Chalbos had confidence in his troops and his well-prepared positions so decided to remain where he was.[15]

At 6am on 13 May a strong rebel column, preceded by numerous cavalry, was seen advancing south of Moncoutant.[16] Quite when the main battle began is unclear, but at some point over the next few hours a large body of rebels, using the cover of hedges, appeared on Chalbos' right flank. He drew his forces together and deployed to face them, later reporting that his troops withstood a sustained fire for an hour and a half, with the Armagnac Battalion taking punishing losses.[17]

Chalbos' right flank was under pressure and at risk of being turned when a second column under Stofflet and La Rochejaquelein was spotted approaching from St-Pierre-du-Chemin. Meanwhile a column under Lescure and Marigny had detoured to the west through Cheffois to move

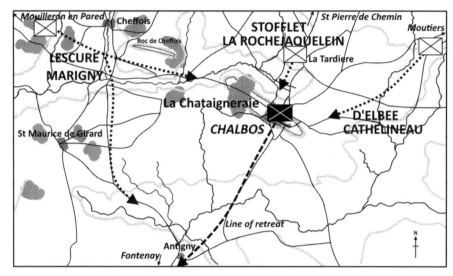

The Battle of La Châtaigneraie.

on Chalbos' left and sent some troops towards Antigny to cut off his line of retreat.

Chalbos later reported that these brigands were very different from those he had previously encountered, with some firing-by-file and others advancing with closed ranks.[18] Their cavalry, he wrote, were well mounted and very bold.[19] Marigny was also proving his worth by directing the rebel artillery with notable success.[20]

Chalbos had no choice but to order the retreat and around noon he withdrew in good order preceded by his artillery and baggage.[21] As he pulled back to Fontenay he was forced to halt and fire on his pursuers on more than one occasion.

Fontenay-le-Comte 16 May

Fontenay was a significant administrative centre, an active republican base, and a clear threat to the Vendéens. Following up their success at La Châtaigneraie they were determined to seize it.

During April units of national guards were hastily organised in the area, including 100 mounted scouts, yet on 7 May there were fewer than 300 men in the town.[22] All male citizens of the Fontenay commune aged 17 to 60 were therefore called up and D'Ayat ordered the open land north of the town to be mown so the troops could use the area as a camp.[23] As early as 1 May a

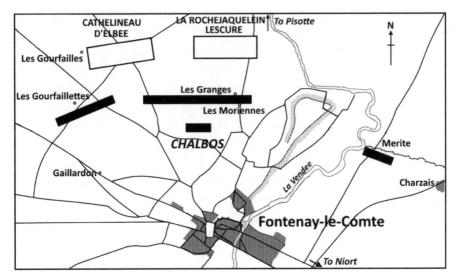

First Battle of Fontenay-le-Comte.

republican engineer had begun constructing earthworks around Fontenay but by 16 May had only completed redoubts at Gaillardon, Les Moriennes and on the Mérité front to the east.[24]

As Chalbos' column arrived from La Châtaigneraie urgent appeals for help were issued and an influx of troops followed as the republicans evacuated several posts. A council of war had even ordered the army to retreat from Fontenay, until Sandoz's arrival from St-Maixent on the 15 May calmed their nerves. Sandoz brought with him 3,000 infantry, 100 horse and some guns.[25] Niort also dispatched between 3,800 and 6,000 men.[26] In total between 7,500 and 10,000 were present when the rebels attacked.[27]

On 15 May the royalists sent out orders from La Châtaigneraie stating,

'We the commanders of the Catholic and Royal Armies order all general officers, colonels and captains of the said armies to reunite their respective corps this evening at 3pm and make a roll call, inspect the arms and ammunition, and distribute supplies for two days'.[28]

It was towards midday on 16 May that large numbers of rebels were spotted at Pisotte, 3km north of Fontenay. The republicans rapidly deployed in prearranged positions covering the northern approaches to the town. With D'Ayat and 150 mounted gendarmes away on a visit to Luçon, Chalbos took command. The infantry were deployed in the centre and placed under Sandoz's orders, his right was commanded by Adjudant General Dufour, and Chalbos personally commanded the cavalry placed in reserve.[29]

The Vendéens were spread out across the relatively flat open land north of Fontenay with their front covered by more than thirty cannon deployed in batteries.[30] Sources differ over the deployment of the columns and although Lescure and La Rochejaquelein seem to have commanded the left wing and D'Élbée and Cathelineau the right, it is not clear which wing Stofflet joined. The cavalry were under Dommaigné and Marigny directed the artillery. There is also confusion over the strength of the royalist army at this battle, ranging from a mere 7,000, according to Madame de la Rochejaquelein, to 15-18,000 noted by the Republicans.

Only a few key events can be pieced together as this battle is poorly documented. Fighting started around the Les Granges and Les Gourfailles Farms with an artillery bombardment that continued for more than two hours and caused some disorder in the republican ranks.[31] Sensing victory, Marigny mounted a horse and with other leaders moved forwards to the attack.[32] Crétineau-Joly, not the most reliable of sources, suggests that Lescure and La Rochejaquelein penetrated Fontenay's suburbs but stalled when the republicans facing them rallied.[33]

What is clear is that Chalbos led an unsuccessful charge against the rebel flank, but subsequently charged again, this time in concert with two squadrons he had left under his chief of staff Nouvion. They caught the rebels to the rear of their right wing and in their centre, causing them to fall into disarray and flee. Chalbos then charged on into the exposed rebel artillery as his infantry charged forwards with fixed bayonets.

It was all over quite quickly and disorder in the rebel ranks was aggravated by D'Élbée falling wounded.[34] La Rochejaquelein managed to cover the retreat and haul away two small guns.[35]

The republicans captured twenty-five guns, including a number of 16pdrs and two 18pdrs, and claimed they suffered only ten casualties to 5-600 rebels killed.[36] The Vendéens admitted that over 240 of their men had been captured.[37]

Chalbos was promoted to the rank of general of division following this victory and on 20 May returned to La Châtaigneraie with 7,000 men.[38]

For the royalists this was a humiliating debacle and a sharp lesson in the risks associated with engaging in more open terrain better suited to cavalry. The loss in artillery and ammunition was especially disastrous, yet only nine days later they took a major gamble and attacked the town once more.

The Second Battle of Fontenay 25 May

On 24 May Chalbos received news that large numbers of rebels were approaching and he once again retreated from La Châtaigneraie. His tired and hungry army reached Fontenay at 6am on the following day.[39]

An estimated 20-25,000 Vendéen infantry and 2,000 cavalry were present, although they only had thirty cannon cartridges and one shot per infantryman.[40]

To oppose them Chalbos fielded 6-7,000 infantry, 250 horse and 35-40 guns.[41]

At about 11.30am the republicans were warned that the rebels were approaching and deployed in the same positions as on 16 May, in three main bodies stretching from Les Gourfailles to Charzais.[42] Their centre deployed behind the redoubts facing Pisotte with a battery placed in the Haute-Roche enclosure and their cavalry were placed in reserve.

The republicans were confident of victory and were told the enemy had no cannon, although Adjudant Major Constantin complained that Chalbos was badly deployed and instead of placing his troops in line in the best possible positions, he deployed where the enemy could approach quite close under cover.[43]

Marching via La Châtaigneraie on 24 May the Grand Army advanced through Pisotte then deployed in three columns, Bonchamps commanding the right, Cathelineau the centre, and Lescure the left.[44]

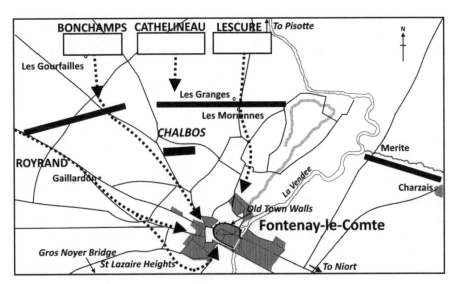

Second Battle of Fontenay-le-Comte.

Dommaigné commanded the cavalry, probably held in reserve.[45] Stofflet seems to have been with Cathelineau in the centre. Some sources place La Rochejaquelein in reserve with the cavalry while others place him on the right.[46] It is most likely that the six guns were split into pairs to support each column. The wounded D'Élbée was absent and Duhoux d'Hauterive commanded his column which probably deployed with Bonchamps. Bonchamps acted as overall commander and before the battle absolution was given to the soldiers.

The battle commenced around 1.30pm with an artillery duel which, from the Vendéen perspective, was brief.[47] Mercier-de-Rocher said the republican artillery started firing too soon and pointlessly wasted ammunition.[48]

With the ammunition exhausted Marigny mounted up and urged his gunners to go for the republican caissons.[49] Lescure led the first column to attack and was obliged to place himself on horseback forty paces in advance of his men to get them to follow. Grapeshot soon rained down around him, but other than some holes in his clothing, a spur shot off, and a great chunk knocked out of one of his boots, he was unharmed and shouted to his men, 'My children the Blues don't know how to fire; you will be fine, advance!'[50]

Inspired by this bravado his men started to run and Lescure moved at a fast trot to remain in the front rank. Tradition suggests that on seeing a large wayside cross his men knelt to pray, even though within cannon range, and on rising they surged towards the enemy.[51]

Goupilleau recalled the enemy's fearless advance and that a strong cavalry force attacked the republican left where he and Chalbos were stationed.[52] The Vendéens had evidently learnt not to expose their flank to the republican cavalry.

After a period of sustained firing, during which the Chasseurs of the Gironde, Compagnie-Franche of Toulouse and 4th Hérault were singled out for bravery, Goupilleau noticed a battalion of volunteers in the second line giving ground. When he and Chalbos attempted to rally them these same volunteers attacked them as they fled.

Goupilleau was furious with the mounted gendarmes who had been deployed in support of the centre and left. At one point he saw the enemy centre waver and move backwards around fifty paces, but when Chalbos ordered the gendarmes to charge only five men advanced and the rest trampled their own infantry in their determination to run away.[53]

Beauvais claimed the Vendéens gave their enemy little time to fire as they had decided to attack quickly, lying flat each time the enemy touched fuses.

He said their cavalry charged almost at the same time as their infantry and the republican artillery was soon overrun.[54] The republican left gave way first, followed by their centre, and eventually their right.[55]

Mercier-de-Rocher wrote that Fontenay was turned 'in the blink of an eye' with enemy columns seizing all the roads into the town.[56] One column descended from the Heights of Saint-Lazare to intercept the Gros-Noyer Bridge and another arrived via the Saumur Gate. The republican agent at Niort recalled the rebels entering in mass via the Porte du Marchaix.[57]

The royalists entered Fontenay around 2.30pm. Lescure's column arrived at the town gates first, but when he entered his troops did not follow. Bonchamps and Forest, noticing this from afar, rushed to join him. These three entered a town crammed with retreating republicans and on reaching the square they split up and called on the republicans to surrender, promising they would not be ill-treated. One soldier appeared to be surrendering to Bonchamps, but snatched up his musket and shot him at close range causing a severe wound. In revenge the rebels killed around sixty republicans before their leaders could calm them down.[58]

The generals and representatives vainly tried to rally the troops as they routed on the Niort road. D'Ayat and Nouvion were both caught up in this rout and managed to rally twenty-five gendarmes, with whom they charged and repulsed 200 rebel cavalry, enabling some of their infantry to escape.[59] Some troops eventually rallied near to Niort.

The Army of the Centre under Béjarry, Cumont and Verteuil had not participated in the first battle, but on appeal from the Grand Army had gathered at Chantonnay on 24 May. They appeared on Chalbos' left flank just as it was giving way.[60] Béjarry claimed that their presence hastened the republican rout and they entered the Luçon Gate as the column led by Bonchamps arrived at the Rue du Leonard.[61]

The battle was over by mid-afternoon although the pursuit on the Niort road continued until nightfall. The Republicans had dispersed on both the Niort and Marans roads.[62]

The Vendéens rounded up 3-5,000 prisoners.[63] Twenty-five guns were captured and they retrieved the famous *Marie-Jeanne* lost at the first battle.[64] The Vendéens also seized 7,000 fusils and a great quantity of powder.[65] Around 440 rebel prisoners, due to be guillotined on the following day, were also freed.[66]

Only a few hundred republican prisoners were retained and, as was now becoming common practice, the Vendéens shaved the heads of the rest and freed them on the promise that they would not serve against them for a year.

The Representatives of the People, Goupilleau de Montaigu, Goupilleau de Fontenay and Garnier de Saintes, all blamed the defeat on the gendarmes who had 'fled like cowards' and the National Convention subsequently ordered their arrest.[67]

Around this time 3,500 men under Salomon marched into Thouars but would not remain long as the Grand Army would soon begin its next enterprise: the advance on Saumur.

The administration of rebel territory

On 27 May the Vendéen leaders created a Superior Council in Châtillon under the overall presidency of the Bishop of Agra, although Charette never officially recognised it. This Council was widely respected and largely obeyed. It had three distinct branches, each under a separate council, covering matters military, ecclesiastical and civil.[68]

The Superior Council had to deal with a wide variety of daily problems within the hundreds of parishes falling within their control. Their responsibilities included ensuring the framework for the divisions; parish companies were in place; protecting and feeding thousands of republican prisoners; overseeing the many hospitals; issuing proclamations and military bulletins; establishing their own system of money (the Royal Assignats); collecting and distributing funds; and addressing evasion from military service, to name but a few of their tasks.

The Military Council, of nine members, comprised the commander-in-chief and the core of the most senior generals. They kept their discussions secret and their prime function was the defence of the region, organisation of the armies, and planning of the campaigns.

With the capture of Châtillon in October, the function of the Superior Council effectively ceased, although supply and military matters would be at the forefront of the Vendéens' attention for the rest of the year.

Coastal Vendée

Palluau 2 May

On 2 May, Joly, leading 3,000 men, launched a sudden attack on Boulard who was than in Palluau.[69] Warned in the early hours that large numbers of rebels had gathered on the Petit-Luc and Beaufou side of Palluau and that columns were moving on the Ligneron and Legé roads, Boulard quickly deployed to face them. Part of the 1st Bordeaux engaged in a lively firefight on the St-Christophe road and the appearance of a cannon forced this rebel column to break off the fight.

Part of the 2nd Bordeaux, a detachment from the 110th Line and a cavalry picket had a tough fight on the Beaufou road with the rebels taking advantage of the cover of hedges. The royalist centre was on the Legé road but rather than advancing it fed troops to the other two columns. When these columns broke off the fight the centre retreated.

The battle lasted most the day and Charette had remained away from the action with a reserve of 2-300 men.[70] He was more interested in recapturing Machecoul and set out that same night with 1,000 infantry, 100 cavalry and 5 small guns.[71] However, these troops became restless on route, and then simply stopped marching, most actually being Vrignault's men. Charette had to abandon his plans and return to Legé.

Meanwhile Canclaux, who had heard of Boisguyon's defeat and had joined Beysser in Machecoul, planned to attack Legé from four directions with a combined strength of around 4,000-4,300 infantry, 180 cavalry and 10 guns.[72] Canclaux would march with Beysser in person, skirting the north of the Touvois Forest before advancing on the Nantes road, accompanied by 7-800 infantry, a squadron of cavalry and two guns; Baudry would march from Challans and St-Christophe with 1,600 infantry, a small number of cavalry and two guns, taking the Touvois road (with orders to make demonstrations to hold the enemy if circumstances made a full attack difficult); Boulard would march from Palluau with 1,200 infantry, a squadron of cavalry and four guns, taking a route left of the Grande-Landes Forest and when near Legé he would detach cavalry towards Retail; finally Labory would march straight down the great Nantes road from Saint-Colombin with 600 infantry, a squadron of gendarmes and two guns, sending a detachment to block the Rocheservière road.

All the columns were meant to arrive before Legé at 11am, but Boulard arrived first, soon followed by Beysser. As Charette had been warned of their approach he withdrew with Vrignault to Vieillevigne.[73]

Over the next few days Charette received another poor reception from the Army of the Centre, and hearing from refugees that the republicans had reoccupied St-Colombin and Pont-James, 15km north of Legé, he decided to set out with his small contingent to attack them.[74]

Pont-James and St-Colombin 7 May

Labory commanded between 300 and 500 men split between Pont-James and St-Colombin. They were reportedly demoralised, lacked supplies and had limited ammunition.[75] Charette marched overnight and on approaching the enemy split his small force in two: the left wing included deserters from 4th Line, followed by men under La Robrie with two cannon; Charette and the cavalry formed the right wing.

Labory claimed he was aware of the enemy's approach and at 7am sent out patrols to scout the roads and some woods to his left.[76] Around 9am he heard loud cries and gunfire so deployed his men and waited in position (probably in Noyers) but it now went quiet and nothing happened for some time. An enemy column eventually appeared on his right but he held them at bay with artillery fire. Then a second column appeared facing his centre, almost immediately followed by a large disorderly mob of armed men on his left. Labory was urged to head for some high ground beyond the village from where he might be able to hold off the rebels, but on route his men became disordered and routed. Only 105 men rallied in Machecoul.

Half of the prisoners joined the rebels and some (notably fifty from the 72nd Line) became firmly loyal to the Vendéen cause.[77] Charette marched his prisoners triumphantly to Vieillevigne where he now received a hero's welcome. On the evening of 9 May he was back in Legé which became his headquarters for the next four months and his recent success enhanced his reputation and would soon increase both his numbers and influence.

The Assault on Palluau 15 May

Although Charette wanted to retake Machecoul, Savin and Joly were not prepared to join him and persuaded him to join them in another attempt on Palluau. They assembled on 14 May and on the following morning advanced in three columns. Boulard's command consisted of three Bordeaux battalions; eighty from the 110th Regiment; forty from the 60th Regiment, one hundred mounted gendarmes and two 8pdrs.[78] Allowing for detachments he fought with 1,184 men.

The first column, under Charette and Vrignault, comprised 2,000 infantry, 80 cavalry and 2 light cannon. They marched on the Legé road and deployed before the other columns appeared. Charette placed himself at the head of the cavalry while his cannon and armed men fired intermittently from behind hedges and trees. Joly was next to arrive and appeared on the Poiré–sur-Vie road.

Boulard had deployed troops north of Palluau on the Legé road and Charette's guns were so badly aimed that the republicans were heard bursting into laughter.[79] They exchanged fire until around 3pm, at which

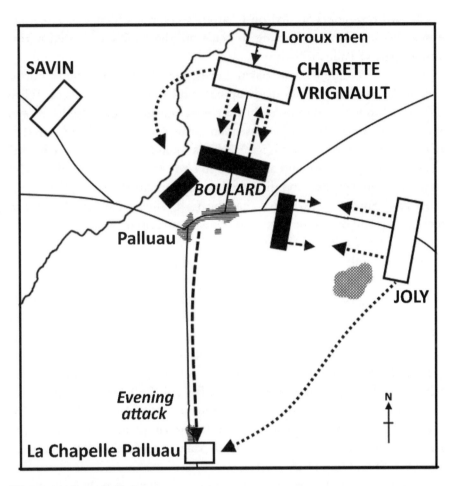

The Assault on Palluau.

point the republican artillery opened up and the Vendéens retreated behind houses and trees along the road and ignored Charette's shouts to advance.[80]

The Loroux area sent 300 armed men to join Charette. They arrived on the Legé road and found themselves pushing Charette's fugitives in front of them. They soon entered into a firefight with the republican tirailleurs.

Joly was making no progress on the right so dispatched 900 men to cut the bridge at La Chapelle–Palluau on the enemy's line of retreat, but this only weakened his force and enabled the republicans to push his column back.[81] A republican battery eventually caused his column to break up and retreat on Poiré.[82]

Boulard now concentrated on Charette's column which was extending around his left flank and trying to penetrate the weakly-defended north-western part of Palluau.

The fiercely independent Savin had deployed on high ground north-west of Palluau but had not made up his mind where best to attack. When Charette's cavalry came into sight they were mistaken for republicans and Savin's men opened fire. As a consequence this cavalry, and then Charette's infantry, rapidly retreated on Legé.[83] Savin's column also withdrew. Charette was pursued by Boulard and attempted to cover the retreat with his cavalry until they were defeated and dispersed by the gendarmes.[84]

Around 5pm Boulard heard that the La Chapelle-Palluau Bridge had been broken and dispatched some troops who surprised and dispersed Joly's detachment and repaired the bridge.[85]

Boulard wildly exaggerated Vendéen strength at 12,000 men and admitted to only 24 casualties against Royalist losses of 150 men.[86]

Boulard now received news of the defeat at La Châtaigneraie and the rebel march on Fontenay. Knowing his priority was to cover Les Sables he dropped back to La Mothe-Achard, where, on 26 May, he received reinforcements totalling 1,500 infantry and 60 cavalry. Nevertheless, three days later he warned Baudry (then in Challans) that he would soon be pulling back on Vairé and Olonne, leaving posts in St-Gilles and La Chaize.[87] Baudry was furious and asked to be put under Canclaux's orders so he could retake the offensive.[88] He had been joined by 2,000 national guards at Challans, who had moved south from Machecoul on 26 May, and a further 600 volunteers were soon to join him from Nantes.[89]

Charette gathered increasing numbers of followers, including Bulkeley's small army from the area of La-Roche-sur-Yon, and in the second half of May republicans in Les Sables were claiming Joly had 20-25,000 men, and although this was far from reality it demonstrates the fear the rebels inspired.

At the end of the month the republicans were holding posts from Challans to La Mothe-Achard, with detachments at St-Gilles, La Chaize-Giraud, Saint-Cyr, Avrillé and Talmont. They were also firmly in control of Paimboeuf and Pornic. Reinforcements were constantly trickling in from La Rochelle and also gathering in Nantes. To oppose them royalist posts included St-Jean-de-Monts, Apremont, Beaulieu, La-Roche-sur-Yon and Poiroux, and constant skirmishes were taking place between Beaulieu and La Mothe-Achard.[90]

Chapter 7

The Republic in Crisis

The National Picture June 1793

Events in Paris drastically and dramatically changed, with direct consequences for the Vendée. The Girondists were ousted from the Convention following the famous *Journées* of 31 May and 2 June and the Paris Commune gained a stranglehold over the Convention for the coming months. The Girondists were blamed for the growing economic crisis, military defeats, and the betrayal of the generals. Following a foolish threat that Paris would be wiped from the face of the earth, pitting the country (the power base of the Girondists) against Paris, the Girondists gave Robespierre and the Paris Commune the excuse to call on the mob to rise up.

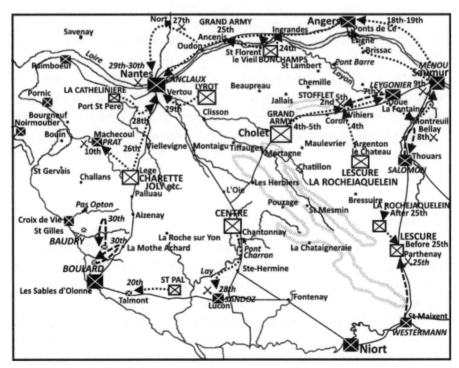

June Campaigns.

The Vendée troubles were cited among the reasons for the arrest of twenty-nine Girondist deputies and the National Convention was now in the hands of the Montagnards, who, influenced by the Paris Commune, would hold power for the next thirteen months and would implement the Terror.

Yet as news of the fall of the Girondists became known, Federalist risings broke out in Marseilles, Bordeaux, Nîmes, Toulouse and Caen. June was to test the revolutionary government more than any month to date and the problems in the Vendée were to escalate significantly.

The *Journées* of 31 May and 2 June also saw the rise to prominence of the Hébértists, who were to play a prominent role in events for the remainder of 1793 and, with the Paris Commune as their base, were dangerous to any who dared oppose them. Key figures included the Minister of War Bouchotte and his ministerial assistants Ronsin and Momoro. As well as infiltrating the armies in the Vendée with agents from the Jacobins and Cordeliers Clubs, one of their own men had already been campaigning in the region: the former goldsmith Rossignol.

In addition to sending representatives on mission to the armies, on 3 May the Executive Council divided France into twenty-nine regions and sent two commissaires to each. Their role was to keep an eye on all that was going on and send in daily reports. Many came into conflict with representatives who, as members of the legislature, were unhappy at this threat to their power, so on 18 May the CPS ordered that they be subordinated to the representatives on mission.[1] However, it was not that simple and the fierce struggles in Paris were mirrored in the regions: not least in the Vendée, which was located between territories sympathetic to the Girondist cause. As far as the commissaires were concerned, all generals of noble extraction were 'suspect' and they were determined to see all such *ci-devants* expelled from the army.

The Arrival of the Duc de Biron

The Duc de Biron was transferred from the Army of Italy to take command of the Army of the La Rochelle Coast, arriving in Niort on 28 May. Canclaux remained in command of the Army of the Brest Coast from his base in Nantes.

Soon after his arrival Biron wrote to the Ministry of War complaining that he found 'a rabble of men that it was impossible to call an army'. He reported that some leaders were acting as if in command of their own private armies and that Niort had no supply wagons and no mobile hospital, 'in a word, no means to make two marches without the certainty of lacking everything'.[2] On 1 June he appealed for staff officers in whom he could have confidence, and was convinced that the greatest and most imminent danger was a coastal invasion. He noted that the rebels had evacuated Fontenay but was most concerned that he was being inundated by the continual arrival of very poor quality volunteers.

Of Biron's 16–17,000 men in Niort nearly 6,000 were in no condition to serve, and of his 1,000 cavalry he felt he could only count on 300 hussars of the Légion-des-Alpes and some Niort and Bordeaux volunteers. On 3 June he set out for Saumur and Tours to meet with the representatives and devise a campaign plan, and on 7 June advised the Ministry of War that several Paris battalions were refusing to join the army until they received their battalion guns.[3]

His campaign plan was to secure communications between La Rochelle and Nantes and deny the rebels any access to the sea. He considered that the greatest risk was the potential aid the rebels might receive by sea, in particular from the British, and remained firmly of this view in the weeks ahead.

The Army of the La Rochelle Coast was extremely thinly spread: stretching from Noirmoutier to Les Sables d'Olonne, Luçon, La Mothe-Achard, Parthenay, Niort, Thouars, Doué, Saumur, Vihiers and Les Ponts-de-Cé. It consisted of two main commands which operated largely independently: the southern under Chalbos stretched from Noirmoutier to Niort, with its main lines of communication to Le Rochelle and Poitiers, and the northern command under Leygonier stretching from Thouars to Les Ponts-de-Cé. National guards held the Loire crossings from Les Ponts-de-Cé to Nantes. Canclaux's army also seemed to be acting in isolation from the Army of the La Rochelle Coast.

Biron was aware of the low morale of the army, after its succession of defeats, and found it rife with insubordination and political in-fighting. The influence of the Paris Commune was now also evident in the person of Ronsin, who took it upon himself to devise a plan which received the backing of a number of representatives. When Biron arrived at Saumur on 3 June he had little option but to fall in line with Ronsin's plan.

Ronsin's plan was to converge on the rebels from several directions while simultaneously covering the coast. Four main columns would be needed:

- 10,000 infantry and 1,000 cavalry would march from Niort on Fontenay, La Châtaigneraie and Ste Hermine;

- 10,000 infantry and some cavalry were to march from Saumur to Doué, before attacking Vihiers, Argenton and Bressuire;
- 8,000 men would march from Les Ponts-de-Cé on Chalonnes and Chemillé;
- 6,000 men would be formed from troops in Machecoul and La Mothe-Achard and between them they would occupy good positions in the area and be ready to take advantage of any opportunity to defeat the rebels;
- A reserve of 6,000 infantry and 500 cavalry would move from Chinon to Thouars to support the other columns in that area;
- National guards from Mayenne, the Loire, Charente-Inférieure and Loire-Inférieure were to move to strategic points in their areas, including along the north bank of the Loire, and be ready to be deployed as needed.

Difficulties were immediately apparent however, because Ronsin's survey on the state of the army, carried out between 10 and 24 May, highlighted its fragile state (see Appendix 2). The representatives also noted that the national guards were disorganised, lacked training, were badly armed, and were ill disposed towards attacking the Vendéens.

In spite of Biron's concerns, the Ministry of War demanded action, but he stood his ground and refused to do anything until he had assessed the state of the army for himself. On 9 June he set out for La Rochelle and visited the posts on the coast. To his alarm he soon discovered that only 2,000 of the army's 15,000 fusils were fit for use.[4]

The Saumur Campaign

After their victory at Fontenay the Vendéens soon dispersed and the town was evacuated on 28 May. The leaders convened a council of war in Châtillon-sur-Sèvres to decide on their next move. There was some disagreement over what to do next, but reports of increased republican activity around Thouars and Vihiers led them to focus once more on that front.

In spite of the poor state of the army it was Leygonier who had made some initial moves on the Vihiers front and he soon became the target of the Grand Army. Summoning their troops once again the Vendéens assembled around 30,000 foot, 1,200 horse and 24 guns in Cholet. Wounds prevented Bonchamps and D'Élbée from joining them in person.[5]

The Grand Army set out from Cholet on 2 June marching in reasonably well aligned closed platoons. At their front were twenty-four drummers led by Drum Major La Ruine. Cathelineau was also near the front with the Guidon-Général that always accompanied the staff.[6] The main body of the army was preceded by the Division of Bonchamps, Marigny marched with the artillery, and the cavalry followed on behind. Boutillier noted that each parish had its own standard and drummer, and gentlemen were seen covered in white scarves and plumes and sporting white lapels.[7]

Vihiers 3 and 4 June

Late on 2 June Stofflet reached Vihiers with seventy cavalry and settled down to await La Rochejaquelein and Lescure who had assembled 3-4,000 men and some cannon at Les Aubiers. Two hours after his arrival a body of republican troops appeared from Concourson and forced him to retreat so quickly that he was unable to warn Lescure or La Rochejaquelein.[8]

Stofflet rallied his cavalry on the Coron road and, when he was joined by 150 more men, he set out to retake Vihiers.[9] The republicans were aware of his approach and deployed in line outside the town above the Lys Bridge, but many were drunk.[10] The shock of the Vendéen assault routed them and a counter-attack by republican cavalry was repulsed. After this small victory Stofflet wisely dropped back and linked up with the advance guard of the Grand Army at Coron.

On 4 June, with his own division now present, Stofflet set out once more for Vihiers, not expecting to encounter any republicans in the town. Informed of their approach Leygonier marched from Concourson with 3,000 troops.

Madame de la Rochejaquelein considered Vihiers a town of 'terrorists' and the civilians certainly cooperated with Leygonier.[11] They left the town on his orders while his troops prepared an ambush on the Doué road.

Lescure and La Rochejaquelein's troops passed through Vihiers having arrived from Argenton a little before Stofflet appeared. According to Deniau they spotted some men on a nearby height moving through the scrubland at a place called Poirier-de-Renard.[12] They assumed these were part of Stofflet's command but, when Lescure and La Rochejaquelein rode ahead to speak with them, the Republicans unmasked a battery of six guns and fired grapeshot at point-blank range.[13] Lescure's horse was hit and some branches were shattered but no one was injured, and instead of retreating the Vendéens rushed and overpowered two guns and captured around eighty men.[14]

On 5 June the rest of the Grand Army drifted into Vihiers.

Doué-la-Fontaine 7 June

The Grand Army set out for Doué on the morning of 7 June in torrential rain. Leygonier claimed he only had 3,500 men, but 5-6,000 was probably nearer the truth; he did, however, lack staff officers.[15]

According to Dupont, Leygonier's troops deployed covering the Layon crossings to the west of Doué.[16] The front of the army was protected by infantry and cavalry pickets; his left flank was around Les Verchers and comprised the Légion-de-la-Fraternité, totalling less than 1,000 men, and the 3rd Republique of 200 men; his centre, at Concourson, was formed by the 3rd Paris of 750 men, 12th Republique (of similar strength) and 4th Orléans of 400 men; his right flank was at Les Rochettes and comprised 15 guns deployed on high ground supported by 598 men of the 14th Charente and 50 from the 8th Hussars. On his extreme right, at St Georges-Châtelaison, was a 750 strong Somme battalion. To the rear, at Soulanger, were two further Orléans battalions totalling about 1,500 men, and east of Doué was a battalion of 800 peasants and a battery of artillery.

As they approached the Layon the Grand Army split into three columns. Stofflet led the left, aiming to capture and outflank the Les Rochettes

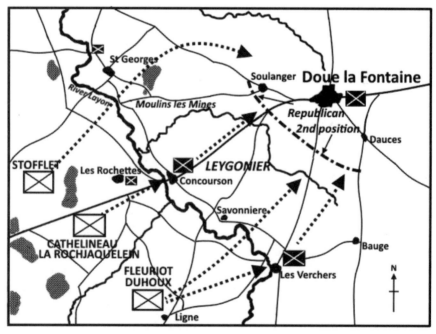

The Battle of Doué-la-Fontaine.

position and cross the river north of Concourson; Bonchamps' division (under Fleuriot) formed the right and aimed to defeat and outflank the Republican positions at Verchers; and Cathelineau was to attack the centre at Concourson.

Towards 10am the commander of the Les Rochettes Camp reported brigands appearing in several columns 'on the right and by a plain that was between the Bois-de-Vallier and Les Rochettes'.[17] He pulled back to high ground east of the Layon.

At that same time Verchers came under attack, and when Leygonier joined them to assess the situation he saw large numbers of enemy deployed on high ground west of the Layon, advancing to cross the river and spreading out to outflank his right.

Leygonier immediately ordered the army to fall back to positions closer to Doué: the right at Soulanger, the centre and cannon at the lime kilns of Minières, and the left around Dauces. His reserve would be placed in Doué.[18]

He planned to deploy his troops in succession. The artillery deployed first, followed by the Somme Battalion and then the two Orléans battalions posted in Soulanger.

Cathelineau had been awaiting developments on the flanks before launching a direct assault on the bridge at Concourson. With 200 infantry, a squadron of cavalry, and a few guns he soon secured the crossing.[19]

The 3rd Paris, 14th Charente, 4th Orléans and 12th République were covering the retreat of the other units, and were withdrawing towards their new positions in square. They became disordered when they saw their right wing in Soulanger routing, having been outflanked by the rebels. These four battalions were subsequently overwhelmed. Leygonier said his right flank had mistaken these battalions for the enemy, and noted that troops that had not yet been engaged in the battle also routed.

The republican left had been successfully resisting Fleuriot and Duhoux, even pushing them backwards, but seeing their rear threatened by Cathelineau and La Rochejaquelein they retreated on Dauces abandoning cannon and caissons on the way.

The engagement spanned several hours and the republicans only rallied near Saumur thanks to the intervention of General Menou and some representatives.

Leygonier complained that his advanced posts were slow to warn him of the enemy's approach, although he proudly claimed that he had saved the artillery, magazines and equipment (later admitting to the loss of two guns).[20] His army suffered 4-800 casualties and a further 1,200 captured.[21]

It is suggested that 500 offered to serve in the royalist ranks.[22] No details of Vendéen losses survive.

Leygonier despaired over the quality of his troops, complaining that some battalions had fewer than half the men armed (excepting the Paris battalions), and that the civilian drivers cut their traces and fled the battlefield.[23] He reported that émigrés had seeped into his units and deserted to the enemy during the battle, highlighting desertions from the 8th Hussars and the Légion-de-la- Fraternité in particular. The day before the battle, reports were already circulating that deserters were fighting with the rebels in small engagements at Martigné and Aubigné.[24] He countered accusations that he had deserted the army during the battle, indicating that he had been abandoned several times by the hussars and cuirassiers and could not get them to charge the enemy.[25]

Leygonier tendered his resignation and left the army. Arrested the following February, he survived the Terror and was released in January 1795. His troops now fell under Duhoux's command, but as Duhoux was wounded Menou took charge.

Montreuil-Bellay 8 June

On 8 June the Grand Army assembled at Doué to consider their next move and after some hesitation they agreed to attack Saumur. Donnissan knew the area well and considered a direct assault along the Doué road too risky as it would expose their flank to republican troops operating in the Thouars area under Salomon. A move on Montreuil-Bellay, then a march north on Saumur, would outflank the republican position on the Bournan Heights near Saumur, allow troops to hold Montreuil-Bellay, and cover the army's rear. This, therefore, was the agreed plan.

Montreuil-Bellay was entered unopposed and Lescure, La Rochejaquelein and Stofflet reached St Just and even crossed the Dive without encountering any republicans. Bonchamps' division, and at least part of Cathelineau's, remained in Montreuil-Bellay.

At 2pm on 8 June Salomon received orders to make for Saumur as quickly as possible and only two hours later he left Thouars heading for Montreuil-Bellay. He halted 3km to its south at La Charpentière, where the road narrowed and entered marshland as it led through Lenay to Montreuil-Bellay.

The walled town of Montreuil-Bellay is perched on high ground overlooking the River Thouet to its west. South of the town is a long east-west ridge which dropped to marshland and fields cut up by numerous water-filled ditches.

Salomon's recently formed brigade was 3,600–4,000 strong.[26] Around 7pm they were spotted by the Vendéens who had deployed among trees and behind hedges at the foot of the ridge south of Montreuil. The front of the republican column was hemmed in by the narrow road as they approached the rebel position, when they suddenly came under attack on their front and flanks.[27] Salomon was able to deploy some troops but the marsh restricted his men and exposed them to gunfire. He managed to deploy artillery on the road, and while Rossignol held that position Salomon attempted to deploy his cavalry on the plain to their right. But bombardment from the Vendéen artillery, and the nature of the terrain, meant the cavalry had difficulty forming up or manoeuvring.

As the battle drifted into darkness the fighting became chaotic and it was only with the arrival of royalist reinforcements that their weight of numbers began to tell. In the dark these reinforcements initially exchanged fire with Fleuriot's troops.[28]

Donnissan had deployed cannon loaded with grapeshot behind the Porte St-Jean.[29] When the republicans reached this gate the doors were swung open and a withering fire tore into their ranks, following which the rebels charged and 'tore them to pieces'.[30]

Running low on ammunition, and with their position being turned, Salomon ordered the retreat back to Thouars, covered by the 35th Division Gendarmerie.[31] Rossignol reported that the civilian drivers left their wagons on the road, cut their traces and fled. The battle had lasted for three to four hours.

Salomon claimed he had faced 12–15,000 rebels, although in the dark it would have been impossible to know with any accuracy. The Vendéens probably began the battle with around 8,000 men, later reinforced by several contingents, although it is not entirely clear which leaders provided this support.[32]

Salomon's column was back in Thouars at 4am on the following morning and subsequently retreated via Parthenay on Niort.[33] He admitted to 200 killed and wounded, although the Vendéens claimed 800 republicans killed, 900 captured, two guns and plenty of supplies.[34] Salomon reported his strength to be 3,200 men when billeted in towns north-east of Niort, suggesting overall losses of perhaps 800.[35]

There are no figures for Vendéen losses, although Deniau suggests they were less than those sustained by their adverseries.[36] Bonchamp's division was so exhausted that they took little active part in the forthcoming battle at Saumur.

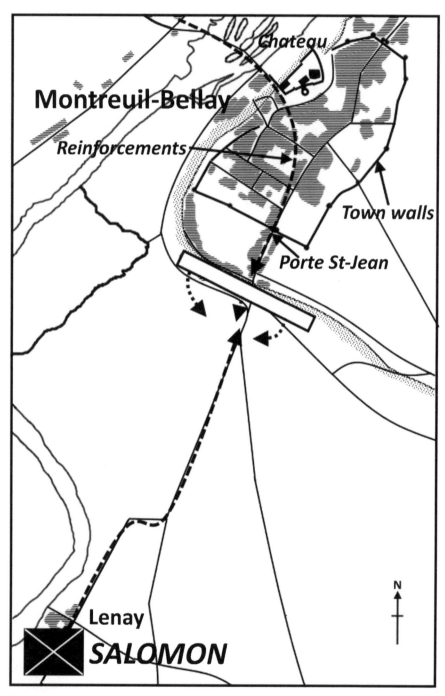

The Battle of Montreuil-Bellay.

This third Vendéen victory in four days had succeeded in preventing Salomon uniting with the republicans in Saumur.

Saumur 9-10 June

Insubordination and disorder in republican ranks was such that Menou had difficulty extracting the Paris battalions from Saumur's taverns, yet with the support of the representatives he was determined to hold the town. General of Brigade Berthier also received orders to assist the representatives in planning the defence of Saumur.[37]

Two redoubts had been prepared on the Bournan Heights, covering the Doué and Montreuil roads, and a third at Varrains east of the River Thouet. Rudimentary entrenchments were also constructed immediately south of Saumur along the Nantilly front.

According to Dupont the republicans distributed their formidable artillery as follows: on the Bournan Heights two 12pdrs were placed on the Montreuil road and two 4pdrs on the Doué road; east of the River Thouet three guns were deployed at Nantilly; pairs of guns were deployed on the Loudan and Chaintres roads, at the Vigneau Mills and at Notre-Dame-des-Ardilliers; six guns were deployed behind the mills near the Château, to enfilade the Fontevrault road; and nine in the Château itself. Around twelve guns remained with their battalions.[38]

The republicans had scraped together at least 8,000 men to cover Saumur.[39] Both Berthier and Coustard arrived the night before the battle and neither knew the terrain nor the troops they were to command. Santerre only arrived on the morning of battle itself.[40]

As the rebels approached the republicans were deployed as follows:

- General of Division Coustard St-Lô held the Bournan Heights with 2,200 infantry, 7-800 cavalry and 6 cannon.[41]
- General of Brigade Berthier covered the south–eastern approach to Saumur with four battalions and 80 cavalry (in total between 1,800 and 2,100 men). His infantry comprised the 2nd and 4th Orléans, 36th Division of Gendarmerie, totalling 1,200 men, and a battalion of Saumur Volunteers.[42] He deployed some of his infantry in the Aunis Farm, his artillery on the heights to his rear and 250 Saumur Volunteers in the church of Notre-Dame-des-Ardilliers. Two Saumur companies were stationed in the Varrains Redoubt.[43]

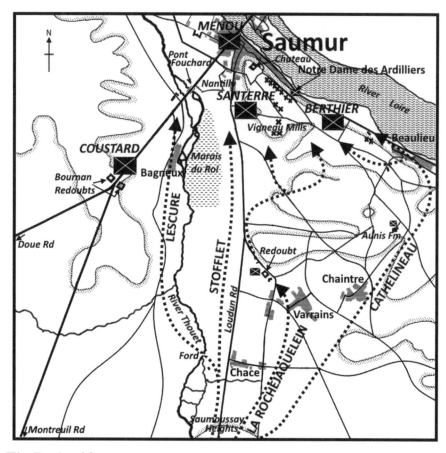

The Battle of Saumur.

- General of Brigade Santerre was given command of two battalions of national guards and 400 gendarmes-à-pied and deployed in entrenchments in advance of the Nantilly Suburb, stretching from the Marais-du-Roi to the Vigneau Mills.[44] These were supported by 250 cavalry (possibly some of the light-cuirassiers of the Légion de la Fraternité).[45]
- General of Division Menou held a reserve of troops in Saumur under his immediate orders. Its composition is not detailed but it probably numbered towards 2,000 and included both infantry and cavalry.[46]

Vendéen tradition suggests that on 8 June La Rochejaquelein reconnoitred Saumur in disguise and reported back that an attack was worthwhile due to the undisciplined state of many republicans. Whether this happened or not the bulk of their army did proceed to cross the Dive and gathered on the

Saumoussay Heights, while 700 men were left to cover the St-Just Bridge in case of retreat.[47]

Fleuriot's division formed a reserve guarding the prisoners and baggage, although some of his men may have received orders to distract Coustard by moving north along the Doué to Saumur road to keep him from moving off the Bournan Heights. Columns were formed under Cathelineau and La Rochejaquelein (right), Stofflet and Des Essarts (centre) and Lescure and Duhoux d'Hauterive (left) and between them they mustered 20-25,000 foot, 1,200 horse and 24 guns.

Towards 3pm Menou was advised that the enemy were near and his deployment indicates that he expected the main thrust to be on the Bournan Heights.

The column on the Vendéen left had both cavalry and artillery support, and received orders to cross the River Thouet at the Chacé Ford, advance between the town of Bagneux and the Bournan Redoubts, seize Pont Fouchard and cut Coustard off from Saumur. The centre would march directly towards the Nantilly Suburb and the right would make for the Fontevrault road and attack along the south bank of the Loire.

Soon after 3pm Lescure was preparing to charge Pont Fouchard when he was struck by a bullet in the left arm just below the shoulder, causing his men to become disordered. Lescure improvised a sling, rallied them, and with cavalry support went on to seize two cannon blocking the bridge.[48]

Coustard ordered two battalions to retake the bridge but the 5th Paris refused to move, even threatening the general's life.[49]

Dommaigné's location in the battle differs between accounts, some placing him on the east side of the Thouet and others on the west.[50] According to Savary and Dupont, he was moving forwards on the Varrains road when he was charged by some of the cuirassiers under Colonel Chaillou. Dressed in the red uniform of an officer of the Maison du Roi, Dommaigné presented a conspicuous target and was killed when his cavalry were thrown back after a fierce mêlée, reputedly shot by Chaillou in person. These cuirassiers were then forced to retreat as a large body of Vendéen tirailleurs moved on their flank.

Deniau suggests Dommaigné actually charged some cuirassiers as he came to the aid of Lescure's troops west of the Thouet. Wherever it took place, both accounts indicate that Dommaigné was defeated and killed. Deniau adds that Marigny, with infantry and artillery support, outflanked the cuirassiers in the ongoing fight west of the Thouet. Lescure's men now reoccupied ground they had lost, but not the bridge.

With his infantry refusing to move unless cavalry led the attack, Coustard ordered Weissen, with some of the light-cuirassiers, to seize an enemy battery near the bridge. Weissen was successful and the Vendéen infantry found their weapons had little effect against the unusual armour worn by these cuirassiers (See Chapter 2). However, this cavalry was not supported by their infantry, even though the commander of the Chasseurs of the Légion-de-la-Fraternité beat the charge for a quarter of an hour.[51] The cavalry therefore fell into a trap: as they charged the enemy infantry the Vendéens opened their ranks and leapt onto the flanks of the horses to unsaddle, and then kill, the cuirassiers. Weissen extracted himself with a handful of men and retreated to the Bournan Heights covered in wounds.[52]

While this confused battle was underway the rest of the Vendéen army continued its march on Saumur.

Moving cross-country in a north-easterly direction Cathelineau was heading towards Beaulieu, and Stofflet's column moved along the east bank of the Thouet towards the Nantilly entrenchments.[53] La Rochejaquelein had been split from Cathelineau's column and ordered to move more towards the enemy centre. Judging by the timings he may have been some way to the rear struggling along narrow country roads and through vineyards.

These moves support Madame de la Rochejaquelein's recollection that the Vendéen attacks were initially badly coordinated and the columns were some distance apart.[54]

Around 4pm Cathelineau's men had gathered on the heights around Beaulieu and the Fontevrault road. Berthier let Cathelineau's men approach within grapeshot range before opening fire from the guns deployed behind the mills.[55] This stopped the Vendéens in their tracks, and as Berthier led his Orléans battalions in a charge the Vendéens retreated in disorder. Cathelineau's men went to ground behind stone walls and in vineyards, ignoring appeals from their leaders to return to the fight.[56]

Berthier, however, was prevented from exploiting his success as his cavalry refused to charge. He was forced to halt his infantry and bring up a third battalion to act in support, but the battle on this flank had reached stalemate and little would change over the next two hours.

Stofflet probably also came into action around 4pm and found his march hampered by republican outposts taking advantage of abattis and stone walls, and by the openness of the marshy valley which unnerved his men. At the head of his cavalry he jostled them forwards but as they came under bombardment from cannon in the château and on the nearby hills casualties started to build and some of his men broke and fled. Stofflet was forced to draw his sword, block their way, and threaten to smash in the skulls of the first Vendéens who did not return to the fight.[57]

Cathelineau sent urgent orders for La Rochejaquelein to attack the Varrains Redoubt and towards 6pm he appeared before that position.[58] The two Saumur companies stubbornly resisted as La Rochejaquelein attacked the east side. Eventually he took a gamble: he threw his white plumed hat into the redoubt and challenged his men to retrieve it. His men now surged over the defences behind him and soon captured the redoubt. Madame de la Rochejaquelein added that her father and a reinforcement of 600 men also attacked the camp. With this small detachment La Ville-Baugé crossed the surrounding ditch, broke down a wall that defended the entrance, and caused the defenders to rout.[59] La Rochejaquelein now marched on Nantilly and the Vigneau Mills.

The sequence of events is confused but it is clear that the rebels were employing flexible tactics as their large columns probed republican defences looking for weak points.

Menou sent reinforcements to support Santerre and made great efforts to repulse the rebels, but his best troops had been neutralised on the Bournan Heights, and the main rebel assault marched in overwhelming numbers against the rest of his army who could not withstand the pressure and were being forced back on the town.[60] The Vendéens were also using the cover of the vineyards, walls and hedges to infiltrate his positions.

Cathelineau was now receiving support from La Rochejaquelein's column as it gradually came into position to his west, and Berthier was forced back as the Vendéens used minor roads to bypass republican positions around the Vigneau and Château Mills. Santerre was being outflanked on his left by La Rochejaquelein and on his right by La Ville-Baugé, who had slid alongside the east bank of the Thouet, and large numbers of rebels were soon descending into Saumur's suburbs.

On the Fontevrault road the republican post at Notre-Dame-des-Ardilliers put up little resistance and fled, although Berthier stalled Cathelineau's advance with some support from the reserve.

Menou sent the 12th République to support Santerre, but this battalion panicked when they saw the Vendéens and soon fled, causing others to follow their example.[61]

Berthier's Orléans battalions deployed under the château walls and he tried to bring some of the reserve artillery on the quay into action.[62] The 36th Division Gendarmerie continued to support his troops while Menou and Berthier assembled some cavalry to launch an assault. The fight was so desperate that both Bourbotte and Choudieu found themselves in the front ranks urging the men on. Probably around this time Marceau, an officer in the Légion-de-la-Fraternité, personally rescued Bourbotte as his horse was killed beneath him and Vendéens flooded around.[63]

Running low on munitions Menou was let down by his cavalry who instead of charging turned and fled into Saumur, dragging the generals along with them and crying treason as they fled.[64] Berthier's infantry, seeing their cavalry flee, were forced to withdraw and did so in good order along the quay and across the Loire.[65] Many republican cannon, however, were abandoned as the gunners were caught up in the general rout. It was now about 8pm.

At Bournan, Coustard had remained undisturbed. Hearing the gunfire fall silent in Saumur he feared that the royalists had won the battle. While he had been marooned within the Bournan Redoubts, Lescure had launched a fresh assault on Pont Fouchard. A republican officer, using two upturned caissons, blocked his path and managed to withdraw four cannon beyond the bridge.[66] Nevertheless, Lescure and Duhoux were soon able to lead some of their men into Saumur to lend assistance to the other columns.

In the confused fighting La Rochejaquelein and La Ville-Baugé, both on horseback, had closely followed the retreating republicans and raced on ahead of their troops. They eventually found themselves near the bridge over the Loire where La Rochejaquelein was being handed loaded fusils by La Ville-Baugé, and fired point-blank at fleeing republicans for around a quarter of an hour.[67] Running significant risks these leaders were fortunate to escape with their lives when Vendéen troops at last made an appearance. Cathelineau's column appeared on the quay around this time and at around 9pm Stofflet and Lescure also arrived.

La Rochejaquelein pursued republicans on the Bourgueil road with 150 cavalry, reputedly rounding up thousands of prisoners. As he pulled back on Saumur he removed some timbers from the bridge and deployed two guns.

Bournan was still in republican hands but now came under attack by Fleuriot and Stofflet's divisions, supported by Marigny. La Rochejaquelein raced to join them only to have a horse killed under him and they all conceded that it was now too dark to continue the battle.

The Republicans fled in several directions and it would take weeks to reorganise them. Menou had been wounded and Representatives Dandenac, Delaunay, Bourbotte, Choudieu, Thibaudeau and La Chevardière, as well as Commissaires Momoro, Saint-Félix, Besson and Minier were all caught up in the rout.[68]

An hour before the Vendéens entered Saumur around 400 republican troops under Lieutenant Colonel Joly were rushed into the château. This futile attempt to retain a foothold in the town simply resulted in their surrender on the following day.

Coustard, however, extricated most of his troops from the Bournan Heights and retreated overnight along the south bank of the Loire to Les Ponts-de-Cé.[69] Berthier also managed to salvage some guns.

In a letter dated 13 June, Commissaire Minier was forthright in blaming the cavalry for the defeat. He said the cavalry of the Légion-de-la-Fraternité were largely composed of Austrian and German deserters and that the 8th Hussars and 19th Dragoons were both newly formed and badly armed.[70]

During the battle Berthier had two horses killed beneath him and both he and Menou were wounded.

The Vendéens claimed an exaggerated figure of 8,000 prisoners, 1,500–1,900 enemy killed and forty-six cannon captured.[71] Only a few prisoners were retained, the rest, once their hair was shaved, were sent away on the Tours road.[72] The Vendéens admitted to light losses.[73]

For his distinguished action Marceau was promoted to Adjudant General Chef-de-Battalion on 15 June and soon took command of the 11th Hussars, formed from the cavalry of the Légion-de-la-Fraternité.[74] Troops from this légion did desert to the enemy, as had some of the 10th Dragoons and national guards.[75]

Reports flooding in to Paris indicated that defeated troops were turning up in towns across a wide area. On 13 June representatives in Le Mans noted the pitiful state of the army, indicating that men in the Orléans battalions no longer wanted to fight the rebels but wanted to return to the frontiers, and that cavalry were selling their horses and men their equipment, leaving troops devoid of effects.[76]

On 13 June Boudon, Reuelle and Tallien reported that the debris of the army was gathering at Tours and being put through military drill.[77]

Vendéen Plans after Saumur

The defeat at Saumur provided the rebels with a significant boost to their morale as well as abundant supplies.

D'Élbée arrived in Saumur on 12 June and Cathelineau was elected the first commander-in-chief of the Grand Army: an army commanded by a peasant elected by nobles. His character, bravery and the confidence the soldiers had in him made him the obvious choice. To quote Deniau, 'The

Republic spoke of equality but did not provide it; the Vendée did not speak of it, but put it into practice.'[78]

The 18-year-old Forestier, also of humble birth, was the preferred choice to replace Dommaigné at the head of the cavalry, but the arrival of the high ranking noble, the Prince de Talmont, meant the rebel leaders felt obliged to offer him the post instead. Forestier was appointed his second-in-command.

There were now significant opportunities for the rebel army to exploit this victory, but it led to serious disagreement over where to march next. Stofflet and La Rochejaquelein favoured a march on Tours then Paris, gathering support on route and striking at the heart of the regime. There were few troops in a fit state to intervene and even Napoleon would later say:

> 'Nothing would have stopped the triumphant march of the royalists. The white flag would have been flying on the towers of Notre-Dame before it would have been possible for the armies on the Rhine to race to the aid of their government'.[79]

Lescure, recognising the reluctance of the troops to march far from their territory, suggested they march on Niort and then seize La Rochelle and Les Sables to gain access to the sea. Cathelineau suggested they march on Nantes to provide them with a major port and enable Britanny, Maine and Normandy to rise up and join them.[80]

One account suggests that the hot-headed Stofflet became so agitated that he drew his sword on Bonchamps and challenged him to a duel, which Bonchamps politely declined saying only God and the King had the right to take his life.[81] Bonchamps, still badly wounded, had arrived in Saumur on 13 June so this may be fictional, but the story does reflect divisions that were to simmer over the months ahead.

It was eventually agreed that Nantes would be the next target and that they would march on 16 June. The Vendéens knew there were significant political divisions within Nantes and with royalist sympathisers in this unfortified city they may have anticipated an easy victory.

La Rochejaquelein was left in Saumur with a garrison of 2,500–3,000 well armed men.[82]

Recruits had been rallying to the Grand Army in Saumur and some able men joined the Vendéens at this time, including D'Autichamp, who became second-in-command in Bonchamps' division; Piron, who had been fighting north of Nantes; and Beauvais who would serve in the artillery and left a detailed account of the war. Small bodies of rebels also made raids as far as Chinon, La Flèche, Loudon and Bourgueil, encountering little opposition.

Many troops headed home for a few days while plans were in preparation for an attack on Angers and the march on Nantes. Lescure's wound, however, was more serious than initially thought and he left the army to recuperate.

The Republicans in chaos

On news of the disaster at Saumur Biron raced from La Rochelle to Niort, arriving on 13 June. However he remained on the southern front and was adamant that an invasion by sea posed the greatest threat. The Bordeaux battalions were also demanding to return home and an anxious Biron put this down to the known Federalist bias of the Gironde.

Biron was immediately working on new plans but the state of the troops, their low morale, and lack of transport hampered any immediate action.[83] Reinforcements arriving from the Army of the North turned up poorly dressed, recruits were arriving untrained and unarmed, and the men raised through the lottery were demanding to go home.

The situation along the southern front was certainly precarious and Boulard did not have enough men to contemplate an offensive along the coast, with posts from Luçon as far as St-Gilles continually under threat. Furthermore Machecoul was isolated and Nantes unable to take any risks.

On 13 June the representatives and generals in Tours authorised the evacuation of the administration and troops in Angers, while Berthier was tasked with reorganising the debris of the Saumur Army in Tours.

The next few weeks were fraught with internal strife as the disaster at Saumur caused underlying tensions between the political factions amongst the representatives and within the army to come to the fore.

Berthier reported an urgent need for a new and properly organised staff. On 14 June Duhoux was named second-in-command of the Army of the La Rochelle Coast, Chabot, Joly and Descloseaux were all provisionally named generals of brigade, and Burac and Beffroy were confirmed in that rank.

Fearing an advance in their direction the Central Commission in Tours ordered Biron to march on Saumur, but he refused. He was adamant that the army did not have the resources they needed to advance and could not risk leaving La Rochelle and Rochefort exposed by marching north.[84]

On 18 June Biron wrote to the Ministry of War and the CPS indicating that he had visited all the posts from Marans to north of Les Sables and found them in a better state than he had feared. He reported that the Bordeaux battalions would not stay beyond 25 June and feared their example would be emulated by others.[85] He also reported that the requisitioned national guards were leaving in large numbers in spite of the efforts of the representatives. His aim now, he said, was to re-establish communications between La Rochelle and Nantes in coordination with Canclaux.

While Biron gave one account of the state of the army, and on 23 June asked to be replaced, the Montagnard Representative Choudieu, then in Tours, gave a contradictory account. He falsely claimed that Biron had 25,000 men (of which he said 16,000 were good troops), Boulard had 12,000 disciplined men, and they had organised 25,000 men in Tours.[86]

The representatives in Niort shared Biron's concerns and highlighted the trouble being caused by Ronsin's agent, Musquinet Saint-Felix. The 'Society of the Friends of Liberty' of Les Sables indicated that two agents had led the respected General Boulard to hand in his resignation. On 21 June Goupilleau of Fontenay, one of the representatives in Niort, was tasked with reporting the truth to the National Convention.

To prove beyond doubt that Biron had lost control of the army, the representatives, generals, assistants to the Minister of War, and commissaires of the Executive Council in Tours, issued the following orders on 25 June:

1. All generals who think they are sufficiently armed and organised should immediately march to the aid of Nantes, threatened by the rebels.
2. The generals ordered to march on the right bank of the Loire are to march in a single mass with a small body of light cavalry acting as flankers.
3. Biron is ordered to cover Tours and make sure this plan succeeds.

Representatives in Tours sent a message to Biron, 'in the name of the CPS', making it clear that it was his responsibility to act as instructed and come to the aid of Nantes.[87]

The generals in Tours separately contacted Biron indicating that in his absence, and due to the threat to Nantes, they had no choice but to act as instructed. Biron accepted their actions and indicated he was sending 3,000 men to cover Tours and would retain 12,000 in Niort. He still felt it imperative to protect the southern front and noted that the departure of the Bordeaux and Midi troops had forced him to abandon his plan to re-establish communications between La Rochelle and Nantes.[88]

Biron now directly challenged the authority of the Central Commission, stating that he would only march on Saumur if given a direct order by the

Ministry. Whatever now occurred, he said, was the responsibility of the commissaires and the Central Commission, not that of the generals.[89]

Hearing that Saumur had been evacuated by the rebels, part of the republican advance guard set out in that direction on 27 June, followed by the rest of the army three days later.

The CPS was astonished by the tone of Biron's letters and in their reply of 28 June they refused his request to resign and ordered him to take control of the plans to save Nantes. Ronsin and his assistants had been recalled to Paris and the Minister of War promised Biron the officers and staff he needed. The CPS also advised Biron that the Convention had now fixed the number of representatives with each army and that their role was to inspire confidence, establish order, and ensure the troops obeyed the generals. However, while Ronsin lost his title as Assistant to the Minister of War, he immediately became an officer under Rossignol's orders.

Rossignol had recently arrived in St-Maixent and was accused of trying to turn the Légion-du-Nord against its leader, Westermann, reputedly saying that if they were true republicans they would not obey him. A municipal officer separately reported that when Rossignol marched through St-Maixent he instructed his gendarmes to forcibly demand wine from a number of houses and had even chased citizens from their properties so he could billet his troops.

Westermann accused Rossignol of undermining Biron when he was in Niort by telling the troops not to obey him, that he was a *ci-devant*, and that it was imperative to stop the plans of someone so dangerous. Westermann, therefore, had Rossignol arrested and transferred to Niort to be judged 'with all the rigors of the law'.[90] However, Rossignol's arrest played into the hands of the Hébértists and would accelerate Biron's fall.

The Coastal Vendée June

Boulard had pulled back from La Mothe-Achard to Olonne at the end of May and only maintained a few posts before Les Sables, while Baudry covered L'Aiguillon, Vairé, St-Gilles and the La Chaize Bridge. Charette, therefore, seized the opportunity to move on the lightly-garrisoned town of Machecoul.

Machecoul 10 June

The rebel column set out early on 10 June and to ensure speed Charette took no artillery. Vrignault, La Cathelinière, Joly, Savin, Du Chaffault,

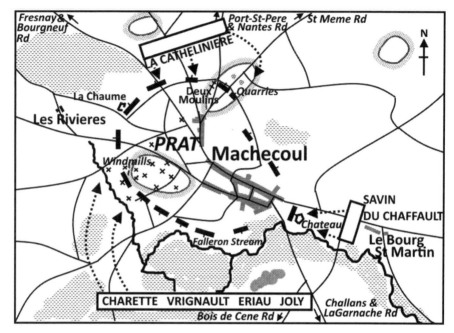

The Battle of Machecoul.

Couëtus and Pajot all joined him and they gathered on the Touvois road with 12-13,000 foot and 200 horse.[91]

Bittard-des-Portes, the best source on this battle, indicates that Machecoul was garrisoned by Chef de Brigade Prat with four battalions, five companies, two platoons of cavalry, two 8pdrs, and a mix of thirteen 4pdrs and 6pdrs. In all he commanded 1,300 men, deployed in defensive positions and entrenchments around the town. One battalion occupied the west and north-west; six guns deployed at the junction of the Fresnay and Nantes roads; two cannon and three volunteer companies were deployed at the post of Deux-Moulins; one battalion guarded the château; two companies were at the hospital and the calvary; and two small battalions, seven guns and the cavalry deployed immediately south of the town north of the Falleron Stream.

La Cathelinière commanded Charette's advance guard and, skirting around the southern and western defences, he deployed on the Nantes road at 2.30pm. Some republican cavalry made a feint against his column and unmasked two guns but were forced back by rebel gunfire. La Cathelinière's men now advanced under cover of some quarries and forced the republicans to evacuate the post of Deux-Moulins. Meanwhile Savin twice failed in attacks on the château.

Charette deployed most of his force along the southern approach to Machecoul and attracted fire from infantry and artillery at Les Moulin-des-Chaume. In spite of casualties his men forced two battalions to fall back to a small hill topped by windmills.

Vrignault's men assaulted this position, but under intense fire Vrignault fell dead and a counter-attack by the republicans caused his men to rout. Charette and Joly now gathered all the cavalry and with sabres drawn moved on the right of this hill to fall on the left flank of the enemy artillery, just as the men of Loroux charged these same cannon. The gunners were cut down and the battery was turned on its supporting infantry who were now forced back into Machecoul by weight of numbers. The battle soon degenerated into desperate house to house fighting.

Savin attacked the château once more, crossing the moat, and climbed its walls to cut down the defenders, some escaping to re-join their comrades in the town.

After four hours of battle, and with ammunition running low, the republicans knew they must cut their way out if they were to escape. Prat hoped to move north on the Nantes road but found this barred by La Cathelinière's men, so headed for the Saint-Même road, doing so through difficult terrain and pursued by cavalry.

At 11pm he reached Port-Saint-Père having lost almost half his force and all his cannon. Next day the Port-Saint-Père garrison and Prat's men withdrew to Nantes. The Vendéens claimed to have killed or captured 750 men and taken 10 guns, 9 caissons, and 20,000 cartridges.[92]

The Vendéens soon retook most of the Pays-de-Retz and Charette's influence in the region greatly increased. He now set out plans for its defence with La Cathelinière at Port-Saint-Père, Couëtus at St-Philbert and Eriau at Machecoul. Barteau was tasked with holding Sorinières, towards Nantes, and to coordinate action with Lyrot.[93]

On 20 June Lyrot fought a small battle at La Louée where he defeated part of the Légion-Nantaise, pursuing them for three hours back to Nantes.[94] Cambronne, of Waterloo fame, distinguished himself in this action, the first by this newly formed légion.

The Nantes Campaign

The Grand Army congratulated Charette on the victory at Machecoul and asked if he would cooperate in the planned assault on Nantes. Charette replied positively and Donnissan was sent to discuss the plans and offer him powder and cannon.

While the Grand Army marched on Nantes, Royrand was to make a diversionary attack on Luçon, La Rochejaquelein was meant to remain in Saumur, and Lescure was in Châtillon, these latter two keeping watch on Republicans to the east.

The March on Angers

Angers had been held by 4,000 men under General Barbazan.[95] When Saumur fell, Ladouce and Talot were in St-Lambert with 2,500 men covering the approaches to Angers, and Gauvilliers was holding the line of the Loire between Nantes and Angers with 1,500 men.[96] However, all troops around Angers had now been withdrawn to Tours. In the chaos that went along with this withdrawal those in Angers abandoned their heavy artillery, munitions and provisions, but did manage to drag away twenty-two cannon.[97] Gauvilliers' men were ordered to pull back to Lion d'Angers.[98] On 13 June, therefore, Angers had been abandoned.

On 17 June the Vendéen advance guard set out from Saumur and by the end of 19 June the rebel army was assembled in Angers. They remained in the city until 25 June, during which time many were permitted time to return home.

On leaving Saumur, Bonchamps had returned to his own territory before receiving orders to seize key towns on the north bank of the Loire preparatory to the assault on Nantes.[99]

The Battle of Nantes 29 June 1793

The city of Nantes was in turmoil when news of Saumur filtered through. They could not rely for help from the army crushed at Saumur, or from troops on the southern Vendée border. Desperate pleas were dispatched across Brittany and beyond and reinforcements trickled in right up until the battle began.

Nantes was a large mercantile city commanding the mouth of the Loire with direct access to the sea. Located at the junction of the Loire and Erdre Rivers, it was dominated by its cathedral and château and had extended beyond its partially demolished medieval walls into extensive suburbs stretching around 3km west, north and east. Bridges connected a series of islands linking to suburbs south of the Loire around St-Jacques and Pont Rousseau. The northern and western approaches to Nantes had numerous hills dotted with windmills and the northern suburbs sloped downhill towards the heart of the city.

It was an extremely difficult city to defend and this weakness was recognised in March when the authorities constructed extensive earthworks enclosing the suburbs north of the Loire and around St-Jacques. The château was a vital arsenal and was well defended with cannon.

There are ample references to high-hedged fields of crops, isolated houses that provided useful cover for the approaching royalists, and many walled gardens in the gaps between the main roads into the city.

The republicans evacuated posts eastward along the Loire to an entrenched camp at St-Georges and on 19 June Nantes was declared to be in a state of siege. Earthworks were repaired and constructed along the main approaches to the city and other vulnerable points, probably adding to the system of defences constructed in March. In and around Nantes,

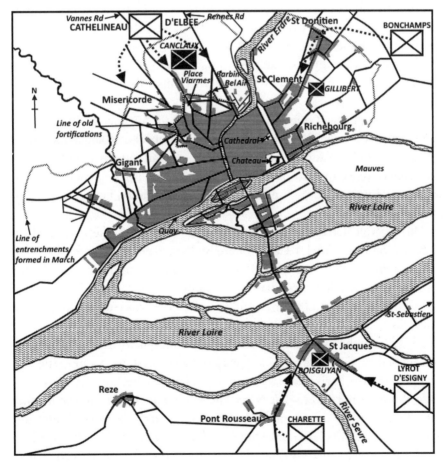

The Battle of Nantes.

roads were blocked with barricades, houses turned into strongpoints, walls toppled to open up clear views for the artillery and works in both earth and stone were prepared on the city outskirts. Improvised defences were set up on the Paris, Rennes, Vannes, Miséricorde, La Bastille and Gigant roads, and three trenches were dug on the open land at Mauves.[100] The northern suburbs were located within and around dilapidated fortifications whose former bastions formed natural defensive points which were used by republican artillery, notably that at Bel-Air.

On 20 June the Vendéens sent a summons to Nantes calling on it to surrender. This was received by Mayor Baco in the night of 23 to 24 June and in collusion with the representatives he kept it secret. The Vendéens had demanded that the white flag be flown from the city within six hours; the surrender of the garrison with its arms and munitions; the town's treasury in the name of Louis XVII; and that the Deputies of the National Convention be handed over as hostages. If they refused and the city fell the garrison would be put to the sword.

Bonchamps occupied Varades, Ancenis and Oudon against limited resistance, and on his march was joined by thousands of men from north of the Loire.

The rest of the Grand Army drifted in to Ancenis to link up with Bonchamps between 24 and 26 June. On 25 June La Rochejaquelein was forced to abandon Saumur, as only a few troops had remained with him, and Labarolière reoccupied it on the following day. La Rochejaquelein's troops soon linked up with those under Lescure in Amailloux, between Parthenay and Bressuire.[101]

On 26 June Charette marched with 5,000 men, Couëtus joined him at St-Colombin, and La Cathelinière at Port-Saint-Père. Two days later they reached Villeneuve with 10,000 men and at midnight on 28 June cattle horns signalled their march on Nantes.[102] That same day Lyrot and D'Esigny assembled 5,000 men and marched towards St-Jacques from the south-east.

By 27 June the Grand Army reached Oudon, but with many republicans entrenched at the Camp of St Georges, north-east of Nantes, the main assault along the Paris road was ruled out. The main body of the army would instead march north, cross at Nort, and launch an assault on the northern suburbs and in so doing outflank the main republican force. Bonchamps would launch a smaller attack along the Paris road and Charette and Lyrot would attempt to force a crossing over the Loire. It was agreed that the combined assault on the city would commence at 2am on 29 June.

Cathelineau arrived before Nort at 8pm on 27 June to discover that it was being held by 1,000 republicans under Meuris who, while appealing for reinforcements, was determined to hold this key crossing.[103] The conflict degenerated into an artillery bombardment, costing the rebels time they could ill afford, and they only made progress once a ford was discovered and some cavalry, with infantry riding pillion, attacked Nort from the north.

Meuris fought heroically and only retreated at 5am on the following day, having taken punishing losses.

At 10.30am Canclaux, then at the Camp of St-Georges, found out about the fall of Nort and that same afternoon deployed most of the 4,000 men under his immediate command in open terrain close to the northern suburbs.[104] The 11th and 13th Seine-et-Oise had been sent on ahead to support Meuris but only arrived in time to cover his retreat. Fortunately for Canclaux it took the Vendéens hours to gather their forces and complete the crossing at Nort.

At 6pm Canclaux was considering whether to march on Nort when he heard that the Vendéens had seized Mauves-sur-Loire to the east of Nantes. That night the post at Sorinières, south of the city, withdrew to Pont-Rousseau.

Overnight 28 to 29 June

By 2am on 29 June Canclaux's troops were deployed and ready for the expected attack. The limited information available indicates that he now commanded 5-6,000 troops covering the northern approaches from the Vannes to Rennes roads. The 11th and 13th Seine-et-Oise were at the Rennes Gate and the 109th Line, Mayenne Battalion and Légion-Nantaise at the Vannes Gate. In support were other units of volunteers and national guards.

Canclaux had deployed a 'great battery' (probably no more than eight guns) on this northern front and the small numbers of cavalry available to him were also on this front. Heavy calibre guns had been set up behind barricades, abattis and earthworks.

Covering the eastern approaches and at St-Donitien were 1,500 men under General Gillibert, supported by more artillery.

South of the Loire, Adjudant General Boisguyon protected St-Jacques with a Côtes-du-Nord Battalion and chasseur and grenadier companies of Charente, Seine-et-Marne and Maine-et-Loire. Some of the Nantes National Guard covered his advanced posts under the command of Chef-de-Bataillon

Mulonnière.[105] This front was strengthened by entrenched artillery. Some units also covered the western approach to the city (see Appendix 2 for order of battle).

Beysser had a roving command and Mayor Baco was present in person at the Rennes Gate.

As Cathelineau was attacking Nort, D'Élbée had remained at Oudon and only followed on later. Cathelineau's forces seem to have spent time recuperating after the battle, and the need to re-establish the river crossing delayed them further still. In the evening of 28 June they camped some 20km north of Nantes.[106] It was clear that they would not be ready for the combined assault at the agreed time of 2am.

Conversely the troops under Bonchamps were ready and in position around Mauves-sur-Loire.

Overnight Charette's main column, preceded by an advance guard, marched cautiously towards Pont-Rousseau. On reaching Trois-Moulins he deployed three guns and also sent two large calibre guns and some cavalry to capture Rezé, with orders to open fire on Nantes across the Loire.[107]

Charette personally reconnoitred towards Pont-Rousseau with 100 cavalry. In the moonlight they spotted a masonry and wooden structure with artillery embrasures closing access to the bridge.[108]

2.30am to 7am

At 2.30am three Vendéen guns opened fire on Pont-Rousseau, which immediately retaliated. Other rebel guns arrived, but while their infantry remained under cover their gunners were using up valuable shot.[109] Meanwhile, the guns detached towards Rezé were silenced by republican batteries across the Loire.

Towards 5am Lyrot could be heard attacking on the Clisson road and around St-Sébastien. Their small campaign guns bombarded St-Jacques.

Charette was concerned that he could hear no gunfire north of the Loire but decided to press ahead with an assault on Pont-Rousseau and formed his peasants in column. Republican 18pdrs enfiladed the road and eventually forced Charette to pull his men back and return to bombarding the works with his artillery.

To the east, Lyrot pressed forwards and penetrated the St-Jacques Suburb, but a counter-attack forced him to retreat and abandon three cannon. Seeing them recoil Charette deployed two cannon and forced the republican pursuit back into the suburb.

Charette and Lyrot continued to bombard Pont-Rousseau and St-Jacques but were increasingly concerned by the lack of action to the north, when around 7am they at last heard the long expected cannonade.

The assault on the Paris Rd 7am to 10am

Bonchamps' column, which must also have been wondering why the northern column had not yet attacked, was led by an advance guard formed from his Breton companies and tirailleurs all under the command of Fleuriot. Further to the rear were the bulk of his 7–8,000 men. Bonchamps was still too ill to mount a horse so remained in a carriage during the battle.

They soon captured St-Donitien and as their attack developed Canclaux transferred a battalion from St-Jacques to bolster the eastern defence. With typical fury the Vendéen advance guard were pushing republican posts back on the St-Clement Suburb when Fleuriot was struck and mortally wounded. D'Autichamp took command but with Bonchamps anxious about the lack of action to the north his assault slackened.

The Northern Front

A lookout in the cathedral spotted the Vendéens advancing on the Rennes road at 6am, but still some distance away.[110] Doré-Graslin suggests that the assault did not begin until around 10am.[111] There may have been light clashes beforehand that possibly included Crétineau-Joly's unsubstantiated reference to the Prince de Talmont making a hasty and unsuccessful attack on the northern suburbs with the cavalry.[112]

Cathelineau was advancing on the Rennes road supported by fourteen guns and D'Élbée advanced to his east, closer to the banks of the Erdre.

Beysser, riding a horse draped with a tiger skin saddlecloth, initially believed Charette's attack was the principal assault until Representative Gillet informed him of the approach of 14,000 men and numerous cannon on the Rennes road. He arrived to find the rebels within 'half cannon range' of the barriers.[113] The republican redoubt at Barbin fell in hand-to-hand fighting, enabling D'Élbée to deploy artillery on high ground facing the redoubts of St-André and Bel-Air. He was soon directing fire into the heart of Nantes.

While this was underway, bodies of rebels moved on the Vannes road. Beysser refers to strong enemy 'platoons' advancing under cover of hedges and crops, seizing isolated houses and using their shelter to fire on the republicans. The republicans in the Rennes, Vannes and Miséricorde Redoubts were now coming under small arms fire.[114]

Canclaux's 'great battery' on the Rennes road included 18pdrs and continually exchanged fire with the Vendéen artillery; during the battle it dismounted two rebel guns. The Vendéens, however, outflanked this battery, forcing republican battalions to divide by sections and fire by platoons from concealed positions.

Fighting with great determination the Vendéen tirailleurs concentrated their fire for a couple of hours on the barricades at the Rennes Gate, Vannes Gate and in the Miséricorde quarter. Among the casualties was Mayor Baco, wounded in the thigh. The Vendéens claim to have broken the barrier on the Rennes road but the republican artillery did not slacken their fire.

Cathelineau was frustrated by the lack of progress at the Rennes Gate and switched the focus of his attack to the Vannes Suburb. With 300 elite men he penetrated this suburb heading for Miséricorde and the Vannes Gate.[115] In the process he forced back the 109th Line and other republicans in the area and succeeded in overpowering a republican battery.[116]

Aiming for the Place-des-Agriculteurs (now the Place-Viarmes), Cathelineau's elite troops swept into the square and could sense victory within their grasp. The 109th Line, 34th Line and Mayenne Volunteers, under Canclaux's direct command, had rallied in this square and stood their ground as the Vendéens began their assault. It was critical that this area be held as beyond the square the roads led downhill to the heart of the city and were more difficult to defend.

According to Crétineau-Joly, Cathelineau had already had two horses killed under him and was now fighting on foot. Surrounded by his most loyal followers, and having made the sign of the cross, he rushed on the forces before him. Just at that moment a bullet fired from a window smashed his elbow and entered his abdomen, causing him to fall to the ground, dangerously wounded.[117] The shock of seeing their 'hero' struck down completely changed the situation. In spite of his pleas, and those of other leaders, the assault ground to a halt. The news of his fall spread rapidly and, picking up their commander-in-chief, the Vendéens withdrew from the square and soon abandoned the suburb altogether.

Around Gigant to the west, 800 National Guards, with part of the Guerche Battalion, were deployed behind their defences, and with support from civilians had also been successfully holding back the rebels.[118]

Although their morale had been affected by the wounding of Cathelineau, D'Élbée and Donnissan endeavoured to renew the assault. From the various accounts it would appear that Cathelineau was wounded in the early afternoon and the attack on the Rennes road gave ground at 1pm when the Vendéens were reported to be seeking cover in surrounding fields. At 2pm Beysser reported that the battle was going well.

In 1795 Gibert, a Vendéen officer and eye witness, wrote that after Cathelineau was wounded the resistance of the republicans persuaded Donnissan to move one of the Vendéen batteries.[119] This gave the republicans a breathing space and when Donnissan came to redeploy the guns he had lost that critical moment. The fighting on the northern front noticeably diminished, although Beysser indicated that the cannon fire only slackened between 5 and 6pm, and Hodanger, a Republican on the northern front, said the Vendéens finally retreated at 9pm.[120]

The Paris road

The assault on the Paris road had diminished by the time the northern assault was developing. Beysser wrote that Bonchamps' troops were repulsed around midday and that the firing slackened by 6pm, then ceased by 9.30pm. It seems clear that republican determination had taken the Vendéens by surprise. Hearing that the northern suburbs had been evacuated Bonchamps reluctantly retired.

The Southern Front

With the fight developing to the north Charette was spurred into renewed action and led forward his parishes several times, but each time the Pont-Rousseau guns forced them back. Canclaux reported that during the great attack in the north only Deurbroucq was employed with the defence of the bridges. Certainly one battalion was transferred to the eastern front, but Boisguyon was still south of the Loire around midday. At one point Lyrot seized some boats and attempted a crossing of the Loire, aiming for Mauves. Firing from republican troops on the northern bank forced him to abandon the attempt.[121]

Volunteers from the Côtes-du-Nord Battalion had attempted sorties but Charette had forced them back with losses. Towards midday Boisguyon attempted a new sortie with this same battalion, aiming to cut Lyrot's line of retreat. Charette hurried to intercept them and picked his moment to throw forward Prudent de la Robrie with 2,000 men, who crossed the Sèvre, rushed the volunteers, and forced them back to their entrenchments.[122]

Charette only heard after nightfall that Cathelineau had been seriously wounded and that the army had retreated; he decided to remain in position for the night.

With daylight on 30 June a republican lookout reported that the enemy were no longer on the Vannes or Rennes roads. Sporadic fighting continued on the Paris road and the southern front over the next couple of days before all the Vendéens eventually withdrew. Charette held his positions until after nightfall. He was not pursued.

Conclusion

The obstinate resistance of the republicans, inspired by determined leadership, undoubtedly led to their victory. The republicans also benefitted from constant updates on rebel movements from lookouts placed in the cathedral tower. Charette and Lyrot could make no headway whatsoever and on the eastern and northern fronts the assaults stalled when leaders fell wounded.

Most of the republican troops were raw and untested and Canclaux would have had no choice but to use entrenchments and rely on his artillery to bolster the defences. His few experienced troops, notably the 109th Line, played a critical role in fending off the most determined rebels and it is clear that the ferocious battle between small bodies of elite troops on either side determined the course of events.

The republicans reported 1,200 Vendéen killed and that the enemy had carried off their wounded. They admitted that their own losses had been considerable but less than that of the rebels. Guin suggests they probably lost about 500 men.[123]

Without doubt the greatest loss to the Vendéens was Cathelineau, who succumbed to gangrene on 14 July.

Westermann's Advance on Parthenay

In mid-June, aware that Westermann and the Légion-du-Nord were in Vienne, Biron secured permission to incorporate them into his army and deployed them in St-Maixent. When Biron heard that the rebels were planning to move on Parthenay and the flour depots near St-Maixent he authorised Westermann to march against them with part of his légion and a detachment from the Légion-des-Ardennes.[124]

It will be recalled that after Saumur Lescure had returned to his own territory, but in spite of his poor state of health he was still actively looking for ways to fight the republicans and expand the Rising. The region around Parthenay was alarmed by the number of republican troops gathering to their east and sent messages to him appealing for help. Knowing this area was keen to rise in favour of the royalists Lescure was eager to oblige and ordered an assembly at Amailloux from where he marched to Parthenay.

Parthenay 25 June

On reaching Parthenay Lescure ordered the cavalry to patrol during the night and deployed four guns behind the town's southern entrance. He also blocked two gates with stone, leaving only the St-Maixent and Thouars Gates accessible. Unfortunately the Vendéens were notoriously lax at patrolling.

Westermann set out from St-Maixent on 24 June and was approaching Parthenay by 2am the following morning. He had been warned that the enemy numbered 5-6,000 infantry and 600 cavalry and had deployed cannon at the town's entrance.[125]

The royalists had little warning when, at 3am, Westermann attacked. Lescure woke to the sound of cannon fire and Le Ville-Baugé galloped to the St-Maixent Gate to find the entrance open, the guns abandoned, and republicans entering the town.

Westermann's account indicated that he marched straight for the St-Maixent Gate, deployed and fired an 8pdr, and ordered his men to assault that entrance. He wrote that the first to enter the gate was his infantry lieutenant colonel who, with sabre drawn, cut down an 'ecclesiastic' who was holding a lit wick and was about to fire a cannon. Le Ville-Baugé was wounded as he made his escape.

With republicans pouring into the streets the Vendéens put up little resistance and fled by the Thouars Gate, some being cut down by Westermann's cavalry who had circled around the town to cut off their line of retreat. Westermann claimed he killed 7-800 men and captured 100.[126] The Vendéens admitted to seventy killed, wounded or captured and the loss of four guns.

Westermann wrote his report after the battle with the sound of the tocsin ringing all around and was warned that 10,000 rebels had gathered to march against him later in the day. He boasted that if they did he had confidence his men would hold firm.[127] Nevertheless his small army soon dropped back to St-Maixent.

The Army of the Centre and the Battle of Luçon 28 June

While elements of the Army of the Centre had participated in the actions of the Grand Army, their primary concern had been to protect their territory and its exposed southern front. With major republican bases at Niort and La Rochelle, the Bocage was under constant threat, especially from republican posts south of the Lay and above all from Luçon. The Vendéens saw an opportunity to seize this position, a key link between Les Sables d'Olonne and Niort and south to La Rochelle. General Sandoz held Luçon with a garrison of less than 2,000 men.

By 27 June an estimated 7,000 men, including 100 cavalry and three small cannon, had gathered in Chantonnay under Royrand, Sapinaud, Verteuil, Béjarry, Ussault, Baudry d'Asson and Des Hargues.[128] Only a small number carried fusils and on the morning of 28 June two Vendéen columns were on the march.

The northern approach to Luçon was largely open agricultural land with a few scattered woods and farms. Although to the north-east of the town was the small Ste-Gemme Forest, overall the Vendéens would have to brave open terrain.

Towards 4pm a lookout in Luçon Cathedral reported large numbers of rebels crossing the Mainclaye Bridge and Sandoz deployed the garrison north of the town. The 5th Charente-Inférieure covered the left flank, the Battalion de l'Union the centre, and the 1st Parthenay the right, each supported by their battalion guns. His cavalry was held in reserve and comprised 160 men, split equally between gendarmes and the 11th Hussars.[129] These sparse forces were spread thinly from the Les Sables road to the approach from Ste-Gemme.

Once across the Mainclaye Bridge Royrand formed three columns and advanced rapidly. The left, under his personal command, moved on the Ste-Gemme Forest; the centre, under Verteuil, marched on the Mareuil road; and the right, under Sapinaud, headed for the Les Sables road. The battle began between 5 and 6pm when the Vendéens were within a few hundred metres of the town.

Sandoz believed he was being turned on both flanks and issued orders for the army to fall back to Luçon, but only his left flank received the order and duly complied. Unaware that this flank had withdrawn, the centre and right fought on and successfully held the Vendéens in check. Meanwhile the rebel right-wing reached the Les Sables road and was approaching the undefended west side of Luçon when it suddenly came to a halt. Their hesitation was provoked by the appearance of enemy troops

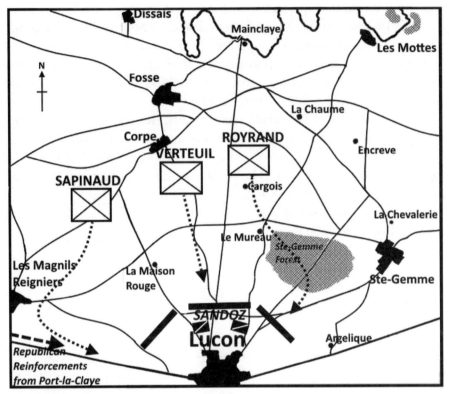

First Battle of Luçon.

approaching from the west, comprising 2-300 men detached from the Vengeur Battalion who had been at Port-la-Claye and were now marching to the sound of the guns.

In the ranks of this rebel column were around 100 deserters from the Regiment de Provence who took the opportunity to desert back to the Republic, causing the column to rout to cries of betrayal. This state of panic spread to the rest of the army which soon broke off the action and retreated in disorder. The republican cavalry was ordered to charge and a furious Sapinaud valiantly, but fruitlessly, endeavoured to cover the rout. Sandoz claimed to have caused 2-300 rebel casualties and captured two cannon.

The Les Sables Front

Throughout June the Republic had been building their forces in Les Sables d'Olonne, but the political troubles in Paris were echoed amongst the troops and politicians in that area and broke out in frequent brawls, resulting in six deaths in the Paris battalions, who it was claimed supported Marat's politics, while the Bordeaux battalions supported the Girondist views of Brissot.[130]

Only minor actions occurred on this front in June, including at the important post of Pas-Opton, when on 15 June 800 Vendéens attacked republican advanced posts but were repulsed.[131]

On 20 June 1,500-1,800 rebels, under St-Pal, attempted a surprise attack on the 1,000-1,200 men garrisoned in Talmont. Knowing this attack was coming 120 republicans moved forwards to Les Moutiers, deploying in a garden in advance of the town. The Vendéens attacked at 10am but after only fifteen minutes they retreated with the loss of fifty-one killed.[132]

Boulard was well aware that his priority was to cover Les Sables and remained very much on the defensive.

Chapter 8

The *Sans-Culotte* Army

The Republic had survived June but July was to shake it once more. On 12 July Toulon opened its port to the English and declared for the royalists and on 13 July Charlotte Corday, a young woman from Normandy and ardent Federalist, gained access to Marat and stabbed him to death in his bath. Both actions handed more power to the extreme elements within Paris. The Vendée also witnessed the escalation of conflict between the different factions represented amongst the generals, troops and local authorities, and Federalist support within Nantes now came to the fore.

As June moved into July the high hopes of the Vendéens, with their remarkable successes at Fontenay and Saumur, drifted back towards a fight for survival against republican columns infiltrating the region and gathering on the borders.

D'Ayat left for another command, leaving Biron with only one divisional general on the southern front: Chalbos. On 1 July the Army of the La Rochelle Coast had a mere 40,000 undisciplined and inexperienced troops covering a line at least 250km long, while at the same time a great expectation was placed upon them to enter the Vendéen heartland.

After his arrest Rossignol had been transferred from Niort to Paris to account for his conduct, but he had nothing to fear from his friends at the Ministry of War. For his actions at Luçon, Sandoz was replaced by Tuncq who was placed under Boulard's orders.

The Federalist Coup in Nantes

On 3 July Canclaux left Nantes to scout the Nort and Ancenis roads and secure news of Biron's movements so he could work in concert with him. He regretted that he did not have fresh troops with which to pursue the Vendéens after his victory at Nantes.

Having arrived at Nort with 2,200 men, accompanied by two commissaires of the Convention, he heard that the Nantes authorities had issued orders on 5 July to oppose the entrance into Nantes of all commissaires sent from the Convention. Beysser, who had remained in Nantes, adhered to this order and Canclaux was invited to do the same. In his reply of 11 July Canclaux refused outright. That same day the representatives gave Beysser a window of opportunity to formally disavow the order of 5 July and appealed to his loyalty and character but, as he did not respond within the required timescale, he was dismissed for revolt and treason.

Beysser issued a proclamation to the people of Nantes saying his 'crimes' were saving Nantes from the rebels and their accomplices the Montagnards, recognising the sovereignty of the people that the '*maratists*' wanted to destroy, and for adhering to an order from the Nantes authorities conforming to the people's voice: namely to distance the Department from the 'dangerous envoys sent to ignite discord'.[1] Yet on 15 July Canclaux was able to announce that Beysser and the Nantes authorities had retracted. They were ordered to the bar of the Convention and somewhat surprisingly Beysser was neither imprisoned nor guillotined, and although placed under surveillance he was sent to hunt down Girondist deputies hiding in the departments of Normandy, La Sarthe and Britanny.[2]

On 18 July Canclaux advised Boulard that he had swept along the north bank of the Loire and communications between Nantes and Paris were now open.

It was in July that Wimpffen, commanding in Calvados, openly declared for Federalism but his shambles of an army, totalling 5,000 men, was routed over 13 to 14 July around Pacy-sur-Eure by General Sepher and soon ceased to exist.

All these actions heightened the pitch of paranoia among the Montagnards, who were fighting both the Federalists and the upsurge of influence held by the Hébértists.

Towards the end of June it will be recalled that troops in Tours, now under Labarolière, were sufficiently reorganised to march on Saumur. On arrival they awaited further orders from Biron.

The Châtillon Campaign

The most immediate threat to the rebels, however, was from General Westermann. A close friend of Danton, and involved in many famous events within Paris, Westermann was determined to make a name for himself. His force comprised the Légion-du-Nord supported by four further battalions: in all between 2,700 and 3,000 men. On 28 June he set out again from St-Maixent, heading for Parthenay. Prior to departure these troops were reviewed by Biron who was impressed by their discipline and quality.

However, Aubertin, who commanded part of this column, recalled the air of trepidation as they set out for the heart of rebel territory.

Westermann was to gain a reputation for burning and destroying settlements wherever he marched, but he did take the precaution of advancing cautiously and with light cavalry covering his flanks. On 2 July his column left Parthenay for Bressuire and aimed to seize Châtillon-sur-Sèvre on the following day, recognising the symbolic significance of seizing the town where the Vendéens had established their Supreme Council. Biron indicated that he would deploy troops in Parthenay and Coulanges to act in support and ordered Labarolière to send 3,000 men to join Westermann.

Bois-aux-Chèvres 3 July

At 6am on 3 July Westermann's infantry were on the march, with the bulk of his artillery following two hours later under cavalry escort.

Between Bressuire and Châtillon were the woods of Bois-aux-Chèvres, at the entrance to which was a large opening forming a long square which tapered away in the distance. It is thanks to Aubertin that we have a detailed account of the action that followed.

At around 11.30am, just after the two Chasseur battalions of the Légion-du-Nord had moved into the open space at the entrance to this woodland, musket and artillery fire opened up on their front and flanks. Having succeeded in keeping order in the ranks Westermann managed to form his men in line with a company of Belgian tirailleurs (probably the fifty-six men of the Légion-des-Ardennes) deployed along the front.[3]

A second body of troops was led by Aubertin and formed up on Westermann's left towards the edge of the wood, and then began to advance under fire. Westermann's third body of troops formed up on his right.

On this right flank Westermann deployed two 4pdrs facing a holloway which led up from the woods. A captain of grenadiers from the 11th Orléans noticed a large body of Vendéens advancing at speed along this holloway, clearly aiming to seize the guns. By a quick and skilful manoeuvre (which unfortunately is not described) he forced them to pull back into the woods.

The republicans were now deployed across fields of crops between the woods. Royalist snipers seemed to be taking pleasure in picking out targets, and Aubertin, who had already lost a number of men, deployed numerous tirailleurs who moved into the woods to put an end to the enemy firing. This manoeuvre was copied by Westermann's centre and right and caused the royalists to give up the fight and disperse.

After this action Westermann's artillery and cavalry arrived and he continued his march on Châtillon.

Mercier-de-Rocher, who was not present, indicated that Westermann had encountered 10,000 rebels supported by ten cannon on a height before La Sauzelière. He wrote that Westermann attacked them, became encircled, but at bayonet point forced the enemy to retreat, capturing six guns and killing 2,000 brigands in the pursuit (undoubtedly a gross exaggeration).[4]

The eye-witness account by the royalist artillery officer Poirier-de-Beauvais describes a different part of what was evidently a series of ongoing actions that stretched from Bois-aux-Chèvres to Châtillon.

On hearing news of Westermann's advance Beauvais was ordered to take two cannon and deploy them on high ground overlooking the Gué-Paillard Bridge east of Châtillon, supported by a large body of infantry.[5] On the morning of 3 July the Vendéen numbers were enhanced by men from surrounding parishes and with these reinforcements they marched on the enemy and encountered them at the Bois-aux-Chèvres, a few hundred metres east of Gué-Paillard. Initially the combat went in the Royalists' favour and caused the republicans to abandon some cannon, but, on seeing two Vendéen cannon being redeployed further from the republicans, the troops nearby mistook this for a retreat and routed. The rest of the troops soon followed and only stopped once across the Gué-Paillard Bridge.

Beauvais was determined to deploy some guns in this excellent position and at first the peasant-soldiers seemed willing to remain, but as soon as the first enemy squadron appeared they broke once more and only stopped in Châtillon. He was quick to point out that many of the troops had not seen action before.

On the Rorthais road east of Châtillon the rebels deployed several guns, with others on a road to its north. The republicans were advancing slowly and cautiously, and Lescure, La Rochejaquelein, Stofflet and the Bishop of Agra were amongst those who did all they could to inspire the troops to fight, but to no avail.[6]

With bullets from republican tirailleurs whistling around, Beauvais advised Lescure that the cannon were at imminent risk and should be harnessed up. La Rochejaquelein, he suggested, could mask this action by making a feint with the cavalry. This manoeuvre was successfully executed but, Beauvais wrote, La Rochejaquelein's ardour got the better of him and some infantry were inspired to join him in his advance.

As Lescure and Beauvais were on their way to harness the guns on the road to the left they noticed that the republican artillery fire had become more intense. Beauvais went to find out what was happening and when he arrived at the eastern edge of Châtillon he discovered that the cannon and the army had vanished. Spotting a single cavalryman approaching he asked how long ago La Rochejaquelein had left, only to be told he was still up ahead in the action.

By his presence La Rochejaquelein had caused the enemy tirailleurs to retreat and had advanced to within close range of the republican guns located in a dip in the ground and out of sight of the town. He was accompanied by a handful of cavalry and a few infantry deployed to either side of the road in the broom. Beauvais warned him that the artillery had left and that he was exposing himself to no avail, and La Rochejaquelein agreed to retire once the wounded had been evacuated.

On that same day Biron advised Westermann that he had placed at his disposal 1,900 men in Parthenay and 1,200 infantry and 150 cavalry in Coulanges.[7] The Parthenay troops joined Westermann on 4 July, bringing his numbers up to about 5,000 men.[8]

Châtillon-sur-Sèvres 5 July

After entering Châtillon most of the republican troops deployed as follows: the Chasseurs of the Légion-du-Nord were posted in the town; the cavalry on the edge of the town on the Mortagne road; a pair of 4pdrs were deployed on the Bressuire road; four battalions were placed in an irregular line facing Mortagne on the Château-Gaillard Heights; and ten guns were placed to their north, on a track leading to some woods on these same heights. Above St-Jouin, in a cemetery on the Cholet road, were more troops supported by some cannon, and in the château and abbey were 2,000 raw levies armed with pikes.[9]

The Château-Gaillard Heights was a dangerous position for a camp, being very steep on its eastern side.[10] Beauvais added that the north side was also quite steep and although their right flank was safe their line of retreat was poor and the position was surrounded by plenty of cover.[11]

The republican leaders hoped that their troops would remain as deployed but indiscipline quickly broke out and a large number returned to Châtillon and began looting. The officers were forced to deploy detachments of disciplined troops in an attempt to control the drunken rampage that followed. Westermann also ignored warnings from local patriots that the constant ringing of the tocsin meant the rebels were gathering in strength.

The Vendéen generals had gathered 25,000 men by the evening of 4 July. Setting out from Cholet an hour before dawn they headed south, aiming to attack Châtillon from the west. At Le Temple, around 4km west of Châtillon, the army split into two columns: that on the left under D'Élbée and Stofflet moving directly on Châtillon and La Frerie; and that on the right, under Lescure, La Rochejaquelein, Bonchamps, Marigny and Royrand, advancing on Château-Gaillard.

As this right hand column drew near it split into three further columns with Bonchamps forming the centre. According to Beauvais the covered country enabled this column to move close to the enemy batteries.[12]

The *Marie-Jeanne* gave the signal for the attack and Marigny's infantry, preceding those of Bonchamps, opened the engagement by assaulting the heights.[13]

Around 11am Aubertin had been invited to dine with Westermann but, concerned about the undisciplined state of the troops, he declined. As he was mounting up he heard gunfire breaking out all around Châtillon. The royalists had crept unseen towards the town through ripe fields of crops.[14] 'It appeared to me that the republicans had taken no precautions and had no outposts,' recalled Beauvais.[15]

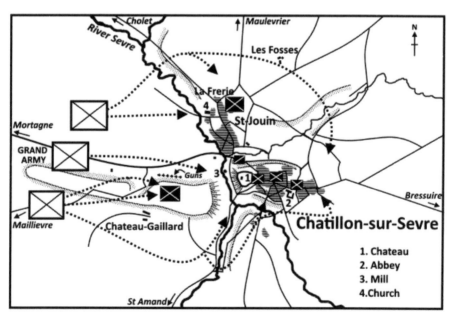

First Battle of Châtillon.

Westermann was enjoying an old cask of Bordeaux in Châtillon when he heard the gunfire open up on the Château-Gaillard Heights. Jean Pernot, maréchal-des-logis of the artillery of the Légion-du-Nord, recalled, 'At midday we were attacked. I was between the two mills at one and a half fusils range from Châtillon on the Mortagne road.'[16] He was with a 4pdr, had an 8pdr about thirty paces to his left, and an Orléans battalion was about 250 paces away when the enemy attacked:

'They came at us in ranks with a badly nourished fire-by-file. The battalions fired over fifty shots before retiring on my right: only sixteen or seventeen men stayed with us to support the guns, the rest dispersed...When the enemy appeared I went to warn the battalion saying, 'Look the enemy!' Several were lying down, others eating soup...I couldn't see their leader. They replied that they could see these troops but did not believe they were the enemy. I returned to my guns which I deployed in battery.'

Westermann galloped to the scene of action but when he reached Château-Gaillard his army was already in trouble.[17]

The rebels seem to have encountered some difficulty fighting over the rudimentary earth ramparts that surrounded the Republican camp on the heights, and could not easily see their enemy, but their screams terrified the Republicans.[18]

On these same heights a battalion in blue coats faced-green (almost certainly one of the Chasseur Battalions of the Légion-du-Nord) formed square and fired on anyone who dared approach.[19]

Jean Pernot continued:

'As they approached and I recognised them I fired grapeshot and pushed them back three times, though they were behind abattis and in a holloway. I fired nearly thirty shots and three of my gunners were shot down. I was also wounded and the fifteen Orléans men who had stayed with us had fled.'[20]

He claimed that he wanted to fight on but was told to retire.

Occupying terrain covered in high standing crops hindered their manoeuvring and Colson, a Republican gunner, recalled:

'Fire rapidly took hold, and seeing that it would reach the caissons and blow us up, as well as being assailed by continuous musket fire, we looked for a way to escape only to come up against a very steep descent. The first caisson tumbled over with its horses and drivers, a 4pdr overturned and fell into a pond, as did some others, and others fell into enemy hands as the gunners fled from the flames. We had no officers with us, the chasseurs-à-cheval were camped on the plain and the infantry were in the town. It was presumed we had been surprised because we had not placed scouts.'[21]

Lieutenant Colonel Friedrichs, commanding officer of the 14th Orléans, was protecting three cannon on the heights and gave a different version of events. He said the rebels advanced unseen up to the 11th Orléans deployed in advance of his position and he summoned the men to arms when a cannon ball landed at his feet. He said the 14th Orléans advanced to support the 11th and these two battalions united and withstood the enemy's fire for over an hour. They then retreated as neither the general nor any orders arrived and they had taken significant losses.

Troops began to rush down the steep eastern slopes in growing numbers, gripped by terror.

Lescure was heading down the Mortagne road and soon arrived at the foot of this steep slope to discover bodies and equipment piled at the bottom. Republicans were running along the riverbank, hoping to cross the causeway at the Moulin-de-Prévie and being hunted down by Renou and the Les Aubiers men.[22]

Frouchard noted that La Rochejaquelein's column appeared on the St Amand road further south, with a third column blocking the St-Jouin and Cholet road to the north.[23]

Marigny and Stofflet had been pursuing fugitives seeking refuge in the town. They penetrated the St-Jouin Suburb and pitilessly cut down their enemy.[24] The republicans on the Cholet road, however, were still putting up a fight and Lescure threw himself against these troops. According to Frouchard this might have failed if La Rochejaquelein and Bonchamps (after leaving contingents from Cerizay and La Pommeraye in the town) had not come to his aid.[25]

Some Republicans attempted to retreat north on the Maulévrier road but were faced by Bonchamps, Lescure and La Rochejaquelein's men and were forced to break up. Many surrendered.[26]

Beauvais said the battle lasted about an hour after which the republicans attempted to escape along the Bressuire road to the east and abandoned their guns and baggage; 'our cavalry held in reserve then advanced.'[27] Marigny led this pursuit with Richard, commander of the Cerizay Division. An enemy unit put down their arms as if to surrender, but facing only a handful of rebels they retrieved their weapons and shot at Marigny's troops: an act witnessed by rebels from the La Pommeraye Parish who massacred these republicans.[28] Overcome with rage Marigny returned to Châtillon, gathered up some gunners he had captured, and fully aware that Westermann had massacred the Vendéen wounded left in the town's hospital, he started to execute them.[29]

Lescure was informed of Marigny's action and was already surrounded by numerous captured republicans clinging to his horse and clothing. Arriving at the prison he encountered the grisly sight of Marigny, sabre drawn and covered in blood from the seventy-five republicans he had personally killed. Lescure ordered him to leave, saying he would defend Marigny's prisoners personally if necessary.[30]

Westermann was witnessing his army being torn to pieces.

Jean Pernot said he tried to join the cavalry when it appeared to be preparing to attack the rebel horse but, added Aubertin, 'Westermann's cavalry, like cowards, abandoned their post…raced into the town and galloped ahead to lead the rout.'[31]

> 'Though vastly outnumbered, the infantry would have been able to retreat if they had been protected by their light cavalry, but seeing that they had been abandoned they threw away their arms and baggage so they could flee as quickly as possible. Many were killed, but some were saved through the humanity of Lescure, D'Élbée and Bonchamps. Nearly all the officers were killed or captured and those mounted formed a platoon and in so doing were able to retreat.'[32]

Westermann's cavalry had difficulty escaping when they were cut off by more parishes arriving on the Bressuire road.[33]

A party of Vendéen cavalry charged vigorously until near Rorthais, and Beauvais recalled:

> 'Here we encountered the Légion-du-Nord retiring in mass. I ordered the cavalry to stop to await two cannons and Stofflet and I quarrelled as he wanted to charge them, but the arrival of a single cannon ended our dispute as its first shot dispersed the enemy. After crossing the Gué-Paillard I took the Bressuire road and many republicans perished on and around this route.'[34]

Westermann retreated on Bressuire then Parthenay.

'I am fairly sure all of Westermann's infantry, artillery and guns were killed or captured,' wrote Beauvais.[35] Savary said the rebels claimed over 2,000 casualties amongst the republicans, 300 in the battle, 600 on the Rorthais road and the rest in the surrounding countryside. He said the republican cavalry were cut off at Amailloux and partly torn to pieces.[36]

The republicans admitted to a loss of 1,200, including 200 killed. Béjarry said 3-4,000 enemy troops were killed or wounded, hundreds made prisoner, and nearly all the guns captured.[37]

Westermann firmly placed the blame for the defeat on the volunteer battalions, above all the 11th and 14th Orléans, and said his légion was reduced to 8-900 men.[38]

Lieutenant Colonel Friedrichs said his battalion of 469 men was reduced to 17. He reported that no advanced posts had been placed and that both the 11th and 14th Orléans fought bravely. Savary cynically wrote that Westermann was trying to pin the blame for the defeat on a battalion that was nearly wiped out.[39]

Biron's Command Struggles July

Biron was informed of the victory at Nantes on 3 July. He now changed his plans and ordered 8-10,000 men to march from Tours and Saumur on Nantes and also ordered Westermann to stop his movements so his troops would be available. Biron was unaware of the disaster that was about to befall Westermann.

Biron had around 16,000 men of which 13,000 were available for use.[40] On the morning of 4 July he set out for Angers leaving Chalbos in charge at Niort. Arriving in Saumur on 6 July he reported to the CPS that he would be marching on Nantes. On 8 July Canclaux reported that he was moving on Ancenis and aimed to meet with Biron at Angers that same night, at which point Biron suggested that they unite their forces, re-establish communications between Nantes and La Rochelle, and then march into the heart of the Vendée.[41]

Biron ordered Boulard to move up to Machecoul promising that a division would march from Nantes in support. Troops were also to march from Luçon on La Roche-sur-Yon to protect the communications of the other columns. Biron was aiming to personally march through Fontenay, attack Pont Charron, and head for Montaigu, and another column was to leave Niort and move to La Châtaigneraie to protect his communications.[42]

The representatives did not support Biron's plan and on 10 July, when he became aware of this, and of Westermann's defeat, he submitted his resignation once again. He said Nantes was no longer threatened and his health no longer permitted him to remain in command.

In discussion with Canclaux, however, he had decided to march a column to Les Pont-de-Cé then on to St-Lambert, Chemillé and Cholet, while the Niort Division would remain on the defensive.[43]

On 11 July Biron once again asked the CPS to replace him but since 23 June they had not replied to any of his correspondence. That same day the troops that had set out from Tours, renamed the Division of Angers, camped at Brissac, and Biron received information that the rebels were aiming to march either on Tremont and Vihiers, or on Chemillé and Cholet. He informed the Ministry that he was heading for Niort and from there would try to link the Niort Division with that of Angers.[44]

On arriving at Niort he counted 10,000 men (including 3,000 untrained recruits) and a further 3,000 at St-Maixent, but for more than eight days he had been running a fever and his requests to be replaced were becoming insistent.[45]

On 11 July the Ministry had written to the representatives with the Army of the La Rochelle Coast with orders for Westermann to appear before the bar; Sandoz to appear before the Revolutionary Tribunal; Rossignol to be released; and Biron to be sent to account for the mistreatment of this citizen. On 12 July Biron received a letter from the Convention summoning him to Paris immediately and he handed over command to Chalbos and was in Paris eight days later. He was detained in the Abbaye Prison and on 31 December would be guillotined for 'having participated in a conspiracy against the external and internal safety of the Republic'.[46]

On 9 July Commissaire Momoro penned a letter to Vincent, assistant to the Minister of War, wondering whether it was deliberate treachery or incompetence that was causing the war to drag on. He singled out Biron and Westermann in his comments and two days later Commissaires Brulé and Besson announced that they were heading to Paris with Ronsin to denounce them in person.[47]

The representatives at Ancenis, Merlin and Gillet, wrote to the CPS informing them that Ronsin and his emissaries had treated Boulard badly and had caused him to hand in his resignation after four months of faithful and successful service to the Republic. 'After having disorganised the Army of La Rochelle, Ronsin wanted to disorganise that of Brest.'[48] They asked that Ronsin and his cronies be recalled to Paris. On 20 July they added that this crowd of commissaries of the Executive Council, who regarded themselves as the directors of the army, were blaming, censuring or exalting the actions of the generals as it suited them. These men, they wrote, had no military experience yet were being elevated to high rank: Ronsin being made general of brigade and the former comedian, Grammont, adjutant general. They also called for the Minister of War's replacement, concluding that 'Bouchotte has been a longstanding friend of Merlin…and will always be an excellent citizen, but he will always be a very bad minister'.[49]

Rossignol would be freed and promoted general of brigade on 12 July, then on 27 July became general of division and commander-in-chief of the Army of the La Rochelle Coast. Westermann faced and survived the Revolutionary Tribunal, undoubtedly due to his influential contacts, even though he was responsible for a disaster not dissimilar in scale to that of Thouars.

The march of the Angers Column

Although Westermann's assault had been crushed, the Vendéens were barely given time to draw breath before reports arrived of further enemy activity to the north-east.

General Labarolière, who replaced Duhoux, had at long last moved to Angers. A detailed return produced by Berthier on 21 June indicates that at that time the Tours troops totalled 16,375 infantry and 1,848 cavalry (see Appendix 2).

Labarolière's division had been rebuilt into brigades under Santerre, Joly, Chabot and a large advance guard under General of Division Menou (this advance guard being led by Fabrefond, Dutruy, Barbazan and Gauvilliers). His cavalry totalled 1,600 men and included elements of the 8th and 9th Hussars, 16th and 19th Dragoons, 24th Chasseurs and Mayenne Volunteers. Labarolière detached 3,000 troops to cover Saumur and Angers and set out from Angers on 11 July with 11,000 men and reached Brissac later that same day. He reported that he would move to the banks of the Layon on 14 July and noted that the enemy were holding the west bank in strength. However, he expressed concern over the indiscipline and insolence of his troops and, having served for thirty-six years with honour, he asked to be replaced.[50]

Ronsin had risen through the ranks with astonishing speed. Within the first four days of July he was promoted from the rank of captain to that of general of brigade. The Hébértists now seemed to be in complete control of military action.

Martigné-Briand 15 July

Labarolière did not attempt to cross the Layon in the presence of the enemy. Having heard of Westermann's defeat he decided to march further south to skirt rebel territory and camp between Chavagnes and Martigné-Briand.[51] His progress was so slow that Bonchamps had time to assemble 16,000 rebels at Chemillé and marched to face this new threat.[52]

At 3am on 15 July Bonchamps advanced to attack Labarolière knowing the republicans were very strung out, but with dawn the temperature rose rapidly on what was to be an extremely hot day. Both Bonchamps and Lescure aimed to take the most direct road until persuaded by an old veteran officer, who reputedly knew the area well, to make a wide detour to surprise the enemy.[53] Under a scorching sun they reputedly marched for six hours to cross the Layon at the Rablay Bridge.[54]

Towards midday they were informed of the enemy positions and according to Beauvais, instead of halting to form up, their column stretched out even further as they rapidly moved towards the enemy.[55]

Labarolière's troops were spread across a distance of about 7km. His advance guard was at Aubigné, his centre and headquarters at Fliné, and the rear in Chavagnes. Bonchamps was leading the advance of the rebel army and immediately saw an opportunity in this undulating and covered country to break through the middle of the enemy position. He left the other leaders the means to mask or reduce Chavagnes as he raced on ahead along the Layon, climbed the vine covered slopes, and appeared near Noyers.[56] Deploying artillery he broke the enemy centre and forced them back towards the Vihiers road. Beauvais recalled that Bonchamps was unable to restrain his troops as they believed themselves invincible, and the battle was already underway when the other leaders arrived.[57]

The Vendéen left took up position on the Jouhannet Heights and bombarded troops in Chavagnes, while their right assaulted and seized Château Fliné, causing the republican headquarters' staff to flee. The Vendéens were close to cutting the enemy in two as the northern part of the republican army was thrown back on the Angers road and the southern on that of Vihiers.[58]

The republican generals managed to summon fresh troops from Aubigné and reformed their lines behind the Vilaine. They also succeeded in slowing the Vendéen offensive, helped by cannon deployed near the Millé Windmills and counter-battery fire aimed at the rebel artillery at Jouhannet.[59]

The initial royalist success continued when General Danican led a cavalry charge at great cost to his regiment.

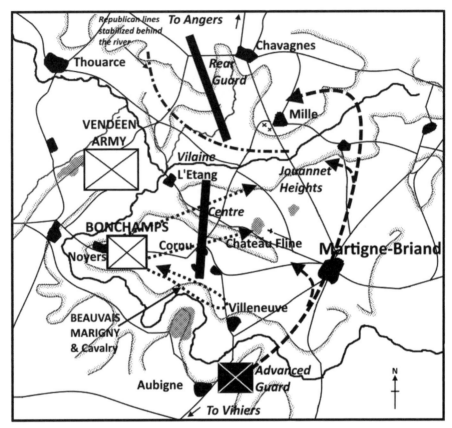

The Battle of Martigné-Briand.

Beauvais was considering moving his six guns to a better position and ordered a reserve of 800 cavalry and 2,000 infantry nearby to cover this redeployment. He took this precaution having spotted some hussars leading a considerable body of enemy cavalry to his right. This cavalry approached to within half range of his guns but dispersed when he fired on them.[60] Marigny joined him to find out what he was doing and told Beauvais he only needed the infantry to cover this move, then set out with the cavalry to charge the enemy's left flank. Hearing that Santerre was in the enemy ranks Marigny was eager to capture him 'and parade around in a cage, as a trophy of war, the man who presided at the execution of the King'.[61]

Beauvais abandoned his plan and joined Marigny and the cavalry. They descended from the high ground, crossed a large stream on their right and took a road to the left, in an attempt to reach Martigné-Briand by marching around Villeneuve. But in this unfamiliar terrain and with no guide they were soon completely lost. When they eventually reappeared they were surprised to see both sides routing, only to be informed that it was the appearance of this very cavalry that had caused their own men to rout. Waving handkerchiefs in an attempt to show they were friends only aggravated the situation. The rout in Bonchamps' ranks caused others to follow and soon the whole army took flight, covered by around forty officers and some cavalry.[62]

Beauvais accepted that it was their actions that had provoked this disaster.

Madame de la Rochejaquelein said few were killed in the battle but around fifty died from heat exhaustion and even Lescure collapsed and was unconscious for two hours.[63] Bonchamps, in his first battle since Fontenay, was surrounded by five hussars during the retreat and wounded again when a bullet shot away the bone at the extremity of his elbow. Beauvais also recalled that although they had captured five guns they abandoned three of their own in the rout.[64]

Writing that same evening, Labarolière reported that he had been attacked on his right and rear as the advance guard had begun its march on Vihiers. He acknowledged that the rebels managed to break through his centre, but said they were repulsed and pursued for over two leagues. The 8th and 9th Hussars, he said, contributed greatly to the success of the day. Ronsin, however, confessed that the republican losses had been quite high and that the battle had been in the balance for some time.[65]

The Vendéen divisions dispersed once again and within a few days their high command was informed that a battle had taken place at Vihiers, but this time none of them were involved.

Vihiers 18 July

On 17 July Labarolière continued his advance and was now marching west on the Cholet road. He camped at Vihiers, leaving his baggage and part of his artillery park at Montilliers 4km to the north-east. That same day his advance guard was repulsed by 600 German and Swiss troops under Baron Keller who were deployed in Coron. The republicans pulled back to Vihiers and on 18 July came under attack.

Labarolière deployed covering the north, south and west approaches to Vihiers as follows: under Menou's command, General of Brigade Gauvilliers deployed on the west bank of the Lys from the Galerne Heights to near the bridge and château lake; a second brigade (under Léopald Hugo, called 'Brutus'), came under Gauvilliers' orders; and one of Santerre's battalions was deployed in support.[66]

On high ground near the Jusalem Farm a second body of troops deployed, with a third deployed close to the southern edge of Vihiers near the cemetery and steep fields at La Dauphinerie.[67] Santerre's troops were both in the town and on the approaches to this cemetery and the cavalry were held in reserve in Vihiers.

With the main royalist divisions dispersed, and the most senior leaders at Châtillon deciding on Cathelineau's replacement, Piron worked wonders in raising peasants from surrounding parishes. Although their morale would have been brittle, all would have been aware of the gravity of the situation. The rebels did, however, have the advantage of terrain that suited their tactics which included woodland, undulating terrain, and plenty of high-hedged fields.

Piron was mounted on a white horse and deployed his men in three columns in copses facing the enemy. He commanded somewhere between 10,000 and 15,000 men.[68] The left was under Guignard-de-Tiffauge; the

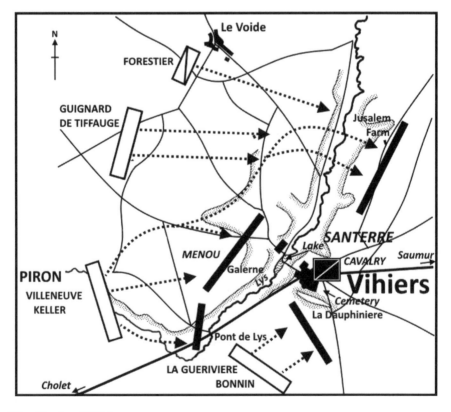

The Battle of Vihiers.

centre under the Chevalier de Villeneuve supported by Baron Keller with the Swiss and German companies; and the right was led by La Guérivière and Bonnin facing the cemetery fields. Piron had the support of Forestier, with perhaps 500 cavalry, who deployed towards Le Voide. Herbault was tasked with deploying their artillery in a favourable position.

Piron placed himself with the centre on the Cholet to Saumur road and launched all three columns in an all-out attack around midday, apparently while Santerre was eating his lunch. Although initially holding well, Menou's men proved unable to withstand the fire from Keller's troops, supported by a turning movement from Piron, and several of his battalions fled. Menou was wounded in the chest as his troops routed.

Piron was soon in command of the bridge over the Lys, with Herbault targeting the enemy as they routed alongside the lake.[69] A squadron of hussars managed to cross the bridge to charge the rebels but by aiming at the horses this charge was disrupted and the cavalry routed.

Forestier had been pinned down in a valley under bombardment from republican artillery until Piron came to his aid. Their combined force caused the republicans' right to panic and rout.

Santerre's Paris battalions led the rout as the republicans pulled back beyond Vihiers.

The republican left put up more resistance but was forced to retreat when the rest of the army collapsed. The official royalist account, quoted in Savary, indicated that the battle in the town was ferocious and 'after forty-five minutes...the victory was complete'.[70]

The entire republican army fell to pieces as the rebels plunged into their ranks. Bourbotte with a body of 1,200–1,500 men tried to stop the rout in Vihiers but dispersed when at risk of being surrounded. Santerre came close to being captured and it was only the ability of his horse to leap a five foot wall that saved him. The republicans routed in more than one direction and were pursued to Montillé and Concourson.[71]

The royalists estimated enemy losses at 2,000 killed, 3,000 captured, and a haul of 7,000 fusils, 25 cannon, 100 horses and plenty of provisions.[72]

An officer in the 6th Orléans reported that the battle lasted around two hours, at which point the right gave way and the rout soon became widespread. They ran so quickly that some appeared at Saumur in three hours.[73] The defeat was blamed on the badly organised battalions under officers with no understanding of their profession; the impossibility of being able to charge in mass in such difficult terrain; and the tactics used by the Vendéens and their great numbers.[74]

Davout, who later become one of Napoleon's finest marshals, was present at this battle. In early July 1793 he had been transferred to the Vendée and joined Labarolière's division. Although recently promoted general of brigade he only commanded a small detachment of cavalry in this action and formed a protective screen that enabled some infantry to escape. He was soon transferred to Niort with orders to escort a detachment sent to reinforce General Tuncq. Arriving at Tuncq's headquarters he received news of his promotion to general of division and his recall to the Army of the North.[75]

Berthier and Dutruy presented a report to the CPS stating that

> 'This army was composed of levies with the few experienced troops forming the advance-guard. Having left 1,500 at Saumur, and 1,500 at Les Ponts-de-Cé, the army went to Brissac where a further post was left to protect their communications. Around the Layon, being near hostile territory, discipline broke down and looting of the area began. The Paris battalions were especially difficult to control and even threatened Santerre's life when he tried to intervene. It was the advance guard that was largely responsible for the victory at Martigné, as some battalions gave way and others showed little willingness to get involved until victory was assured. The bread due did not arrive and this prevented the army marching on 16 [July].
>
> 'Some of the generals were concerned about marching with the murmurings among the troops, saying it would be better to head for Doué or Argenton, but Labarolière said they would camp at Vihiers and defend themselves if attacked.
>
> 'Towards 1pm the enemy appeared in force; the advance-guard fought with valour, but all the rest retreated in spite of contrary orders. The Paris battalions retired without having fought, threatening their leaders and crying treason! Two battalions, being led to support the advance-guard, turned back like cowards on sight of the enemy. The rout soon spread through the army.
>
> 'The advance-guard had lost some of its best infantry. The army lost five or six cannon.'

They noted that the drivers abandoned their guns and concluded that the war needed a new approach, asking for four experienced light infantry battalions who could be employed as tirailleurs; eight line battalions; two battalions of workers armed with good tools; two companies of sappers; four howitzers and a regiment of chasseurs-à-cheval or dragoons.[76]

Berthier's republican credentials, however, were now being questioned and he felt it necessary to add that he was not related to two other Berthiers (one being the former king's secretary), that he was at the Tuileries on 10 August 1792, that he had a certificate of bravery for action on the northern frontier, and that he had the full confidence of the representatives and commissaires with the army in the Vendée. But according to Savary, Ronsin now made sure Berthier was no longer employed in the Vendée and that his report was ignored.[77]

The rout of the army at Vihiers was an embarrassment to the extremists both in the army and in Paris but, as it was the *sans-culotte* officers and troops who were evidently responsible, no action was taken against them.

On 19 July, when ordered to occupy the positions around Doué, Labarolière's battalions refused and wanted to cross the Loire; that is until the artillery and cavalry were deployed to persuade them to remain.

Once again the Vendéens had a breathing space and the initiative had swung back in their favour.

The Election of a new Vendéen Commander-in-Chief

With Cathelineau's death the Vendéens convened a council of war in Châtillon on 19 July to elect his replacement. Some generals sent substitutes to act on their behalf.

Two leaders stood out from among the divisional generals: D' Élbée and Bonchamps. However, as both Bonchamps and Lescure were wounded they were absent and it was relatively easy for D' Élbée, with broad support, to secure the appointment.

In addition to appointing the commander-in-chief, rebel territory was split into four principal commands, each under a lieutenant general: Bonchamps for Anjou; Lescure for Poitou; Royrand for the area of the Army of the Centre; and, most surprisingly, Donnissan for Bas-Poitou. The first three were obvious choices, but to assign Donnissan command of an area he had no connection with could only have been due to the lack of unity evident in the coastal Vendée, with some leaders unlikely to accept Charette in that role. Donnissan would certainly have given them a voice at the Superior Council and as he was not one of the more active field commanders he left them to run operations as they saw fit.

Four men were appointed second-in-command in each area: La Rochejaquelein under Lescure, the Chevalier Fleuriot under Bonchamps, Cumont under Royrand, and Charette under Donnissan.

Les Ponts-de-Cé 26 July

After Labarolière's rout, Angers was again exposed. On 20 July Bourgeois, who commanded the 8th Paris, was ordered to occupy the strongpoint of Roche-de-Murs on the south bank of the Loire. He placed 600 men and two guns in that position and dispersed the remaining 377 men of his battalion to cover the Moulins d'Érigné, a redoubt at the junction of the Brissac and St-Lambert roads, and the Pont-du-Louet (two more guns being deployed at the latter). The 6th Paris Battalion held an entrenchment at the side of the Chêne road.[78]

On 23 July, Duhoux placed a further 1,500 men at Les Ponts-de-Cé and spread 3,248 men in posts stretching along the north bank of the Loire as far as Ingrandes. He also put Angers in a state of siege, declaring that every day spies were trying to find out all they could about his forces.[79]

Bonchamps was acutely aware of the need to watch Les Ponts-de-Cé as it was the springboard for many republican assaults. He therefore placed his 10-12,000 strong division under D'Autichamp's command and ordered him to seize it. This would not be easy as in addition to the republican entrenchments covering the approach, three bridges separated Érigné from the north bank of the Loire. Nevertheless the Vendéens marched overnight and were in position for a dawn attack on 26 July. D'Autichamp's right wing soon routed the republicans on the Chêne road and at the Pont-du-Louet, pushing forward with 'dreadful cries'.[80]

Scépeaux, commanding the left wing, dispersed republicans at Quincé and then met with limited resistance when he assaulted those at Roche-de-Murs, many falling to their deaths down steep rocky slopes.[81]

The Vendéens crossed the first bridge and captured St-Maurille as General Desclozeaux and the Jemappes battalion fled after only limited resistance.[82] The Vendéens closely pursued them and captured the second bridge and then the third, some even pursuing to the suburbs of Angers.

The administrators of the Department of Maine-et-Loire condemned the cowardly behaviour of the troops, reporting that they bayonetted Desclozeaux in the foot when he tried to rally them. Others accused Desclozeaux of being drunk and falling from his horse as they fled.[83]

The situation was stabilised by a counter-attack from the national guards who although outnumbered managed to push the rebels back on Les Ponts-de-Cé and then wisely held the approaches from this town to Angers.

This series of battles ended around 10pm and D'Autichamp cut the bridge to the northern bank and dug in. The royalists claimed 900

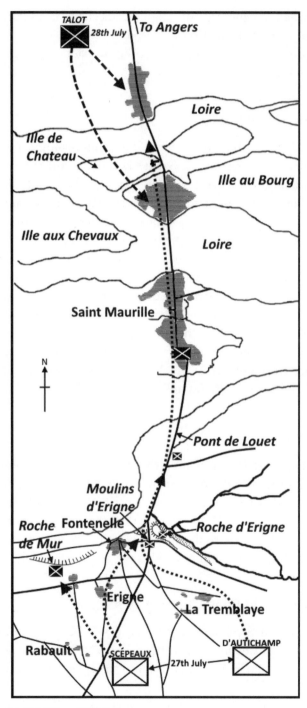

Les Ponts–de–Cé 27 and 28 July.

republicans killed or captured, although Hostis suggests a figure of around 450 is probably nearer the truth.[84]

All was quiet on the following day as the two sides watched each other but made no move.

Les Ponts-de-Cé 28 July

At 5pm on 28 July, Adjudant General Talot commanding the 6th Paris, the 'Vanqueurs de la Bastille', a Sarthe Battalion, and the debris of the Jemappes Battalion, launched a sudden attack on Les Ponts-de-Cé.[85] The official Republican account states that he crossed the Loire in some boats, seized the far bank, then overcame strong resistance and fought his way into Château. He pressed on, pushing the rebels back beyond the Érigné Heights where he established a new post before pulling most of his troops back at around 9pm. The Vendéens vigilantly watched this post from this date while the republicans constructed stronger defences supported by many guns.

With Labarolière clinging to the banks of the Loire and calling for more help, General Barbazan wrote that the only solution was to ensure all the generals were *sans-culottes* both in morals and principles, and that they should remove all reminders of the Ancien Regime.[86] He would have been heartened, therefore, with Rossignol's appointment.

Southern Front

While all this intrigue continued, the army along the southern front proceeded with the plan established by Biron, and in his absence Chalbos advised Boulard that he would head for Châtillon on 21 July, marching via St-Maixent, Parthenay and Bressuire with the 8,000 men under his command. However news of the catastrophe at Vihiers immediately curtailed his plans and he indicated that he would now await the army's reorganisation.[87]

Pont-Charrault and Pont-Charron 25 July

Tuncq had replaced Sandoz on 1 July. On 8 July he said he only had 700 infantry with him in Luçon and was expecting to be attacked at any moment. Chalbos therefore sent him some battalions to replace ones sent on to Les Sables.

Impatient for action Tuncq planned a surprise attack on Pont-Charron, a frontier post held by the Vendéens under Sapinaud-de-la-Verrie. The

Vendéens had constructed redoubts and entrenchments along the north bank near the stone bridge. Centred on Chantonnay Sapinaud's 4,000 troops formed the advance guard of the Army of the Centre.

The republicans marched in two columns: one under Adjudant General Canier comprising 480 infantry, 100 mounted gendarmes and two guns, and the other under Tuncq's personal command formed of 780 infantry, 80 cavalry and a single 4pdr.[88] In the early hours of 24 July Canier had been ordered to march on Pont-Charrault, overpower its 100 strong post and single gun, and then attack the eastern side of the entrenchments covering Pont-Charron. Tuncq was to head directly north from Ste-Hermine on the main Pont-Charron road.

Canier set out at 4am and Tuncq at 11am. At 2am on 25 July Canier crossed the Grand Lay at an undefended ford at La Solissonnière and appeared above the town of St-Philbert, while some of his men crossed at a ford west of Pont-Charrault. His troops may have been marching disguised as rebels.[89]

The Vendéens spotted the enemy approaching from the south and were ready to resist them, but suddenly found themselves under attack from the north as Canier's main force appeared. They put up little resistance as Pont-Charrault fell to the republicans.[90] Canier's men then massacred a post at La Gué.[91]

As soon as he heard gunfire Sapinaud and thirty cavalry raced from Chantonnay to Pont-Charron. Finding it undisturbed he headed towards Pont-Charrault via Vildé.[92] They spotted some republicans lying flat on a path not far from Les Gabardières, clearly waiting to ambush them. As

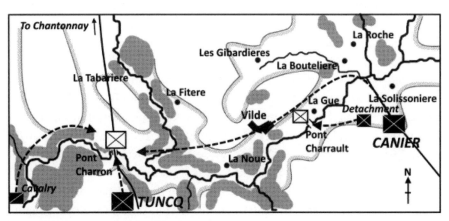

Pont Charrault and Pont Charron.

they turned to withdraw, Sapinaud was struck by gunfire and cut down by republican cavalry before the others could come to his aid.

Canier continued his march on Port-Charron and picked up speed when he was told rebel reinforcements were on route to the two bridges.[93] He attacked Pont-Charron just as Tuncq launched his attack from south of the river. Tuncq had also sent cavalry across a ford further to the west.[94] The rebels now came under attack from three directions at once and after initial resistance they retreated via Chantonnay to St-Vincent.[95]

Losses were light but the death of Sapinaud-de-la-Verrie was a terrible blow for the Army of the Centre.

Tuncq advanced to Chantonnay, destroyed rebel supplies, and then sensibly withdrew back to Luçon. The Vendéens soon reoccupied the lost ground. This small action was hailed as a great victory for the Republic at a time when they had little else to celebrate.

Luçon 30 July

With the area around Les Ponts-de-Cé stabilised by Bonchamps' division, the Vendéens still had their eye on Luçon. A second assault would now see part of the Grand Army linked to the Army of the Centre and would involve D'Élbée, Lescure, La Rochejaquelein, Stofflet, Royrand, Talmont and Marigny. Charette was asked to join in the attack but declined, claiming that he had to defend his area against republicans from Nantes and Paimboeuf.[96]

Tuncq had warning on 28 July that large numbers of rebels were assembling, giving him time to plan his defence with the meagre forces he had to hand. On the following day the Vendéens set out from Les Herbiers, and that evening, having spotted rebel cavalry, Tuncq deployed his troops. The rebels gathered at Chantonnay, marched through Ste-Hermine and then crossed the River Smagne at the Mainclaye Bridge.[97]

Tuncq had the confidence to deploy in open country north of Luçon, covering the area from Corpe to north of the Ste-Gemme Forest. His command consisted of little more than three volunteer battalions and a few squadrons of cavalry: in all 1,170 infantry, 400 cavalry and 6 guns of the newly formed horse artillery.[98] He was being approached by thousands of rebels supported by 800 cavalry and 6 guns.[99]

The republican left comprised 350 men from the 6th Charente-Inférieure under Sagot, supported by 250 men from the 11th Hussars.[100] Sagot's Grenadiers were deployed north of Corpe.

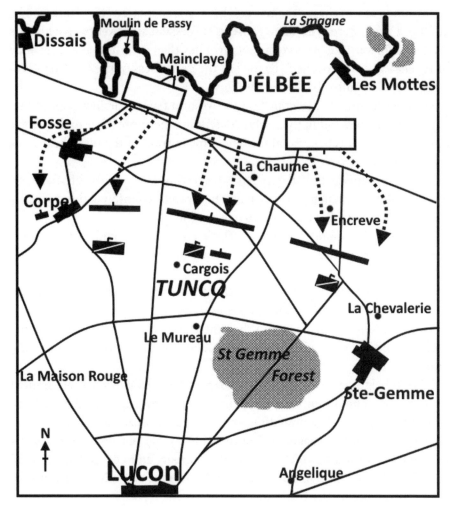

Second Battle of Luçon.

Their centre comprised 420 men of the 3rd Charente-Inférieure covering the roads leading to Luçon from Mainclaye and Les Mottes. This weak battalion was supported by around seventy-five mounted gendarmes and possibly some volunteer companies from Parthenay.

The right flank was deployed to the north and north-west of the Ste-Gemme Forest and comprised Lecomte's 400 strong battalion (*Le Vengeur*) supported by around seventy-five mounted gendarmes.

Tuncq deployed numerous posts so had plenty of warning of the enemy's movements. Once again the Vendéens had to face the open terrain north of Luçon.

Around 11am three enemy columns were spotted by Tuncq. The advanced posts were ordered to retire in succession and twenty-five hussars were sent forwards to observe the enemy. They then withdrew as a large body of rebel cavalry approached. To the left the grenadiers of the 6th Charente-Inférieure also pulled back towards Corpe.

The battle initially developed on the western flank as artillery opened up and the grenadiers found themselves defending the approaches to the village against swarms of rebels. Soon the landscape in front of the republicans was thick with enemy troops.

Sagot recognised that the rebels were trying to turn his left flank, so while holding the enemy to his front he bravely countered this move by obliquely marching his battalion to new positions.

Lecomte also found his eastern flank under threat and (although his manoeuvres are not recorded) by advancing his troops he managed to stop the Vendéens.

In the republican centre part of the 3rd Charente-Inférièure wavered and then broke under Royrand's onslaught, losing a gun in the process. The supporting republican cavalry in the centre and two companies protecting their second cannon seized back the higher ground and recaptured the gun.

The rebels seemed to hesitate and may have exhausted their limited ammunition. The discipline and tactical skill of the small republican force took advantage of this hesitation and frustrated what should have been an easy rebel victory. Sagot had been firing-by-file but now advanced his battalion with fixed bayonets and cavalry support and charged and routed the rebels facing him. On the eastern flank Lecomte also advanced and with their centre rallying the battle was won.

Talmont came to the aid of the rebel infantry and charged the republican cavalry several times with only fifty horse, dispersing successive republican squadrons.[101]

Tuncq claimed that the Vendéens rallied 3,000 men at the bridge but could not hold it against his troops and boasted that over 2,000 rebels 'bit the dust', yet by contrast Beauvais claimed that Talmont's heroism meant their losses were limited.[102] Three rebel guns, two caissons, and a wagon full of munitions also fell into Tuncq's hands.

D'Élbée's first battle as commander-in-chief had been a shambles. Their own bulletin claimed that the stragglers at the rear of the columns spread panic and caused the disaster, but this setback was a reminder that good leadership was more important than numbers. It was also a reminder just how vulnerable their troops were in open terrain.

The Vendéens had not given up hope of seizing Luçon and as July slipped into August the Grand Army opened discussion with the armies of the coastal Vendée as they planned yet another assault on that town.

The Coastal Vendée

Les Sables Front July

The Les Sables front was quiet during July due to republican setbacks elsewhere and the political troubles in Nantes. There were several minor skirmishes at Château-d'Olonne and Le Pas-Opton and a 400 man reconnaissance on St-Julien and La Chapelle-Hermier on 24 July was attacked by 1,500 Vendéens and forced to retreat in disorder.

The republicans of Les Sables, however, were beset by serious political divisions that surfaced among the troops and many volunteers were coming to the end of their period of service. The condition of the troops was also abysmal and many were falling ill.[103] On 27 July the two Bordeaux battalions left Les Sables for La Rochelle by sea and on 30 July the Lot-et-Garonne Battalion, under Baudry's command, left their post without orders aiming to head home. Baudry set out from Vairé with 600 men to stop them and forced them at bayonet point to put down their arms. A number of the battalion's officers were arrested and led away to prison.[104]

It was near the end of July that Boulard, in very poor health, had his resignation accepted.

The *Sans-Culotte* Council of War, Saumur 27 July.

In late July Labarolière was busy once again reorganising the army in Tours and Chinon, and Chalbos and Duhoux remained stationary in Niort and Angers respectively. Labarolière again asked to be replaced and appealed for veterans if this war was to be ended.

Following the latest succession of defeats a council of war was held in Saumur on 27 July. This meeting was dominated by the Hébértists: namely Ronsin, Rossignol and Commissaires Momoro, Hazard, Millié, Bodson, Laporte and Parrain, some of whom were among the most unsavoury characters to appear during the French Revolution. They clearly anticipated another rebel attempt on Saumur and met with the officers responsible for the area before issuing the following orders:[105]

1. Saumur was to be put in a state of siege.
2. The town's citizens were ordered to assemble in the town square, with all available weapons, on pain of being declared traitors.
3. Commissaires were to be sent to all the communes north of Saumur, from Tours to Angers over a distance of ten leagues, and to assemble all men in a state to fight with all possible weapons (including pikes and pitchforks). They were to be in Saumur in twenty-four hours with supplies for eight days. The tocsin would be sounded to raise people for the republican cause.

Ronsin also ordered Saumur to be fortified, the bridges over the Thouet to be destroyed, and announced to the Minister of War that he and the *sans-culotte* Rossignol were taking measures to save the Republic and not betray it like the former *ci-devant* generals.[106]

Chapter 9

'Destroy the Vendée!'

Towards the end of July the beleaguered garrisons of Mayence and Valenciennes surrendered to the Allies. Although both capitulations were significant blows to the Republic, the Convention did not consider the Vendée to be part of the Coalition formed against France so saw no problem with redeploying the Army of Mayence and troops from Valenciennes to fight in the region.

While this was under organisation the CPS issued the following orders, published in Saumur on 4 August:

1. The staff and commissaires of war of the Army of the La Rochelle Coast are to be 'purified' and substituted by strong patriots.
2. The generals are to rigorously execute the law with regard to deserters, traitors, those that flee, those that throw away their weapons, and those that sell their *habits* (military jackets).
3. The organisation of companies of pioneers and workers…will only be recruited from strongly patriotic communes.
4. The generals are to form bodies of *tirailleurs* and *chasseurs*.
5. Inflammable materials are to be sent by the Minister of War.
6. The forests are to be cut down; the lairs of the rebels destroyed; the harvest gathered by the companies of workers and carried to the rear of the army, and the beasts seized.
7. The women, children and elderly are to be conducted to the interior for their 'subsistence and safety with all due regard for humanity'.
8. The Minister of War will take measures to equip the army with arms, munitions and cannon in preparation for the next general move on the rebels.
9. As soon as the army is ready the representatives in the Departments around the rebel area will sound the tocsin and ensure all men, aged 16 to 60, march on the rebels.
10. All women will be expelled from the army.
11. Wagons will be reduced to the absolute minimum necessary for transporting strictly necessary effects and munitions.

12. The generals will only use patriotic expressions in their orders, in the
    name of ancient republicans or martyrs of freedom, and never in the
    name of a living person.[1]

Twenty-four companies of workers and pioneers were also to be organised.

On his appointment as commander-in-chief, Rossignol was praised for
his patriotism. Ronsin was to act as his chief of staff and assist in planning
the campaign. Rossignol asked that Ronsin and Santerre be promoted to
the rank of general of division and asked for 15,000 veteran troops; even the
sans-culottes recognised that the quality of the army was poor.

On 30 July the new command structure of the Army of the La Rochelle
Coast was announced and showed a marked dominance of sans-culottes. At
the same time Commissaires Grammont and Hazard were busy informing
against all activity they considered suspect. Niort's public spirit, they said,
was 'counter-revolutionary'; La Rochelle needed careful watching as the
mayor was an intimate friend of Biron, General Verteuil was a 'man of straw',
his nephew was a rebel leader, and the commander of the town's national
guards was suspect.[2] They added that General Tuncq was an 'arrogant…old
general of the Ancien-Regime' who had dared to say to them that 'a general
at the head of a victorious army does not need to be lectured.'[3]

This was as much an ideological war within the army as it was a campaign
against the rebels, and when Representative Cavaignac, who was attached to
the Army of the Brest Coast, wrote that the new sans-culotte generals were
talentless and would prolong the war, he was soon recalled.[4]

The Vendéens were known to be planning a large expedition but the
republicans were in the dark as to where this might be directed. General
Duhoux was reporting rebels in Brissac, Doué and Thouars, and also indicated
that his posts on the north bank of the Loire were coming under attack.

At the beginning of August Grouchy was in command of 4,000 troops to
Duhoux's west (deployed in posts stretching from Nantes and Ingrandes)
and over the next few weeks he was fully occupied preventing rebels crossing
the Loire to communicate with sympathisers to its north. His command
consisted of twelve companies of grenadiers, a 'German' regiment and two
Paris battalions – all part of the Army of the Brest Coast. He felt this force
was coping reasonably well, but as most of the boats were in rebel hands
there were many minor actions along the banks of the Loire and on its many
islands.[5] Nevertheless, by early August an active field Army of 6-7,000 men
had been organised in Nantes and an advance guard was ready to move
against the rebels.[6]

Rossignol's Army Advances

Rossignol's Saumur Division started to move on 5 August, aiming to pierce rebel lines near Doué. Ronsin and Salomon marched in advance with 2,700 infantry and 300 cavalry, and Santerre, with 7–8,000 men, deployed on the Bournan Heights to cover their retreat if that was found to be necessary.[7]

Rossignol's lack of confidence in his troops is evident in the instructions he issued to his generals. In case they needed to retreat they were advised to familiarise themselves with the roads they advanced along, keep them clear of obstacles, and place a reserve of cavalry to the rear. He also ordered that all non-essential baggage be kept well back from the army and that the batteries of artillery must always be protected by infantry.[8]

Doué-la-Fontaine 5 August

In spite of this lack of confidence the campaign began well. On 5 August Ronsin's advance guard defeated royalist posts under Piron's command encountered on the Montfort Height and pursued them all the way to Doué. Salomon estimated the enemy to be 7–8,000 strong and after a further hour of battle they forced them back to Concourson.

Their advance now ground to a halt, as instead of urging the army forwards Rossignol and the Hébértist commissaires became obsessed with 'purifying' the army of suspect generals. On 8 August Rossignol made a series of denunciations: Rey, Duhoux, Menou and Gauvilliers, he wrote, were suspect, and Commissaires Grammont and Hazard were closely watching Chalbos and Nouvion.[9] Momoro went so far as to say that Rey was a Bironist who should be guillotined.[10]

On 19 August Labarolière would have been considered fortunate when he at last got his wish and left the Vendée.

Coastal Vendée

August was a quiet month in the coastal Vendée, not least because many of the rebel contingents joined in the forthcoming attack on Luçon.

The only action of note took place on 10 August when La Cathelinière led 6,000 men, supported by a single 4pdr, in an attack on the 700 strong battalion of the Loire-Inférieure, garrisoned in the Château d'Aux on the south bank of the Loire. La Cathelinière's aim was to intercept supplies to Nantes. His troops, however, were repulsed and he was wounded.[11]

The Southern Front

Luçon 14 August

From 1 August Tuncq was expressing concern about a new gathering of rebels reported at La Roche-sur-Yon and one week later he was notified that they were planning a third assault on Luçon and were also assembling at Châtillon and Vihiers.[12] He appealed for help and on 9 August Chalbos sent 1,800 infantry, 200 cavalry, light artillery and a howitzer to the camp of Les Quatre-Chemins.[13]

Bonchamps and Lyrot remained in the north to cover the Loire and Layon, while 30-35,000 rebels and 22 guns were assembled to attack Luçon.

On 12 August the Grand Army linked with the Army of the Centre at L'Oie, and on the following day moved to Ste-Hermine where Charette, Joly and Savin added a further 6,000 men. On 14 August they advanced in three huge columns, each at least 12,000 strong.

Awaiting this vast army was General Tuncq with 5,371 infantry, 414 cavalry, 203 gunners and 14 cannon, all but one of which were 4pdrs. This force included battalions present at the last battle and the 11th Hussars, 14th Chasseurs and some gendarmes.

Once again Tuncq deployed from Corpe towards Ste-Gemme and, although not specified, it is probable that he deployed in two lines: one behind and in support of the other. Most of the cannon were dispersed along his front, with the horse artillery limbered behind the left wing. From the available information it is known that two squadrons of gendarmes and two of hussars supported the centre and cavalry pickets were deployed north of La Fosse.

Following a plan proposed by Lescure the Vendéens were instructed to deploy in echelon, from left to right, as they arrived on the battlefield.[14] Charette then Lescure would form the left wing; Royrand then D'Élbée the centre; La Rochejaquelein then Stofflet the right. Talmont would deploy to the rear of the right wing with the cavalry. The artillery would be dispersed in front of the three columns. Knowing the terrain was largely open this would be the first significant attempt by the Vendéens to fight in regular order, but, with the exception of a handful of companies, the men were unfamiliar with regular forms of deployment or manoeuvring. Madame de la Rochejaquelein, who usually praised her former husband's skill, noted that none of the officers, including the commander-in-chief, could quite comprehend Lescure's plan.[15]

Charette and the contingent from the coastal Vendée were on the march by 6am, crossed the River Smagne, and rapidly passed through the village of Les Mottes. They deployed in several loosely formed lines when they

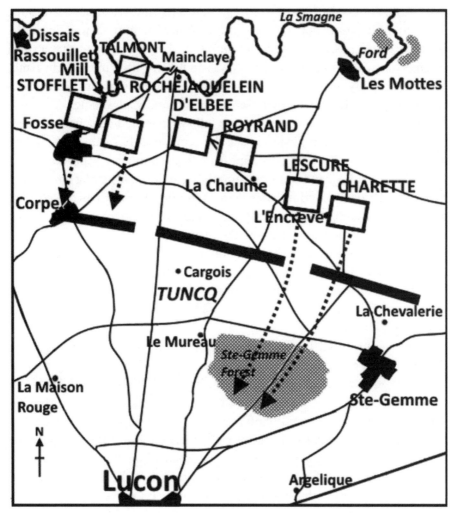

Third Battle of Luçon.

reached L'Encreve Farm, and Charette planned to direct the troops towards the east side of the Ste-Gemme Forest.

Lescure followed on Charette's heels and deployed close to his right flank.

The cannon arrived next, crossed at the Mainclaye Bridge and began to deploy from east to west. Unfortunately the artillery train was delayed by a broken caisson and Marigny halted deployment until this was addressed. Stofflet, in his haste to get to the battlefield, marched straight through the artillery train, delaying its arrival even further.

Beauvais noticed Charette starting to advance and raced across to warn him about the confusion in the centre, calling on him to wait until the artillery was in position with its ammunition. He also advised that a third column was still to the rear. Beauvais was on his way back to the right flank, Stofflet was only just reaching the battlefield, and the caissons were at last appearing, when Charette's men were spotted rapidly advancing.[16]

Lescure felt he had no choice but to follow Charette's advance and these two columns were soon pushing back the republican left wing and moving through the Ste-Gemme Forest, capturing five cannon in the process.[17]

D'Élbée and Royrand were last onto the field of battle having crossed the Mainclaye Bridge sometime after 9am. Assuming the timings are correct, this was two hours after Charette had launched his attack.[18] When at last they deployed, wide gaps separated the three columns.[19]

Beauvais indicates that the plan was to put several guns on the right and he noted that Talmont deployed a large body of cavalry behind the right flank and then promptly abandoned them to join La Rochejaquelein in person. Probing attacks by their right did however disperse some chasseurs-à-cheval.

Beauvais informed La Rochejaquelein that the enemy's line was wider than their own and he could easily lengthen theirs. Talmont wisely advised La Rochejaquelein to do this discreetly, but while these troops had been ponderously deploying, Charette and Lescure's attack lost momentum and Tuncq had been able to send reinforcements to counter their advance.

The enthusiasm of the Vendéen right meant they could no longer be restrained and the men kept moving forwards shielding their guns.[20] In clear evidence of the use of combined-arms Beauvais had these guns limbered and moved forward with the troops, while some cavalry were ordered up in support to prevent the republicans rallying if broken. However, Marigny now arrived and abruptly halted the advance, reminding Beauvais that the army was meant to be attacking in echelons with the right wing advancing last of all.

The Vendéen centre and right were under continual artillery bombardment and there is little evidence that the Vendéen artillery retaliated. While enduring this bombardment D'Élbée, some 800 metres south of the Mainclaye Bridge, spent time trying to align his troops in loosely formed columns twelve to fifteen ranks deep, to the bemusement of the men.[21] Part of the centre column was unaware of the decision to deploy in regular order and had moved forwards, only to become isolated in the middle of the open terrain.[22]

While D'Élbée had been struggling to get his troops into position the right wing was left standing and without orders. Whether D'Élbée's centre started to move forward before the right is not clear, but Beauvais indicates that when the right did start to move forwards again they had lost their initial ardour. The stress of the bombardment was now causing problems in the centre, where the poorer quality troops started to give way, and when the right wing spotted them they also began to withdraw. The cavalry led their retreat.

Tuncq made a feint with his cavalry on D'Élbée's troops and unmasked a battery of horse artillery which fired into the rebels at close range. With no cavalry to repel them, or counter the republican horse, the fate of the Vendéen centre was certain. Republican infantry had taken advantage of the rolling terrain to shelter in the dips and behind what trees and bushes there were in the open landscape. They now fixed bayonets and went on the attack.

Béjarry estimated that barely twenty shots had been fired by their own artillery before the gunners fled with their horses, leaving the infantry exposed.[23]

With their line of retreat threatened, Lescure and Charette pulled back towards the Mainclaye Bridge, linking with Royrand's men on the way. Charette's troops managed to maintain some order as they covered this retreat.

A cannon became jammed at the Mainclaye Bridge, preventing access for other guns and the vast number of troops retreating in that direction, all now coming under bombardment. Beauvais managed to divert some troops to a ford and succeeded in removing the cannon and withdrawing some guns.

On reaching L'Encreve, Charette was charged by Tuncq's hussars and gendarmes and dispersed but then rallied behind some copses. Crossing the Mainclaye Bridge he deployed on the opposite bank and Beauvais records that a handful of officers and men, including both D'Élbée and La Rochejaquelein, held the republicans back for over half an hour before making their escape northwards.

Beauvais blamed Marigny for the defeat, saying he should not have stopped the right flank's advance. He added that Marigny's violent temper was a liability in battle and argued that if Charette had not attacked so rashly, and the two wings had been left to outflank the enemy, then the enemy's centre would never have attacked as it did and victory would have been certain.[24] He also criticised the attempt to form up in echelon rather than allow the troops to fight in their normal manner.

Madame de la Rochejaquelein recalled that the Vendéens lost most of their artillery and 2,000 men and the army blamed Lescure for a plan the troops were incapable of following.[25]

A few days later the republicans were back in Chantonnay and the troops of the coastal Vendée returned to their own territory.

Mieszkowski replaces Boulard

When Boulard left Les Sables a third of his division was sick with fever.[26] He was replaced on 20 August by the Polish-born General Mieszkowski, Biron's former ADC and friend. How he managed to avoid immediate dismissal for this association is not clear. He had originally been sent to command Chalbos' advance guard, but was directed to Les Sables on Boulard's departure. Baudry, like Boulard, was exhausted and left the army around 7 September.

Mieszkowski moved his 5,000 men to La Mothe-Achard and was soon reinforced by 960 men from the 24th Charente-Inférieure. There was still trouble in the Les Sable Division as the 3rd Paris had gained a reputation for indiscriminate looting, such that when they were seen marching towards Les Sables on the Olonne road they were refused admittance and cannon were deployed ready to stop them by force if necessary. All of Mieszkowski's troops refused to serve with this notorious battalion.[27]

La Roche-sur-Yon 26 August

In late August Charette retained a few troops in Legé and marched with 500 infantry and 150 cavalry to support Joly and Savin in an assault on La Roche-sur-Yon.[28]

A Battalion of the Marne formed the core of the town's garrison and on 26 August came under attack by three rebel columns approaching on the La Mothe-Achard, Poiré and Les Essarts roads. Charette combined his horse with those of Savin and advanced to assault the town, followed at a distance by their foot. However, this cavalry was vigorously repulsed and their infantry became disordered and withdrew. Charette had no option but to cover this retreat and among those helping him was Madame Bulkeley, wife of one of the rebel leaders and not unfamiliar with combat herself.[29] The Vendéens suffered about eighty casualties.[30]

Charette's camp was notorious for drinking and dancing and he was surrounded by a number of women, drawn in some cases by his charismatic personality and striking looks and referred to as his *Amazones*. Any frivolity was to be short lived however, as new republican assaults were already underway.

Battles around Sorinières, Naudières and Vertou 26 to 31 August

On 26 August Canclaux was beginning his move south from Nantes hoping to re-establish communications between Nantes and Les Sables. He gathered 5,000 men at Naudierès and grenadiers under Adjudant General Blosse seized Sorinières, routing some of Lyrot's men after a brief combat. Lyrot's cavalry made a diversionary attack on the Les Sables road but were routed by Grouchy and the Dragoons of Ille-et-Vilaine.

That same day Chef de Brigade Radermacher seized the Château of La Maillardière following stubborn resistance from the parish of Vertou.[31]

Canclaux established a camp at Naudières, at the junction of the Montaigu and St-Philbert roads, and placed an advance guard in Sorinières under

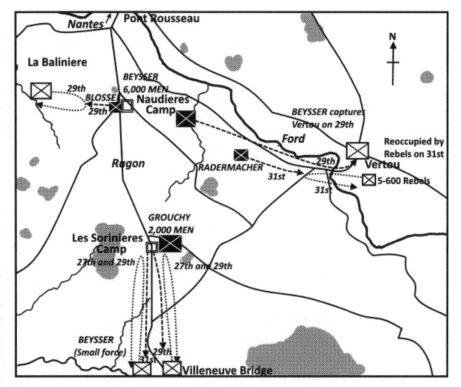

Engagements south of Nantes: 26 to 31 August.

Grouchy. Alarmed by these developments the Vendéens were determined to force the republicans back to Nantes.

On the following day Lyrot's officers Goulaine, Massip and La Sécherie went on the offensive.[32] Grouchy reported that his advance guard faced several attacks. Around 4pm the rebels marched in force on Sorinières along the Les Sables and La Rochelle roads, flowing around the enemy's flanks and forcing their tirailleurs back. Grouchy arrived from Naudierès and Adjudant General Cambray, sent to find reinforcements, succeeded in forming two columns to stabilise the flanks.

Although reinforcements had yet to arrive, two columns advanced: Blosse commanding the right and Grouchy the left. The rebels were firing from ditches and hedgerows but were eventually charged by these columns and pursued to entrenchments at Villeneuve. The first entrenchment and a prepared house were captured and a second entrenchment carried at bayonet point by grenadiers from the 9th and 109th Regiments. With nightfall closing in the Republicans dropped back to Sorinières.

Beysser returned to the army and was given command of 6,000 troops at Naudières on 28 August, while Grouchy remained at Sorinières with 2,000 men.

On the following day Canclaux warned Beysser that the enemy were aiming to cross the Sèvre to attack the camp on the following morning. Leading the 77th Regiment and two Paris battalions, Beysser went on the offensive and seized the Château of La Bretèche. As he continued to advance he came under attack from an enemy column which fell back to a second château and after a prolonged firefight they were charged and routed by Republicans. Beysser went on to seize Vertou, but wisely retired to Naudières towards midday having taken no casualties.

While Beysser had been thus engaged, Blosse discovered a large number of rebels threatening the right of the camp. He advanced with a fresh brigade to discover them in prepared positions in some woods and a house. In less than an hour the rebels were overpowered, pursued to a place called Moulin-Cassé, then dispersed.

In the evening numerous bands attacked Grouchy's advanced posts but were unsuccessful once again and pursued by the Republicans to Villeneuve.

Beysser enthusiastically reported that this was the first time his troops had marched without their artillery and believed such courage, unhindered by baggage and artillery trains, would speed up the end of the war.[33]

On 31 August Canclaux left for Saumur to discuss the campaign plans and on that same day Beysser discovered rebels moving in strength to seize, cut, and dig in at the Villeneuve Bridge. He marched from Naudières leading a few hundred infantry with some cavalry and artillery support. As he approached, the rebels fled.

Over 500 Vendéens appeared at Vertou that day, aiming to threaten the left of the camp. Chef de Brigade Radermacher repulsed them and forced them back across the Vertou Bridge.

Unlike the Army of the La Rochelle Coast, the troops of the Army of the Brest Coast had sustained numerous assaults and had held firm.

Chapter 10

'The Promenade of the Sovereign People'

The Saumur Conference 3 September

The Saumur Conference, between the generals, representatives and commissaires, would determine the course of events over the next month. Two campaign plans were debated: the Nantes Plan, prepared by Grouchy in discussion with Beysser, Canclaux and Representatives Philippeaux, Gillet, L. Turreau and Cavaignac; and the Tours Plan put forward by Ronsin in discussion with Bourbotte, and Choudieu.

The first stage of the Nantes Plan would be to cut rebel communication with the sea in cooperation with the Les Sables Division. Part of the Army of the Brest Coast would be attached to the Army of Mayence and this large body of troops would be split into three columns to advance concentrically on Mortagne. Here they would link up with the Army of the La Rochelle Coast in a joint march on Cholet. This concentration would be completed by 14 September and Grouchy predicted that 'with the Army of Mayence reunited to that of the Brest Coast, the rebels will submit within fifteen days.'[1] While those on the southern front would join in the advance, Grouchy added that the Army of Tours and Saumur would form a reserve and cover the Loire.

Cavaignac presented the Nantes Plan to the CPS on 14 August. He also expressed disgust at the Army of La Rochelle Coast and was particularly critical of Fabrefond (brother of Fabre d'Églantine) who had bought a property worth 100,000 francs to serve as a 'place of pleasure' for six courtesans kept with him during his military expeditions.[2] The Dantonist Representative Philippeaux shared Cavaignac's view:

'The brigands committed no more atrocities against peaceable citizens than our own soldiers... It is a strange thing that the royalist soldiers who fight for despotism are the real *sans-culottes*, without gratification, unpaid, with only a morsel of bad bread to eat, while ours, for the sublime cause of *liberté*, make war with slaves and sybarites.'[3]

On 23 August the CPS voted in favour of the Nantes Plan and Philippeaux raced back to the army to give them the news.[4]

On 29 August, however, Ronsin was in Paris and met with the CPS to promote his Tours Plan. After a tirade against the undisciplined rabble that made up the royalist army, he claimed that a combined and vigorous attack would liberate the area in fifteen days.

His plan suggested that they should advance in five columns, two of which would be formed from the Army of Mayence. These two columns, each 7,000 strong, would assemble at Tours and Doué respectively: the first would head for Mortagne via Argenton and Châtillon; the second on Cholet via Vihiers, Coron and Vezins. A third column, of similar strength, would march from Brissac direct on Clisson via La Jumelière, Chemillé, Jallais and Beaupréau. They would cover the north bank of the Loire in case the enemy, repulsed by the first two columns, moved on Nantes. A fourth column would move from Chantonnay to Montaigu, via Puybelliard and Mouchamps, and a fifth column would camp between Les Sables and Machecoul to cover La Rochelle and move on the rebels if they attempted to seek refuge towards the sea.[5]

Choudieu indicated that the Tours Plan could be enacted on 4 September, whereas the Nantes Plan would take longer to be put into effect.[6]

As a consequence of this second proposal the CPS advised Philippeaux that although they supported Grouchy's Plan they recognised there were strong opinions on both sides and ordered that the two plans be put before the generals and representatives at a council of war to be held in Saumur.

The following were present: Representatives Reubell (chair), Merlin de Thionville, Richard, Choudieu, Bourbotte, L.Turreau, Cavaignac, Méaulle, Philippeaux, Ruelle and Fayau; Generals Rossignol, Canclaux, Duhoux, Menou, Santerre, Aubert-Dubayet, Chalbos, Salomon, Rey, Mieszkowski and Dembarrère.

The decisive argument was presented by Vergnes, chief of staff of the Army of the Brest Coast who, although not part of the debate, was allowed to answer questions directed to him.

He argued that the only decent road in the Vendée ran from Nantes to La Rochelle. The enemy, he added, had the advantage of knowing their terrain intimately and it was cut up with ravines, streams and woods that were particularly difficult late in the season. He advised, therefore, that this territory be penetrated in mass and in a single army corps.

He described the organisation and fighting methods of the rebels and estimated that they had 10,000 capable troops, 30,000 armed peasants, and an abundance of cannon.

He indicated that the Army of the La Rochelle Coast risked being overwhelmed by vastly superior numbers if they attacked in separate columns, adding that these columns would not be able to come to each other's aid.

The disciplined Army of Mayence, however, reinforced by 6,000 seasoned troops taken from the Army of the Brest Coast, would create a formidable force. Their first step should be to clear the coast, which would be relatively easy as the republicans already held Paimboeuf, Noirmoutier and the Château d'Aux. He also pointed out that the roads from Nantes to La Rochelle via Machecoul, and from Nantes to Clisson, were good for moving supplies.

After this first step the Army of Les Sables would link with the main column, followed in turn by those of Luçon and Niort, until they arrived before Mortagne. This march would retain the army's supply line to Nantes, and after the capture of Mortagne, and by holding the Loire, they would force the rebels to surrender or drown.

Merlin de Douai and Gillet du Morbihan had ensured that the army was well supplied from Nantes; cannon had been manufactured in Rennes to supply the Army of the Brest Coast and twenty-four guns were available for the Army of Mayence. It was also pointed out that the morale of the Army of the La Rochelle Coast was low due to its frequent defeats, unlike that of the Army of the Brest Coast.

It took two rounds of voting to conclude with support for the Nantes Plan, but due to his influence Vergnes was placed under surveillance by Ronsin and while Canclaux and Rossignol worked on the campaign plan, orders were in preparation to dismiss all *ci-devant* officers.

South of Nantes 5 September

Informed that Canclaux had left for the conference in Saumur Charette, Lyrot, Couëtus and La Cathelinière planned more assaults on the Naudières Camp which had been burning property south of Nantes, but as many of Lyrot's men were busy harvesting, the date for the attack was postponed until 5 September.[7]

Coincidentally, Canclaux was back in Nantes in the early hours of 5 September and ordered Beysser to go on the offensive. At 5am Beysser clashed with Lyrot who was advancing on Naudières from the east – hours before the time agreed with Charette.[8] Canclaux ordered Beysser to attack their left, with a column consisting of the 77th Line and five companies

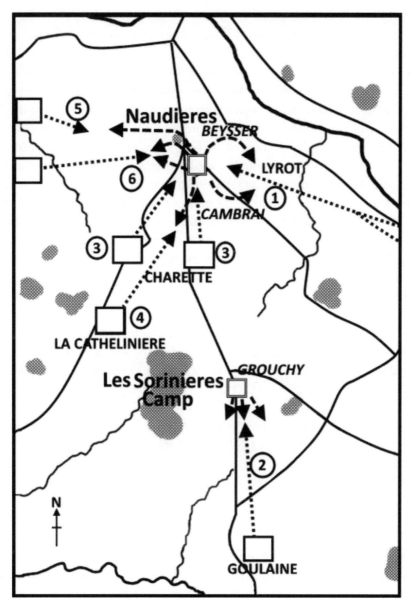

Engagements south of Nantes 5 September.

of grenadiers, while Cambray with the 13th Seine-et-Oise and the 12th République, attacked their right.[9] Lyrot was repulsed and pursued to Vertou.[10]

A second rebel column under Goulaine was ordered to contain the enemy in Sorinières while Charette attacked Naudières. Goulaine successfully pinned Blosse's advance guard, even after it was supported by Grouchy with the 34th Line and 12th Seine-et-Oise. Eventually, however, Goulaine was repulsed.

Charette marched with 2,000 men. At 5am, as he passed close to Villeneuve, he heard cannon-fire to the north-east as Lyrot's premature attack went in. His troops attacked Naudières in two columns along the La Rochelle and Les Sables roads. Those on the La Rochelle road were forced back at bayonet point and pursued for over a league by Verger's grenadiers; they lost a cannon and flag to the Hussards-Américains.[11] The column on the Les Sables road was pursued as far as Villeneuve by Grouchy and Blosse.[12]

La Cathelinère led a fourth column, which the Republicans claimed was 10,000 strong, and came into conflict on the Ragon Heath south of Naudières. Once again the Vendéens were defeated.[13]

A fifth attack developed north-west of Naudières but was contained by two battalions of the 109th Line sent by Canclaux.[14] Then a sixth column advanced between Canclaux's advance guard and La Belinière to attack the right and rear of the Naudières Camp held by General Vergnes. During this assault the 12th Seine-et-Oise retreated and had to be replaced by the 3rd Orne. Beysser, who had been victorious on the left, now transferred his troops to the right, fell on the flank of the Vendéens, and forced them to retreat.[15]

By nightfall the Republicans had conclusively repulsed all attacks. Naudières was much too tough a target, and Charette, who had been suffering from a fever all day, fell back to Legé.

To the south, however, a more significant battle had been underway near Chantonnay.

Chantonnay 5 September

On 4 September General Tuncq seized the line of the River Lay with 8,000 men and established a large entrenched position at the Camp-des-Roches north of Chantonnay. He placed detachments at Chantonnay, Puybelliard, St Vincent-Sterlinges and Pont-Charron.

In retaliation the Grand Army and Army of the Centre gathered 25,000 men and 21 guns under La Rochejaquelein, Stofflet, D'Élbée, Royrand, Lescure and Fleuriot (commanding in place of the wounded Bonchamps), and approached Tuncq's forces from the north, south and east. The rebels marched through the night of 4 to 5 September, and while Royrand was ordered to make a feint on the Camp-des-Roches from the north to hold the

Above: The Abbey of St Florent-le-Vieil. The Rising officially began in the square adjacent to this abbey.

Right: The sacre-coeur: the emblem under which the rebels fought.

Fonteclose. Home of Charette, from where he reluctantly joined the Rising. Now a museum.

Pont Neuf, Thouars. Marigny and Donnissan attacked across this bridge.

Châtillon-sur-Sèvre (modern day Mauléon). The Royalist administrative and military headquarters and symbolic capital of the Rising.

Above: Diorama of the Assault at Coron, September 1793. The rebels frequently ambushed columns in this manner. Courtesy of Josh Harper.

Below: Windmill at Alouettes, Haut-Bocage. The rebels used windmills to signal the presence of the enemy by setting the sails at different angles.

The battlefield of La Tremblaye looking south from the Vendéen centre towards the Republic positions. The terrain is typical of many of the battlefields.

Torfou battlefield looking from Kléber's positions towards Tiffauges, with its church visible in the distance.

A column built after the Restoration to commemorate the Vendéen victory at Torfou. It is located on the main road east of Torfou where it joins the road to Cholet.

Detail from a plaque commemorating the Battle of Cholet located to the north of the battlefield.

The Loire at St-Florent-le-Vieil, where the Royalists and thousands of refugees crossed the river after their defeat at Cholet.

The bridge at Château-Gontier. Although a more recent bridge, it was at this point that La Rochejaquelein led the assault after defeating the Republicans at Entrammes.

Above: Laval: occupied by the rebels twice during the campaign north of the Loire.

Left: Granville. The Grande Porte at the western end of the Rue-de-Juifs and the focus of fierce fighting during the siege.

Above: Old buildings in Dol. The Royalists faced a critical few days here in November 1793.

Right: Memorial to Battle of Dol-Antrain. Located at the centre of critical fighting east of Pont Galou. The Republicans and Royalists are commemorated by the Phrygian Cap (popular with the Republicans) and the Sacre-Coeur respectively.

The bleak landscape of the coastal Marais, cut up with many waterways, hindered Republican marches.

Above left: The settlement of Bouin from where Charette escaped in December.

Above right: La Rochejaquelein leads the assault into Cholet on 17 October. From a painting by Paul-Emile Boutigny, 1854. By courtesy of the Musée d'Art et d'Histoire, Cholet.

Below: The tomb of General Bonchamps, located in St Florent-le-Vieil, with its famous epitaph 'Grace aux Prisonniers!'. The sculptor, David d'Angers, was the son of a Republican soldier, one of several thousand spared by order of Bonchamps in October 1793 as he lay mortally wounded.

enemy's attention, most of the army converged on the republicans from the south and east.

The timing of these attacks worked perfectly and by 3pm on 5 September all possible escape routes were securely in rebel hands and Fleuriot had evicted the 4th Dordogne from Pont-Charron.[16]

The main body of Vendéens deployed in three columns with Fleuriot on the left, Stofflet on the right and D'Élbée in the centre. Both sides recalled that the battle was ferocious and the republicans were well aware of the desperate position they were now in.

Lecomte, with no more than 150 cavalry, raced to support the solitary Lorient Battalion facing the approach of Royrand's 2–3,000 men moving south from St-Vincent-Sterlinges. On arrival he saw that these rebels had been repulsed and were being pursued, unaware that Royrand was simply making a feint.

Lecomte now received news that other columns were closing in from the south and east. He raced back to the Camp-des-Roches and dispatched 150 cavalry and the Chasseurs de l'Oise towards La Réorthe (9km south of Chantonnay) to secure his line of communications, and the 7th Orléans was ordered to Pont-Charron to reinforce the 4th Dordogne.

News now arrived that the 4th Dordogne had abandoned its post, and Marceau, who had been ordered to rally them and retake Pont-Charron, found them near the Camp-des-Roches with the 7th Orléans, both retreating.

Chantonnay had also fallen into rebel hands and Marceau deployed two battalions in line to its north (east of the road to St-Vincent-Sterlinges), with orders to hold the enemy and support two light guns and a body of cavalry that were to their front. Beauvais recalled that the republican artillery fought well and caused the Vendéens problems as they debouched from Chantonnay, yet in spite of this they managed to capture two batteries a little beyond the town: one on the road and another in a field to its east.[17]

While these Vendéen troops were moving through and beyond Chantonnay, D'Élbée and Stofflet were forming up the two main columns of their army. Fleuriot was unable to break the troops to his front but Stofflet had more success and after obstinate resistance overcame two battalions beyond Puybelliard. With their left flank now uncovered Marceau vainly tried to rally these battalions. He ordered the hedgerows to be held to slow the enemy's advance and Lecomte sent the 10th Orléans to temporarily secure this flank.

The line of battle now seemed to stabilise and stretched from near Puybelliard to the St-Vincent-Sterlinges road north of Chantonnay. It

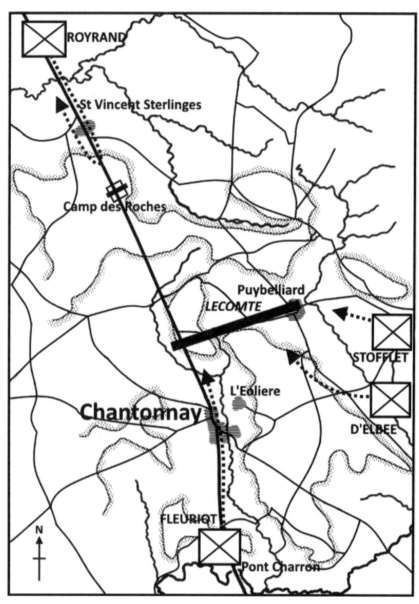

The Battle of Chantonnay.

had been secured by the 10th Orléans, L'Union, L'Égalité and Vengeur battalions. Marceau believed now was the time to send in the cavalry, held in their centre, but he could not get them to charge.

Beauvais was with Fleuriot's column when they were reinforced by the Swiss and German Companies and witnessed the Vendéen cavalry charge in the centre but stop short under heavy fire. Seeing that his artillery could do little more on the left Beauvais was permitted to join the cavalry, and found them badly deployed and in range of the enemy as nightfall rapidly approached. He sent men to find cannon in Chantonnay and eventually an 8pdr arrived and began to cause problems for the republicans.

Lecomte had meanwhile ordered the 3rd and 6th Charente-Inférieure to advance on the Vendéen right as it appeared to be faltering. They skilfully swung into the exposed rebel flank and if their cavalry had charged the republicans might have defeated them, but once again they refused and Beauvais recalled that when their 8pdr fired on the enemy cavalry they retreated to their rear as quickly as they had appeared.

Dense smoke and darkness now obscured Vendéen movements, although Lecomte still held his troops in line as musketry erupted along the whole front once again. However a gap formed in the republican centre, after a Calvados battalion routed under sustained infantry and cannon fire, and the Vendéens poured through the breach and cut the republican army in two.

The Vengeur and 3rd Deux-Sèvres soon found themselves under attack from all sides and the republican right flank collapsed as men fled into nearby woodland in search of safety. Lecomte remained alone with two Charente-Inférieure battalions and some gendarmes, and more than an hour passed as they stood their ground against vast numbers of rebels. Marceau cut through the enemy to re-join Lecomte and brought news that all the republican troops in the centre had vanished. Lecomte therefore withdrew through woodland and successfully saved the debris of the army.

The battle fell silent around 9pm with republican losses almost certainly in the thousands and most of their artillery in royalist hands.[18] Lecomte gathered what remained of his army in Luçon but they had been dispersed across a wide area, including 2,000 who turned up in Les Sables trailing five guns and seven caissons.[19]

This remarkable victory was to have direct consequences for the republican campaign plan.

The Advance of the Army of La Rochelle

On 7 September a huge levy was summoned across a wide area north and north-east of rebel territory as all able-bodied men were ordered to gather in Saumur and Angers ready to support the planned invasion of the Vendée-Militaire.

Érigné 7 September

The Vendéens had been in control of the Érigné Heights for some weeks, cutting communications between Angers and Doué. Salomon and Turreau had orders to seize this post as a first step in their move south and set out from Angers around 4am on 7 September with 1,800-2,000 men.[20]

The 8th Hussars and a division of Gendarmerie led the assault, successfully expelling the Vendéens from their camp at Roche d'Érigné. Salomon returned to Angers and Turreau was repairing the bridge when at 9am his advance guard was assaulted by three enemy columns totalling around 3,000 men. His tirailleurs were forced to retreat and the central rebel column came within 300 paces of the Érigné Redoubts but, says Turreau, they were routed by a charge from this redoubt and a flank attack by the hussars. Danican and the 8th Hussars came in for particular praise and pursued the rebels for a considerable distance.

Saumur Council of War 11 September

News of the disaster at Chantonnay made Rossignol hesitate and he convened a council of war in Saumur with the few generals to hand. Although he claimed that he did not diverge entirely from the agreed plan he now changed key details without informing Canclaux. His aim, he claimed, was 'to avoid defeat by putting up a solid defence and enable his army to present a more active mass if they took the offensive'. He ordered the following:[21]

- 10,000 men were to occupy Doué, 3,000 Les Ponts-de-Cé and 3,000 Thouars.
- In second line positions new levies would occupy extensive areas to the right and left of each of these bodies of troops. 12,000 would deploy from Brissac to bridges over the Thouet in support of those in Doué; 6,000 from Ferrières and fords on the Thouet as far as St-Gemme, in support of those in Thouars; and 8,000 in woods and thickets stretching to Juigné and the island from St-Maurice and Port-Godard, in support of those in Les Ponts-de-Cé. If it was felt necessary to advance the 3,000 in Les Ponts-de-Cé to the heights beyond the Érigné Mill, then these 8,000 would be deployed from Rochefort to Avrillé.
- Chalbos was to be notified of these dispositions, with orders to follow the same principle (i.e. unite the mass of troops in the centre of his area and hold two main posts to his left and right).

- The Les Sables Division was given the same instructions.
- Finally, Saumur was to be garrisoned by 1,000 men supported by 3-4,000 summoned by tocsin.

The most significant consequence of this change of plan affected Chalbos' command. On 14 September he advanced on La Châtaigneraie in accordance with the 3 September orders, but on 16 September he received Rossignol's orders to return to his original positions and was back in Fontenay two days later.

The Luçon column had been rebuilt after Chantonnay and placed under Beffroy's command. He advanced beyond Ste-Hermine around 13 September, encountering plenty of resistance. On receipt of Rossignol's orders he pulled back to Luçon three days later. Mieszkowski, however, advanced to St-Fulgent and when he received the same order, instead of retiring he remained where he was to consult with Canclaux first.

By retreating, Chalbos and Beffroy would not be in position to link up with Canclaux and Dubayet's column as they marched in an anti-clockwise direction from Nantes to south of Mortagne and risked leaving these generals isolated. But it was already clear that the 20,000 levies marching with Chalbos' troops were a significant liability and were guilty of indiscriminate pillaging and violence. Complaints were such that on his return to Fontenay he disbanded them.[22]

The advance of the Saumur Division

Martigné-Briand 11 September

Ronsin had persuaded Rossignol that Santerre's Saumur column was best placed to seize Cholet while most of the Vendéen forces were busy fighting Canclaux, even though this does not appear to have been part of the Nantes Plan. Santerre's division totalled 16,500 men, of which 10,000 were raw levies. As these levies had no uniforms they were given tricolor ribbons to tie to their shoulder belts to distinguish them from the enemy.[23] Santerre proudly described them as his 'military men in *carmagnoles*' marching in 'a promenade of the Sovereign People' who he reported were enthusiastically chanting 'To Cholet, to Cholet!'[24]

Salomon commanded Rossignol's advance guard and had already set out from Saumur with orders to watch the Layon. He was accompanied by troops of the new levy and a detachment of the 8th Hussars.[25] According to Savary he exceeded his orders and marched to attack Martigné-Briand where La Rochejaquelein had linked with D'Autichamp. The Vendéens were caught by surprise when Salomon suddenly attacked with 1,200-1,300 men. Madame de la Rochejaquelein noted that both armies were small, although Rossignol claimed the rebels were 4-5,000 strong.[26] A long and obstinate battle ended with Salomon being repulsed. During the battle La Rochejaquelein had his thumb smashed by a shot and was obliged to wear a sling for months to come and to take time out to recover.

Érigné and Les Ponts-de-Cé 12 September

The strategic significance of Érigné and Les Ponts-de-Cé was such that Bonchamps again ordered its recapture and, thanks to Beauvais, who accompanied this expedition, we have a detailed account.

As the battle of Martigné was underway to the south-east, 8,000 men under D'Autichamp and Talmont, accompanied by six guns and the cavalry, assembled in Brissac.[27] D'Autichamp was detached to Mozé and Beauvais accompanied him with the cannon. On route they came across a large number of cavalry which Beauvais' guns dispersed.

Commandant Bourgeois had been dispatched with 500 men and a handful of cavalry and had orders to repulse enemy posts occupying Soulaine and surrounding communes south of Érigné.[28] Around 6am they came into contact with some rebels and repulsed them, but on the arrival of D'Autichamp's column the situation changed.

Approaching the republican camp at Roche d'Érigné, Beauvais deployed his battery on high ground and although at long range he began to cause noticeable damage to the enemy position. Meanwhile D'Autichamp marched on the left and rushed the enemy infantry, who fled as soon as the rebels opened fire. The republicans failed to remove timbers from the bridge over the Louet in time to prevent the rebel pursuit and Bourgeois was wounded while desperately trying to throw some planks in the river.

The rebels crossed the bridge and captured both St-Maurille and the Île-aux-Chevaux but were unable to take the next bridge as the enemy had deployed cannon and occupied a watermill and houses on the opposite bank.[29] Deploying artillery along the south bank the Vendéens began to bombard them, but counter-battery fire put some of their own guns out of action.

At this point more of the Grand Army arrived. D'Autichamp and Beauvais wanted to continue the assault on news that the river between them and the enemy was fordable. Talmont, however, convinced Stofflet and others that the republican column in Doué posed the greater threat.

The battle therefore ended around midday and most of the Vendéen army moved south on 13 September, abandoning Érigné to the republicans.

The *Lévee-en-Masse* joins the Army of La Rochelle

By 13 September tens of thousands of raw levies had assembled in the area around Saumur, Angers and Thouars, many armed with farmyard weapons and in civilian dress. From this vast pool of levies three columns were created: as already noted 10,000 joined Santerre, 20,000 were gathering towards Thouars under Rey, and around 5,000 were added to Duhoux's command. Tens of thousands were also flooding into St-Maixent, Niort and Fontenay, and as has been seen Chalbos dissolved those with his column.[30]

Representative Richard boasted on 14 September that 'In two days 20,000 Republicans will plant the Tree of Liberty in Mortagne.'[31] As far as they were concerned the war would be over in days.

Thouars 14 September

In the Airvault and Thouars area General Rey's division was to be the nucleus around which the 20,000 levies would rally and Lescure was determined to launch a pre-emptive strike on these assembling troops from his camp at Saint-Saveur where he had gathered 3,000 men and two guns.

Lescure attacked around 3,000 patriots in Thouars, including reinforcements from Airvault led by Rey in person.[32] These 3,000 must have formed part of the 20,000 levies being assembled in the area.

Lescure launched his attack at the Vrines Bridge at 8am. After hand-to-hand fighting, and with artillery support, they overcame the republicans. With most of the levies armed with pikes they were no match for Lescure's men.[33] However, as Lescure approached Thouars, he came up against Rey and a reinforcement of 5,000 troops who had arrived at the Paris Gate. Rey had been warned in the night that the rebels were marching on Thouars and raced from Airvault to its support. Reluctantly Lescure was forced to abandon the fight, being tentatively and ineffectively pursued.[34]

Beauvais remarked that Lescure had an obstinate character and in this battle had such contempt for the enemy that he handled his men carelessly and came close to being turned. He added that he only retired after inflicting 1,200 casualties on the republicans and losing 200 casualties and two cannon.[35]

The advance of the Saumur Division continues

Doué 14 September

Sweeping down from Érigné the Vendéens were without the injured Bonchamps, D'Élbée and La Rochejaquelein. Stofflet took command of both his and La Rochejaquelein's troops.[36] Santerre's troops in Doué were nominally under Turreau's command but were being directed by the more experienced General Dembarrère. Turreau was forewarned that the rebels were on their way and deployed at dawn on 14 September between Doué and Soulanger with most of his army behind earthworks constructed under Dambarrère's direction. In total he led 6,500 infantry, 500 cavalry, two 12pdrs, two howitzers and several battalion guns. An additional 5-6,000 levies were kept well to the rear.

Stofflet split the army into two columns as he approached and they advanced on the Angers and Doué roads respectively. Most of their artillery was left well to the rear, although two guns supported their right and four were deployed on the road in their centre. The battle began around 11am.

Perrault and Beauvais soon advanced the guns in their centre to counter an enemy battery holding up their advance but under a hail of shot and shell some ammunition received a direct hit 'throwing men over twenty feet in the air'.[37] The rebel gunners, however, calmly fought on.

The Vendéen right had been successfully pushing the republicans back when they were caught by cavalry in their flank, thrown into disorder, and forced to retreat. Their left had failed to make inroads and with the retreat of their right they soon followed. Around 2pm their army withdrew on the Brissac and Vihiers roads.

Beauvais complained that the army had been too large for its objective, was badly handled, and that the two columns were too far apart and failed to stay in touch. They lost around 500 men and Stofflet was wounded in the thigh.

Coron 18 September

When Santerre's 16,500 strong column subsequently advanced, its 6,500 more experienced troops comprised an advance guard under Turreau and brigades under Chabot and Joly accompanied by around twenty-four guns and a modest cavalry force. Under Ronsin's direction they marched in a single column. It is not clear whether the new levies were interspersed with these brigades or formed a separate mass of troops.

They were in Vihiers on 17 September and on the following morning continued their march on Cholet. Around noon, on reaching Château des Hommes, Turreau could hear cannon fire coming from Coron. When he asked for orders he claimed he received none and when he insisted they should stop and scout before advancing further he claimed Ronsin ignored this advice and ordered him to march on.

Coron is located at the bottom of a valley, through which ran a single narrow road hemmed in by buildings and streams, and Turreau now marched through this deserted town. Scouts warned him that the enemy were marching towards them in great numbers and at speed. Turreau claimed that he seized some high ground above Coron and advised Santerre of his movements and those of the enemy. Santerre makes no mention of this indicating that he was at the head of the column with Ronsin, Turreau and Representatives Bourbotte and Choudieu where, he claimed, the front of the column halted in a bad position at a dip in the road through Coron.[38]

With the main Vendéen leaders facing Canclaux, Piron found himself once again in command; although this time he was supported by Laugrenière. They assembled around 15,000 men and deployed in a crescent largely concealed by the terrain. Their centre was supported by three 8pdrs deployed on the Cholet road. Turreau claimed he deployed two 12pdrs and two howitzers to oppose this artillery and told Ronsin he must deploy immediately.

The bulk of the republican army was congested on the main road with their infantry interspersed with their artillery. Santerre endeavoured to turn eight guns to move them to high ground a short distance east of Coron only to have this order overruled by Ronsin. The Vendéen tirailleurs came right up to the cannon to shoot the gunners, and the republicans found their line of retreat blocked by caissons attempting to turn on the narrow road. Piron may have led some parishes in a charge to cut the enemy line and the battle soon turned into a massacre as the Vendéen forces converged on the trapped republicans.[39]

Turreau was wounded and fell from his horse, Ronsin disappeared into the mass of troops, and General Dembarrère had his coat riddled with bullets. The republicans were routed after no more than an hour of combat. The talentless Santerre had suffered another disastrous defeat.

The Vendéens seized nearly all the republican artillery and a large number of pikes but, due to the nature of the terrain, losses were focused on the advance guard and were therefore limited.

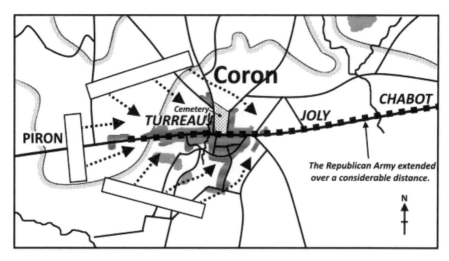

The assault on Coron.

On news of this defeat Rossignol ordered Salomon to hold a position in advance of Doué with four battalions and refuse passage to the fleeing troops.[40]

In their official bulletin the Vendéens claimed nine cannon, three howitzers, nineteen caissons and three thousand killed.[41] Whatever the actual cost this was yet another blow to the Republic.

Duhoux's Angers Column

As Santerre left Saumur, Duhoux's division, conforming to the 3 September Plan, set out from Angers heading for the Layon. He led 11–15,000 men of whom at least 8,000 were new levies mostly armed with pikes.[42] The rest of his forces included the Angers National Guard and a handful of volunteer battalions, supported by at least nine guns and a small body of cavalry.

By the evening of 17 September Duhoux had crossed the Layon and was in St-Lambert preparatory to marching on Chemillé and La Jumellière the following day.[43] However, Duhoux was now informed of the disaster at Coron and re-crossed the Layon to deploy on its eastern bank.

Pont-Barré 19 September

The Vendéen forces were led by the Chevalier Duhoux d'Hauterive, nephew of the republican general he was now about to fight. His contingent from the Chemillé Division was joined by others under Cady, La Sorinières and

Piron (who sent cavalry and a few thousand infantry from his victory at Coron). In total he appears to have mustered 9,000 men, including a few hundred horse and some cannon.

Having assembled in Chemillé they advanced in two columns and brushed aside some republicans in St-Lambert before pressing on towards the Layon.[44]

They found the enemy deployed along the east bank. The Vendéens sent detachments across unguarded bridges at Bézigon and Les Planches to either flank of the republican positions while Cady and La Sorinière's troops held their attention at Pont-Barré.[45] The Vendéens had deployed their cannon near La Bodière and the republicans at Moulin-Brûle, and towards 11am the cannonade began.[46]

Planks at Pont Bézigon had been removed so their cavalry swam the river and replaced them, enabling 300 Vendéen infantry to cross. Les Planches was crossed by 100 men and these two groups, who must have been formed from the elite of their army, now attacked the republican flanks. Panic soon took hold of the republican flanks causing them to pull back on their centre which was deployed on high ground facing Pont-Barré. However the rebels had also managed to force Pont-Barré and overpower the enemy gunners, the Jemappes Battalion and the Angers National Guards. When the republican flanks arrived on the high ground east of Pont-Barré they found themselves facing rebel cavalry and a contingent of Duhoux d'Hauterive's troops who

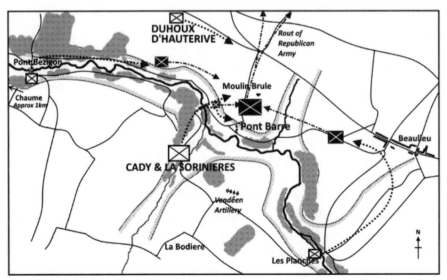

The Battle of Pont-Barré.

had crossed at Chaume.[47] The landscape was soon littered with hundreds of republican dead as their army routed in several directions.

Beauvais recalled this being one of the bloodiest battles he had yet experienced. He wrote that the republicans were soon broken and although some of their troops retreated in orderly fashion towards Les Ponts-de-Cé the levies fell to pieces.

The republicans had prematurely removed timbers form the bridge at Les Ponts-de-Cé, cutting off their own routing troops who now faced a massacre as Beauvais recounted 'we no longer took prisoners'.[48]

The Vendéen Bulletin of 20 September boasted:

'In an instant all the enemy were beaten and around 4,000 were ground to dust. Nine cannon, six caissons and three hundred wagons full of wheat and other pillaged effects were the fruit of this victory. No one could count the number of enemy patriots who perished in the Loire.'[49]

Casualties were certainly in the thousands and on 21 September only 5,500 men from Duhoux's column could be accounted for in Angers.[50] This victory enabled the Vendéens to seize the Érigné Heights once more.

General Duhoux was sent to face the Revolutionary Tribunal and was in prison throughout the Terror, probably only saved from execution due to his heroic defence of Lille in 1792.[51]

The March of the Army of Mayence

Santerre and Duhoux had been routed, Rey had been stalled, and Chalbos and Beffroy had pulled back as instructed. Yet Canclaux was completely unaware of these unfolding disasters as he fought the Vendéens to the west and advanced in accordance with the Nantes Plan.

At long last a large force of veteran troops, the heroes of the long Siege of Mayence, would face the Vendéens and, it was assumed, would quickly put an end to the war.

As the *Mayençais* and part of the Army of the Brest Coast advanced through the coastal Vendée, leaving death and destruction in their wake, the men under La Cathelinière fell back from St-Philbert-de-Grandlieu on Legé. The republicans pressed forwards at speed and it did not take long for Pornic, Bourgneuf, Vertou, Aizenay and Chapelle-Palluau to fall into their hands.

After the victory of Chantonnay the leaders of the Grand Army held a council of war at Les Herbiers. D'Élbée divided the region into four areas under the overall command of Bonchamps (northern Anjou and banks of the Loire); La Rochejaquelein (southern Anjou); Lescure (Haut-Poitou); and Charette (south of Nantes and Bas-Poitou). Independent leaders in the coastal Vendée (notably La Cathelinière, Joly and Savin) reluctantly accepted Charette's command at this time of crisis.

Charette was soon forced to abandon Legé and cover the withdrawal of refugees as everyone moved eastward.[52] He personally commanded his rearguard and withdrew shortly before Kléber and Beysser linked up in Legé.

Joly, Couëtus, Savin and La Cathelinière had all joined Charette and increased his numbers to around 5,000 men. They marched through Rocheservière and gathered in Montaigu on 14 September. Some troops were deployed in St-Georges-de-Montaigu and others placed on the Nantes road to the north.

On that same day Beysser was ordered to Vieillevigne and sent a demi-brigade south to Mormaison. Kléber camped that night at La Grolle, 3km east of Rochservière. Persistent rain, however, slowed the pursuit and left republican troops scattered and exhausted.

On 15 September the bulk of the Mayence column joined Kléber at La Grolle and he was ordered on to Remouillé, 15km to the north. Here he came into contact with a Vendéen post which fell back on Montaigu. Beaupuy was sent to Vieillevigne that day and plans for a three pronged attack on Montaigu – from the north, west and south – were agreed for the following day.

Montaigu 16 September

On the morning of 16 September the republican army approaching Montaigu comprised Kléber and the advance guard, formed from two demi-brigades supported by cavalry and totalling around 2,500 men; Aubert-Dubayet with Vimeux's division of two brigades, totalling 3,700 men; and Beaupuy's division formed from a single brigade of 1,400 men. The cavalry comprised companies formed from several chasseur regiments, totalling 280 men, along with small detachments of volunteer light cavalry. The Mayence artillery numbered twenty-four guns.

General Beysser's detachment from the Army of the Brest Coast was formed into an advance guard and three demi-brigades, along with two squadrons of the 15th Chasseurs and detachments of mounted gendarmes, volunteer dragoons and a company of the Hussards-Américains. In total Beysser commanded 5,800 infantry, 380 cavalry, eighteen 4pdrs, two 12pdrs and two howitzers.

To face these troops Charette commanded a mere 5,000 infantry, 230 cavalry and a handful of guns (mostly of small calibre but including an 18pdr and 36pdr).

Although 17,000 republicans were close by it would be Kléber and Beysser's 8,500 men who would be ordered to advance on Montaigu: Kléber from the north and Beysser from the south. Both columns received orders at 7am and were soon on the march.

Cambray commanded Beysser's advance guard, largely formed from combined grenadier companies led by Blosse. They overcame obstacles strewn along the road as they marched in column on Montaigu, supported by two cannon. La Cathelinière had orders to defend St-Georges-de-Montaigu, but after a short firefight his men pulled back towards Montaigu.

Kléber's column was bearing down from the north but was delayed when part of his artillery train broke down en route. Marigny, commanding his advance guard, first came into enemy contact a few kilometres north of Montaigu. Kléber soon joined him and urged him to advance rapidly with his cavalry in a south-easterly direction, to threaten the enemy's line of retreat or assault their right flank. Kléber marched eight companies of light infantry on his left 'obliquely and in echelon' in support of Marigny.[53] He sent a second battalion to his right to clear farms and a château occupied by some rebels.

The Vendéen troops defending the outskirts of Montaigu were unable to resist Kléber's advance and he entered the north of the town just as Beysser entered from the south.

Beysser had used his cavalry to good effect on the southern approach to the town, but in the lower part of Montaigu a large body of the enemy supported by two 4pdrs stopped his advance. Cambray's grenadiers outflanked the enemy position via the St-Jacques Suburb, compelling the Vendéens to withdraw on the Tiffauges road.

In a limited pursuit republican cavalry cut down some fugitives and captured three cannon, although most rebels withdrew unmolested and casualties were light. They reached Tiffauges that same evening.

Beysser's troops now pillaged Montaigu and instead of placing outposts Kléber noted that he was more intent 'on the pleasures of the table and those of women'.[54] Unable to stop the pillaging Kléber withdrew on the Remouillé

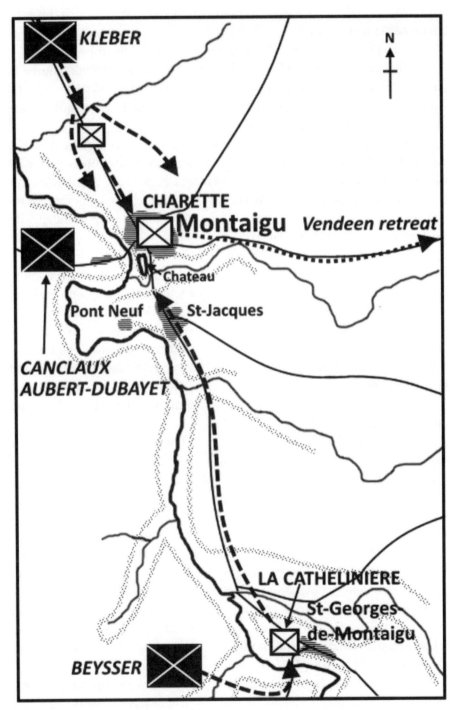

First Battle of Montaigu.

road only to witness a bizarre caravan of Beysser's troops marching by encumbered with booty.

Aubert-Dubayet's main column camped outside of the town.

Little was achieved on 17 September as the republicans endeavoured to identify the enemy's movements. Canclaux's next target was Clisson, and Kléber marched there on 18 September. On route he faced dreadful roads in very difficult country and found Clisson evacuated.

News however now reached them of the first defeats sustained by the Army of the La Rochelle Coast. Canclaux had to now carefully consider his next moves and decided to continue with his advance. He ordered Beysser to march on Tiffauges, while Kléber was instructed to cross the Sèvres and advance to Torfou from where he would be able to keep in touch with Beysser's column south of that river.

The main body of the army was ordered to Clisson, while the 2nd Division was detached to the west to clear the country along the Clisson to Nantes road in concert with the Reserve. To achieve this they were ordered to move to Pallet and seize rebel positions at Croix-Moriceau, La Louée and Vertou. They were then to return to Pallet, while the Reserve would camp at Le Hallay, keeping posts at La Louée and La Chapelle-Heulin. The Légion-Nantaise and a grenadier battalion were instructed to move on Basse and Haute-Goulaine.

These dispositions would close down rebel activity in the area and ensure units could support each other if attacked.

However, Canclaux's plans were about to unravel as Kléber came under attack.

Torfou 19 September

Kléber set out early on 19 September to march eastwards along of the north bank of the Sèvre. After crossing the village of Gétigné he detached his chasseurs-à-cheval and Marigny's light-infantry with orders to advance and report back as soon as they spotted Beysser's column across the Sèvres.

Around 9am, after two hours' march, Kléber heard firing up ahead and urged his troops forwards. Marigny, at the head of his two légions, had encountered and defeated 400 Vendéens stationed by Charette in Boussay. These rebels fell back on Torfou.

At the entrance to Boussay the road split and although both led to Torfou the left was more practicable for artillery. Marigny was sent with the Light Advance Guard on the right and the rest of the column moved on the left.

Kléber, with Merlin and his staff, was at the front of the main column. They were soon in densely covered countryside, cut into many small fields, and with the road gradually narrowing. Kléber, his staff, and a handful of cavalry had advanced some way ahead of the column when they were warned that enemy scouts were near. They cleared them away with carbine fire and Kléber sent orders to hasten his column forwards. He advanced a few chasseurs-à-cheval and as more troops arrived they were rushed forwards in support. He issued orders to seize the heights at Torfou and hold them while the infantry caught up, and although his cavalry occupied these heights they had to abandon them as the infantry were delayed by the difficult terrain.

The republicans were now in the presence of Charette's men with some deployed as tirailleurs to cover Torfou and its valley (with perhaps 300 infantry and 200 cavalry) and some locals deployed in Torfou itself.[55] Unknown to the republicans Lescure and his men were a short distance to the east and a large contingent of the Grand Army was racing to Charette's aid down the Cholet road.

The Vendéen forces were initially 5,000 strong and would increase during the battle to upwards of 20,000 including part of the Army of the Centre and divisions under Lescure, D'Élbée and Bonchamps.[56]

Kléber recalled:

'Torfou was on quite an elevated height and the holloways leading to it were completely concealed. Ditches, hedges and bushes surrounded each field; the woods that were in front and on its flanks appeared to make this position impregnable'.[57]

Around 10am Kléber's infantry finally arrived and he ordered one battalion to attack the right of Torfou, one the left, and some companies of the Légion-des-Francs the centre. Two battalions were held in reserve to support the assault.[58]

Lucas Championnière recalled that his troops were deployed on the road east of Torfou when he received orders to race into the battle underway above the town. Unfortunately their bravest men were too prompt: they ended up some way ahead of the rest and were routed before support arrived.[59] Kléber's assault forced Charette's men out of Torfou around midday and they broke up and retreated on Tiffauges, most ignoring Charette's attempts to hold them together.[60]

At this moment the heavily covered country meant the republicans were unaware just how few rebels were ahead of them. The plight of the fugitives

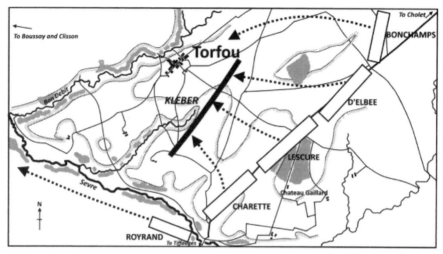

The Battle of Torfou.

in Tiffauges was desperate as defeat could have led to their massacre. With pleas, and even violence, women prevented the men from fleeing beyond the Tiffauges Bridge and forced them to return to the fight. Some women joined the ranks as men moved back towards the Torfou plateau. Around this time Lescure may have made a feint with his cavalry while his infantry stayed to the rear.[61]

Kléber was intent on holding the heights east of Torfou from where he had a reasonable view of the area beyond. He sent two cannon forward: one on the left where Merlin was in command, and one on the right under Marigny.

Lescure and his officers, witnessing Charette's rout, were determined to hold their ground. Dismounting amongst the 1,700-strong Parish of Échaubrognes, considered 'the grenadiers of the army', Lescure would hold firm for around two and a half hours.[62]

While holding his ground, undoubtedly supported by other parishes and with Charette's men drifting back into the action, Lescure would eventually receive support from D'Élbée and Bonchamps.

Kléber recalled that the Vendéen lines stabilised when they rallied in a good position beyond a ravine and occupied woods near Torfou. He also noticed their numbers increasing and soon faced 20,000 men with 2,500 and his back to the wooded valley of the Bon-Débit Stream in terrain perfected suited to rebel tactics. Alarmingly they could see the Vendéen right-wing extending ever further to the north as their numbers increased.

With Torfou around a kilometre to their west the Vendéen line now stretched over 4km. Charette formed the left, Lescure then D'Élbée the centre, and Bonchamps the right.[63]

Bonchamps, still suffering from his previous wound, had arrived by coach and set out on reconnaissance. With D'Élbée and a small group of officers he only managed to get 500 paces when fusil fire whistled around their ears. Part of Kléber's left flank was en route to attack them and some gendarmes and tirailleurs had been concealed in a nearby thicket.[64]

D'Élbée immediately gave orders for the army to attack. Beauvais found the army advancing 'in the best possible arrangement' but, taken by surprise when encountering republicans sooner than expected, their right flank began to fall back and spread alarm among the rest of the troops. They may have fallen back following a bayonet charge by a company of the 7th Chasseurs-à-Pied but the rebels now simply spread even further north to turn the republican flank and forced them to pull back.[65] Beauvais recalled how their own front ranks held firm and was encouraged to see the centre and left still advancing.[66]

Kléber felt confident that the two battalions he had placed in reserve could deal with the threat to his left flank but he knew he was running a great risk if Beysser's column did not appear as his only line of retreat was the difficult route back to Boussay. As a precaution he ordered Targes to move a battalion to secure their line of retreat and another, under Chevardin, to seize a wood to their left. He then decided to move men forwards into the ravine between the two armies and to attack the rebels once more. Just when he was giving these orders he received news from Merlin that the two battalions on the left had fled and but for the determination of a handful of men they would also have lost the cannon on that flank.

The rout of these two battalions was undoubtedly caused by Bonchamps' column, although a charge by some Vendéen cavalry is said to have been repulsed by some grenadiers.[67] Bonchamps had been giving orders from a stretcher and now stood to lead his men into combat. Charette, with his clothes torn by bullets, mounted his horse and with his hat on the point of his sword called on his men to rally around him and follow him back into the fight.[68]

All the Vendéen army was advancing. To stabilise the situation Kléber ordered Boisgérard to switch one of his battalions from the right to support the exposed artillery on the left, but as they set out the other troops on his right thought this battalion was retreating and became disordered.[69] Kléber said many on his right flank now used this excuse to flee.

Firing could now be heard to the rear of the republicans and men were shouting that they had been cut off. A furious Kléber used all means possible to hold his men together. Racing to his left he found Torfou in rebel hands, but fortunately he could see his soldiers contesting every foot of ground as they fought at close quarters. Kléber said he had never experienced so cruel and relentless a fight and with the left stabilised he returned to his right to try to push them forwards once more, but this proved impossible against the vast enemy numbers.

Kléber was now struck in the shoulder by a musket ball but managed to remain in command as he ordered the retreat. His priority was to extract the artillery and he intended to redeploy his men on the Boussay Heights, still hoping that Beysser's column would appear on the enemy's left flank.

Kléber set everyone around him to work clearing the way for the guns, but a caisson broke on the narrow road forcing them to abandon their efforts. The capture of two howitzers emboldened the Vendéens and a further four cannon and four caissons fell into their hands. Royalist accounts talk of their men racing to get amongst the artillery to kill the horses and capture the guns.[70]

Royrand had been moving along the south bank of the Sèvre with orders to cut the republican line of retreat by crossing at the Boussay Bridge. Kléber had the foresight to send Chevardin with the battalion of the Chasseurs Saône-et-Loire to hold that bridge at all costs.

Championnière was full of admiration for the Mayence troops, recalling that they never retreated more than thirty paces without turning to face them. 'Their fire-by-file resembled a roll of drums' and 'wherever they found space they deployed in line.' But, unlike the republicans, the Vendéens were only suffering light casualties as they slid close alongside the flanks of Kléber's men, exploiting the cover of hedges and ditches 'never more than thirty paces from them'.[71]

D'Élbée, who moved parallel to the republicans, reached L'Éraudière but Kléber managed to reach Boussay before him.

Chevardin's stand at the Boussay Bridge held Royrand's column in check and enabled the rest of Kléber's men to struggle back to the heights west of Boussay, but this heroic defence cost the Chasseurs Saône-et-Loire devastating losses and Chevardin his life.[72]

Earlier in the day Kléber dispatched messages to Canclaux and Aubert-Dubayet calling for reinforcements and as he approached Gétigné, Vimeux's 2,500 men appeared led by Canclaux in person.

Kléber formed his men in line between the Sèvre and Moine, rallying on the high plateau of Garenne less than a kilometre from Clisson, and now stood in reserve.[73] Meanwhile Vimeux advanced aggressively against the Vendéens and some of Kléber's men joined in as they forced the rebels back. Around 5pm Canclaux's cavalry infiltrated Gétigné and clashed with Charette's men who had been pillaging abandoned military supplies. Charette rallied his men and by putting up a determined front drew the battle to a close.

The republicans had taken heavy losses with the Vendéens claiming between 1,200 and 1,500 killed.[74] They also lost six cannon and two howitzers.[75]

The rebels had decided beforehand not to take prisoners from the Army of Mayence who, they said, had broken the terms of their parole by fighting within a year of their surrender.[76] When looking for wounded on the following day General Decaen noted that the bodies of their troops were in part reduced to ashes.[77] The Vendéens suffered around 600 killed and wounded.[78]

With odds so much in their favour the Vendéens ought to have achieved more, although the battle did boost their morale as they could now legitimately claim to have defeated veteran troops in battle. Kléber was certainly impressed with their fighting ability.

Eager to know why Beysser had not advanced on Tiffauges, Kléber was told by Canclaux that Beysser was under the impression he needed to await a second order before marching.[79] As he must have heard the battle in the distance his failure to race to Kléber's support is inexcusable.

On the following day Kléber pulled back to Clisson.

On the evening of their victory the Vendéen generals gathered in Tiffauges. They agreed to follow up their success with further aggressive action and decided to coordinate an attack on Canclaux's troops in and around Clisson. Bonchamps was to attack their northern flanks, D'Élbée their front, and Lescure and Charette, after first attacking Beysser in Montaigu, would attack their southern flank. Lyrot and D'Ésigny, whose bands were between Clisson and Nantes, would cut their line of retreat.[80]

First, however, Bonchamps was asked to complete the assembly of his parishes which had been interrupted by the urgent need to race to Torfou.[81] He set out on the evening of 19 September, while also making contact with Lyrot's troops preparatory for the forthcoming assault.

While the battle of Torfou had been underway Beaupuy had continued with his orders and by the evening of 19 September was at the Château of La Galissonnière, between Clisson and Nantes. His troops had skirmished with rebels during the day. Canclaux apprised him of the current situation and intended to use his troops to take revenge, with support from Grouchy and the Reserve.[82] Grouchy had encountered Vendéens around La Plée and La Louée as he moved forwards in support of Beaupuy. The Légion-Nantaise had meanwhile cleared the villages of Haute and Basse-Goulaine as instructed.

Canclaux ordered the army to rest in their current positions on 20 September while the advance guard moved beyond Gétigné, pushing forward patrols on its flanks and front. He was confident that Grouchy was now protecting his line of communications with Nantes.

However, on 21 September he received news that Mieszkowski's division had been ordered to retreat from St-Fulgent. Concerned that this would leave Beysser exposed he ordered him to move his cannon and baggage under escort on the Clisson road and the rest of his men on Boussay by the Montaigu road, to deploy between Boussay and the Sèvre. Kléber's advance guard, now totalling 1,800 men, was ordered to move forwards to the heights near Boussay, and Vimeux's 1st Division was ordered up to Gétigné. The horse artillery was to march at the head of the column while the rest of the artillery would follow on behind.[83] Beaupuy's 2nd Division was ordered to occupy Clisson.

However Beysser, who was busy ransacking the area around Montaigu, did not move as promptly as ordered and was caught in a Vendéen onslaught.

Montaigu 21 September

In accordance with the agreed plan, Lescure, Charette, Joly and Savin left Tiffauges to attack Montaigu, supported by part of D'Élbée's forces. D'Élbée's plan was to act as a reserve to Charette and Lescure, who would be supported by Des Essarts.[84] Royrand, meanwhile, was tasked with escorting the bulk of the artillery back to Les Herbiers.

Early on 21 September the Vendéens were on the march and Beysser was entirely oblivious to the forthcoming attack. Joly formed the advance guard with Charette following behind. Splitting from the rest of the army at Treize-Septiers they took up position in hilly terrain north of Montaigu on the Clisson road and took shelter while they awaited cannon fire that would signal Lescure's attack.[85]

In his report to Canclaux, Beysser said his advanced posts were attacked around 9am to the north and east of Montaigu. He deployed his troops and sent out scouts but as nothing seemed to happen over the next couple of hours he took advantage of this respite to find something to eat.

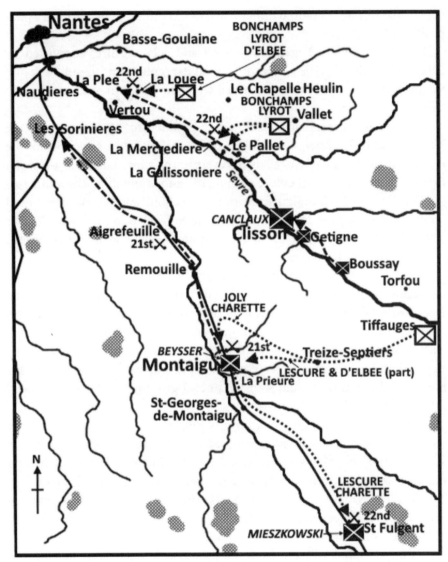

Second Battle of Montaigu, St-Fulgent and the pursuit of Canclaux.

He claimed that he only now received Canclaux's letter ordering his artillery on the Clisson road and the rest of his troops to Boussay, but due to his current predicament he decided to wait until 3pm before marching, when suddenly he was attacked.[86]

Beysser's advanced posts were repulsed by the Swiss, German and French Companies under Lescure's direction.[87] Representative Cavaignac managed to rally these posts and halt Lescure's advance near the edge of the town while Beysser deployed under its walls (according to Beauvais in a poor position).[88]

Lescure's artillery began a sustained and accurate fire, supported by Charette's artillery to the north, and forced the republicans to pull back into the town. Beysser had at last managed to deploy his own guns on the two fronts.

The Vendéens were now deployed in a wide arc stretching from the Nantes road to Le Prieuré south-east of Montaigu.[89] The salvoes from the republican artillery led the rebels to revert to their usual tactic of throwing themselves to the ground before rushing the guns and killing the gunners.

They stormed Montaigu from three directions and at one point fired on their own troops as the columns became embroiled in the town. Beysser claimed that it was the retreat of the post on the Boussay road that spread disorder amongst his troops.

While Charette was fighting in the northern part of the town Joly and Du Chaffault attacked the Château held by 500 republicans. Beysser ordered the *Dragons-de-Lorient* to rescue them but they panicked and fled on the Nantes road. Beauvais deployed some guns on a height overlooking Montaigu, but with men racing on ahead he was forced to follow on and came up against Beysser's troops fighting fiercely in the town. Auguste de Béjarry had his horse killed beneath him but went on to lead growing numbers of Vendéen infantry into the battle.

Although giving ground on all fronts Beysser managed to force his way out of Montaigu on the Nantes road, led by the 79th and 109th Regiments and with the rest of his disorganised column followed behind. Charette pursued with his cavalry, harassing the republican rearguard which was now formed by the same two regiments. Once again the Vendéen infantry slid alongside either side of the republicans, using the cover of hedges to continually snipe at their column.

On high ground a league from the town, Beysser had some respite and put some order back into his column, deploying some guns to cover their further withdrawal. At one point some Vendéen guns were deployed and a large body of their infantry were poised to charge in once the republican guns were silenced but, making no progress, Beauvais then outflanked these republicans with this infantry and caused them to abandon their guns and flee in disorder.[90]

Beysser failed to rally and deploy on the Remouillé Heath and congestion at the Remouillé Bridge cost him a large quantity of equipment and a number of cannon. Beauvais was now ordered to restrain troops as D'Élbée did not want the victory compromised by counter-attacks, especially as Canclaux was still believed to be in Clisson.

Beauvais caught up with the pursuing troops and aimed to stop them at Aigrefeuille. Here, once more, the republicans deployed and a fierce fight developed. Two rebel guns eventually arrived and their fire swept aside an enemy column. An attempt to turn the republican position by an outflanking march caused Beysser to continue his retreat.[91]

With nightfall the pursuit ended and as Beysser's troops marched on to the Sorinières Camp the Vendéens pulled back to Montaigu.[92]

A grenadier corporal named Broussais left a particularly interesting description of the battle and subsequent retreat, demonstrating how chaotic the day's events had been.[93] Having initially been deployed in a village outside the town, where he had been sent on reconnaissance with a party of grenadiers, they were forced to fight their way back into Montaigu only to find it evacuated. Under continual fire they managed to reach the rearguard. He described nearly being surrounded, being separated from the main column, having to leave the wounded behind, and experiencing moments when the enemy burst on them as they were often only a few paces away. The retreat, he said, lasted five hours.

Beysser complained to Canclaux about the conduct of the Battalion of Bas-Rhin: 'The officers were more cowardly than the cowards they commanded,' he wrote.[94] However, within a matter of days Beysser was sent to Paris and would be guillotined in April 1794.

The rebels claimed fourteen cannon, two howitzers, twelve caissons and a vast haul of supplies.[95] There are several reports that the Vendéens massacred hundreds of prisoners in Montaigu, hurling 400 alive into the château's well in retaliation for republican brutality.[96]

Broussais wrote, 'I am unable to evaluate our losses. Some say 1,200, others 1,500 to 1,800, several 2,000. I reckon we had lost 1,500.'[97]

Canclaux's Retreat: 22nd September

A council of war was held in Montaigu at dawn on 22 September. At the opening of the meeting D'Élbée reminded those present that Bonchamps was to attack Clisson that same afternoon and that he was counting on their support. In fact Bonchamps and Lyrot were already on route with 7–8,000 men. Overnight, however, those in Montaigu received an appeal from parishes to their south reporting that Mieszkowski's division had advanced to St-Fulgent and was laying waste to the area.

There is disagreement between sources over who was responsible for the decision to attack St-Fulgent: some say Charette, others Lescure. One of them argued that St-Fulgent was an open town and would be easy to attack, while Clisson was walled and protected by the River Sèvre.[98]

They debated for some time and while D'Élbée urged them to stick to the agreed plan, Lescure and Charette ultimately disobeyed. D'Élbée was evidently a commander-in-chief without the strength of character to enforce obedience. So while D'Élbée and part of the army marched north, Lescure and Charette headed south. Charette sent a message to Royrand asking him to cut Mieszkowski's southern line of retreat.

With Beysser's defeat Canclaux knew he must act quickly and pull back to Nantes to avoid being surrounded. On 22 September he ordered Vimeux to move from Gétigné and camp that night at La Plée and at 1am Kléber received orders to follow him. The supply train was ordered to march next, with Beaupuy bringing up the rear, again with orders to camp at La Plée. Haxo, then in Pallet, received orders to follow Beaupuy once he had safely passed by.[99] This 12,000 strong column was preceded by two battalions escorting the ambulance train.[100]

Canclaux moved as quickly as he could, with his southern flank covered by the Sèvre. When the front of the column reached La Galissonnière, just beyond Pallet, Bonchamps and Talmont launched an attack to cut their line of retreat. Deniau indicates that Bonchamps expected Charette to simultaneously attack from south of the Sèvre and when there was no sign of anyone he appeared to hesitate.[101] However they soon pressed an attack near La Mercredière and Lyrot's men began killing the wounded until Bonchamps personally intervened.

Aubert-Dubayet sent some troops forwards to assist the front of the column and succeeded in forcing the enemy to pull back, capturing two cannon in the process. The Chasseurs of Mayenne and twenty-five dragoons of the Ille-et-Vilaine had successfully stalled the Vendéen assault, enabling the column to continue its march.

An hour later cannon fire on the La Louée Heights indicated that the Vendéens were attacking once more. Aubert-Dubayet once again attacked with part of his column and Kléber wrote that the soldiers no longer marched but ran at the enemy, charging in with the bayonet. Under both infantry and cavalry attack the Vendéens withdrew once more, losing two more cannon in the process.[102]

Deniau suggests that when Bonchamps and Talmont next attacked, D'Élbée had joined them with reinforcements. Between them they launched a vigorous and determined assault on both the front and flank of Kléber's men, held respectively by Targes and Patris.

Kléber recalled that his soldiers were burning with determination to avenge the killing of their wounded and forced the rebels to retreat once more. Kléber's rearguard was attacked next, as the Vendéens sought to break the column and separate him from Beaupuy and the baggage train.[103] They were beaten back, but not before they had seized part of the artillery train and several wagons. Kléber's light infantry killed many before others slipped into woodland. Kléber now deployed his whole brigade in line alongside the road to enable the baggage train and the troops under Beaupuy and Haxo to move by safely. He now formed a new rearguard.

They reached the camp site at nightfall after eight hours of fighting and on the following day received orders to cross the Sèvre at Vertou. Kléber was instructed to occupy Sorinières and the rest of the column Naudières and all were in position on 24 September.[104]

Having fought from La Glassonière as far as La Louée, Bonchamps was forced to pull back around 4pm and retired to Vallet.

Madame de la Rochejaquelein wrote, 'our generals only took or broke 100 wagons but achieved nothing more and were very dissatisfied.'[105] However, fighting with 7,000 men against nearly twice their number it is remarkable that the Vendéens only lost 500 men.

Kléber praised the skill of Canclaux and Aubert-Dubayet and the firmness of the troops but admitted that the republicans sustained many more losses.[106]

The Vendéens had failed in their objective and the blame has been placed firmly in the hands of Charette and Lescure. Beauvais remarked that 'this one day had perhaps changed the destiny of the Vendée.'[107]

St-Fulgent 22 September

In accordance with the plan of 3 September Mieszkowski had set out from his headquarters in La Mothe-Achard on 11 September. He did not wait for the arrival of the men from the *levée-en-masse* and captured Aizenay that same day against limited resistance.[108] He then captured Beaulieu and Poiré before marching to St-Fulgent.

Mieszkowski's column included a handful of regular troops, 200 mounted gendarmes and volunteer cavalry, and about a dozen 4pdrs and an 8pdr. His total force numbered towards 5,000 men. On the night of 20 to 21 September he received Rossignol's order to pull back, but instead sent Dufour to confer with Canclaux. Dufour arrived as Canclaux was retreating but apparently too late to return and alert Mieszkowski.[109]

Mieszkowski's men now faced Charette and Lescure at the head of 15,000 men.[110]

The republicans were camped on high ground north of St-Fulgent when towards nightfall on 22 September gunfire could be heard from their advanced posts. Mieszkowski quickly deployed his men to either side of the main road just north of St Fulgent, with a number of 4pdr guns in their centre.[111]

The Vendéens arrived as the sun was setting and their advance guard, under Joly and Savin, deployed their guns and began an ineffective exchange of fire with the republican artillery.[112] When one of their guns was put out of action the peasants took shelter in nearby ditches. Charette arrived and urged them to attack straight ahead which they did with some reluctance and little effect.[113] They gradually spread out and after Lescure's men arrived the extent of the line was such that St-Fulgent was at risk of being surrounded.[114]

Beauvais recalled that in the darkness the Vendéens formed a column on the main road, and to divert enemy artillery fire drummers gathered around 100 paces to either side.[115] This column now advanced undisturbed and captured the enemy guns.

With the rebels continually firing into the darkness, and making terrifying cries, the republicans' morale plummeted and their troops began to pull back.

The Vendéens were approaching the houses when suddenly they heard cries of 'Advance! Long live the King! Long live religion!' Charette was spotted on horseback accompanied by lit torches and with a drummer mounted pillion beating away furiously. He was followed by Joly, Savin and around thirty soldiers racing up the main road to the town, soon followed by large numbers of peasants.[116] The republicans desperately fought their way to the southern edge of St-Fulgent and took the Les Quatre-Chemins road, abandoning many guns and supplies on route.

The Vendéen cavalry bypassed the town and charged Mieszkowski's column, and although they were repulsed they captured two more guns. Using their customary tactic the Vendéens were sliding alongside the republicans concealed by the hedges and continually firing on them. Baudouin, the military administrator of the army, recalled that the troops became disordered, no longer obeyed their leaders, and used the cover of darkness to run away. However, the Vendéens had blocked the roads and were butchering troops.[117]

The Comte de la Bouëre recalled:

> 'It was difficult to explain the impression that our near continual cries…had on the Republicans. The many hills in this area echoed with cries of 'Vive le Roi!' such that the enemy felt they were being attacked from all sides by huge numbers; and while this had a terrible effect on the enemy, it gave great confidence to our soldiers…'[118]

The pursuit continued overnight and they rounded up 700 prisoners.[119] Although Royrand did send some cavalry they arrived too late to block the vital junction at Les Quatre-Chemins.

The republicans limped into Luçon with 2,000 men and six guns and Mieszkowski was back in Les Sables on 24 September. He denounced the performance of the mounted gendarmes saying that after retreating in good order to La Mothe-Achard 'they then fled, cutting their way through their comrades to escape more quickly'.[120] Mieszkowski was dismissed in early October and was fortunate to escape the guillotine. He was replaced by Dutruy.

From 5 to 22 September the Vendéens fought fifteen battles against numerous columns advancing from the north, south and east. The fact that they survived this onslaught is clear evidence that the disorganised rabble of March had developed into armies capable of defeating an all-out assault on their territory.

Canclaux only found out about the routs at Pont-Barré and Coron because Representatives Richard and Choudieu wrote to their counterparts in Nantes who in turn notified him on 21 September.

These numerous defeats should have led to Rossignol's dismissal and Representative Philippeaux was outspoken in his attack on his incompetence. Ronsin, however, leapt to his defence and the Hébértists were too powerful for action to be taken against him.

To demonstrate that this retreat had not broken the morale of his troops or his confidence in their ability as a fighting unit Canclaux ordered a new advance on 25 September. As one tumultuous campaign ended so another would immediately begin.

Disunity in the Vendéen Armies

Detachments from the Grand Army returned home after the Battle of St-Fulgent and the failed attempt to crush the Mayence column. They stopped on route at Les Herbiers to gather supplies before marching on to Châtillon.

Charette also withdrew in that direction, but on reaching Les Herbiers found that nearly all the supplies had gone. On 24 September a furious Charette set out for Montaigu with a strong escort to claim what he believed was his rightful share of captured supplies, but once again he found little available. This was too much for this prickly character and giving no warning he broke with the Grand Army and left for Legé, in spite of having made arrangements to attack Chantonnay with Lescure and La Rochejaquelein on 25 September. So when Lescure turned up at the agreed rendezvous, Charette's troops were not there.[121]

Cooperation now completely and irreparably broke down. When Charette's men reached Legé on 26 September they found it largely destroyed and were forced to disperse to find food and rest.

The attack on Noirmoutier 29 September

Shortly after his arrival in Legé, Charette heard that Noirmoutier was being held by a single battalion and a few cannon. Capturing Noirmoutier might enable him to establish communications with the English and receive much needed supplies. So on 28 September he gathered 2,000 men and marched to Machecoul, then towards Noirmoutier via the Île-de-Bouin on the following day.[122]

Charette aimed to attack along the causeway using local guides and disguised a number of his men as fishermen who were sent on ahead to land at La Maison-Rouge. Charette was at the causeway for 1.30am (low tide being 3am) and as they marched along it they came under fire from a battery on Noirmoutier and a nearby gunboat. His troops panicked and fled and could not be rallied and those landed at La Maison-Rouge had to escape as best they could.[123] By 3 October he was back in Legé.

Chapter 11

'The rebels fought like tigers and our soldiers like lions'

The Cholet Campaign

Following the succession of defeats, reprisals inevitably followed, and the political situation in Paris would directly impact on military appointments and strategy over the weeks to come. Ronsin, responsible for the debacle at Coron, was not a man to be crossed, and orders to remove *ci-devant* officers were about to be enacted. Representative Philippeaux who had denounced Ronsin as the cause of the disasters would end up being guillotined.[1]

Back in Nantes on 24 September, Canclaux prepared a new plan of campaign with the support of the local representatives and communicated this plan to both the CPS and Rossignol.

He advised that they form two large bodies of troops, one in Nantes and the other in La Châtaigneraie, and march them rapidly into the heart of the Vendée where they would link up. The plan was accepted, and although part of the Army of the La Rochelle Coast was in no fit state to fight, a considerable body of troops would form up under Chalbos and would cooperate.[2]

Early on 25 September the Army of Mayence and part of the Army of the Brest Coast were on the march. Their advance guard was ordered to move to Remouillé and their main body to Aigrefeuille. They were to remain in these positions until 27 September when the advance guard was moved to between Ste-Hilaire-du-Loulay and Montaigu. The headquarters was established at Ste-Hilaire-du-Loulay, where it would remain until 30 September, and Kléber was ordered to Montaigu with his Light Advance Guard.

Kléber's command was reinforced at Montaigu by the seventeen companies of grenadiers under Blosse, the 4th Rhin, a battalion of grenadiers from the Army of Mayence and the 32nd Line. He was now over 3,000 strong.

On 28 September Canclaux and Merlin marched with a demi-brigade towards Clisson and brushed aside a small Vendéen post.[3]

Although Chalbos remained in La Châtaigneraie for the time being, Westermann was ordered to make a reconnaissance on Réaumur. Towards

11am on 30 September he set out from La Châtaigneraie with his Légion-du-Nord and a detachment of infantry from the battalion of Haute-Vienne.[4] On the road near Réaumur a brief combat ended with his men 'forced to retreat with the resolve of true republicans'.[5] In reality some of the republican infantry threw away their weapons so they could flee more quickly. The Légion-du-Nord held firm and were soon reinforced, but as night was falling nothing more occurred.

The Reorganisation of the Army

Chaumont had been sent to examine the extent to which 'suspects' had infiltrated the army staff and on 30 September he ordered Aubert-Dubayet to report on the state of affairs in the Vendée. Savary indicated that this was simply a pretext to give Chaumont sufficient time to organise the replacement of officers that had already been determined.[6] On the same day, General L'Échélle, who had recently replaced Verteuil as commander of the 12th Military District, was ordered to report to Nantes. L'Échélle was an unknown quantity as far as military talent was concerned but he was considered a true *sans-culotte*.

On that same day orders were initiated to suspend Salomon, Rey, Gauvilliers, Grouchy, Mieszkowski, Beffroy, Nouvion and Burac. Menou and Duhoux had already been removed. Turreau left the Vendée, Adjudant General Muller was promoted to general of division, and Canuel was made general of brigade.

On 1 October L'Échélle was appointed commander-in-chief of the newly designated Army of the West, which combined the Army of the La Rochelle Coast, the Army of the Brest Coast south of the Loire, and the Army of Mayence under a single overall commander. Rossignol was given command of the Army of the Brest Coast north of the Loire and Canclaux was left without a post. Prieur, member of the CPS, was dispatched to Nantes to explain the intentions of the Committee.[7]

On 1 October Rossignol wrote to Canclaux setting out the orders determined by a council of war held in Saumur on that day (neither general being aware of the changes about to come). In summary they were as follows:

- The divisions commanded by Rey, Salomon and Chalbos were ordered to merge as a single army at Bressuire on 7 October then march on Châtillon.

- Chalbos was ordered to La Châtaigneraie, and Rey to Thouars, for 5 October. Salomon was ordered to leave Doué on 4 October. Lecomte's men, and troops in Parthenay, were also ordered to join Chalbos.
- Beffroy and Mieszkowski were ordered to remain on the defensive to protect Luçon and Les Sables.
- Once in Bressuire, Chalbos, Rey and Salomon were to await further instructions.

On arrival at Bressuire, Rey and Salomon would leave the army, to be replaced by Muller. Beffroy was replaced in Luçon by Bard, but Mieszkowski was yet to receive notice of his dismissal. Similarly Canclaux continued his movements.[8]

The Vendéens had lost valuable time in recriminations following the failure to crush the Army of Mayence and as the republicans marched into their territory at the beginning of October the unity evident weeks before no longer existed.

While Charette had been attacking Noirmoutier, Royrand was busy covering the southern front. Lescure and La Rochejaquelein meanwhile protected Châtillon by positioning themselves at Bois-aux-Chèvres and only Bonchamps and D'Élbée rallied their men at Cholet and marched on Tiffauges then Treize-Septiers in response to news that the Army of Mayence was once more on the march.

On 1 October Kléber wrote that the Light Advance Guard was at St Georges-de-Montaigu, with the bridge and ravines guarded by Blosse, and the 1st Division and Reserve near Montaigu.

Targes attacked the Vendéen advanced posts on the following day. Canclaux ordered Marigny's Light Advance Guard to march at 2am on 3 October and clear the route to St-Fulgent as he still feared an attack by Charette. Canclaux, Kléber, Beaupuy and Merlin accompanied this expedition and were present as the Château of La Chardière was captured and burnt after fierce resistance by its small garrison. With Canclaux and Beaupuy returning to Montaigu, Merlin and Kléber continued on to St-Fulgent where Marigny attacked and repulsed a Vendéen rearguard.

Some inhabitants informed them that a republican column was at Chantonnay, and Marigny set out with a handful of cavalry to make contact, reporting to Canclaux that he had found them at Mouilleron.

Before hearing of the deliberations of the latest council of war, Canclaux had endeavoured to coordinate movements with Mieszkowski and Beffroy in Les Sables and Luçon. Mieszkowski declined any involvement saying his troops were completely disorganised, a third were sick, and he could not risk the threat to Les Sables by advancing. Beffroy wrote that 3,000 men from his division were currently with Chalbos and others were in Les Sables and had largely been replaced by raw and unarmed soldiers. He was also exhausted after fifty years of military service and still suffering from a wound received in May. His suspension was about to be announced.

On the south-eastern front General Lecomte had been summoned by Chalbos to La Châtaigneraie with a large part of the Luçon Division (the rest remaining under General Bard and Adjudant General Marceau's command).

All this confirmed that Canclaux could expect little immediate help from this area, except from Bard's column now with Marigny. Even this limited contribution encouraged him to order Kléber to march on Tiffauges at midnight on 5 October with instructions that if forced to retreat he was to pull back towards the rest of the army deployed to his rear.[9]

Treize-Septiers 6 October

Bonchamps and D'Élbée had gathered 10-12,000 men, but appeals to Charette proved fruitless.

Beauvais had been in the process of trying to organise a body of disciplined troops and found himself with the Compagnie-Francaise in Tiffauges at dawn on 6 October. He was about to march to join Bonchamps and D'Élbée at Treize-Septiers when he heard feeble gunfire in the distance.[10]

At 11pm on 5 October Kléber formed his men in three columns. He commanded one column in person and Targes and Blosse led the others. Canclaux and Merlin sent him two cannon from the horse artillery and provided Scherb's 1,200 men to act as reserve and cover his line of retreat if that proved necessary.

When Kléber's column arrived at the height of Treize-Septiers they were greeted by well executed enemy fire. Targes also clashed with rebel advanced posts and when he pursued them he discovered their Army on the heights. Kléber ordered him to deploy and await the arrival of Blosse, who subsequently formed up on his right.

Kléber was determined to make up for the defeat at Torfou and when his men called out to him that they had no cannon, he replied that they could go and recapture those they had lost at Torfou: a response that was greeted with cheers.[11]

With Targes on the left, Blosse on the right, and the rest of his men in the centre, Kléber now advanced. They encountered the Vendéens moving down from the heights and in positions behind hedges and broom firing at the republicans from all along their line. Kléber immediately deployed eight grenadier companies in line with their left flank facing some thick woodland to counter any attempt to turn them. The other battalions remained in column by platoons, ready to move wherever they might be needed.

Just as these dispositions were completed some of Targe's light infantry were seen retreating, but they rallied when they saw the advance guard deployed ready to support them.[12] These same chasseurs now raced towards the Vendéens at bayonet point causing the rebels to give way. Kléber advanced his grenadier battalion to support this attack and deployed the rest of the battalions in column ready to move on the enemy's left.

Canclaux now arrived with Scherb's troops and Kléber deployed them on the left of the 4th Haut-Rhin and a battalion of the 62nd Line, with orders to turn the enemy's right flank. The success of this move caused the Vendéen right to rout, but their left still held firm, even after the château and church towers were seen to be in flames. Seeing the church on fire, Kléber wrote, enraged the 'fanatics' who were constantly seeking ways to turn the republicans.

Blosse and the right flank successfully seized some high ground before the rebels could reach it, thereby stalling their advance.

Finally, after two hours of combat, Kléber ordered all the troops to advance and beat the charge all along the line. They moved 'over hedges and across ditches, using partial then general attacks to the front and flanks; the cavalry also made daring moves.'[13] He recalled that both sides were in such a mêlée that cannon could not be used. The Vendéens eventually gave way and withdrew to Tiffauges, but were not pursued.

Beauvais wrote that 2,000 republicans had appeared before the royalist camp at dawn. Although initially exchanging fire, he said many of the Vendéens were taken by surprise and instead of uniting to fight they fled, forcing those who had engaged with the republicans to break away and follow behind.[14]

The republicans captured two guns and by the end of the battle Kléber's troops were completely out of cartridges and used bayonets alone.

Having taken the heights, Kléber rallied his men and moved on St-Symphorien. He was starting to march on Tiffauges when Canclaux urged him to pull back to Montaigu as he had received a letter from Aubert-Dubayet suggesting that Charette was attacking from Legé.[15]

However, Blosse and Targes, with 1,500 men, were ordered to move on Tiffauges, but only take it if the rebels were no longer there and to retire on Montaigu if they encountered resistance. Targes moved on the left and seized a height overlooking Tiffauges. He saw that the Vendéens had rallied at least a part of their army behind entrenchments and had deployed some large-calibre cannon, from which ineffective shots were fired. Blosse had moved on his right, but both then pulled back on Montaigu as ordered.[16]

Dismissed on the Evening of Victory

Orders for the removal of the *ci-devants* Aubert-Dubayet, Canclaux and Grouchy arrived that same evening, and to avoid causing any trouble all three quietly departed for Nantes. When it did become known, the troops were furious.

Vimeux, as the most senior in the army, was appointed interim commander-in-chief; Kléber was appointed interim commander of the Army of the Brest Coast; Beaupuy was given the advance guard; Scherb was ordered to take temporary command of the 2nd Division; and both Blosse and Dusirat were given temporary commands in Remouillé and Nantes respectively. For the time being Kléber was effectively in command and would remain so over the next couple of weeks, even after L'Échélle's arrival.

L'Échélle arrived on 8 October accompanied by Representative Carrier and General Dembarrère. A council of war was held in Montaigu that same evening involving L'Échélle, Dembarrère, Kléber, Vimeux, Beaupuy and Representatives Carrier, Merlin and Turreau. In this meeting Kléber gave an update on the state of the army, and a detailed description of the plans they had been following, using a map laid out on the table.

Kléber noted that L'Échélle said nothing and did not even look at the map during the whole proceedings. When he had finished, the new commander-in-chief simply stated, 'Yes this project seems to my taste, but I observe that there is the need to march in order, in mass and majestically.'[17] With that the meeting ended and Kléber was left wondering what sort of man had been placed in command.

On 9 October the army was reviewed and harangued by Carrier and L'Échélle. As they finished, Kléber could see men in the ranks calling out, 'Long live Dubayet!' He was convinced this response fuelled the hatred that L'Échélle now held against the Army of Mayence.[18]

This reorganisation at Montaigu meant that L'Échélle's army was only ready to march on Tiffauges on 14 October. Political interference had lost them a week of time.

After the setback at Treize-Septiers, Bonchamps and D'Élbée dug in around Tiffauges and Donnissan was able to send reinforcements gathered in Cholet. However they now received urgent appeals from Lescure and La Rochejaquelein to come to their assistance as they were under attack. Leaving behind a weak force covering Tiffauges, with orders to make the enemy believe the army was still there in force, they slipped away to Cholet during the night of 9 to 10 October.

Bois-aux-Chèvres 9 October

After the split with Charette, Lescure decided to march on La Châtaigneraie but had insufficient strength to attack it. He did, however, remain nearby for several days, winning a number of skirmishes. Informed that Westermann was assembling in Bressuire he made a vain attempt to attack him before marching from St-Sauveur to Châtillon with his 4,000 men.[19]

While the Armies of Mayence and Brest Coast had been marching on Tiffauges, Chalbos had been gathering his forces in Bressuire, and also carried out a purge of ci-devant generals. The division in Fontenay was strengthened to 5,000 men, formed in two brigades under Lecomte and Westermann, and set out for La Châtaigneraie on 5 October.[20] On the following day they were joined by 6,000 troops from Saumur and camped between La Châtaigneraie and Bressuire.

The day before they left for Châtillon General Rey was dismissed and replaced by Muller.[21] News soon spread among the troops that Muller was a former dancer from the Paris Opera, and as the representatives were assembling the Saumur Division, to announce that Muller was their new commander, the soldiers shouted that they would not recognise him and ignored the representatives' threats. Rey agreed to encourage the soldiers to do their duty and was given a day to sort out the mess.[22]

The two divisions assembled some distance apart as the terrain prevented a march in parallel columns.[23] Chalbos' division was formed into three brigades: the 1st under Chambon, the 2nd led by Lecomte and the 3rd under Westermann.[24]

Chalbos' division was about to set out when they heard that the Army of Saumur still obstinately refused to accept Muller. Rey had to appeal to them again. At last, at 9am on 9 October, Chalbos set out for Châtillon. Approaching Moulin-aux-Chèvres his scouts warned him that the enemy were near. According to his own account he deployed his tirailleurs 500 paces in advance, placed a cannon on high ground, and marched at the head of the centre column which he deployed in line. The Grenadiers of the Convention deployed on his right.[25]

Lescure had been awaiting the republicans, with around 6,000 infantry and 2-300 cavalry, concealed in the woods on high ground at Bois-aux-Chèvres.[26] Both Stofflet and La Rochejaquelein were present.

On reaching Bois-aux-Chèvres the front of the republican column was attacked by rebels pouring out of the woods. The republicans managed to form line while under fire and, in spite of their growing losses, they did not retreat. Chambon was killed early in the action. The two cannon from the 1st Brigade had deployed in broom too far to the right and at that moment were unable to fire. A large number of royalists were heading for these guns and would have captured them but for the 160 Grenadiers of the Convention who withstood the Vendéen assault, but in so doing sustained over 100 casualties.[27]

Lecomte's troops now arrived, but as he was deploying his brigade he was mortally wounded and this promising general was to die in Bressuire a few days later.

In spite of their losses the first two brigades managed to form up. Both sides were engaged in an ongoing firefight, with that on the Vendéen left especially intense. Contrary to their usual tactic Lescure had placed his best fighters on the left and not the right; as a result the republican right was suffering badly. The Vendéen right was formed of their newest levies, who were probably instructed just to hold their ground.[28]

Aubertin recalled that the Vendéen firing was more sustained as their ranks were more numerous and their losses were being replaced by reserves posted in the woods. The rebel lines were also three times as wide as their own.[29]

Chalbos found it necessary to deploy the front of Westermann's Brigade towards his right, but against orders they made a half turn to the left and then a diagonal march towards the royalist right. Westermann was on horseback at the head of his column, urging his men on towards the extreme right of the enemy, apparently not even bothering to check whether all his troops were following.[30] Aubertin noted that the royalist centre and right did not take the opportunity to envelop this 'unwise general', especially as they heavily outnumbered his spread out and disordered troops.[31]

Chalbos, who was at that moment with his right wing, spotted Westermann's manoeuvre and immediately sent Aubertin to order him back to his designated place in the line. A very anxious Aubertin recalled that in this grave situation they still had no idea where the Saumur Division was, and with less than 4,000 men still fighting, 'all anticipated defeat'.[32] When he eventually reached Westermann, the latter, without even stopping, simply told him that he was going straight to Châtillon.[33]

Remarkably Westermann's disordered advance had the desired effect and the Vendéen right dispersed, followed by their centre, seemingly to the complete surprise of the rest of the republican army. Lescure was obliged to cover the retreat with his left wing.[34]

A further encounter followed at Gué-Paillard (Pont-Paillet), but once again the Vendéens were forced to pull back and Lescure was wounded.[35] Few Vendéens were killed in this action.

Châtillon-sur-Sèvres 11 October

On arrival in Châtillon, Westermann's troops wasted no time in burning the town. The rest of the division only arrived on 11 October, in company with the Army of Saumur and its new general.[36] Their combined strength totalled 10-11,000 men with 14 guns of varying calibre and the generals were confident the royalists would not attack such a strong force.[37]

However, the Vendéens called for urgent help and managed to gather around 18,000 men to launch a counter-attack.[38] Crétineau-Joly lists Bonchamps, La Rochejaquelein, Stofflet, La Bouëre, Beauvais, Du Chaffault, D'Élbée and Talmont amongst those coming to Lescure's aid.[39]

The Vendéen Assault

Early on 11 October Westermann received orders to reconnoitre towards Mortagne and set out with part of his brigade.[40]

Towards 1pm the troops in Châtillon heard cannon fire in the distance. Sending an officer to find out what was happening, Chalbos was informed that Westermann said it was nothing but asked for a small reinforcement and two guns. As a precaution Chalbos called the men to arms.

Beauvais wrote that the Vendéens assembled in Cholet and repulsed some enemy tirailleurs at Temple as they marched on Châtillon. They then formed into two columns as they continued towards Châtillon.[41]

The gunfire grew in intensity and was approaching the town. Chalbos and his staff mounted up and moved to the foot of the height on the Mortagne road (almost certainly the Château-Gaillard Heights). A battalion was under arms in a small a field to the right and extending along the road.[42]

Westermann's column suddenly appeared, retreating at speed and being pursued by the Vendéens.

> 'Everywhere the soldiers were fleeing in disorder, pursued by Westermann galloping behind them; he had removed his *habit*, and the right sleeve of his shirt was rolled up; he sabred both republicans and royalists; one of the latter managed to seize his horse's tail, trying to stop it; Westermann, seeing him, sabred him several times to make him let go.'[43]

The Vendéens now appeared in great numbers and were moving fast.

Beauvais, with the left-hand column, recalled the enemy being deployed in line in a good position on the heights before Châtillon. An exchange of artillery fire achieved little, he said. The Vendéen soldiers were heading down the road to Châtillon, 'making for the left and marching in closed columns as far as the river', but were exposing themselves to fire as they moved to outflank the enemy's right.[44] They crossed the river at a ford with arms held high and rushed on the enemy, firing as they ran.

Bonchamps and the right wing also raced into combat and the republicans were soon overpowered all along the line.[45]

Aubertin, who was with Chalbos and the staff, recalled,

> 'The battalion under arms, the staff and cavalry escort all looked to Chalbos for orders, but to the great surprise of all none were given; he about-turned and re-entered Châtillon. The rout then became general. We abandoned cannons, caissons, baggage, causing an indescribable blockage in the middle of Châtillon…We had put 2 guns in battery on the Bressuire road, which served to cover the retreat of our troops…The Republicans were overlapped to either flank by hundreds of tirailleurs.'[46]

D'Élbée ordered Beauvais to pursue the enemy on the Rorthais road. Beauvais wrote,

> 'I had dislodged the enemy from some houses and hedges on the road where they had dug in, and I returned with everyone satisfied that I'd completed my task, when Beaurepaire and Richard made the few cavalry we had charge.'[47]

They continued the pursuit for a considerable distance when suddenly they came under fire, were charged by hussars, and retreated in disorder 'throwing trouble amongst our infantry and causing everyone to flee'.[48] Being on foot, Beauvais was forced to run for over two leagues. At Gué-Paillard he successfully rallied the men thanks largely to the small numbers in pursuit.

Most of the republican troops, Aubertin wrote, had not panicked when they retreated and felt completely let down by their generals. 'One could only attribute the loss of the beautiful artillery, the caissons, and all of the *équipages* of the two divisions to the incompetence, inability and cowardliness of General Chalbos.'[49]

Counter attack 11 October evening

Aubertin and Nouvion were busy reforming the two divisions around Bois-aux-Chèvres when men began demanding that they march back to Châtillon to catch the royalists by surprise.[50]

The Chef-du-Battalion of the 9th Orléans, furious that Chalbos was not responding to his soldiers' demands, seized the battalion flag and cried, 'To Châtillon! To Châtillon!', a chant 'taken up by 2-3,000 brave men who raced towards the rallying sign'.[51]

The representatives and Chalbos, seeing the resolution of the troops, agreed to risk a detachment of 6-700 men for this expedition under Westermann's command.[52]

Beauvais noted a sense of panic amongst the Vendéens that only increased after nightfall. Racing back to Châtillon he told the senior leaders that less than 100 Republicans were in pursuit and would be able to chase them all from the town while the men were so fearful. He urged them to deploy cannon and soldiers at the bridge of Gué-Paillard, but ignoring his advice they just sent a post.[53] The Vendéen soldiers had become undisciplined, barrels of brandy had been broken open, and many fell asleep. None were expecting further trouble.[54]

An hour before nightfall Westermann's detachment received orders to march in complete silence. When they encountered the enemy advanced posts, in response to the challenge 'who goes there?' they called back, 'Armée d'Anjou, Vive le Roi!' and charged on.[55]

Less than half an hour after Beauvais had given his warning, the Vendéen army was routing. Beauvais, with fifty cavalry and some infantry, re-entered Châtillon in the dark and witnessed the town being ransacked and burnt, before pulling back. Westermann's troops were committing atrocities and may have killed over 2,000 Vendéens.[56]

On 12 October, instead of advancing further, the republican army returned to Bressuire to be reorganised and recuperate. L'Échélle now sent orders to Chalbos to cooperate with his movements, and the Vendéens, rallied by their leaders, reoccupied Châtillon.

The 3,000 infantry and 330 cavalry under Bard and Marceau had seized St-Fulgent and Les Herbiers and approached Mortagne against little opposition. Royrand had retreated as they advanced, moving north through Mallièvre and reaching Mortagne on the 14 October. His men were exhausted and Royrand sent warning to the Grand Army that the enemy were close on his heels. Considering Mortagne too difficult to defend, Royrand and Sapinaud headed for Cholet where they united with the Grand Army.

La Tremblaye 15 October

On the night of 14 October Kléber camped north of the Sèvres near Tiffauges. On the following day he marched on Mortagne. On route he scoured a wide area, encountered and repulsed some Vendéens in La Romagne, and marched on through Langeron to Mortagne which he entered unopposed.[57]

Events were moving rapidly as the republicans closed in on Cholet from the south, west and east. The Vendéens, by a supreme effort, managed to assemble 30,000 men in Cholet. They headed south-west on the Tiffauges road, believing the republicans to be in that direction.[58] Towards La Romagne they were informed of the enemy's march on Mortagne so retraced their steps and near Cholet split into two columns. The left column under D'Élbée, Stofflet, Royrand, Forestier and Marigny returned to Cholet then headed straight down the Mortagne road, deploying 2km to its north along high ground at La Renardière. The right column under Bonchamps, Lescure and La Rochejaquelein, seem to have initially moved towards La Séguinière and La Romagne, and although some enemy were encountered, Bonchamps and a few thousand men then returned to Cholet.[59] Meanwhile Lescure, in command of the rest of this column, made for St-Christophe-du-Bois and occupied high ground around Le Grand-Chambord, north-west of D'Élbée's column.

The republicans were feeling their way forwards in search of the Vendéens. In Mortagne, Kléber and his officers were told the enemy were more to the north. They spotted Bard's column moving on Mortagne, and L'Échélle

urged them to march straight on for Cholet, promising him support from
Kléber's troops.[60]

North of Mortagne, Bard's advance guard, under Marceau, came under
attack as D'Élbée's tirailleurs swooped down from concealed positions.
Marceau pulled back towards La Haie as Bard raced to his aid. Both were
nearly enveloped by weight of numbers and part of Bard's column broke and
retired on La Haie where they were rallied.

Towards 2pm Beaupuy also received orders to march on Cholet, and
when south of La Haie he reached a junction but had no idea which road
to take. Hearing gunfire towards La Renardière he sent the battalion of
the Chasseurs-de-Cassel in that direction to support the Luçon column,
while he headed with the rest of his advance guard for St-Christophe-de-
Bois. He also asked Vimeux to send him six battalions to act as support.
Reaching the edge of the high ground he spotted the Vendéens holding Le
Grand-Chambord and, although there in strength, he felt they were badly
deployed, being scattered over a wide area and with a couple of hundred
cavalry moving about quite a bit but not attacking.

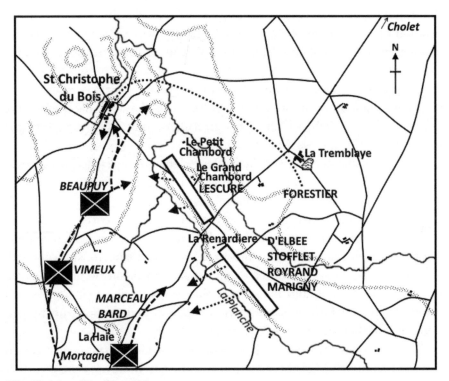

The Battle of La Tremblaye.

The Légion-des-Francs deployed facing Le Grand-Chambord, in positions out of sight of rebel artillery (probably in the valley of the La Planche), with the 1st Grenadiers-Réunis to their right, both being supported by artillery and having a combined strength of 900 men.[61] Under a hail of artillery fire, and attacked from two sides, the Vendéens were eventually forced to pull back on La Tremblaye.

Beaupuy, with Vimeux's supporting battalions, moved into the valley between St-Christophe-du-Bois and Le Petit-Chambord. Occupying the crest in strength he sent two battalions under Dubreton to occupy St-Christophe-du-Bois and protect his left flank. A detachment of the Chasseurs Côte d'Or, on his left, had been under pressure and needed support.[62]

On the right, the Chasseurs-de-Cassel had successfully extracted Marceau and Bard, but were also under pressure from the Vendéens, even after Marceau deployed two guns on the great road to blunt their attack.

Towards 5pm D'Élbée noticed that the Vendéen right wing was falling back. He ordered Forestier, with part of the reserve, to attempt to outflank the republicans by passing around St-Christophe-du-Bois. From his position on the heights, Beaupuy could see the white flags of this reserve moving in a long column from the Château of La Tremblaye towards St-Christophe-du-Bois.

In spite of grapeshot from two captured guns, Forestier managed to reach, and then move beyond, St-Christophe-du-Bois. But his troops were forced to disperse when Dubreton's grenadiers, dug in on the Mortagne road, opened fire at close range.[63]

While the Vendéen left still held, their right now stretched backwards, anchored on the Château of La Tremblaye. Lescure, on horseback, was on this line trying to ascertain the enemy movements as the light began to fail. Some republican troops had managed to move under cover close to his position and, opening fire, a musket ball struck Lescure in his left temple, exiting through the back of his head near his ear. Dangerously wounded, he fell to the ground, unconscious and soaked in blood. Renou managed to staunch the blood, and his servant Bontemps, seeing that he was still breathing, placed him on a horse, riding pillion and propped up by two soldiers, and they slowly set off northwards.[64]

Beauvais wrote, 'Lescure, rash as always and too far from his men, received a mortal wound.'[65] Madame de la Rochejaquelein, however, remarked that the leaders were always forced to act like 'enfants-perdu' (a forlorn hope).[66]

News quickly spread that Lescure had been killed, discouraging troops who were barely hanging on. The Vendéens clinging to St-Christophe-du-Bois were now forced out by Dubreton, and Marceau finally managed to push D'Élbée's men off the heights. With nightfall the Vendéen columns retreated on Cholet.

The Vendéens had not been routed and the exhausted republicans only cautiously pursued. A strong counter-attack, under Bonchamps and La Rochejaquelein, pushed the republicans back to La Tremblaye, after which the Vendéens returned to Cholet.[67] Beauvais noted that their numbers were much stronger now than at the start following Bonchamps' arrival.

According to Kléber the battle lasted five hours and the republicans lost 500 killed to 1,500 Vendéens casualties. He also claimed that they captured seven cannon, including three 8pdrs.[68] It was noted, perhaps with a hint of sarcasm, that L'Échélle only appeared at the end of the battle.

After the battle the rebels took the precaution of deploying a strong guard and barricading the Cholet Bridge with wagons.[69]

Kléber, fearing a counter-attack, deployed the troops south of Cholet on 16 October. All that day the tocsin rang, urgently calling all available men to gather in Beaupréau. It was to this town that the Vendéen army now withdrew, considering Cholet too difficult to defend.

Cholet 17 October

Everything was chaotic in Beaupréau and the Vendéens' morale was low. At a council of war the generals held widely differing views: D'Élbée agreed with La Rochejaquelein that they should attack but first wanted to await the arrival of 5,000 men under Lyrot, not due to arrive until the evening of 17 October; Royrand was all for marching to link up with Charette; while Stofflet advised dispersing the troops to harass republican communications, and by doing so force their withdrawal.[70]

Bonchamps convinced them to carry out the following plan: 3,000 men would secure crossings over the Loire, at St-Florent-la-Vieil and Ancenis, and escort the bulk of the artillery north of the river via Ancenis in case of defeat. The bulk of the army would meanwhile march south to launch an all-out assault on the republicans, hoping to catch them off guard and achieve a crushing victory.

Approximately 35,000 men, therefore, marched south to attack the republicans, but they were probably unaware that Chalbos' troops were about to unite with those under L'Échelle.[71]

Kléber's division cautiously marched into the abandoned town of Cholet during the 16 October.

On the following morning Kléber's troops, along with a further contingent under Marceau, were camped in a semi-circle on a ridge north of Cholet. Beaupuy's advance guard was further north still. Chalbos' troops arrived during the night and camped south of Cholet, bringing the total forces in the area to nearly 23,000 men.[72] Haxo, acting in reserve, was near La Treille watching the roads to his north-west; Saint-Suzanne and Jordy formed the left and were deployed along the edge of the St-Léger Wood; Marceau covered the centre near Bégrolles Farm; Bois-Grolleau and the Saumur road were covered by Vimeux and Scherb. Cannon were deployed on approach roads. Marigny and the Light Advance Guard were deployed as far as the town of Le May to the north, with Beaupuy and the advance guard to his rear on the La Papinière Heath. They were not expecting to be attacked.

Numerous small enclosed fields marked the approach to Cholet from the north and there was a large area of woodland to the north-west, which meant that neither artillery nor cavalry would be easy to use in the forthcoming battle.

The La Papinière Heath

Beaupuy was resting in his tent when around 1pm scouts reported vast numbers of rebels approaching. An experienced and able commander, Beaupuy immediately deployed his troops and sent a rider to Cholet calling for reinforcements. Blosse and his united companies of grenadiers were deployed in advance towards the left, Targes on his right towards the farm of La Jominière, and Dubreton in reserve supported by a battery of light artillery. It is likely that many of Beaupuy's troops spread out across the heath as the Vendéens approached. In Cholet, Kléber called the men to arms and raced to join Jordy and Sainte-Suzanne at what he considered to be the weakest part of their line.

Around 1pm Stofflet and Marigny's men (Marigny commanding Lescure's troops) approached along the Le May road, leading the march of the entire Vendéen army which was advancing in one huge column. After passing the farm of La Préverie they were momentarily stalled by fire from Verges' Grenadiers.[73] The Vendéens now began to deploy vast numbers of tirailleurs. Spreading to left and right the majority of Stofflet and Marigny's men moved in a south-easterly direction, sheltered from the republicans by the brow of the low hills north-east of Cholet. They passed the crossroads

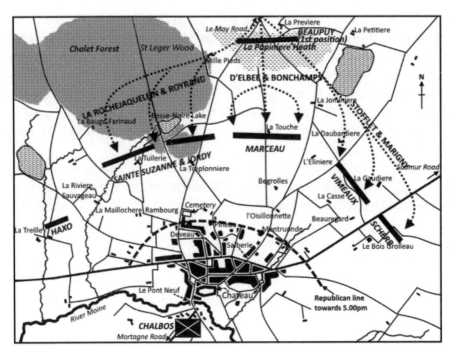

The Battle of Cholet.

that led to La Jominière and, while continuing their south-easterly course, launched a furious attack on Blosse's right flank, throwing his grenadiers back in disorder.[74] Beaupuy recalled how a multitude of peasants inundated the heathland.[75]

Stofflet's men now skirmished with Targes' battalions around La Jominière, throwing them back as they continued to head south-east.[76]

Meanwhile Bonchamps and D'Élbée slowly appeared on the heath, planning to march directly on Cholet. Bonchamps made some attempt to deploy his men in regular order, probably in rudimentary massed columns shielded by large numbers of skirmishers.

With the Vendéens continually massing to his front, Beaupuy threw forward his light artillery, which fired rapidly into the rebel ranks. Although effective, the cannon fire set light to the dry heathland and with the wind blowing towards the republicans they were blinded by the smoke and forced to pull back.[77] The smoke was so dense that men reported only being able to see those immediately adjacent, and while this confused fight developed, the third Vendéen column, under La Rochejaquelein and Royrand, appeared at Millé-Pieds and in the adjacent woods, aiming to threaten the republican left.[78]

Unable to use his artillery Beaupuy ordered two battalions forward from his reserve, refusing his left and advancing his right. Intended to unsettle the royalists, and buy him time, this manoeuvre failed immediately because his men were unnerved by the enemy numbers. Although his flanks initially held, his men were being jostled back on La Touche. Beaupuy tried to charge with some chasseurs-à-cheval, but they refused to follow him. In the ensuing confusion he was nearly captured, being rescued by a Hérault battalion sent by Marceau.

Seeing his troops retreat, Beaupuy gave orders to pull back on the Cholet road and redeploy closer to the town. Although he had earlier appealed for reinforcements Kléber had declined to send any as he did not want to commit troops without being sure of the direction of the main Vendéen attack. Experience had shown him that this was usually from the Vendéen right, and this had yet to appear. By now Beaupuy and Marceau were probably deployed just north of Cholet, at the point where the ground dropped away behind in a long downward slope to the town square.[79]

The Vendéen Onslaught on Cholet

The republicans gained valuable time because the Vendéens only split into smaller columns as they appeared in succession on the battlefield.

With Beaupuy's situation clearly precarious, Kléber asked Chalbos to send some men forward to strengthen their centre. General Muller was dispatched with 4,000 men and began his march through the town heading for the Rambourg Suburb.

Stofflet's men had appeared on the Saumur road and towards Bois-Grolleau. His sudden and impetuous attack on the flank of Scherb and Vimeux unbalanced the republicans who, outnumbered by perhaps four-to-one, suddenly broke in a disorderly retreat on Cholet. Stofflet then advanced on La Casse and La Gaudière.[80] Vimeux and Scherb had been deployed in advance of Bois-Grolleau, with their artillery park sheltered in a field next to the ruins of the château. Six cannon in this park were captured.

La Rochejaquelein dislodged republican skirmishers in the St-Leger Wood and, moving around the heights of La Bordage-Farinaud and the Bosse-Noire Lake, he forced both Sainte-Suzanne and Jordy to pull back.[81] Kléber, who was still on this flank, and under extreme pressure, rallied a battalion but was forced back on the La Treplonnière and La Tuilerie roads.

It was around this time that Muller's reinforcements arrived, but seeing the battle raging at La Treplonnière they panicked, fled, and spread alarm in the streets of Cholet.[82] They continued their flight over the Moine Bridge and along the Mortagne road. Representative Carrier fled with Muller's men, although he would later claim he had been trying to rally them.

In the centre, Bonchamps and D'Élbée threw forward their troops with artillery support. The farms of La Touche, La Jominière and La Dabardière fell to them, and Marceau's battalions were forced back on Bégrolles Farm and the outskirts of Pineau, l'Oisillonnette and Montruonde.[83]

La Rochejaquelein progressed even further, the front of his column fighting its way into the Rambourg Suburb.

The Republican Counter-Attack

Around 4pm, with dusk approaching, most of Kléber's division was disorganised in the streets of Cholet.[84] If Kléber had lost his nerve the battle would have ended in disaster. Vimeux and Scherb had their backs to the Moine and Stofflet was skirmishing around the eastern edge of the town.

Supported by Beaupuy, Marceau, Vimeux, Travot and Targes, Kléber managed to stabilize the line from La Maillochère, through Bégrolles, to the Saumur road.[85] Abandoning any hope of further reinforcements from Chalbos, he ordered Haxo's reserve forward. They had remained concealed in low ground near the Château of La Treille and now fixed bayonets and descended into the valley of the La Rivière Sauvageau, unnoticed by the Vendéens. Marching up the slopes of La Maillochère, and led by a battalion of the 109th Line with their band playing the *Marseillaise,* they suddenly appeared on La Rochejaquelein's exposed flank.[86]

La Rochejaquelein's column stretched back to the St-Leger Wood, with the bulk of his less courageous troops towards the rear.

With his best troops engaged in street fighting far in advance, it was the troops to the rear that took the full force of Haxo's assault. Thinking a second republican army had appeared, they immediately broke and fled, some to the north and others eastwards into the column under D'Élbée and Bonchamps. The panic was infectious and many rebels began to break away to retreat northwards, including Stofflet's troops to the south-east.

La Rochejaquelein's front line troops had no option but to pull back, although some now linked up with the elite troops under Bonchamps and D'Élbée who largely held in spite of the commotion to their rear. Again a critical point had arisen.

It was now towards 6pm and D'Élbée and Bonchamps, seeing La Rochejaquelein's column crumbling and night drawing near, began moving their troops forward led by the Swiss and German Companies. Through this attack they hoped to deflect attention from the crumbling flank. Vendéen cavalry, perhaps a few hundred in number, may have made a feint, which caused Marceau to pull back his infantry. Other Vendéens, seeing this move, swept forward.

Kléber and Damas had rushed to the centre and placed five battalions in echelon in case they had to cover a retreat.[87] Marceau, having deployed his infantry in line, suddenly withdrew them to unmask some cannon deployed in a holloway near Bégrolles Farm. Firing grapeshot at close range whole files of rebels fell, including both Bonchamps and D'Élbée who were both hit multiple times. The 400 or so men that these royalist leaders had rallied for the attack had been decimated, yet they still managed to cover the withdrawal of their wounded leaders under La Rochejaquelein's direction. Kléber now advanced the battalions he had deployed to cover a retreat, and although fighting continued until around 8pm a republican victory had been secured.

It was already dark when Bonchamps and D'Élbée were carried from the field and Beaupuy was sent in pursuit. He mercilessly hunted down fugitives until General Lyrot's reinforcement of 5,000 men intervened and covered the rout of the royalist army.

Kléber soon called off the pursuit as his troops were exhausted.

The Results

The Battle of Cholet was one of the most fiercely contested of this war. Kléber wrote that the Vendéens 'fought like tigers and our soldiers like lions'.[88] The losses are not recorded but were probably evenly balanced, with those killed being in the hundreds rather than thousands. The republicans claimed to have captured twelve cannon.

Kléber had lost fourteen senior officers over the previous few days, but the loss of D'Élbée and Bonchamps, coming so soon after that of Lescure, left the Grand Army devoid of nearly all of their most senior generals. It would be down to Stofflet and La Rochejaquelein to pick up the pieces. For their conduct at Cholet, Marceau and Blosse were promoted to the rank of general of brigade, and Kléber to general of division. Marceau was attached to L'Échélle's staff.

Securing of the Loire Crossings: Ancenis and Varades 17 October

Before the Battle of Cholet, Bonchamps ordered D'Autichamp to secure key Loire crossings with 3,000 troops, in particular those at Varades and

Ancenis. Ancenis would provide the necessary access for their artillery train and thirty-six guns and numerous caissons were sent in that direction.[89]

At 4am on 17 October 400 men crossed the Loire at St-Florent-le-Vieil to seize Varades, moving silently from island to island. They took the 4th Seine-et-Marne, who formed its garrison, by complete surprise and forced them to evacuate westwards. Some hours later these same republicans, reinforced by a few hundred men, failed in an attempt to retake the town and pulled back to Nantes.

Ancenis was also easily captured, as were other fords along the river between Champtoceaux and Ingrandes.[90]

That the Vendéen army survived the flight from Cholet, with their backs to the River Loire, is remarkable. The speed and skill with which they secured key crossings, gathered small craft, and then ferried both the demoralised army and thousands of refugees across the river, would later draw the admiration of Napoleon.

Bonchamps died at Varades, having barely survived the crossing of the Loire. D'Élbée, covered in wounds, was smuggled under escort to the relative safety of Charette's territory. Lescure's mortal wound rendered him barely conscious.

The Vendéens were faced with the dilemma over what to do with 4–5,000 republican prisoners being held in St-Florent. As Bonchamps lay dying he became aware that the army was contemplating their execution and as a last dying act demanded that they be spared and set free. This remarkable act of mercy, by a general held in such high esteem, ensured their survival.

The number of troops and civilian refugees who fled north of the Loire has been the subject of extensive debate. On balance the men able to fight totalled around 40,000 and they were probably followed by at least 20,000 civilians.[91] Several thousand rebel fighters remained in the Vendée, some cut off and others taking the opportunity to head home.

Chapter 12

The Coastal Vendée stands Alone:
October and November

While the main action was focused on Cholet, the royalist leaders of the coastal Vendée gained some respite.

The capture of Noirmoutier 12 October

On 9 October, the day before General Haxo's column entered Legé, Charette's 3,000 men had set out south then west, marching via Palluau and Commequiers on St-Gilles. The republican garrison in St-Gilles fired on his column causing him to divert to St-Jean-de-Monts and Bouin, where he camped on 11 October.

Weilland's garrison in Noirmoutier consisted of two companies of gunners and the 5th Manche.[1] To avoid a repeat of his previous debacle, Charette timed the march on the causeway for 1am on 12 October, just as

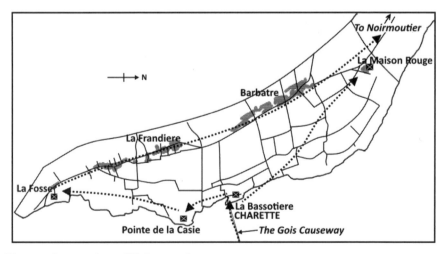

Charette's assault on Noirmoutier.

the tide was beginning to rise and therefore aimed at preventing his men from retreating.

The republicans held posts to the south of the island at La Bassotière, La Casie, La Masion-Rouge and La Fosse, all supported by cannon, in addition to troops within the town of Noirmoutier itself. As Charette's advance guard headed for Barbâtre his rearguard seized the guns at La Maison-Rouge. After a desperate fight La Bassotière was captured, followed by La Casie. A final action took place at La Fosse where two guns were posted. By 4am all these posts had fallen and by 5am Charette was ready to march on Noirmoutier.[2]

They had to cover around 8km through flat and exposed country, cut up by narrow raised walkways between vast salt marshes. Part of the 5th Manche was deployed with two guns at the bridge south of Noirmoutier, but as the Vendéens approached they fled to the town. Weilland tried to organise resistance but was compelled to seek refuge in the château with many of his men. They surrendered when Charette arrived.[3]

The capture of Noirmoutier was a major coup for Charette. He garrisoned the island with 1,500 men under the Chevalier René de Tinguy, supported by batteries and more defences, while he departed for Bouin on 15 October taking the remaining 1,500 men and escorting 300 prisoners. These prisoners were executed on the orders of Pajot, having been implicated in an earlier massacre of royalists in Machecoul.[4]

By 16 October Charette was back in Machecoul and would remain there over the following week, during which time he heard of the defeat of Cholet. D'Élbée was taken to Noirmoutier under escort of 1,500 men, in the hope that he might recover from his many wounds. A few weeks later this escort returned to Anjou and must have contributed troops to a small army being formed by Pierre Cathelineau, younger brother of the former commander-in-chief.[5]

A new Army of the Centre was also in embryonic form under Prudhomme, one of Royrand's officers, but did not have the strength to unduly worry the republicans.

Anjou had been devastated, many people had fled the area and many villages were in ruins. The region was soon placed under military occupation with small republican garrisons in Cholet, Mortagne, Châtillon, Bressuire, Cerizay, Vihiers, Chemillé, Jallais, Beaupréau and St-Florent. Commaire, based in Saumur, was placed in overall command.

Pierre Cathelineau initially lay low, but had some success against Adjudant General Desmarres, the local commander of the Bressuire and Cholet area. For weeks to come his numbers were rarely above 400 men.[6]

The Les Sables Front: November to December

After Torfou, Joly had returned to his own territory and spent the autumn and winter maintaining pressure on the republicans in and around Les Sables, and harassing the post at Pas-Opton. Most of the time all Joly could do was watch as the republicans embarked on a ruthless campaign to seize crops, cattle and goods from his territory, while he rounded up whatever cattle and supplies he could find.

The Convention were under the illusion that the Vendéen rebels were no longer operating south of the Loire, but Les Sables reported increasing activity in the Challans and La Roche-sur-Yon area.[7] Les Sables took the precaution of improving its fortifications and was still receiving reinforcements in early November.[8]

St-Gilles 31 October, Joly, Savin and du Cloudy

Joly's single significant action in the autumn was an attempt to seize St-Gilles on 31 October in coordination with Savin and Guerry-du-Cloudy with 6-8,000 men. He advanced early that morning via Vie and Pas-Opton to attack St-Gilles with around 5,000 of these men, while another column advanced to attack Croix-de-Vie.[9] Adjudant General Charlery was in command at St-Gilles. To cover the town he had constructed earthworks containing ten cannon between the Vie and Jaunay Rivers; a 36pdr, barrier and chevaux-de-frise beyond the cemetery on the Pas-Opton road; an 18pdr covering the Les Sables road; and eight cannon at regular intervals behind entrenchments in a low-lying area of wetlands.[10]

Croix-de-Vie was covered by an entrenchment and three cannon and the only route to this settlement was by the Sion road, closed by a chevaux-de-frise and a 36pdr. Two more cannon, at the extremities of the entrenchment, commanded the Sion plain. The road from St-Hilaire had been cut and made unusable.

The garrison comprised the 9th Gironde, a Lot-et-Garonne battalion and the 5th Charente-Inférieure: totalling 2,000–2,200 men, supported by 250 local patriots.[11]

The Vendéens approached in three columns supported by three guns. Joly led a column on the St-Révérend road, Savin led another towards Croix-de-Vie, and a third (mistakenly thought to be commanded by Charette) advanced from Villeneuve to Pas-Opton with all three guns.

Towards 4pm outposts announced the approach of the right and left columns, while the third was slowed by the tide which blocked the passage

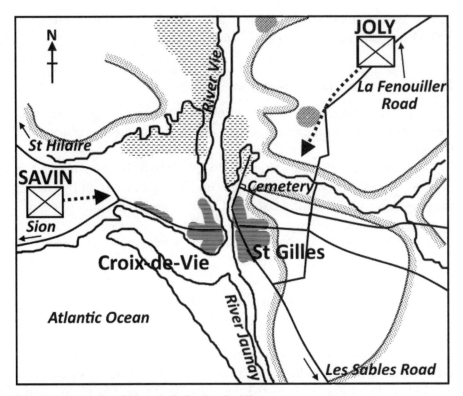

The attack on St-Gilles and Croix-de-Vie.

at Pas-Opton. 150 men of the 9th Gironde, deployed on the left bank of the Vie, retired in good order on St-Gilles after coming under bombardment. Two of the Vendéen columns merged at La Fenouiller and advanced on St-Gilles at speed and to the beat of drums.

The attack began around 6.15pm, in complete darkness, a gale and torrential rain. Charlery's tirailleurs pulled back to the town and shut the barrier and a few discharges of grapeshot from the 36pdr was sufficient to discourage a rebel assault.

The Croix-de-Vie column attacked at the same time but another 36pdr had the same effect. Charlery did not pursue.[12]

Build-up of Republican troops

By mid-November the republicans had gathered 5,000 men in La Mothe-Achard, over 2,000 in St-Gilles, and 2,400 in Les Sables. On 21 November more reinforcements appeared: a 900 strong Orléans battalion, 120 sappers and the Barbézieux Battalion, followed a few days later by 700 men from the 110th Line, who joined the Army when at La Garnache.[13]

Haxo verses Charette: November

The republican priority south of the Loire was to crush Charette, but they were hampered by having to keep an eye on the Loire and the actions of the Grand Army.

Over the last weeks of October Charette did little from his base at Touvois, simply keeping a close watch on the republicans and gathering supplies. After Cholet, both Haxo and Dutruy were placed under Vimeux's overall command, operating from his headquarters in Nantes. Haxo was given orders to recapture Noirmoutier, defeat Charette, and re-establish communications between Nantes and Les Sables. Generals Dutruy (Les Sables), Duval (Niort), and Dufour were ordered to cooperate with him. Haxo first planned attacks on Port-Saint-Père and Machecoul, and gathered gunboats, corvettes and a frigate near the mouth of the Loire to assist in the recapture of Noirmoutier.

With 6,000 men Haxo set out from Nantes on 8 November and met with little initial resistance as he scoured the region for rebels. They occupied St-Philbert and Legé, and crossed the Forêt-de-Prince. On 16 November a small republican force was repulsed at Port-Saint-Père by part of La Cathelinière's Army.[14]

On 21 November Vimeux ordered Dutruy to begin his offensive and over the next few days he retook La Roche-sur-Yon, Aizenay, Le Poiré, Palluau, Legé and Challans.[15] His march had forced rebels from the southern area to join Charette further north.

Collinet recorded on 24 November that there were now 18,000 Republicans on the march from Paimboeuf, Nantes, Montaigu and Les Sables.[16]

Aubertin was back in command of the 11th Orléans and had been relocated to Les Sables by 18 November. He formed part of Dutruy's force and on 23 November they linked up with Haxo's men at Legé. The 11th Orléans now fell under Adjudant General Guillaime's command and on 24 November they were camped near Touvois. On the following day, when near Paulx, he heard that Haxo had established his headquarters in Machecoul to coordinate the assault on Noirmoutier. On that same day Aubertin took temporary command of Guillaime's troops and camped half a league from Machecoul near the Challans road, in company with other troops.

Around 25 November the 8th Bas-Rhin, forming part of Jordy's command, captured Port-Saint-Père by rowing across the river under enemy fire. This action forced La Cathelinère to abandon his artillery and retire on Ste-Pazanne.[17] When Jordy pursued him he came under attack from Guérin's cavalry and was forced to pull back to Port-Saint-Père.

La Garnache 27 November

Charette, now joined by Joly and Savin, failed to reach Machecoul before Haxo, and seeing republicans on the Challans to Machecoul road he took up position at La Garnache.

On 27 November, in freezing weather, Aubertin and Jordy were marching south on the Challans road. Aubertin's column consisted of a single 4pdr and about 1,200 men, of whom 255 were from his battalion and the rest a mix of numerous detachments (including part of the 110th Line, 109th Line and Grenadiers-Réunis from the Army of Mayence). Jordy's column was of similar strength.[18]

Aubertin was constrained by strict orders not to engage in combat when encountering the enemy. Somewhere near La Garnache he spotted Charette's army, which he overestimated to be 8,000 strong. Following orders he hastily withdrew, but this emboldened the Vendéens to attack, and to avoid a panic he deployed his men by sections in a closed column (this being the only formation the width of the road allowed). He placed tirailleurs at the front, masking and protecting the 4pdr behind them. Marching at the *pas de course* they managed to secure some high ground between the opposing forces and, although heavily outnumbered, they unmasked the cannon and the tirailleurs spread out to act in support. The Vendéens spread to right and left but then dispersed towards Challans.

Aubertin was unable to pursue as he had no cavalry, although he did follow them and camped on high ground just outside La Garnache. It is unclear whether Aubertin had repulsed Charette or, as seems more likely, the royalists simply withdrew to gather at St-Gervais.[19]

On 27 November Jordy seized Ste-Pazanne and then marched on Bourgneuf and Beauvoir to support an attempt to destroy La Cathelinière's Army. On 2 December the Forêt-de-Prince was scoured and rebel supplies seized. Although the Republicans were closing in on La Cathelinière, Charette, Joly and Savin, they were finding it impossible to pin them down.[20]

Chapter 13

The March on Granville

The campaign north of the Loire is commonly known as the *Virée de Galerne*, from a name of Celtic origin used to describe a variable west and north-west wind, and used to symbolise the nature of the campaign as the armies marched and counter-marched in different directions.

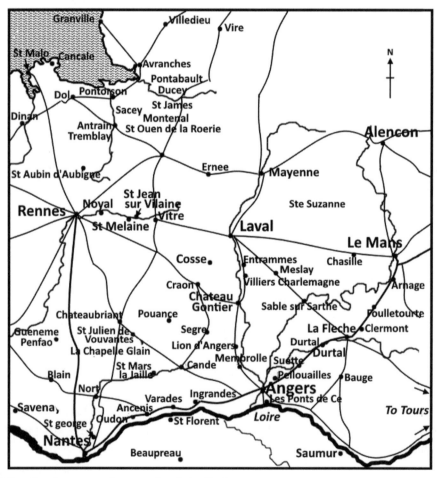

Map for the campaign north of the Loire.

General Fabrefond, responsible for holding the north bank of the Loire, had failed to stop the Grand Army and when L'Échélle's army approached St-Florent they were surprised to be met by the freed republican prisoners marching south, and even more surprised to see that their prey had eluded them.

A council of war in Beaupréau concluded that they must protect Angers and Nantes in anticipation that the rebels would attempt to seize either city in a bid to re-cross the Loire, in addition to covering the more direct crossings. On 19 October Beaupuy force-marched to Les Ponts-de-Cé via St-Florent to reinforce the republicans in and around Angers under Olagnier's command. On 20 October, the Luçon column, temporarily under Canuel's command, received orders to cross the river at St-Florent and track the enemy. Representative Merlin moved to cover Ancenis while the rest of the army marched to Nantes.

On 19 October the Vendéens were still in Varades. The senior officers considered Lescure to be their new commander by right, but as he felt his wound would prove mortal he asked that they support La Rochejaquelein instead and this request was accepted.

The 21-year-old La Rochejaquelein accepted the role with great trepidation, but would be ably supported by Stofflet who was now confirmed as his second-in-command. Their first priority was to find food, rest and reorganise the army, but with republican advanced posts appearing in St-Florent they had to move quickly.

La Rochejaquelein wanted the army to make an attempt on Angers or Nantes. Lescure, in agonising pain and barely conscious, urged them to stick close to the banks of the Loire.[1] At this critical moment an émigré, Le Haye-Sainte-Hilaire, was presented to a council of war with important information. He had travelled from England with news that the British government was prepared to intervene and provide the Vendéens with military support.

This decision by the British was made with some reticence and following long debate as to how they should support French opposition to the Revolution. There was division over whether they should focus their energy on the campaign in the Low Countries, support the émigré army in the field or, with recent evidence suggesting that the Vendée Rising was far more extensive than they had originally assumed, support the rebels directly. There was also long discussion over whether they should allow the Comte d'Artois to lead the rebels in person, which was his professed wish.

A handful of émigrés lobbied the Vendéen cause, and a report by Tinténiac, who had returned to England from a visit to rebel headquarters in September, convinced the British government that they merited support. The Comte d'Artois wrote to the Vendéens on 7 October indicating that he had the blessing of the Prince Regent and asked that they now regard him as their leader and companion-in-arms.[2]

The scale of the Rising came as a complete surprise to the British and a plan to send an army to their support was now put into action. However, time was slipping by, and communication between the rebels and England was painfully slow. To achieve a successful landing the rebels would need to control a port and Dundas favoured St-Mâlo. La Haye-Sainte-Hilaire conveyed this news to the rebel leaders and indicated that the English fleet was ready to sail but securing a port was imperative.

This news convinced them that they must march north. They decided to head for Talmont's homeland centred on Laval, to gain recruits, secure supplies, and put some distance between themselves and the enemy. Being in Laval also kept their options open: to move on Rennes, march back to the Loire, progress north, or move into Britanny.

On 19 October they were on the march, led by an advance guard of cavalry and light guns. Stofflet commanded the rearguard as their lumbering column marched via Ingrandes and reached Candé that same day, having brushed aside republican detachments on route. The following day they gathered supplies and on 21 October marched in pouring rain to Sergé then Château-Gontier. The republicans in the area dared not attack such a large column and a feeble attempt to resist them at Château-Gontier was beaten off with ease. The following evening they set out once again and reached Entrammes towards midnight.

Laval 23 October

The Vendéens approached Laval towards 8am on 23 October and at the entrance to the town came up against 5-6,000 republicans behind improvised defences and supported by two guns.[3] These troops were nearly all national guards and levies and the Vendéens immediately attacked. First they obliterated a barricade with their light guns and then their cavalry moved into action. At risk of being outflanked the republican commander, Adjudant General Letournoult, gave orders to retreat on Mayenne.[4] The battle was brief and republican losses may have been as high as 600 men.[5]

Beauvais wrote that the Vendéen advance guard was formed from their best soldiers and was around 6,000 strong. With the bulk of the army providing support to their rear, they marched on the enemy with bayonets fixed. The Vendéen cavalry pursued on the Mayenne and Craon roads and had orders to spare the levies, identifiable by their civilian dress.[6]

Laval was largely sympathetic to the Vendéen cause and, with Talmont being an influential figure, Chouan bands began to arrive over the following week. Madame de la Rochejaquelein wrote that they called these men the *Petite-Vendée*, recognisable by their clothing which was generally black or formed from hairy goat skins.[7]

Talmont was responsible for their organisation and appointed the former head of Laval's National Guard, Besnier-de-Chambray, as overall commander. Besnier had been in hiding having declared for the Fédéralist cause at the start of June. The Vendéens had already received 200 recruits when they reached Château-Gontier and at Laval bands under Jean Cottereau, Aimé de Boisguy, Louis de Hercé, Lecomte, Allard and Louis Hubert brought their numbers up to around 1,500.

The contingent, under the former salt smuggler Jean Cottereau, better known as Jean Chouan (the name by which many bands north of the Loire came to be known), only recognised Talmont's authority and did not want to be seen as part of Besnier-de-Chambray's command.

The recruits who joined the Vendéens north of the Loire seem to have numbered only 3–4,000.[8] However, these troops were considered well-armed, performed a vital role in the battles, and often acted as rearguard.

Republican moves 21 to 22 October

On 21 October the republicans were deployed as follows: Kléber, with perhaps 4,000 men, was in advance of Nantes at the Camp of St-George; Chalbos and Westermann were in Nantes with around 12,000; Canuel was in St-Florent with 2–3,000 men; Beaupuy was in Angers with 3,000 men, and Olagnier, also with 3,000, was moving west from Angers on the Ancenis road.[9] From Nantes and Saumur, Vimeux and Commaire had orders to watch the south bank of the Loire; Marigny was put in charge of troops from Nantes to Paimboeuf, and Blosse was ordered to scour the south bank of the Loire before following Canuel in pursuit of the rebels.

On the next day Beaupuy marched on Candé, Westermann moved on Nort with 2,500 men, and Kléber marched to Ancenis. Along with Canuel and Olagnier, Beaupuy had orders to pursue the brigands relentlessly.[10]

La Croix-Bataille Night of 24 to 25 October

The Vendéens needed time to rest and reorganise before heading north, but the republicans were closing in. Beaupuy marched from Candé on to Château-Gontier, arriving around 5pm on 24 October, but had received no news of L'Échélle's movements. Westermann joined him after a long detour and was eager to attack the rebels immediately. As the troops were in need of rest, and Château-Gontier was over 30km from Laval, Beaupuy tried to dissuade him suggesting that they wait until Canuel arrived on the next day, especially as they would be fighting in the dark. Westermann, the senior by length of service, would not be dissuaded and gave orders to march immediately, hoping to repeat his success at Châtillon.

In the late evening the Vendéens heard the sound of distant gunfire, warning them of the approaching republican forces. Towards midnight Westermann and Beaupuy arrived on the heath at La Croix-Bataille with 4,000 men, and it was the sound of gunfire between republican scouts and a Vendéen outpost that alerted the royalist army to their approach.

Forestier and some officers set out to scout the enemy and returned around 1am with news that the republicans were marching straight on Laval. La Rochejaquelein deployed a strong division on the Le Mans road, to cover his left flank, and with the rest of his troops headed south on the Entrammes road, his right protected by the River Mayenne.

With the advantage of surprise gone, Westermann was in the process of deploying Beaupuy's forces when the Vendéen army bore down on them and a fierce firefight commenced. The rebel forces gradually grew in strength as more arrived from Laval.

The two armies could only distinguish each other by the flashes of gunpowder. The Vendéens were helped by a local guide who was able to lead them by side roads around the heath at La Croix-Bataille to attack the enemy's rear. The battle degenerated into a confused mêlée at close quarters, with accounts of both sides taking cartridges from the same caissons. Forestier even recalled fighting for several minutes at the side of a republican officer.[11]

At one point two republican 4pdrs unsettled the royalist ranks and at another their left flank came under severe pressure. Westermann's cavalry was so badly harassed that they refused to charge after an initial encounter.[12] In the early hours Stofflet broke the republican left flank and forced their withdrawal.[13] The German and Swiss Companies were especially distinguished in this battle and Chouan bands under Aimé du Boisguy and Jean Cottereau fought courageously alongside the Vendéens.

Westermann had stubbornly refused to retreat until he realised he might fall into rebel hands. Abandoning two cannon he withdrew to the bridge at Entrammes, where Vendéen guns caused further losses to his depleted forces. Westermann may have lost as many as 1,600 men in this battle, although most were probably dispersed rather than killed.[14]

After this victory the Vendéens returned triumphantly to Laval to the great joy and relief of the refugees.

On 25 October Kléber rallied most of the advance guard at Château-Gontier and held a meeting with the commander-in-chief. He was astonished to see that L'Échélle had failed to deploy the troops in good positions or provide them with food. Kléber moved his troops to Villiers-Charlemagne, 10km beyond Château-Gontier.

Chalbos, with L'Échélle and the headquarters staff, camped at Saint-Germain de l'Hommel, while Westermann, with the Light-Advance Guard under Danican, returned to Entrammes and pillaged its château. Westermann only obeyed Kléber's order to return to Villiers when he received it for the third time.

Kléber now received orders from L'Échélle which indicated that the army would move on Laval 'majestically and in a mass'. Kléber had no idea what L'Échélle had in mind and no further instruction was given. Both Savary and Kléber thought that the army should regroup and rest for a day or two before pursuing further action. Kléber ordered Blosse and Beaupuy, still in Château-Gontier, to join him, but to leave a strong post at that town's bridge.

He dined that night with Westermann, Savary, Marceau and Danican. Westermann complained that the army should have advanced to the Entrammes Heights, but Kléber wanted to rest the troops and would have preferred a coordinated attack from multiple points with support from 4,000 troops then at Vitré.[15]

Entrammes 26 October

L'Échélle ordered Beaupuy to command his column's advance guard, and gave orders that the army was to deploy only when it arrived on the heath at La Croix-Bataille. Kléber felt these orders demonstrated a complete lack of military understanding and wrote that all the generals were furious. To march an entire army in a single column, without making feints or diversions, left them completely exposed to attack on either flank. They had no option but to obey L'Échélle.

There was an old wooden bridge on stone piers at Entrammes, and a wooden bridge and two fords further to its east. As the banks of the river were steep and rocky they were passable only to infantry and the fields were surrounded by high hedges.

Entrammes is a small stone-built village largely focused on a single street with a church at its northern end. The river valley to its north is quite wooded, and the château is hidden in woodland on the north bank of the river to the west of the bridge. The whole area is claustrophobically focused on the low point by the bridge, tucked down in the valley north-west of the church.

The land between Entrammes and Château-Gontier rolls in long uphill then downhill stretches. The land drops away to either side of the road between these settlements, with the lower ground and river crossings being noticeably woody. The area today still retains many hedges and flattens out around Villiers-Charlemagne.

The opposing forces were of similar strength: roughly 18,000 Vendéens to 19-20,000 republicans, but when the battle began the republicans were spread out over many kilometres. A large part of the Vendéen army remained in Laval protecting the refugees.

With five representatives and several commissaries accompanying him, L'Échélle would have had little freedom of action. His most experienced troops remained the ever-diminishing veterans of the former Army of Mayence, and once again these bore the brunt of the fighting. Yet discipline was beginning to break down amongst Kléber's troops and over the preceding days he had been repeatedly forced to issue strict orders against pillaging.

Beaupuy led a strong advance guard of around 4,000 men supported by 4 guns; Kléber's 1st Division totalled around 7,000 and 12 guns, formed from two brigades under Scherb and Damas, and 17 companies of grenadiers under Blosse; Chalbos' division was also around 7,000 strong, supported by 12 guns, comprising: a light advance guard under Danican, Muller's Saumur Division, brigades under Canuel and Chabot, and light troops under Westermann.

L'Échélle had specifically ordered the men to march in two files along the road and ignored advice that the army be split in two to use alternate minor roads. Dubbed 'the Incapable' by his troops, he seemed to be living up to his name.

The sequence of events in this battle are difficult to unravel as once the fighting began it was fast-paced and eventually spread over many kilometres.

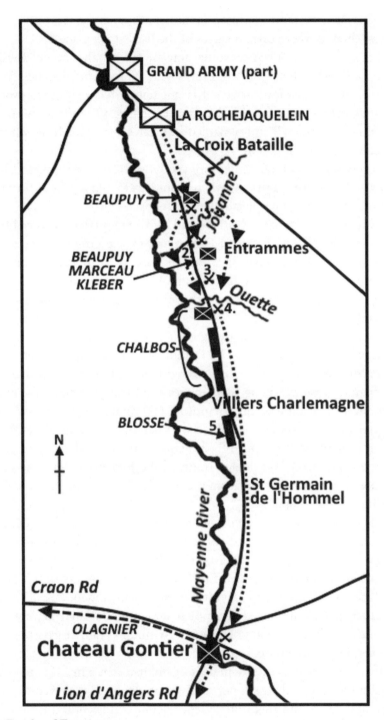

The Battle of Entrammes.

Historians have therefore confused a number of events and it is only possible to guess when or where certain stages of the battle took place.

Beaupuy led the advance some way ahead of the other divisions. Kléber came next, then Chalbos, each separated by some distance. Where Westermann and Danican marched is not noted, but they were probably now with Chalbos' division, as indeed was L'Échélle. Olagnier seems to have received no orders at all and remained in Château-Gontier from where, in the evening, he left for Craon.

Beaupuy was marching straight up the Laval road. According to Gréau, he crossed the River Jouanne and when about 1km to its north he encountered an advance party of La Rochejaquelein's troops.[16]

La Rochejaquelein had set out around 9am on news that the republicans were on the march. As a strong contingent of the Grand Army set out from Laval the dangerously ill Lescure wanted to mount up and join them, but was dissuaded by his friends. He managed to gather enough strength to encourage the troops with words and gestures from a window as they filed by.[17]

For some time the battle focused around two republican cannon deployed by Beaupuy near the Château of La Drujotterie and which had been tearing holes in Stofflet's ranks. Stofflet managed to seize these guns with a small detachment of cavalry, killing the gunners and turning them on the enemy. His division then repulsed an attempt by 600 republicans to retake them, with even La Rochejaquelein and his staff helping to defend them.[18] After this determined fighting the rebels gained the upper hand and forced Beaupuy to pull back and deploy south of the Jouanne River. The Grand Army now deployed their forces on the heights north of the Jouanne River, facing Beaupuy's troops.

As Royalist cavalry scouted the republican positions they deployed artillery along the heights and formed up in three main bodies: to the left Forestier, Royrand, Des Essarts, La Ville-Baugé, De Hargues and the Chouan contingent; in the centre, Stofflet, Fleuriot, Duhoux, and Marigny; and on the right, Talmont and Lyrot. Perrault commanded the artillery.[19]

La Rochejaquelein allowed Beaupuy to deploy unmolested, aiming to pin him while he infiltrated around his flanks. At around 11am he gave the signal for the artillery to open fire.

Marceau was with Beaupuy in person and had sent a message to Kléber urging him to race to their support and was undoubtedly relieved to see his column appear around this time. Kléber deployed to left and right of the road (probably on Beaupuy's flanks) and in turn sent a message to L'Échélle asking him to send Chalbos' troops to outflank the enemy left. As Chalbos was still several kilometres to his south this was a futile request.

Perrault deployed four 12pdrs and was causing increasing losses in the Mayence ranks, when he was wounded and replaced by La Ville-Baugé. With the cartridge bags nearly exhausted Royrand galloped away in search of more and on his return was seriously wounded when a musket ball struck him in the head. Royrand's wavering troops were steadied by La Rochejaquelein.[20]

In spite of the overwhelming enemy numbers Beaupuy held his ground for a couple of hours. Gréau[21] indicates that towards midday La Rochejaquelein launched an attack with his right flank, crossing at the Châteliers Ford to attack Beaupuy's left and his centre pressing forwards under Stofflet's lead. Forestier meanwhile moved forwards with the left. The republicans were being turned and, in spite of the efforts of Beaupuy, Kléber and Marceau, they had no option but to pull back as best they could; some fell into disorder and some formed square to fend off the rebels.[22] If Gréau is correct, they managed to organise some limited resistance on high ground around La Bétonnière, between Entrammes and the Ouette Bridge, supported by six guns deployed by Representative Merlin.

Beaupuy and Marceau, with the support of Merlin and Turreau, wanted to rally the fugitives on the Ouette Heights south of the bridge and Kléber dispatched his two reserve battalions to secure the crossing.

Chalbos had set out from St-Germain-de l'Hommel around midday and sometime after 3pm his column reached the Ouette Heights. As the Vendéens appeared, Chalbos' men, formed in mass on the main road, found it impossible to deploy in the difficult terrain and many simply fled.[23] The Chouan leaders, Jean Chouan and Boisguy, used minor roads to march around the republican right flank and appeared towards their rear, undoubtedly provoking this rout. Having witnessed the rout of Chalbos' column, Kléber's men 'fled like a flock of sheep',[24] abandoning their cannon along the way, cannon that were now turned on them once again.

A republican soldier named Broussais recalled, 'Each feared to be wounded, knowing that if they suffered this misfortune no one would have the humanity to help them escape.'[25]

By 4pm the republicans were in full retreat.

At some point in the flight Representatives Merlin and Turreau rallied a few hundred men and used an abandoned baggage train as an improvised fort, until weight of numbers forced them to make their escape.

Beauvais said, 'several of their corps fled to left and right, saving themselves in the countryside; their main body retreated on the great road with their artillery and baggage, which soon fell into our hands.' He recalled that they were unable to fire grapeshot on the republicans for fear of hitting their own men and that the fight was so closely engaged that they were seizing republicans by the scruff of the neck and using the bayonet.[26]

Prior to the battle La Rochejaquelein issued strict orders that the Vendéens were not to disperse but to fight in massed columns close to their leaders. This decision had a telling effect and whenever the republicans tried to make a stand the rebels simply swarmed around them.

Around midday L'Échélle had sent orders to Blosse to march north from Château-Gontier on Villiers, but when they eventually set out, his grenadier companies collided with the troops leading the republican flight, L'Échélle amongst them. Blosse tried to block their path but was forced back by weight of numbers.

The pursuit continued for six hours as La Rochejaquelein drove the republican flight on Château-Gontier. Here Kléber, Marceau, Blosse and Beaupuy attempted to organise serious resistance. It was probably after 10pm and in complete darkness that the Vendéens approached this town.

Château-Gontier is split by the Mayenne River. The old walled town is on the western bank, on ground rising up from the bridge to the church, with a suburb on the east bank. Once again accounts are confused but in the darkness some events can be pieced together. Stofflet, at the head of his tirailleurs, is said to have slid behind an enemy column, driving them back onto the Mayenne, drowning some and forcing 300 Mayençais to swim for their lives.[27]

The royalists were temporarily held back by two guns that Blosse deployed on high ground overlooking the approach to the bridge, and they found some republicans dug in along the opposite river bank. Kléber desperately tried to organise resistance at the bridge but only 100 men rallied to him, supported by others in surrounding houses.

Surprised that the bridge had not been cut, and fearing a trap, the Vendéens hesitated. At great personal risk La Rochejaquelein seized a standard and led the assault, reputedly crying out, 'Advance my friends, advance! Will you let these men who chased you from your country escape?'[28] Storming over the bridge they seized some cannon and a confused melee developed. La Rochejaquelein called for artillery support and Beauvais appeared with four 4pdrs, two being directed on the Lion d'Angers Gate and two on the church.[29]

Blosse and a handful of chasseurs-à-cheval made a futile attempt to recapture the bridge at the cost of their lives. Thus, said Kléber, 'one of the most brilliant and valiant officers in the army perished.'[30]

Beaupuy reputedly led some regiments towards the bridge but was seriously wounded by a shot that cut through his body. 'I have been unable to gain a victory for the Republic,' he is reported to have said, 'but at least I die for her.'[31] His bloody chemise was taken to his grenadiers to inspire revenge and they placed themselves in ambush in the roads and houses beyond the bridge, firing into the Vendéens from the windows and causing them to hesitate. Kléber joined these troops and the Vendéens at one point wavered but were stabilised by La Rochejaquelein and Stofflet. The ever increasing tide of rebels kept pressing forwards and a separate body appeared and captured the gate on the Craon road, possibly helped by locals.[32] The republicans could take no more and were seen to be routing in several directions. Those on the Lion d'Angers road were pursued until around 11pm.

The Vendéens discovered that their wounded, left behind in Château-Gontier only a few days previously, had all been massacred. There was therefore no appetite to take prisoners.

The Vendéens had achieved an overwhelming victory. The republicans admitted to losing nineteen cannon and plenty of supplies. When they eventually managed to reorganise their army there were only 16,000 in their ranks, implying they suffered around 4,000 casualties. By contrast the Vendéens lost an estimated 400 killed and a further 1,200 wounded.[33]

For the time being the republicans were broken as a fighting force and were scattered far and wide. Only 7,000 were rallied behind the Oudon River by Kléber on the day after the battle. On that same day Kléber wrote to the CPS and acknowledged the outstanding quality of Henri de la Rochejaquelein:

'We faced their truly admirable impetuosity and élan communicated to them by a young man. This young man was Henri de la Rochejaquelein, who was made their general-in-chief after the crossing of the Loire... He demonstrated in this unfortunate battle a military science and aplomb in manoeuvres that we have not seen with the brigands since Torfou.'[34]

'L'Échélle the Incompetent' was sent on leave to Nantes, purportedly to recover his health, but only to take ill and die on 11 November.

The representatives invited Kléber to take command, but he deferred to the more senior Chalbos who became interim commander-in-chief while more formal arrangements were considered.

On 29 October the republicans held a Council of War at Lion d'Angers. Merlin, Turreau and Dembarrère were amongst those eager to strike back at the rebels in Château-Gontier, but it did not take Kléber long to convince them that the army was in no fit state to fight and needed to fall back to Angers to reorganise and be resupplied. The debris of the army therefore pulled back to Angers on 30 October.

Over the next six days Kléber worked tirelessly to rebuild the army. However he was now under close surveillance as in a parting gesture L'Échélle had denounced him as a royalist.[35] Undoubtedly as a deliberate act of spite, orders were given to dissolve the former Army of Mayence once and for all. Kléber was however able to use the demi-brigade system to strengthen less reliable troops with a core of decent battalions. His division was rebuilt to a strength of 7,000 men, formed into the Light Advance Guard under Marigny (now back with the army having been in Nantes) of 1,600 foot and 100 horse, and brigades under Marceau and Canuel. Muller's division was of similar strength and Adjudant General Klinger commanded a reserve of 1,500 men.

The Convention was horrified by news of the defeat and orders were issued to block the Loire crossings to ensure the enemy did not re-cross the river, and scour the Vendée for supplies for the Army of the West. Barère railed against the exaggerated lies, 'half successes' and 'coloured victories' being reported by the generals and civil authorities.[36]

The Vendéen plans after Entrammes

The Vendéens now had options and perhaps the most sensible would have been to re-cross the Loire. However Talmont, and others from north of the river, were pushing for a march on Normandy or Rennes: either might enable them to gain recruits, and a march on Rennes would keep open the option of a march on Nantes or into Britanny. D'Autichamp urged them to seize the moment and march on Paris.

Curiously, almost as if he had been waiting in the wings, it was the influence of another émigré, named Prignet, who settled the debate. He appeared at headquarters with news that help from England was near, even claiming that he had seen their fleet anchored off Portsmouth ready to sail. The possibility of military aid and safe passage for the refugees proved decisive and Prignet set out for Jersey to inform the English that the rebels were marching north.[37]

The appearance of these émigrés at each critical moment seems almost pre-planned by those, such as Talmont, eager to march to the northern coast. How true their reports were is also questionable and raises suspicion that some may have been double-agents.

While in Château-Gontier the Vendéens received news that 5,000 republicans were in Craon under Olagnier and Chambertin. They had been sent there by L'Échélle on the evening of the Battle of Entrammes. La Rochejaquelein decided to seize the opportunity and attacked them on 28 October with 8,000 men.[38] He was accompanied by Stofflet and D'Autichamp.

Craon 28 October

Accounts of this battle are poor.

According to Royalist sources Olagnier and Chambertin believed that resistance would be useless, but were ordered by Méaulle and Esnue-Lavallée, commissaires of the Convention, to cut the bridges on the Château-Gontier to Craon road to obstruct La Rochejaquelein's march. In reality they probably had no time to carry this out, assuming the Vendéens were already on the march.[39]

Beauvais indicated that a large body of troops awaited them at Craon, supported by the levy from surrounding parishes, but held their positions for less than fifteen minutes, their right wing fleeing on the approach of the first Vendéens. He did acknowledge that the republican artillery covered their retreat quite well.[40]

As the Vendéens entered Craon they found that royalist prisoners had been shot just before the republican retreat, and as a consequence few prisoners were taken.[41]

On 29 October La Rochejaquelein returned to Laval and on 1 November the Vendéens began their long march northwards from Laval.

General Lenoir had been ordered to hold Mayenne and had under his command 17,000 completely disorganised levies. He considered resistance futile, due to the dreadful quality of his troops, and as a Vendéen advance party approached he evacuated the town in the direction of Alençon where he managed to rally 6,000 men.[42] The Vendéens marched into Mayenne unopposed.

Ernée 2 November

On the following day the royalist army marched on Ernée. This town was being held by some levy battalions and the 8th Calvados, sent from Fougères on the evening of 1 November, but they abandoned Ernée before the rebels arrived. Fougères then sent the Chasseurs d'Imbert and two guns to replace them and they arrived just as the Vendéen advance guard reached the town. Beauvais said that they did not expect to encounter enemy troops on their march to Ernée so their column was strung out over some distance. Their advance guard was led by some cavalry, followed by some infantry and half a dozen guns, and this small body of troops was soon a considerable distance ahead of the main body of the army.[43]

The rebel cavalry were tying up their horses in Ernée when they were suddenly warned that the chasseurs had entered the western end of the town, so they quickly mounted up and evacuated eastwards. Beauvais was with the advance-guard artillery on a height near Ernée, hidden from view, and the cavalry formed up to his rear.[44] At this location the road narrowed. Beauvais advanced four cannon to counter fire coming from the chasseurs, who had advanced within close range, but the republicans dared not approach any nearer as they could only see a few of the rebels.

As more Vendéen infantry arrived, Beauvais deployed them in ditches and behind hedges on his wings. Soon, with only part of the advance guard present, their infantry went onto the attack, followed up by a cavalry charge. Beauvais pursued the republicans beyond Ernée and when the Chasseurs eventually limped into Fougères they had lost more than half their original strength.

Fougères 3 November

The Vendéens camped in Ernée that night and scoured the area for supplies before marching on Fougères the following day.

The garrison of Fougères was commanded by Adjudant General Brière. Before the encounter at Ernée it was composed of a battalion of the 19th Chasseurs-à-Pied, three battalions of volunteers (6th Côtes-d'Or, 3rd Calvados and the grenadiers and gunners of Coutances), a company of Paris gunners, and 3–4,000 national guards, half of whom were armed with pikes.[45] Their situation was not helped when the commander of the Fougères National Guard was imprisoned as a suspect and, although the available troops totalled 6,500 men, many were new levies.

The rout of Ernée spread alarm in Fougères and the troops spent the night under arms. Campaign guns were placed at all the town's gates and they began constructing entrenchments. Two battalions were deployed over a league to the east, on the Ernée road. The engineer officer, D'Obenheim, prepared some earthworks on high ground near the town and the two battalions were advised that if necessary they could fall back to rally at that position.[46] The Paris gunners deployed in the republican centre with the various battalions to either flank, all covered by poorly constructed earthworks.

Around 2km from Pellerine, the Vendéens clashed with the 19th Chasseurs, and reputedly only a third of them escaped to rout on Fougères, entering by the St-Léonard Gate.[47] None of the troops sent on the Ernée road rallied at the position prepared by D'Obenheim.

The Vendéens marched to Fougères in three columns and at speed. Their weakest column was on the Ernée road while the other two marched along roads to either side. Talmont and 4–500 cavalry were behind the centre. The royalist army soon appeared on the eastern approaches to Fougères. Beauvais recalled that the republicans were deployed in the gardens and behind hedges at the entrance to the town. At about 3.30pm the rebels attacked. They initially faced stubborn resistance and their centre came under sustained fire from the Paris gunners. While this fight was underway the Vendéen cavalry circled around the town to attack via the Rennes road and repulsed 400 men holding the Rennes Gate, forcing them to seek refuge in the château.

The republicans facing the main Vendéen assault were soon breaking up under the strain. D'Obenheim managed to rally some troops at the

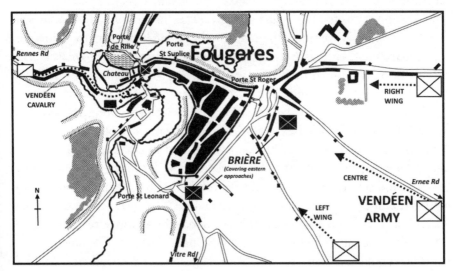

The Assault on Fougères.

Vitré Gate, but they only held their ground for a quarter of an hour and disintegrated when the rebel cavalry appeared to their rear. While most fled on the Vitré and Rennes roads, 100 hid in the town's cellars and attics.[48] After three hours of combat all positions had been seized and all republican guns captured.[49]

Around 800 republicans were made prisoner, and those identified as having previously fought against the Vendéens were shot.[50]

On 4 November, in the parish of La Pellerine between Ernée and Fougères, Lescure succumbed to his wound and was secretly buried.

The Pursuit of the Royalist Army

When the republican army was reorganised in Angers the troops were formed into demi-brigades: not strictly, according to the *Amalgame*, but combining one reliable battalion (whether regular or volunteer) with two less steady battalions. Kléber found time to prepare a valuable treatise detailing how to fight the Vendéens, leaving us with important insights into the tactics used by both sides (see Chapter 3). Rossignol was also notified that he had been appointed to replace L'Échélle as commander-in-chief of the Army of the West, no doubt to the dismay of many of the troops.

At a council of war held on 5 November it was evident that the republicans had no idea where the rebels were or what they now intended. They concluded by a move to cover Le Mans, which they assumed to be at risk, and the following orders were issued: the advance guard (under Marceau and Marigny) was to march via Durtal, La Flèche and Foulletourte, to reach Le Mans for 9 November; the main body of the army was to follow on a day's march to their rear, until nearer the enemy; Lenoir was to march on Le Mans for 8 November, then Bonnétable for the 9th; Danican was to march on Laval, then Ste-Suzanne, for 8 November.

Precautions were also being taken to cover towns along the northern coast:[51] General Thevet-Lessert, with troops from the Côtes-du-Nord, was ordered to cover Dinan; 1,700 troops were sent to cover St-Mâlo, Cancale and Château-Neuf; Tribout was ordered to march toward the same stretch of coast and set out from Brest on 6 November with 4,000 men and 10 guns; and General Sepher (Army of the Cherbourg Coast) was instructed to leave Caen and march on Falaise on 6 November. He was in Viré from 9 to 13 November then marched via Thorigny-Saint-Lô towards Coutance.

The republican army set out from Angers on 6 November. The Light Advance Guard reached Durtal, as did the 2nd Brigade, and the rest of

Kléber's division moved up to Sablé. Muller reached Lion d'Angers, and the Reserve, Membrolle.[52] During 7 November they modified their march on news that the rebels were making for Fougères, being ordered to gather at Laval on 10 November. A council of war decided that they must protect Rennes, to avoid the rebels recruiting from further west, so marched in that direction on 12 November. General Vergnes, the commander in Rennes, had 5–6,000 fit to fight.

The Vendéens in Fougères

After the victory at Fougères, the Vendéens took full advantage of the respite to reorganise their army and carefully plan their move towards a port on the northern coast.[53] The structure of the army was also reorganised (see Appendix 3).

D'Obenheim, who had been captured and was now fighting for the Vendéens, noted that a dozen leaders formed a General Council but none had real authority. Stofflet, by force of character, tended to dominate discussions, supported by half a dozen peasants acting as his adjutants.[54] The army, he said, had little confidence in this Council.

He would later note that D'Autichamp, Scépeaux, Duhoux and Des Essarts were brave and could inspire the troops in battle. He added that Perrault skilfully handled the artillery, which in general was well led, but the individual gun commanders were not well controlled.

During their stay in Fougères a further 1,500 men joined their ranks.[55]

On 6 November the Vendéens marched to Antrain, although Stofflet, opposed to the march north, caused some confusion when he initially set out on the Rennes road. On 7 November they reached Dol. Two days later another council of war was convened as the army was becoming increasingly unsettled the further north they marched.

A letter was dispatched from the Vendéen generals, addressed to George III, appealing for him to keep true to his word and send support quickly as they were now approaching the coast. Émigrés appeared at this council of war, with letters signed by Dresnay (émigré commander in Jersey), countersigned by Pitt and Dundas, promising generous and immediate support if they seized a port.[56]

After acrimonious debate they took D'Obenheim's advice and agreed to march on Granville: a port at the south-western corner of the Cotentin Peninsula, with the potential to provide relatively easy communications with the Channel Islands. The émigrés were sent back with the message that they would signal the capture of Granville by flying a white flag between two black flags, and by three cannon shots separated by two minute intervals.

On 10 November the Vendéen advance guard camped near Pontorson, followed by the rest of the army on the following day. They reached Avranches on 12 November, where they brushed aside limited resistance. General Tribout began his move eastward from Dinan that same day, with his advance guard reaching Dol. Over the next day the royalists rested, and on 14 November a large contingent began its move on Granville.

The Siege of Granville 14 to 15 November

Granville is a walled medieval town perched high on a peninsula of land and with impressive defences. The town had developed beyond these defences at its south-eastern corner. Granville had a population of around 8,500 people at the time of the siege, although many were evacuated before it began. The garrison totalled 5,335 men, of whom 3,183 were armed.[57] They were supported by formidable artillery, totalling 68 guns, with additional support from three gunboats.[58]

On 5 November, Le Carpentier was at Coutances and set out for Granville four days later. To defend Cherbourg he assembled the cavalry of Valognes, Cherbourg and Carentan, and moved them to Saint-Côme-du-Mont, where redoubts and batteries were raised.[59]

Only a portion of the Vendéen army advanced on Granville. Fleuriot remained in Avranches with around half of the troops and most of the artillery train. His role was to protect the refugees and cover the army's rear. Béjarry led the march on Granville with an advance guard of 2-3,000 men, followed by 6-7,000 men under Stofflet, and a similar number under La Rochejaquelein accompanied by part of the artillery train.[60]

Unknown to the Vendéens, Representative Laplanche and General Sepher were marching from Cherbourg to come to the aid of Granville, but were not rushing and seemed to be awaiting events rather than attempting to directly intervene.[61]

Beauvais was clear that only the elite of the army marched on Granville, but no one had indicated how they intended to attack this walled town. He wrote that Des Essarts and several other leaders believed the town would surrender as soon as they appeared, leaving him thinking they must have intelligence from friends within the town he knew nothing about.[62] Around 9am General Peyre, the garrison commander, was given warning that an estimated 15,000 rebels were heading in his direction.

At Croissant, 4km from Granville, the Vendéen advance guard halted to rest and the Vendéens issued a proclamation giving the republicans one hour in which to surrender the town and port to spare it from the ravages of a siege.[63] It was now around 12.30pm.

The Action of La Calvaire

In an astonishingly risky move the republicans decided to send 2,000 men out from Granville in three columns to cover the approaches to the town. Vendéen scouts gave warning of their approach, having spotted the republicans downhill from their position marching on both sides of the road and partially hidden by the terrain. Beauvais estimated them to be within half a cannon's range.[64]

The republican advance guard was led by Adjudant General Vachot and accompanied by some 4pdr guns. They were followed at a distance by the main body under Peyre, General Varin, Commandant Coffy, and Representative Le Carpentier.[65] Peyre made sure every approach to Granville was guarded by parties of troops. Around 1pm Vachot reached the high ground north of the Vendéen position.

On news of the enemy's approach Beauvais convinced La Rochejaquelein to organise two squadrons with infantrymen riding pillion. These would be used to rush the enemy, hopefully cause them to panic, infiltrate the town as they routed, and seize the gates. Beauvais was given command of Bonchamps' cavalry to set about this task.[66]

La Rochejaquelein ordered the cavalry forward to overpower Vachot, with the artillery and infantry instructed to follow on close behind. Some of the Vendéen cavalry were detached to outflank the republicans by heading for Houles. The Vendéens also outflanked the republicans on the Saint-Pair road.[67] Peyre claimed he was quick to notice these moves and sent a cannon and a half battalion of Somme Volunteers to reinforce the post of La Haguette towards the sea.[68] Soon afterwards he sent the rest of this battalion on his left with orders to slip alongside some houses bordering high ground on the Villedieu road, deploy in line in an adjoining field, and fire on the enemy cavalry if they dared approach.

As this order was being given, Peyre noticed Le Carpentier and Varin retiring at the head of a column just as the Vendéen artillery was heard to open up. Varin had been on the St-Pair road and claimed that his careful observation of the enemy columns meant he prevented them out-pacing and cutting off the Somme Battalion, Aunis Battalion and part of the Manche Battalion, deployed under La Roche-Gautier.[69]

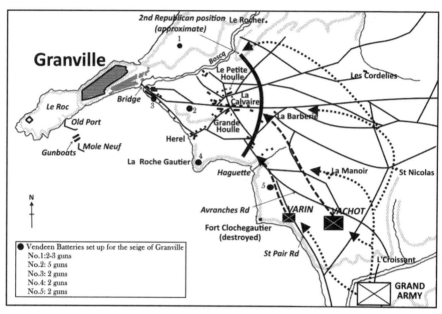

The action at La Calvaire.

It did not take long for Vachot, with only a few hussars and gendarmes and a handful of 4pdrs, to be pressed backwards on La Calvaire; he could do little against the overwhelming enemy forces. Peyre said he had to warn him to pull back to avoid being cut off, and then claimed he now fooled the enemy into thinking they were about to be counter-attacked by sounding the charge all along the front. This, he claimed, stalled them long enough to enable him to disengage and pull back successfully.

The Vendéens claimed the enemy were soon routed and rushed back over the bridge into Granville. They retreated so quickly that they denied Beauvais the opportunity to seize the gates as planned.[70] Chief of Staff Coffy reported that after around two hours of fierce combat they had retreated due to the superiority of the enemy's artillery and their large numbers of cavalry.[71] By 3pm they were safely within the town walls.[72]

The Vendéen advance now came under bombardment from two gunboats in the harbour near Mole-Neuf. Peyre says the principal objective of these gunboats was to sweep the area around the bridge over the Boscq, the shore between that bridge and the old port, and to supress the fire from a Vendéen battery set up near La Haguette.[73] Two 18pdrs covered the Rue des Juifs, although these guns reputedly opened up prematurely, killing troops from both sides.[74]

While this action progressed along the Rue des Juifs, Vendéens were also following other routes to infiltrate the lower town.[75] In an astonishing oversight, or act of treachery, no one could find the key to the entrance in the curtain wall between the two demi-bastions on the Isthmus, so the republicans were forced to improvise and block the entrance as best they could.

Peyre reported that he had deployed three 8pdrs and a 12pdr on the jetty of the old port to support the gunboats; the old quay had been fortified to prevent the enemy from seizing the Esplanade de Roc, and the houses of these old quays were occupied by the 9th Manche.[76]

The first part of the action was over and the siege was now about to commence, but when the Vendéens looked out to sea no English ships could be seen.

The Siege

The Vendéen established their headquarters at La Calvaire and Beauvais indicated that three Vendéen batteries were set up, but they only had 4pdrs, 8pdrs, and a couple of 12pdrs: all too weak for a siege.

A contemporary sketch of the siege shows five guns deployed on high ground west of Grande-Houle, two closer to the town near the west coast, and three north of the Boscq Stream.[77] Peyre also mentions two guns on the south-east reverse of the height at La Haguette, two on the site of the old fort of La Roche-Gautier, and two north of the Boscq. In all the rebels only had fifteen guns and Beauvais set up some bellows to produce heated shot.

Although the republicans had a vast superiority in cannon, many would have been in fixed positions facing away from the eastern approach to Granville. There were a number of cannon deployed behind a barbette[78] near the main gate at the west end of the Rue des Juifs. This barbette was on a raised earth platform (a cavalier), but as it was overlooked by nearby houses on the Rue des Juifs it quickly became vulnerable to snipers and those manning it took punishing losses.

Having suppressed the fire from this battery the Vendéens focused their efforts towards the nearby battery of Marché, where they were planning to undertake their first assault.[79] It was manned by naval gunners and comprised two 24pdrs behind a hastily constructed knee-high parapet.[80] Once again heavy casualties were inflicted and by 9pm the Vendéens were infiltrating the lower defences around the Isthmus and north of the Rue des Juifs.

Unperturbed by a fusillade from the ramparts, Forestier led his men in an assault, but came up against walls fifteen metres in height. The ladders from nearby houses were found to be too short and they were forced to use bayonets hammered between the stones to improvise steps. Some managed to climb up and over the ramparts, but Forestier fell wounded and the demoralised attackers withdrew, sliding down the steep banks north of the Rue des Juifs. Near to 300 Vendéens ended up piled in a tangle of bodies in the huge ditch at the bottom.[81] Forestier remained unconscious in the ditch for some time before he was evacuated to safety.

The rebels had managed to move onto the covered way near to the demi-bastions and curtain wall on the Isthmus. Rochejaquelein made a tentative attempt to attack these defences but the fighting soon degenerated into an intermittent exchange of gunfire and shouted insults.

After dark the Vendéens attempted to move a 12pdr towards the town gate, but when the limber horses were killed at the bridge they were forced to give up.[82]

At around 2am Peyre ordered red-hot shot to be prepared and fired into the suburbs to clear the enemy from these positions, but without a furnace to heat the shot it took some time to carry out this order. At 4am he repeated the order in writing. Property near the ramparts eventually caught

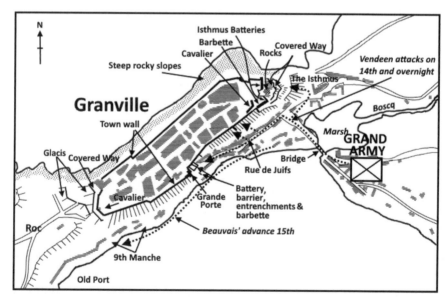

The Seige of Granville.

fire, but at more risk to the republicans as the wind was mainly blowing in their direction.[83]

During the night the Vendéens attempted more than one assault on the Isthmus, but a full moon and clear sky meant they could be easily spotted. Beauvais went to the Isthmus at 10pm and found La Rochejaquelein standing upright and exposed, firing on the republicans, until he managed to persuade him to take cover. Beauvais indicated that from the covered way near the demi-bastions the men could open fire on the ramparts, and using this covering fire they could then deploy ladders and storm the defences. By making diversionary attacks elsewhere it was felt this might just succeed, so this was the plan agreed for the following day.[84]

All through the night Peyre and his staff toured the defences encouraging the men. An intermittent cannonade continued but infantry fire largely petered out and many Vendéens went in search of sustenance and sleep.

15 November

As the second day arrived Beauvais went to the headquarters. The news was discouraging. Although their losses in men were not considered high, they had lost fifteen distinguished officers. Marigny had also been forced to return to Avranches to secure more ammunition, leading to further delays.

Looking across the port, Beauvais noticed that the tide was out, and suggested crossing this area to attack the town from the high ground at Le Roc. They decided to carry out this attack immediately. Experience had taught them that their men were not intimidated by cannon fire and, once they were at the base of Le Roc, Beauvais believed they would be under cover. He also mistakenly thought the area would only be lightly defended. Stofflet was put in command of this attack, with Beauvais accompanying him to help identify the easiest route. The men assigned to this task were assembled at the battery at Lude.[85]

Unknown to Beauvais, there was no access from Le Roc to the town, which was also defended by outworks and ramparts. D'Obenheim was familiar with the town's defences so must have known this, so his loyalty to the Vendéens was evidently questionable.

When the troops selected for this attack were pulled back from the front line, others thought they were retreating and took flight. This flight left the selected troops thinking an enemy army must be approaching, only adding to the panic. Beauvais said he retained fewer than 100 men to make the attack.[86] This small group began their advance and confronted the 9th

Manche dug into the houses along the quay. Facing artillery, infantry, and gunboats this was a pointless enterprise and they were forced to take cover behind grounded boats. When at last they managed to reach Le Roc it became evident that it would not be easy to climb its steep slopes.

The Vendéens had been unnerved by troops seen approaching Granville earlier in the day. They turned out to be levies from surrounding communes who withdrew once they realised the size of the royalist army. However, with no sight of the English Fleet, a lack of siege equipment, and the failure of the first day's attacks, the troops were demoralised and began leaving in large numbers.

Rumours had spread that Talmont and other officers were aiming to take ship to England, and that is why they had marched to Granville. With the command structure breaking down, La Rochejaquelein conceded to the inevitable and ordered the retreat around 1pm.

The batteries at La Calvaire and on the old Coutances road continued to fire until 5pm to cover the withdrawal of the army.[87] As night fell on 15 November the republicans in Granville were content to sit tight.

Béjarry and his men had not been made aware of the army's retreat and discovered at 10am on 16 November that they were alone before the town. Setting off at some risk, they eventually caught up with the army when it reached Pontorson.

Losses totalled around 400 republicans killed and wounded and 600 Vendéens killed.[88] Beauvais regretted the loss of several cannon that were abandoned in the hasty retreat.

Where were the English?

The failure of the English to appear has been the cause of acrimonious debate. They are blamed for having betrayed the rebels and missed a perfect opportunity to come to their aid. Unfortunately the promises given by the émigrés were exaggerated and the English were far from ready to offer the required support as quickly as the rebels were led to believe.

While the Siege of Granville was underway the Earl of Moira was about to be appointed commander of the planned expedition. He was in Portsmouth on 24 November, nine days *after* the siege had ended, when he received his orders and was appointed major general of forces destined for the expedition. These comprised four brigades of infantry, totalling less than 6,000 men, supported by ten cannon. They were to be reinforced by a Hessian contingent, totalling a further 3,500 infantry and 500 cavalry, but on

24 November these Hessians were still with the Duke of York on mainland Europe.

On 31 November, Admiral McBride passed through the Needles and out into the Channel.

Lieutenant Charles Stewart of the 28th Foot picks up the story:[89]

'2 December: At daylight was off Cherbourg...the admiral sent the *Druid* and *Eurydice* frigates close under the land...in hopes that the royalists might have possession of some tenable port, or to receive and answer concerted signals, but instead the frigates were fired on from two small batteries close on the shore. We have since learnt that the *carmagnoles* were much alarmed at so unexpected a visit as we were. Along the shores of a rich and fertile looking country we could perceive the signals of alarm spreading from one post to another; being thus disappointed we shaped our course for Guernsey at 12 o'clock.'

He summed up what seemed a half-hearted attempt at an invasion as follows:

'Thus ended...the Expedition for the Coast of France...an expedition which upon its departure from England the greatest advantages were hoped for..., there remains but little doubt that the royalists of France were too sanguine in their expectations, and represented to the government of Britain the situation of their affairs in a far more flattering and forward state than what they actually were.

'It requires not one moment's reflection to decide on the impossibility of eleven British battalions and five thousand Hessians, the latter of which had not at this time arrived, attempting an invasion without prompt, united, and vigorous assistance from those to whose aid they had come...they possessed not a single port upon their coast, and along the whole shore from Cherbourg to St-Mâlo, nothing was observed but the tricolor flag...and moreover it was said, that there reigned in the army of the royalists that spirit of equality so destructive of good order and military discipline; their chiefs were even afraid to promise the intended succour from England and lead them to the coast lest should the British forces not that moment be in sight they might fall victims to the fury of their soldiers, as men designed to betray them.'

On 16 December Moira advised McBride that they had received news of the royalists' retreat on the Loire.[90] Although he remained in the Channel Islands until the end of the year, still hopeful of being able to provide some assistance, on 17 December the expeditionary force set sail and returned to Spithead.

The commander of the British forces in the Channel Islands questioned the credibility of Monsieur de Solérac, suggesting he had betrayed the royalists at the attack on Granville.[91]

This whole debacle was caused by a failure of the British government to fully comprehend, or be fully convinced by, the news filtering across the Channel. When at long last an expedition sailed, it was already three weeks too late. In the circumstances the conclusions penned by Lieutenant Charles Stewart could deservedly be met with derision by the Vendéens.

As a final painful reminder of the pitifully sluggish response by the British it was only on 4 January 1794 that the convoy from Ostend carrying the Hessian troops anchored in Spithead.

Mutiny

The Siege of Granville had failed and on 16 November elements within the royalist army mutinied. A breakdown of trust was already evident before Granville and may have influenced the decision to keep a large part of the army at Avranches during the battle. Some Vendéens were even boasting that they could have taken Granville but decided not to because they believed the rumours that their leaders would then desert them with their 'fine ladies'.[92]

Small groups of peasants began to march south, and while a level of order was restored thanks to the intervention of Abbé Bernier, the bulk of the army refused to follow an order by La Rochejaquelein to march on Caen and remained in Avranches on 17 November.

In spite of this disobedience, La Rochejaquelein, Stofflet and D'Autichamp set out in the direction of Caen, but followed by less than 1,000 men. Stofflet, furious with this setback, was nevertheless determined to head for a port and had his eyes on Cherbourg. They managed to reach Villedieu, and while La Rochejaquelein returned to Avranches that same evening and re-joined the troops in time to lead them into combat at Pontorson, Stofflet only pulled back on the following day. This was crucial for what now followed, as he was in Avranches when news came in that a mounted party led by Talmont was reportedly heading for the coast.

Talmont and a group of around twenty men, women and children, instead of marching south with the army, did indeed head towards the coast west of Avranches between midnight and 1am on 19 November. Talmont appears to have prearranged transport to Jersey.

It is true that Talmont, being from the high nobility, would have made an excellent ambassador for the Vendéen cause. This had been considered at the council of war in Fougères, but the aim had also been to transport the refugees to safety at the same time.[93]

Stofflet managed to seize them before they could escape and, although there is some doubt over what followed, one source suggests that Talmont was brought before Stofflet and accused of cowardice and treachery and told he would be put on trial. Marsonnière may even have drawn his sword and advanced towards Talmont declaring, 'If it wasn't for respect for your bloodline, I'd run you through with my sabre.'[94]

Talmont had gained a reputation as a womaniser which, according to Madame de la Rochejaquelein, dishonoured the Catholic cause and he now lost what respect he had left. However, whether he was aiming to desert or, as he claimed, simply escorting others to safety, he was to play a crucial role in saving the army over the next few days.

Stofflet led the rearguard out of Avranches early on 19 November and with the republicans closing in, the Vendéen leaders had to urgently regain control of their men if the army and refugees were to survive the trap closing around them.

Chapter 14

The Race to the Loire

W hile the Vendéens were before Granville, republican forces had indeed been closing in. Rossignol's army reached Rennes by 15 November where orders were given to merge the troops in Rennes with his own.

Rossignol's army was now reformed under Divisional Generals Kléber and Muller, and brigades under Marigny, Marceau, Boucret, Legros, Westermann, Canuel, Chambertin, Amey and Klinger: in total 21,000 men. Chalbos was granted a period of sick leave and Kléber confessed to being in despair having 'never seen a collection of men with such little ability to lead troops'.[1]

Informed that the rebels were before Granville, they were ordered to march on the Fougères and Antrain roads (the stronger column, the Army of the West, taking the Antrain road). Sepher was instructed to move on Viré and Ville-Dieu; Tribout was ordered to hold Dol; and General Cadene, with 2,500 troops and support from local national guards, was ordered to take command in St-Mâlo. General of Division Tribout was currently in Dol and Dinan with 4,400 men, and Sepher was approaching Coutances with 6,000 men.

Kléber reached Saint-Aubin d'Andigné on 16 November in dreadful weather. On news that the Vendéens had failed in their assault and were moving back on Avranches, a large part of the republican army concentrated around Antrain on 18 November: Marceau at Tremblay; Chambertin at Sacey; Marigny's cavalry at Montanel, and his infantry at Saint-Ouen-de-la-Roërie.

Rossignol's aim was to cover Antrain and enable the army to scout in the direction of Avranches. He sent troops to check the roads towards Pontorson, the Selune crossings, and bridges at Bault, Ducey and Pontaubault. The Pontaubault Bridge had been partially broken by the rebels, so engineers were dispatched to report on the state of alternative routes.[2] General Marigny used the opportunity to distribute printed proclamations amongst troops from the former Légion-de-la-Fraternité who had left rebel ranks. These men were now returned to the Vendéen army to lure more men to desert.

On 18 November Rossignol sent Canuel and Amey on the Fougères road to cover St-James, march around the rebel left flank, and hinder any attempt to move in that direction. With Tribout holding the enemy's western flank, he was ready to march on Avranches on the following day.

The Vendéens were evidently marching into a trap. Apart from 10,000 republican troops in the vicinity of Antrain, Tribout was approaching Pontorson with 4,400, Peyre was in Avranches with 5,000, Sepher was at Coutances with 6,000, and 8,000 were covering the Fougères road under Amey and Chambertin: in all around 34,000 men. However, although Sepher had marched towards Granville on 16 November, on news that the siege had lifted, he was ordered back to Coutances to cover Cherbourg and would remain there until 23 November. Only then would he march on Avranches.

Pontorson 18 November

Tribout reached Pontorson on 17 November. Following days of rainfall the roads were in a terrible condition and the fields flooded. There was torrential rain on the evening of 18 November, and as the Vendéens approached Pontorson they soon became aware of the presence of republican troops.

The wider area around Pontorson, south of the famous landmark of Mont-St-Michel, is largely flat. The landscape was broken up into a grid of hedged fields, and the main road to Dol through Pontorson runs east to west and slopes gradually downhill towards the River Couesnon. Beyond the town, to north and south, the landscape dips downhill, providing plenty of opportunity for the rebels to slide unnoticed around the republican flanks.

Tribout had deployed in line behind hedgerows at Caugé, a village close to the eastern edge of Pontorson. He said four of his seven guns were placed on the St James road, one in front of the right of his line and the other two behind the Couesnon Bridge.[3] He deployed a long line of skirmishers on the northern and southern flanks of the town and kept small reserves in the town and on the west bank of the Couesnon River.

Vendéen troops under Forestier overpowered a small advance guard sent by Tribout on the Avranches road. Thinking the road ahead was now clear they were surprised to come face to face with republicans deployed in advance of Pontorson. Forestier goaded the peasants into action by saying they had abandoned their leaders at Granville so he wanted to see what they could do now.[4]

Around 1km from the republicans many of the rebels split into two columns to march around Tribout's flanks and, following a lively

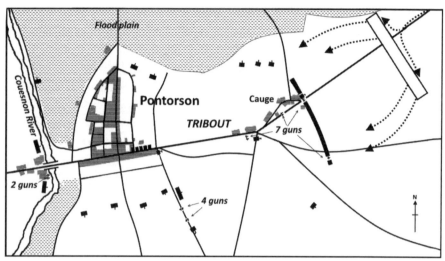

The Battle of Pontorson based on a contemporary map.

cannonade, some deployed behind an embankment to fire on the enemy.[5] After some hesitation they were spurred into action by the appearance of La Rochejaquelein in person and were soon up against the hedgerow screening the enemy.[6] The republicans had been outflanked and were now facing a withering fusillade from around 6,000 men of the highly experienced Vendéen advance guard, and during the battle perhaps 2–3,000 more rebels arrived to join in the combat.

Tribout claimed that the battle began around 4pm; with sunset around that time, and with clouds overhead, almost the entire battle would have taken place in the dark.[7]

Unfamiliar with Vendéen tactics, Tribout's troops formed square to resist the assaults coming in from all sides. In spite of taking heavy losses they hung on until about 7.30pm, by which time their artillery had used up their ammunition and they were forced back.

The Vendéens now closed in and accounts talk of a mêlée lasting for around an hour, until the republicans could take no more and gave way. Many were cut down in the rout that followed.

Some Vendéens bypassed Pontorson and cut off Tribout's line of retreat at the Couesnon Bridge, leaving part of the republican army encircled within Pontorson itself. Towards 9pm, thanks to moonlight from a break in the clouds, some republicans counter-attacked the Vendéen left flank, causing rebels to take cover behind some hedges. La Rochejaquelein took immediate control and led them back into the attack, although some republicans had managed to escape in the direction of Antrain.[8]

Tribout's troops had taken punishing losses and the main road through the town was strewn with their dead. Madame de la Rochejaquelein arrived as the battle ended and before the dead had been cleared off the road. Her coach jolted over their bodies to the sound of breaking bones.[9]

The Vendéens were delighted to find a large supply of bread, shoes and trousers. They captured all of Tribout's artillery, several caissons, and some flags. Their own casualties were reported to be light.

Tribout blamed the cavalry for his defeat, saying they deserted the army at the start of the battle and left the rest of his troops exposed. Kléber, however, put it down to Tribout's incompetence. All Tribout should have done, he said, was hold the line of the River Couesnon, but against 'all the rules of war' he deployed where his flanks were exposed and in terrain perfectly suited to rebel tactics. Instead of overseeing the battle, Tribout was reputedly found with his main battery passing grapeshot to his gunners.[10]

In Tribout's defence, he had sent urgent messages to Antrain as soon as he became aware that the Vendéens were marching in his direction. Kléber would have heard the sound of battle as he was only 12km away. However Chambertin had been sent towards Pontorson that same morning but fell back due to the awful state of the roads. So either the bad roads, or Kléber's excessive caution, contributed to Tribout's defeat.

The Vendéens had recently discovered that the republicans had massacred 800 prisoners and demanded that those captured at Pontorson be put to death. In spite of some resistance, nearly all were executed the next day.[11]

On 19 November the rest of the Vendéen army arrived from Avranches. Tribout, meanwhile, fell back to Dinan where he would be reinforced by troops from St-Mâlo, but would take no part in the fighting over the next few days.[12] After nightfall the Vendéens headed for Dol and drifted in throughout 20 November. The Vendéen artillery train was lined up along the main road and the refugees and troops sought food, shelter, and sleep.

On the march towards Dol, La Rochejaquelein had set out with a handful of men to scout the road ahead. Encountering some enemy cavalry he was forced to cut his way out to escape.[13]

Dol-Antrain 20 to 23 November 1793

At a council of war on 19 November, Kléber presented a plan that aimed to prevent the rebels obtaining supplies, close in on them using four mutually supporting columns, and throw them on the sea.[14] The representatives accepted this plan, and orders were being issued, when an emotive letter arrived from Westermann announcing that he was marching to attack the Vendéens who were reported to be in a terrible state in Dol. He claimed that if he was supported by a column on the Antrain road, Dol would become 'the last tomb of the rebels'. The representatives enthusiastically acted on this letter, immediately cancelled Kléber's plan, and at midnight ordered Marceau to prepare to march on Dol.

The Terrain

The weather compounded terrain already difficult for artillery, cavalry and regular manoeuvres. The approach to Dol from Pontorson was formed by a series of hills and valleys with most of the country broken up into small irregular fields. The Antrain road, although less hilly, was not dissimilar in the area west of Trans. The valleys were generally wooded and marshy, and the only open land consisted of patches of heathland on high ground. However, although this type of terrain favoured the Vendéens, Dol was the last town before the wide plain to the sea.

The series of engagements over 20-23 November make up the greatest single battle of the counter-revolution in the west of France and witnessed some of the most ferocious fighting of the revolutionary war. The chronology below highlights the key phases and demonstrates the fighting skills of the Royalist elite, honed over eight months of continual warfare. The accounts by Kléber and Savary are particularly valuable and many of the place names they describe have been identified in Jamaux's work on the battle.

Night of 20 to 21 November

Between 6 and 7pm Marigny and Decaen, with 400 cavalry, 300 infantry, three cannon and a howitzer, launched a surprise attack on Dol from the Pontorson road. They were quickly beaten back but had now warned the Vendéens that the enemy were on their way. Towards 10pm part of their army marched out and deployed near the eastern edge of Dol: Stofflet, D'Autichamp and Talmont with 3,000 men and thirty cannons on the Antrain road, and La Rochejaquelein, probably with a similar number, on the Pontorson road.[15]

Westermann and Marigny now linked up near Begauds to await Marceau's approach on the Antrain road. Possibly provoked by the

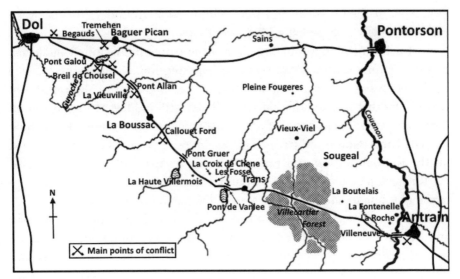

The landscape for the Battles of Dol-Antrain.

Vendéens, Westermann's troops advanced around 1am and encountered La Rochejaquelein's forces close to Dol, but quickly retreated to Baguer-Pican against overwhelming numbers. Westermann now deployed near large bivouac fires at Tremehen, but these fires only served to illuminate their positions. By 3am they were in full retreat eastwards, closely pursued by some Vendéens under La Rochejaquelein. Westermann eventually rallied at around 6am, about 2km west of Pontorson, having lost an 8pdr and two howitzers.

Around 3am Stofflet began to advance on the Antrain road and about an hour later encountered Marceau's troops marching through Pont Galou.[16] Quickly deploying into line, Marceau would fight for around three hours shrouded in darkness and thick fog.

Daytime 21 November

Towards 7am La Rochejaquelein returned to his original position, followed by successive detachments. He now moved to support Stofflet.

Aware of his precarious position, Marceau skilfully pulled back to better positions behind the Guyoche. Unknown to Marceau the fog now helped him as Stofflet's force had mistaken its own cavalry, returning to Dol for munitions, for the enemy's and most of his men broke and fled to Dol. Talmont, 400 Chouans and a handful of cannon held their ground along the west bank of the Guyoche and were reinforced at around 7.30–8am by La Rochejaquelein with perhaps 700 more troops.[17]

La Rochejaquelein was in despair over the army's predicament and began to advance on a causeway between the opposing forces, intent on dying in battle. He was restrained and went on to lead 300 men in the capture of two 12pdrs that blocked this causeway. Then, still hidden by fog, he moved north along the west bank of the Guyoche and after some skirmishing launched an assault on Marceau's larger force. The 12pdrs had been turned on the Republican left and rallied Vendéen troops had by now increased La Rochejaquelein's strength. Around 10am Marceau faltered under the onslaught, but stabilised his line a mere 150 paces further east.[18]

Both sides increased in numbers as the Vendéens rallied more men and Muller's division arrived to support Marceau. Muller, arguably more incompetent than L'Échélle and Santerre, was drunk, and his division blundered into Marceau's position causing complete chaos. Around 11.30am Kléber and Rossignol arrived and issued orders to pull back to better positions further east. This time the fog appears to have hidden the Republican vulnerability from the Vendéens.

Kléber had already deployed 4,000 men at Pont Allan, but on seeing troops retreating in their direction, these troops routed. Some Vendéens cautiously followed but stopped in the vicinity of Pont du Gruer around 4pm.[19] Kléber managed to rally the army and ordered Chambertin to replace Marceau's tired brigade.

Night of 21 to 22 November

During the night, the Vendéens drifted back to Dol. Thousands had earlier retreated west of the Dol, in company with many of the refugees, and also returned to the town. While celebrating their survival there was a brief panic when outlying troops from Klinger's column were spotted some distance south of Dol. They had probably been deployed to block the rebels' line of retreat in that direction rather than engage in any aggressive action.

A more defensive plan was now put forward by Kléber, and agreed, but while Kléber and Prieur de la Marne issued orders in the early hours for all forces to fall back on Antrain, Westermann was advancing once again, this time supported by Marigny and Amey.

Marigny's advance guard, followed some time later by Westermann and Amey, left Pontorson at 10pm and occupied Baguer-Pican at 4am. At 4.30am his scouts prudently advanced on Dol and were surprised to hear the call to arms being beaten. This was Stofflet calling everyone to assemble ready to leave Dol. They were led by the elite troops, followed by the artillery, the non-combatants, and finally a rearguard under Marigny. Around 7.30am the Vendéens set out on the Antrain road, unaware of the enemy's proximity. At 8am, with their advance guard around the Clos du Gibet, they were suddenly ordered to halt as reports arrived that Westermann was on their northern flank.[20]

While the bulk of the Vendéens remained on the Antrain road, La Rochejaquelein peeled off with some of his best officers and a body of troops. Towards 8.30am Vendéen cavalry threw panic among the republican scouts and Amey's troops fled on sight of the enemy. This rout was emulated by the other republicans, who failed in an attempt to rally north of Baguer-Pican, and were now pursued beyond Pontorson. The republicans on this flank lost all their cannon and both Marigny and Westermann narrowly avoided capture.

Daytime 22 November

Around 8.30am the main republican army at Trans was preparing to retire on Antrain when they heard the cannonade at Baguer-Pican, but with the staff, generals and representatives split between Trans, Antrain and elsewhere it took some time to agree what to do. Around 10am Kléber set out with sixty hussars to scout towards Dol. Stofflet, meanwhile, had deployed the bulk of their army on the spine of high ground amidst the scene of the previous day's battle.

At about 10.30am Kléber scouted their position and decided it was safer to deploy further east. The Vendéens were content to follow the hussars (who were deliberately slowing their advance) while Kléber sent orders to Chambertin to deploy at Pont Allan.

By 11.45am this deployment was complete, but the subsequent encounter did not last long. The Regiment la Reine refused to fire and fled. Nattes, attempting an outflanking manoeuvre on the Vendéen left, was also abandoned by his troops. The republicans had in fact been outflanked by a body of cavalry on their right, while Chambertin's left flank was threatened by Vendéen tirailleurs. Kléber immediately set about delaying the Vendéen advance while calling up more troops, this time aiming to deploy near the Callouet Ford.[21]

Canuel's experienced troops arrived first and Kléber deployed them to cover the successive deployment of the rest of the army. Stofflet and Talmont spread out opposite and harangued their troops.

This battle began at about 12.30pm (around the time La Rochejaquelein was entering Pontorson). The Vendéens now faced their greatest test as cannon bombarded their dense ranks. Their own artillery replied in kind but the battle appears to have reached a stalemate. After around three hours the republicans were sufficiently confident to deploy, ready to charge in with the bayonet. With perfect timing, La Rochejaquelein, Forestier, and 2,000 troops now appeared on the republican right flank and took them by complete surprise. The Vendéens may have simultaneously attacked their enemy's left flank (possibly under Marigny). When some battalions were being moved from their front to redeploy against La Rochejaquelein others mistook this for a retreat and panic set in. Their subsequent withdrawal was covered by a combined grenadier battalion.

Night of 22 to 23 November

The Vendéens pursued into the night, with the grenadiers stubbornly fighting swarms of enemy tirailleurs until they were thrown into disorder around 9pm.

As Chambertin's Light Advance Guard rallied at La Vaulée, Kléber gave orders to hold that crossing for half an hour to enable the army to escape, but two 8pdrs deployed by La Rochejaquelein soon broke them up. By 9.30pm the republicans were routing through the Forest of Villecartier.

The bulk of the republican army retreated beyond Antrain. Marceau, however, assembled a mixed body of infantry from various units on the banks of the Couanon, replacing Canuel's troops who had withdrawn from that position without orders. A fierce fight now developed in the early hours of 23 November around the various entrances to Antrain, involving perhaps 4,000 Vendéens and Chouans against a few hundred republicans. Before Forestier could get into position to block the enemy's retreat however, other Vendéens stormed into Antrain and routed the republicans.

By 2am the battle was over and a half-hearted pursuit began on the Rennes road, petering out towards 3am. During the night Dol was evacuated by the Vendéen rearguard and refugees, and by noon on 23 November the last rebel troops drifted into Antrain.

The republicans probably suffered in excess of 5,000 killed or wounded and the Vendéen victory is all the more remarkable considering their desperate plight.

The Vendéen march on Angers, and reorganisation of the Republican Army

The republican army took the road south, cutting the bridge at Romazy behind them, and reaching Rennes on 23 November. That same day the Vendéen advance guard arrived in Fougères, followed by the rest of their army on 24 November.

Rossignol tendered his resignation but it was refused. At a council of war it was agreed that the wounded would be evacuated to Nantes and the arsenal in Rennes moved two leagues in that direction. Kléber recalled with distaste that Prieur de la Marne philosophically announced that each republican defeat increased rebel losses and, as they had less opportunity to replenish their ranks, this could only benefit the republican cause.[22]

Rossignol wrote to the commanders in Laval (Danican), Coutances (Sepher), Granville (Peyre), Dinan (Tribout), Angers (Fabrefond), Saumur (Commaire), Le Mans (Chabot) and Nantes (Vimeux). He informed them of the recent defeat and ordered them all to be ready to stop the enemy.

Having made preparations to cover the approach from Antrain to Rennes, the republicans held a further council of war on 25 November. Following Kléber's advice the army's command structure was changed to ensure a single overall commander, and generals in command of the infantry, cavalry and artillery. Another general was made responsible for the Rennes garrison and local policing. Under Rossignol's overall command Marceau was assigned the infantry, Westermann the cavalry, Debilly the artillery and Damas the Rennes garrison. Kléber, Marceau's friend, recognised that Marceau had the charisma, courage and ability, to which he might add his own coolness of character and calming influence.[23] It is curious that throughout his time in the Vendéen War Kléber repeatedly declined the most senior roles, always finding an excuse for others to be promoted in his place. Self-preservation seems the only logical justification for his actions.

When Sepher arrived in Rennes he was immediately dismissed for having failed to support Rossignol at the Battle of Dol–Antrain and would be replaced by Tilly. A further council of war was held on 28 November, following news that the rebels seemed to be heading for Angers, and orders were issued for the army to march on Châteaubriand. When Tribout arrived in Rennes he was ordered to remain there with his troops, while Tilly and Westermann were dispatched to Châteaubriand two days behind the main army. To gauge the tension at Republican headquarters, Prieur loudly proclaimed that even if Rossignol lost twenty battles he would remain 'the cherished child of the Revolution and elder son of the Committee of Public Safety'.[24] Yet Rossignol did not march with the army but remained in Rennes.

The army reached Châteaubriand on the evening of 30 November to news that Angers was under direct threat. Marceau immediately wrote to Rossignol asking for orders, but none were forthcoming. Early on 2 December he again asked for orders, indicating that Angers was now under siege, but Rossignol's only response was to say he would join them on the following day.

Rossignol had been too engrossed in political manoeuvring with Bourbotte, Prieur and Turreau against Danton's friend Westermann, who they considered to be unprincipled and against wnom Rossignol still bore a personal grudge. Late on 3 December Rossignol and the representatives arrived at Châteaubriand, and when asked why he had not ordered the march on Angers, the commander-in-chief simply blamed Marceau. After an angry confrontation Prieur concluded that it was less Marceau's fault but rather Kléber's, and announced that they would set up a military tribunal and have him guillotined.[25]

When Marceau passed on this news to Kléber he was furious, and in a state of near despair he confronted the representatives and told them some home truths about Rossignol. Their response was to order both Kléber and Marceau to march forthwith, and Rossignol was sent back to Rennes where he was quietly sidelined. At midnight, between 3 and 4 December, the army was on the march and great fires were lit along the way to provide moments of respite during a very cold night.

The Vendéens meanwhile had set out from Fougères on 25 November, passed through Ernée with their advance guard, and reached Mayenne that same day. Dysentery was taking hold as the weather closed in and many refugees and stragglers fell behind. It became a common sight to see bodies by the side of the road.

Their best cavalry resembled a band of pirates: each trooper armed with swords, carbines and several pistols, and many dressed in captured overcoats.[26] A Council of War held in Mayenne on 26 November concluded with an agreement to march on Angers to force a breakthrough to the Vendée.

On 27 November the first of the rebels reached Laval and the rest drifted in over the following day; their rear was now continually harassed by 300 horse and 100 foot under Marigny and Decaen.

As the Vendéens advanced, so Danican dropped back towards Angers. On 29 November the rebels covered a considerable distance to reach Sablé and arrived at La Flèche on the following day, where they rested on 1 December.

Never was the army so eager to march: both to escape the republicans and to get back to their home territory.

On 2 December they passed through Durtal and camped that evening under heavy rain around 10km north-east of Angers.

The Siege of Angers 3 to 4 December

The garrison of Angers was about 4,000 strong, including Boucret's Brigade that had been dispatched from Rennes on 26 November, and Danican's 2,000 troops who arrived two days before the siege.[27] General Beaupuy, still recovering from the wound received at Entrammes, was also present.

Angers was surrounded by medieval walls interspersed with fifty-seven towers and many gateways, although the Vendéens only attempted to attack the part of the city on the east bank of the River Maine. The republicans had hastily walled up the Port Cupif and Port Saint-Michel, and had patched up areas of the town walls in particularly poor condition. They deployed six guns at the Port Cupif (two 8pdrs and four 4pdrs), a 36pdr at the Haute-Châine, and one in a redoubt on the opposite bank. The weakest points were protected by large ditches and earth ramparts. At the Port Cupif they constructed an inner defensive wall in dry stone, and two great ditches were cut on the Paris road, roughly 2km from the city, and another on the Saint-Serge Quay.[28] A cutting was also made on the La Flèche road around a kilometre from Angers, served by two 4pdrs.[29]

The republican troops included two battalions of the 28th Line, one battalion of the 29th, one of the 78th Line, the 5th Paris, the Battalion de l'Unité, and a battalion of Veterans; all under the command of Danican and Boucret. The Angers National Guard was commanded by Captain Ménard who expressed concern that they did not have enough men to hold the length of the town's walls.[30] They had few cavalry.

Beaupuy played an important role advising on the defences and instructed the troops to place sacks of earth on the parapet to absorb enemy musket fire. However the defences were still incomplete when the Vendéens arrived.

Marigny filled in the ditches near Mortiers to enable the Vendéen artillery to move forwards and their army arrived under the walls of Angers early on 3 December.[31] Around 9.30am part of their army was seen heading towards the Port Cupif.[32] This was considered the weakest point of the city and suggests the Vendéens may have had some prior knowledge from their many sympathisers within Angers.

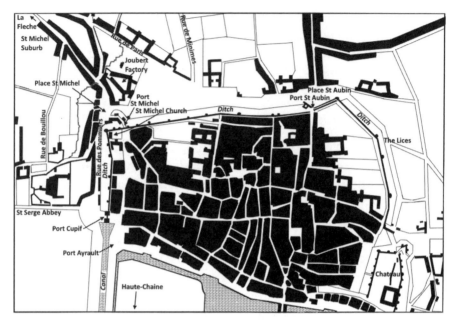

The Vendéen Assaults on Angers.

Their baggage was left around a kilometre back on the main road and the cavalry dismounted to join with the infantry. All those not fighting dispersed to find shelter and food, cramming into the buildings in the eastern suburbs.

Deniau indicates that the Vendéens deployed 8pdrs in the Rue des Pommiers, a cannon on the Rue de Paris, another on the Rue de Bouillou, and one above the course of the Pigeon Stream, near to a mill.[33]

The Departmental authorities recorded that the rebels attacked the Port Cupif 'with audacity in spite of a well sustained fire-by-file and that of two 4pdrs posted on the ramparts'.[34] The attack failed.

By 11.30am the Vendéen rearguard had arrived and moved into the area around the Joubert Factory and the vicinity of the Minimes, preparatory to attacking the Port St-Michel. Some guns were pushed forwards to target this entrance.[35]

A column of royalists, deployed on a nearby road ready to make an assault on this gate, was taking casualties from the republicans around the St-Michel Church.[36] O'Daly provided covering fire so these royalists could advance, but the men would not cross the square as they had no ladders and no breach had been formed. Eventually some were pressed forwards and Beauvais recalled crossing the square and a ditch to reach the town gate, soon joined by Cady, Stofflet, several other leaders and more men. All they could do, however, was hurl insults at the enemy beyond the gate. In hindsight Beauvais regretted that they had not prepared explosives to help create a breach.[37]

The 36pdr at the Haute-Châine fired grapeshot and dismounted an 8pdr that had advanced along the Rue des Pommiers, and another gun was dismounted on the La Flèche road.[38] The Vendéens had by now largely fallen back to the Saint-Serge Church and its neighbouring houses.

In spite of the lack of success at the Port St-Michel and Port Cupif, a third attack was made on the Port St-Aubin further south. Here the royalists took advantage of cover from houses that had not been demolished before the siege and which limited the effect of republican artillery from nearby towers. Nevertheless they could make no progress, as the republicans covered the approach and dismounted two cannon deployed on the road to fire on the gate.[39]

Ménard later reported that twenty cannon, supported by infantry, countered the Vendéen fire all the way from the Haute-Châine to the Port St-Aubin, and that the interior of the gates had been lined with further walls supported by heavy guns.[40]

Several times during the night the Vendéens near the Port St-Michel sent for news from their left, but with no response. It was clear that the attacks were not being coordinated, enabling the Republicans to race to each point in turn as they became the focus of battle.

4 December

Beauvais remained near the Port St-Michel until 2am, in the vain hope that someone would find a way to form a breach, but the plummeting temperature forced him to pull back. Under cover of darkness the rebels had managed to sneak across the St-Aubin Square, armed with axes to beat in a chevaux-de-frise protecting the Port St-Aubin, but once the firing recommenced, 'all who dared to advance were shot.'[41]

Around 9am rebel fire once again intensified at the Port St-Michel, where Marigny, Herbault and Piron were then located.[42] By keeping careful watch on this area the republicans noticed that during the night, under the cover of some houses near the gate, the enemy had moved forwards, filled up two ditches, and had been busy picking away at the dry stone walls.

The danger became more imminent when a column was spotted gathering behind these houses to await the call that the gate was open to rush into the town.[43] A wall ten to twelve feet thick was constructed behind this gate in a matter of hours. Combustible material was also gathered, its smoke soon filling the area and forcing the rebels to withdraw. Ménard was praised by

Benaben for having fascines smeared with tar, resin and pitch, and having these thrown down onto the Vendéens.[44]

At one point in the battle an 8pdr, placed on a roof near the Port St-Michel, fell through and crushed some of the defenders.[45]

La Rochejaquelein was furious that the soldiers did not join him in an assault on a small breach made near the Port St-Michel. Dismounted, and with fusil in hand, he called on them again, but as only a handful of officers joined him the attempt was soon abandoned.[46]

At the Port Cupif a number of Vendéens were gathered by Perrault and La Ville-Baugé but their attack was beaten back and groups of Vendéen cavalry were cut down by the 36pdr firing from the Haute-Châine.[47] Another small breach seems to have been formed at Lices, south of Port St-Aubin, but when a group of attackers attempted to break in they were cut down by grapeshot.[48]

Groups of Vendéens were starting to slip away from the action to find shelter in the suburbs away from the fighting and soldiers were even resorting to firing pebbles as they were running so low on ammunition.[49]

With little progress being made, and with no siege guns, the Vendéen leaders discussed various options, including building up fascines to make an attempt to escalade the Port Cupif; operating a diversion on Les Ponts-de-Cé to secure an escape route in that direction; or leaving 1,500 men to cover Angers while they made a feint on Les Ponts-de-Cé while moving on Ingrandes.[50]

Les Ponts-de-Cé was protected by 1,800 soldiers and ten guns, but D'Autichamp was adamant that his division could secure the crossing. When La Rochejaquelein sent cavalry to scout out the area they reported back that such an attempt would be futile.[51]

While a final attempt on Angers was underway reports were coming in that the rear of the Vendéen army and their baggage train was under attack. La Rochejaquelein set out with the cavalry, but the Republicans were only forced to retreat once Stofflet had joined him with a few hundred infantry and some cannon an hour or so later.[52]

General Moulin, who commanded at Les Ponts-de-Cé, now appeared with around sixty cavalry and a detachment of infantry in the Bressigny Suburb, surprising the Vendéens in that area.[53]

With republican detachments to the north and east, and their main army beginning to arrive from the west, the Vendéens were in imminent danger and quickly lifted the siege. Between 4 and 5pm they departed in a north-easterly direction, camping that night in a village at the junction of the Baugé road.[54]

At midnight on 3 December Kléber and Marceau had set out for Angers and began arriving at 4pm on the following day.

The heavily outnumbered Republican garrison had been quite content to sit behind their defences and await their main army.

Ménard wrote:

'All of the troops deserve praise, and especially the national guards. The veterans policed the interior. The old, young girls, women and children, carried munitions and supplies to the soldiers on the ramparts. The military men and the inhabitants formed a family that day.'[55]

The Vendéens lost 600 killed, an unknown number of wounded, and left behind three cannon and a vast quantity of fusils. The republican losses, in killed and wounded, totalled around 400.[56]

Benaben accused General Danican of treachery, indicating that while the battle was underway Danican was in bed claiming to be recovering from a fall from his horse, and when the town was in the greatest danger he moved his effects by wagon to the Port St-Nicholas on the far side of Angers. He also accused Danican of deploying his cavalry and a battalion of the 38th Regiment in the vicinity of the bridge, which he had illuminated as a signal to the brigands that he had withdrawn his regiment from the Port Cupif, thus encouraging them to make one more assault. As a result, he claimed, that gate was only guarded by five soldiers between 10pm and 1am. Ménard apparently had the position occupied by the 2nd Battalion of the 38th Regiment.[57]

Although Danican was now considered suspect, with some justification he claimed that it was the 2,000 men he sent to Angers that had saved the town. Danican was dismissed, having been accused of deserting his post at Entrammes and of aiming to abandon Angers during the siege.[58]

General Marigny, one of the finest officers in the republican army, was sent in pursuit of the Vendéens as they moved north from Angers. Aiming to take advantage of their disorder he charged a large column with 150 men but was struck by a cannon ball and killed.

Marceau's column finally reached Angers around 10pm on 4 December, followed the next day by Westermann and Tilly. Kléber and Marceau rested the troops that day while, in company with Westermann, they investigated which road the Vendéens had taken and came across many men, women and children who had died from cold and hunger. They massacred other stragglers and brought others back as prisoners.

Chapter 15

The Death of an Army

The March on La Flèche

The Vendéen army spent the night of 4 to 5 December at Pellouailles, and Suette and a council of war failed to reach agreement over what they should do next, so they headed to Baugé in the hope of securing provisions.

It was on 5 December that Marceau was confirmed as general of brigade, brevet general of division, and interim commander-in-chief of the Army of the West, with orders to pursue the Vendéens until the arrival of General Turreau. Representative Turreau headed for Saumur to coordinate its defence with General Commaire as he feared it might be a potential target for the rebels.[1]

Marceau had received orders to suspend a number of officers including Kléber, but also received a secret communication from the Minister of War not to reveal Kléber's suspension as they still believed he could be of service to the Republic. Marceau and Kléber had both been in a precarious position for several days, Kléber even dryly joking that they would at least be guillotined together.[2]

Kléber's division was sent along the north bank of the Loire to cover Saumur, and Tilly was sent towards Suette. Westermann received orders to harass the enemy and Muller was ordered to follow him with his division, to occupy strong positions in case they were attacked, and to protect Westermann's cavalry if they were forced to retreat. Under no circumstances was anyone permitted to take unnecessary risks. The republicans were on the march in the early hours of 6 December.

The Vendéens entered Baugé unopposed and on route Royrand died, having at last succumbed to the wound received at Entrammes.

On 6 December republican chasseurs and horse artillery appeared before Baugé. Madame de la Rochejaquelein wrote that these troops were posted in a small wood at the end of a plain that surrounded the town. From her window she watched as a body of Vendéens crossed the plain at great speed to attack the enemy. The republicans quickly fled.

When the Vendéens assembled on the following day, they believed that they were about to march on Saumur, but with no explanation the order was changed and they took the road to La Flèche instead.[3]

La Flèche 7 and 8 December

By the time the Siege of Angers was underway, General Chabot, previously at Alençon, became commander-in-chief of troops in Le Mans. With Representative Garnier, 700 infantry and 160 cavalry, he marched to La Flèche to cut the bridges over the Durtal and Lude Rivers.

Towards midday on 7 December a detachment of Vendéen cavalry, that was leading their advance guard, approached La Flèche. They were spotted by some national guards who had now been reinforced by Chabot and were supported by two guns. The Pont-des-Carmes had been cut and the republicans deployed along the north bank of the Loire to prevent various fords being used.[4]

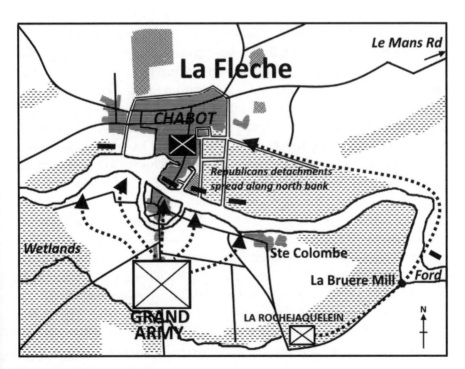

The assault on La Flèche.

A cannon deployed on the Pont-des-Carmes opened fire, as did troops deployed nearby. For two hours the Vendéen advance guard exchanged fire with the republicans, hoping to find a way across the river.

At around 1pm three large Vendéen columns appeared, supported by many cannon. On 8 December, writing to his colleague Letourneur, Garnier-de-Saintes would claim that they were attacked by 18,000 Vendéens at four or five points.

When La Rochejaquelein arrived with the bulk of the army he knew they needed to cross the river urgently as Westermann was harassing their rearguard around Clefs. Sending men along the river to test its depth, he was advised that a crossing was possible downstream at La Bruère Mill and that it was only weakly guarded.[5]

According to Bordereau and D'Obenheim, some Vendéens crossed the river in small boats, under covering fire from artillery and small arms, and soon repulsed a detachment of republicans that attempted to stop them. Madame de la Rochejaquelein, however, suggests that this crossing was very much in the hands of the commander-in-chief, indicating that he took 400 cavalry, each with an infantryman riding pillion, and dashed to the ford. They crossed the river with the water reaching up to their necks and, she states, encountered no resistance. They then marched under cover of fog to the edge of the town, where the infantry dismounted and were all instructed to cry 'Vive la Roi!' before being ordered to rush into the town.[6] When this column was spotted, Chabot's men quickly retreated to Foulletourte on the Le Mans road.

Although La Flèche was now in their hands, most of the army was still on the wrong bank and they urgently needed to construct a bridge to escape Westermann's harassing attacks. La Rochejaquelein had some beams placed across the gap in the bridge to enable the foot and horse to cross. Overnight more substantial repairs were completed under D'Obenheim's direction, enabling the artillery, baggage, and rearguard to follow. Towards midday on 8 December the alarm was sounded as Westermann's cavalry and some light infantry appeared near the town.

Piron commanded the Vendéen rearguard and had been holding his own against Westermann on 7 December, but on the following day he was being pushed back. La Rochejaquelein had great difficulty assembling a small core of fighters to go to his aid, although on arrival great cheers of 'Vive le Roi!' greeted him. He made the sign of the cross, something he only did when the situation was perilous, and charged into the republican ranks followed by his troops.[7] Westermann was soon overpowered and forced to retreat 'for over a league and a half'.[8]

D'Obenheim noted that the bulk of the Vendéens followed with great reluctance and at some distance. The lack of close support caused their leading troops to lose courage and, when Westermann counter-attacked, his horse artillery caused the Vendéens to rout. This rout spread to the main column and it was only the huge disproportion in numbers that obliged Westermann to pull back.[9]

That same evening the Vendéens were again called to arms as troops were seen approaching on the Le Mans road. Although this column was small and quickly brushed aside, its appearance compounded their state of nervous exhaustion.

D'Obenheim observed that many Vendéen soldiers were no longer willing to fight. They seemed to be believing rumours that it was only their leaders the republicans wanted, and that if they were captured without arms they would be spared. Bands of men were also forming up to leave the army and head their own way. The leaders were forced to issue a proclamation at La Flèche announcing that only those men retaining their arms would be fed.[10] La Rochejaquelein was furious at the lack of willingness to continue the fight, especially among the officers. In open council he reproached them saying, 'You contradict me in council and abandon me at the cannon's mouth!'[11]

The royalist army remained in La Flèche for two days, gathering whatever arms and provisions they could find and putting some order back into their ranks. Royrand was replaced by Amédée de Béjarry in command of the former Army of the Centre.

Kléber, who had been covering the Loire, headed north when he was advised that the Vendéens had marched on La Flèche. On 10 December he arrived at Baugé and met up with Marceau.

After La Flèche, D'Obenheim indicated that the Vendéen leaders did not know which way to turn. Some were for crossing the Loire between Les Ponts-de-Cé and Saumur, others for crossing at Blois. Some, without rejecting either of those options, wanted first to rest and resupply the soldiers and considered Le Mans to be their best option for that purpose. They also hoped they might receive new recruits in that area. On 10 December they destroyed the temporary bridge behind them and headed for Le Mans.

Clermont 9 December

The loss of La Flèche caused great anxiety in Le Mans. The Sarthe and Huisne rivers were considered too long to defend and had many fords.

Nevertheless the old bridge at Pontlieue was cut and the Pont Neuf was strewn with planks covered with spikes and *chevaux-de-frise*.[12]

General Chabot was supported by Representative Garnier-de-Saintes and the army at his disposal totalled 4,000 men, although few had experience of fighting the Vendéens. Two thirds of this force were national guards (with many carrying pikes due to lack of muskets), or raw conscripts.[13] They included 300 grenadiers from various companies; the Battalion L'Égalité; part of the 4th Sarthe; battalions from Le Flèche, Belesme, Le Mans and Saint Denis d'Orques (probably the national guards); new levy battalions from Fresnay and La Ferté-Bernard; fifty mounted Paris Gendarmes; 100 cavalry from the 7th Chasseurs and 9th Hussars; two companies of gunners from the Armée-Revolutionnaire and about fourteen cannon (all 4pdrs).[14]

Taking 1,600 men and two guns, Chabot planned a pre-emptive strike on the Vendéens camped at La Flèche and was on the march at 2am on 9 December. Preceded by a strong cavalry picket, the head of the column was formed by the grenadier companies with one cannon, followed consecutively by the battalions of La Flèche, Belesme and Le Mans. The Paris Gendarmes brought up the rear.

Around 6am an exchange of cannon fire commenced at the Clermont Hill. The Vendéens sent a large body of troops to cut Chabot's line of retreat, but spotting the enemy's tirailleurs the republicans withdrew to avoid being surrounded. La Rochejaquelein had led this attack in person.

Retreating once more on Foulletourte, it was now clear to Chabot that Le Mans was the rebel target, so vedettes were dispatched to watch all the approach roads; a levy battalion was placed with four cannon and fifty cavalry at a redoubt at La Terte Rouge; the Maulny Ford, protected by abattis, was placed in the hands of the Valenciennes Battalion; other Valenciennes troops were placed at La Croix-Georgette, and a masked cannon was deployed in an entrenchment near La Mission. Some defences were also occupied at the L'Epeau Wood.[15]

This deployment covered the four key southern approaches to the city and, while Chabot's defeated and demoralised column occupied Pontlieue, the majority of the remaining troops waited in Le Mans. At Pontlieue four guns were placed in one rudimentary redoubt and fifty men in a second.

On the night of 9 to 10 December the defences were completed, albeit not particularly well, and would now be tested by the entire royalist army. Static defences, occupied by 2,000 largely inexperienced troops, in an area covered with hedges and woods, perhaps indicates how poor a general Chabot was.

The royalist army probably numbered 18-20,000 at this date, supported by around 35 guns. They were still encumbered by thousands of refugees and

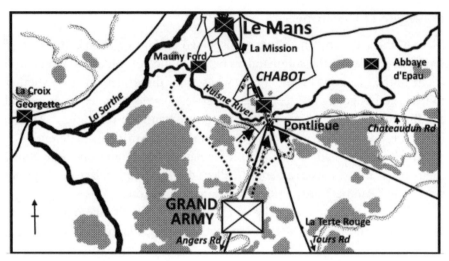

The Vendéen assault on Le Mans.

the cold weather, lack of food, and spread of dysentery was causing the army's morale to plummet. The head of the column, however, was still formed from the hardened elite led by La Rochejaquelein and Stofflet in person.

Pontlieue 10 December

At 11am on 10 December cannon fire was reported on the La Flèche road, probably when the battalion at La Terte Rouge fled on the first discharge of Vendéen fire. Chef-de-Battalion Houdiard wrote that the engagement started at Pontlieue around noon, others suggest towards 2pm. What was clear, however, is that both Pontlieue and the Mauny Ford were coming under attack, and according to Commissaire Rochelle 1,500 armed inhabitants held well, along with the gunners and the Saint Denis d'Orques Battalion, but after a while they were obliged to retreat. The Fresnay Battalion was also praised for its efforts. Desmarres, commanding the artillery, put up a determined fight but with his gunners being laid low by cannon fire and snipers, he was forced to withdraw.

After the Vendéens seized the bridge at Pontlieue the battle continued in the nearby settlement, until republican defence collapsed around 4pm. The Vendéen cavalry entered Le Mans hot on the heels of the republicans as Chabot and Garnier-de-Saintes fled with the bulk of the garrison on the Alençon road.[16] The Vendéens now poured into Le Mans, leaving a detachment to cover Pontlieue.

Pontlieue 12 December

Most of the army and the refugees dispersed around Le Mans, in search of food and rest, while the commanders held a council of war at the Hotel de la Biche in the Place des Halles. There was serious disagreement as to whether to take the Baugé or La Flèche roads, between factions under Talmont and La Rochejaquelein, which ominously ended without resolution. All the leaders, however, were well aware that Le Mans was difficult to defend.

The Vendéens had virtually no information on republican movements, their troops were in disarray, and the Place des Halles and Place de l'Éperon were soon crammed with artillery, caissons and wagons.

Kléber marched on La Flèche on 11 December, his advance guard moving as far as Clermont and Mareuil. On that same day a large body of national guards approached Le Mans from Alençon, but were easily repulsed by 1,500 Vendéens.

On the following day Marceau moved to Foulletourte, while towards 11am Westermann's hussars and chasseurs appeared on the heights facing Pontlieue. He was under strict orders not to engage in a general fight, but once again he disobeyed.

With the alarm raised, La Rochejaquelein, Stofflet and Lyrot managed to assemble 3,000 troops (including 100 cavalry) and raced to the defence of Pontlieue.[17] La Rochejaquelein placed the core of his men in the republican redoubts and deployed his tirailleurs in pine covered hills south of Pontlieue. He covered the Tours, Angers and Châteaudun roads and, with the bridge at Pontlieue only 2km from the Place des Halles, it was imperative that this position be held.

Westermann's troops numbered around 2,000 and deployed facing the rebels in woods between the Angers and Tours roads.[18] The battle commenced around 1pm with a Royalist attack. Madame de la Rochejaquelein states that the republicans were repulsed after a stubborn fight, which was probably of brief duration. The republicans retreated over a league, with their infantry covered by their cavalry and artillery.[19]

Muller's 4,000 men had been called up from Foulletourte to support Westermann but, seeing him retreating, most of his men broke and fled (according to Westermann, after the first discharge of fire). Kléber, then at Parigné-le-Polin, came across Muller and his staff on the Foulletourte road openly blaming Westermann for the defeat.

Not all of Muller's men fled however, as part of Carpentier's 3rd Brigade, comprising men from the Haute-Saône Battalions from the former Army of

Mayence, had held firm.[20] Benaben recalled that they had been marching on poor roads for four or five hours when they arrived on a height covered in pines around a league from Le Mans. Carpentier deployed his brigade and ordered Benaben to move on some woods to the right of a hill where Vendéens' artillery had deployed (between the Angers and Tours roads). Benaben successfully turned this wood, but suddenly found himself in the midst of a complete rout. Carpentier managed to retain 200 men who came back to Westermann's support. Westermann, however, now withdrew towards La Terte-Rouge.

The rest of Muller's men fled south over a wide area, although most were eventually rallied at Foulletourte.[21] At long last, and after an abysmal record, Muller was immediately dismissed.

Arnage Mid-afternoon

The republicans were fortunate that many of the royalists, thinking the crisis over, now drifted back to Le Mans, rainfall and the cold weather undoubtedly encouraging them to retire. Only about 400 joined La Rochejaquelein in his pursuit of the republicans, but did so in separate bands and without order.[22]

At Arnage the royalists came across Tilly's troops who had been on the march since 8am. Vachot, commanding Tilly's advance guard, wrote that they formed their two brigades in attack columns, either side of the Arnage road, and a discharge at forty paces stopped the Vendéens in their tracks.[23] Some Vendéens who had taken the Tours road found themselves caught in the flank. Charged at bayonet point by the Aunis and Armagnac regiments, the Vendéens fled to Pontlieue, some cut down by Westermann's cavalry.[24]

Pontlieue Late afternoon

La Rochejaquelein, Stofflet, Lyrot and Forestier were amongst the elite of the army who now disputed every foot of ground as they once again dug in around Pontlieue. They were heavily outnumbered but sustained the fight for at least an hour, at which point the advance guard of the Cherbourg column, supported by fifty of the 9th Hussars, carried the four enemy entrenchments at bayonet point.[25]

The royalists immediately rallied across the Huisne, but the head of the Cherbourg column soon seized the bridge. Vidal was forming his men up in the streets of Pontlieue, but his advance seems to have been delayed when he heard that Westermann had crossed the Huisne at a ford and had got into difficulties when attempting to turn the enemy position.[26]

The Vendéens fought from hedge to hedge as they were gradually forced back towards Le Mans, abandoning two cannon in the process. Stofflet was urging his men on with shouts of 'victory or death' as the battle was even now in the balance. By 4pm, with night rapidly falling on a dismal and cold day, they were at last in retreat on Le Mans. La Rochejaquelein may have provoked this retreat when he temporarily handed over command to Allard and Forestier while he returned to Le Mans to find reinforcements. When he arrived at the Place des Halles he soon witnessed troops fleeing from the battle.[27]

Vidal reached the edge of the city but faced withering fire from the houses and gardens on the outskirts and was forced to pull back to La Mission.[28]

The assault on Le Mans Night of 12 December

Marceau ordered Westermann to deploy before Le Mans, ready for a general assault the next day, but Westermann said they must exploit the opportunity and assault the town immediately. Taking his hand Marceau promised him support and gave orders for the Cherbourg Column to back Westermann's attack.[29] It was now nearly 5pm.

Following the earlier retreat from Arnage, panic began to spread amongst the refugees. The commanders had not considered which road they would take if forced to retreat and did not have a plan on to how to defend Le Mans. La Rochejaquelein now had to give urgent priority to both, but faced with complete confusion in the darkness he was overwhelmed by the gravity of their situation.[30]

Towards 4pm, even while fighting was still underway south of Le Mans, the rout from the city began. The roads from the southern side of Le Mans, however, converged on a single three-metre wide bridge across which they could escape on the Laval road, and the tortuous and narrow roads in Le Mans were difficult to navigate in the dark.

Chardon described the chaos that followed as a 'Dantesque scene which defies all description'.[31] Thousands of people, wagons, limbers and even cattle were crammed into the roads down to the bridge. People were being crushed, cannons and limbers overturned, and the wounded abandoned. The shouts of the leaders had little effect and both Stofflet and La Rochejaquelein were swept along in the rout, over the bridge, and away from the battle: neither returned.

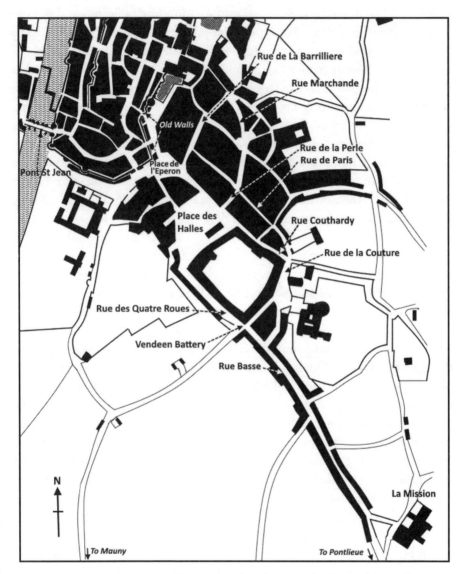

Plan of the southern part of Le Mans showing the final area of combat.

Blavette wrote that the republicans split their troops into two bodies, to enter the town via the Rue de la Couture and the Rue de Puits-de-Quatre-Roues, and hard fighting was soon underway along both roads.[32]

The Vendéens had thrown up an entrenchment with four cannon at a crossroads on the Rue de Puits-de-Quatre-Roues (also known as Rue des Quatres-Roues), but after fierce resistance the republicans captured the position.[33] The defenders dispersed into surrounding buildings and poured down such withering fire that republican progress stopped.[34] The Vendéens had also deployed artillery enfilading all the roads leading to the Places des Halles. When Westermann's cavalry and a small body of infantry appeared in that square, they came face to face with deployed artillery and were forced to retreat.[35] The republicans were also stopped twice in the Rue Basses, having evidently not cleared all the buildings of rebels.

The Vendéens were still able to call on enough men to hold their enemy back and secure more time for fugitives to escape, and the republicans were being forced to take one house at a time. At one point they captured all of the Place des Halles, but were expelled by a counter-attack and pushed back beyond the entrenchment in the Rue de Puits-de-Quatre-Roues, losing an 8pdr in the process.[36]

The entrenchment in the Rue de Puits-de-Quatre-Roues was recaptured towards 10pm, by which time the royalists had again been forced back to the Place des Halles, and had lost the Rue de Couture and exits to the Champ des Casernes.[37] All of these exits, however, were covered by royalist artillery, barricades and wagons.

With his losses increasing, Marceau decided to dig in to his position on the Rue du Puits-de-Quatre-Roues and await Kléber's reinforcements. His aim was to blockade the Vendéens in the Place des Halles and turn their position by blocking all the roads between that square and the rest of the city. Marceau did send a column to seize the Paris road while Westermann held all the approaches to the Place des Halles. For the rest of the night the two sides exchanged occasional artillery fire, and there was some fighting in the Rue Marchande and Rue de la Barillerie as the republicans tightened their grip on the eastern side of the two squares.

Towards midnight the Vendéens were reported to be infiltrating towards the rear of Marceau's position. Lacking troops, Marceau feared the rebels might launch an assault on his flanks or rear at any moment, and only had the main Le Mans to Pontlieue road secure as a line of retreat.

D'Obenheim, who slipped away from the royalists during the battle, recalled that the republicans were in a very dangerous predicament as there were Vendéens in several roads to their rear, still holding out in a number of buildings.[38] It would have been easy for them to swamp Marceau's positions if they had the leadership to coordinate such an assault, but neither Stofflet nor La Rochejaquelein were present, and Marigny had also abandoned the artillery and followed the flight.

Kléber received desperate orders to race to Marceau's support.

Le Mans midnight to dawn 13 December

Some of the Vendéens were unaware that many of the refugees and most of the army had retreated. In command of those still fighting were the Vicomte de Scépeaux, Allard and Duhoux, with perhaps 6-700 troops.

Beauvais was overcome with exhaustion by 11pm but his servant kept him up to date with developments. At 1am he heard that most of the caissons and cannon had been withdrawn from the Place des Halles and then departed on the Laval road. Some artillery had been moved back to the Place de l'Éperon, from where it continued firing during the night, to fool the republicans into thinking that the army was still present.

Kléber's division arrived in the early hours and found Marceau overcome with exhaustion; he was furious that Marceau had shown such reckless disregard for his troops. Kléber had set out from Parigné-le Polin towards midnight, having first spent some time rounding up Muller's routing column. His arrival enabled Marceau to replace Tilly's men at dawn with Kléber's troops. Delaage, commanding the 600 men of the Chasseurs-des-Francs and Chasseurs-de-Cassel, replaced Carpentier's 1,500 men. Kléber's other troops took up position in the surrounding area and nearly up to the gates of Le Mans.

The Final Assault Morning of 13 December

Delaage came under attack from some royalists, but three rounds of grapeshot stopped them. He soon overwhelmed them and captured two cannon.

At 7am the charge was beaten all along the republican lines. Delaage had advanced along the Rue de Puits-de-Quatre-Roues. Other columns advanced along the Rues de Saumon and La Perle and managed to cut off those in the Place des Halles from the Place de l'Éperon. Kléber marched his troops towards the Sarthe to seize the bridge and Westermann advanced along the Rue de Couthardy.

After the fall of the Place des Halles some still put up a fight in the Place de l'Éperon. Delaage led the attack on the left and Westermann that on the right by the Rue de la Mission and the Rue de la Couture. This last stand involved hand-to-hand fighting. Scépeaux, personally firing a cannon, declared that while he still had a grain of powder and a cannon ball he would remain. He was wounded at his post. Even at this late stage some royalists managed to escape over the Saint-Jean Bridge, but others fought until they were cut down.[39] 'The enemy no longer held, and then the butchery began,' Delaage recalled.[40]

Le Mans was at last in the hands of the republic, but the city now experienced the horror of a town taken by assault. 'It was no longer a fight, but a bloody orgy,' wrote Chardon.[41]

The Cost

'Never was there a butchery to equal this since the Vendéen War began,' wrote Prieur de la Marne, Bourbotte and Turreau on 13 December.[42]

The battle of Le Mans was a decisive defeat for the Grand Army and the pursuit that followed on the road to Laval witnessed the massacre of men, women and children.

Maignon states the Vendéens lost near to 2,300 killed and Gabory claims that between 10 and 12,000 people would be massacred as a result of this catastrophic defeat. Madame de la Rochejaquelein estimated 15,000 casualties, 'very few of them fighters'.[43] Gréau gives the more conservative figure of around 4,000 killed.[44] In 2009-10, archaeologists came across nine mass graves in the Place des Jacobins, about 500 metres north of the Place de l'Éperon. These graves contained 159 bodies of men, women and children identifiable as some of the victims from the battle.[45]

D'Autichamp managed to evade certain death by being merged into the ranks of one of the republican cavalry units. It is suspected that his masonic links, and recognition of a relative in their ranks, may have saved his life.[46]

Apart from the human cost, the rebels lost around sixteen guns: half of their remaining supply.[47]

The republicans suffered about 500 casualties.[48]

Les Mans to Nort 13 to 18 December

On 13 December the last of the Vendéens left Le Mans, and all through that day and into the following they drifted into Laval in complete disarray and haemorrhaging troops on route. Many of those who had joined them north of the Loire were leaving the army.

With Le Mans secured Marceau sent Westermann and Decaen in pursuit at the head of some cavalry and light artillery, supported by Delaage and the Chasseurs Francs-de-Cassel. They headed for Ste-Suzanne, pushing patrols towards Laval. Westermann was struggling with two wounds and asked to be given some time to recover.

Kléber and Tilly's troops crossed Le Mans and moved to the village of Chassillé later in the day. Muller's troops, who had taken no part in the battle, remained in Le Mans with orders to march to Saumur and strengthen its garrison, his better battalions (three of Haute-Saône, one of Jura, and one of Vosges) were transferred to Tilly and Klinger. D'Obenheim provided the republicans with valuable information on the state of the rebel army and reported that the rebels still retained 14,000 armed men and about a dozen cannon.

The Vendéens no longer resembled an army; many were in despair, exhausted, sick and hungry. They were facing attacks from locals, who feared the consequences of being seen to collaborate with the royalists. On the morning of 14 December they left Laval, marched through Cossé, and reached Craon that same night. At a council of war it was agreed that they would make an attempt to secure a crossing at Ancenis and set off in the early hours of 15 December.

Marceau was near Le Mans by the evening of 15 December. All garrisons on the Loire had been ordered to firmly hold their positions. Correctly identifying Ancenis as the most likely enemy target, Marceau ordered Boucret to leave Angers, race along the south bank of the Loire, and block the crossing. Marceau's cavalry reached Château-Gontier that night having marched via Laval. Westermann reached Puancé, followed by Decaen.

Marceau next marched through Laval to Crossé and reached Craon on 16 December, but always a step behind the rebels. Westermann moved forwards to St-Mars-la-Jaille.

On 16 December a Vendéen advance party set out for Ancenis to secure boats, the rest following on behind. As soon as they reached the Loire small groups of Vendéens began the hazardous crossing, but were soon coming under attack from gunboats.

La Rochejaquelein and Stofflet both slipped across in the hope of rallying support for the army, but soon after they reached the far bank republican patrols attacked and forced them to flee inland. Gréau estimates that around 2,000 made the crossing before an assault by Westermann on 17 December, even though repulsed, caused the remaining Vendéens to head towards Nort.[49] Marceau reached Châteaubriand that day. The royalists abandoned more guns at Ancenis and avoided Nantes, knowing it to be far too well garrisoned. They reached Nort on 18 December.

Nort to Blain 18 to 21 December

On 18 December Scherb was sent ahead with orders to make for Ancenis as rapidly as possible, but near Saint-Mars-la-Jaille he was recalled as

Westermann had reported that the rebels were heading for Blain. Scherb was now directed to Saint-Julien-de-Vouvantes where the bulk of the army gathered. The weather was awful.

Haxo, in Charette's territory and preparing to assault Noirmoutier, was ordered to divert his troops to cover the south banks of the Loire. On 19 December he was in the process of working out how to cover all the crossings from St-Florent to Champtoceaux when he received a counter-order to proceed with the capture of Noirmoutier.[50]

Westermann's relentless pursuit caused more rebel losses between Nort and Blain.

The Vendéens were desperately trying to reach Morbihan, a region known to be fiercely loyal to the royalist cause. On 20 December they held a council of war in Blain and elected Fleuriot as the new commander-in-chief. Talmont saw this as a personal slight and left the army with some of his supporters. The rebels took the precaution of cutting the bridge and took the opportunity to rest for the day.

That same day most of the republican army moved to the area around Derval, and Scherb reached Guémené-Penfao. Delaage skirmished with the Vendéens at Blain but was repulsed, and Westermann stopped four leagues from Blain to await the rest of the army.

On 21 December the republicans marched on Blain and, as the rebels were still there, they halted a league from that town to eat and unite the different columns. Kléber made a detailed reconnaissance and was advised by a local woman that the rebels were in strong positions, deployed on open ground before the town, and waiting to be attacked.

The troops advanced quickly and when Kléber's column arrived he deployed them in line. He recalled that a sudden torrential downpour slowed the march of the Cherbourg Division as it moved to turn Blain by the right. They only reached their designated place an hour after nightfall. Westermann was ordered to march on Blain along the Nantes road and the plan was that they would all attack at dawn on 22 December.

The March to Savenay 22 December

At dawn a republican reconnaissance found that the town had been abandoned. The rebels had quietly left during the night, heading for Savenay. Forestier, Sapinaud and a small band of followers took the opportunity to leave the army and would later succeed in crossing the Loire.

Fleuriot's decision to move on Savenay, instead of marching west, may in hindsight have been a serious misjudgement as it limited his options and left the army with its back to marshland.

The numbers remaining with the Vendéen army were now down to around 6,000 men capable of bearing arms, and ten to twelve guns, but more significantly there were still thousands of refugees entirely dependent on their protection.[51]

The republican pursuit was hampered by heavy rainfall that swelled a ford between Blain and its château and the troops were forced to unload the caissons and wade across the river carrying ammunition above their heads.

Lyrot and the royalist advance guard brushed aside some republicans encountered between 6 and 7am at La Moëre, and the Vendéens arrived at the small town of Savenay around 9am.[52]

The troops deployed north of the town and immediately set about preparing defences as best they could. They were helped by three areas of woodland which provided them with excellent cover. Lyrot deployed to the north-east, forming the right of the line, and his men took advantage of the cover of the Touchelais Wood. To the west Laugrenière grouped his men in the Matz Wood, and Fleuriot deployed in the centre and towards the town, using the Amourettes Wood.

The remaining Vendéens cannon were deployed on the main approach roads, two being placed on the Guérande road and two in the centre on the road next to the Amourettes Wood.[53] Even at this late stage locals from surrounding parishes came to fight with the rebels.[54]

Refugees crammed into the small town, although some began to retreat even further west.

Kléber recalled the march on Savenay being extremely gruelling, along difficult roads, and in terrible weather. Marceau and Kléber set out in advance to join Westermann, closely followed by the advance guard under Scherb.

Westermann's troops and Kléber's advance guard arrived towards 11am and deployed on a hill facing the rebels. Their small force comprised a party of grenadiers, an 8pdr, Westermann's cavalry, and twenty hussars led by Kléber's ADC.[55] They were content to unlimber the 8pdr and fire on the enemy.

A sudden rebel onslaught from the woods pushed Westermann's troops back as far as the stream at Le Pont Bouvronnais, causing him some losses.[56] The royalists now returned to their original positions, probably thinking they only had Westermann to contend with.

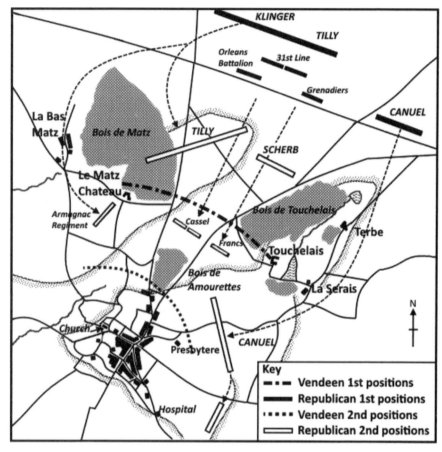

The Battle of Savenay based on a contemporary plan.

Kléber arrived in person later that morning and reconnoitred as far as the village of La Serlais in the hope of discovering a good road for the artillery. Shots from Vendéen snipers forced him to dive for cover when a musket ball pierced his hat. Kléber wrote:

'I sensed then that they [the Vendéens] had not thought through their plans, as they needed to hold the heights occupied by our cavalry ready for the battle the following day. I thus made 300 of Blosse's grenadiers advance, as well as the 8pdr. I split them into two bodies and ordered Chef-de-Battalion Duverger to attack in the front, while I put myself at the head of the others. I turned the wood from where the enemy had set out.'

This manoeuvre was successful and the rebels were forced to pull back towards Savenay, abandoning the woods of Touchelais and Matz. Marceau reported that an 8pdr was captured on the great road to Savenay.[57]

Kléber had succeeded in securing the high ground commanding the town and towards midnight the rest of his troops arrived.

The Republicans deployed as follows:

- Westermann was to the west of the Blain road with his cavalry and Blosse's 300 Grenadiers (commanded by Verger);
- Legros commanded the Orléans formation to the right of Westermann;
- two battalions of the 31st Regiment (part of Tilly's column) formed up in a second line in support;
- the light artillery was to their north-east, near the Blain road;
- Scherb formed up in the centre and was in command of the advance guard comprising the 32nd Line, a detachment of the 13th Line, parts of five battalions of Haute-Saône, and three cannon;[58]
- Canuel deployed east of the Blain road, with a detachment of the 9th Hussars covering his flank. His command is unknown but a contemporary plan of the battle suggests four battalions or formations (it seemed to be common practice in the Vendée War to merge smaller battalions into larger formations to retain some cohesion in unit size);
- A further cavalry detachment, including more of the 9th Hussars, covered the right wing;
- Marceau and Kléber deployed in the centre and were accompanied by the Légion-des-Francs and Chasseurs-de-Cassel, both placed in the front line.

The Vendéens were deployed in a more constrained arc facing the republicans: the left holding the exits from the Matz Wood, the right facing the Touchelais Wood, and the centre supporting itself on the Amourettes Wood.

Prieur, Turreau and Bourbotte now arrived and were astonished that the advance guard did not attack immediately. They had the drums beaten and called on the troops to advance. An urgent council of war was held and Kléber discreetly told Marceau that they must not attack until the following morning when all the troops would be rested and in position. He did not want another carefully considered plan compromised by a sudden impetuous one. Westermann was not helping as he was in vocal agreement with the representatives.

Exasperated with Prieur in particular, Kléber quietly said to Marceau, 'If you don't stop this lawyer's ranting, tomorrow we will be in Nantes with the enemy following behind us.'[59] Marceau tactfully asked the representatives to leave the front line for their own safety, and fortunately for the republican troops they did.

In a moving account Madame de la Rochejaquelein recalled how Marigny seized the bridle of her horse, urging her to flee immediately on the Guérande road. 'We are lost,' he said, 'It is impossible to resist tomorrow's attack, in twelve hours the army will have been exterminated; I hope to die defending your flag. Take flight and save yourself this night, Adieu! Adieu!'[60] He was carrying the flag she had made. Her father, Donnissan, also urged her to leave and she was never to see him again.

The rest of Tilly's Cherbourg Division arrived around 2am and initially formed up behind the centre, but in the morning deployed on the right wing towards Matz.

Marceau's forces now totalled around 10,000 troops, but they were exhausted, wet and cold, with many poorly clothed and without shoes. Nevertheless they must have recognised the significance of the moment and the opportunity at long last to destroy the Vendéen army once and for all.

All night Marigny and Lyrot walked through their ranks encouraging the men and, according to Béjarry, although sombre and silent, the men remained resolute.[61] Sporadic cannon and musket fire continued to be heard through the night.

Monday 23 December

The Vendéens must have realised that this was a battle they could not win and they fought with a mixture of despair and desperation. A breakthrough could mean some might be able to join with Chouan bands in Britanny, or even escape to the Vendée. Some must have fought to enable as many refugees as possible to escape on the Guérande road.

Kléber wrote:

> 'At dawn, when everyone was still resting, I mounted my horse and with Westermann and Canuel carried out a reconnaissance around the town and indicated to each the roads they should use for the attack. Having completed this reconnaissance, the cannonade and fusillade began.'

At 8am the Vendéens launched a sudden surprise attack on the Touchelais Wood, which had been occupied by Verges' troops during the night.[62] Even the Royalist wounded who could bear arms joined in this attack. They overpowered the republicans, and pushed them back from the area around the Château de Touchelais, capturing two guns in the process.[63]

Arriving at the scene of the attack Kléber found Duverger and his grenadiers fleeing. Duverger cried out that they had no more cartridges, to which Kléber replied that they should use their bayonets and ordered them back to the charge. He promised them support, and immediately ordered the 31st Regiment to advance, even though they were not part of his command. The Vendéens were now pushed back to their original positions.

With Canuel marching to turn Savenay by its left, Kléber advised Marceau that it was time for the centre to charge. He also sent an ADC to order the Cherbourg Division to charge on the right. But as he did not command that division, and as Tilly was absent at that moment, he ordered the ADC to say to the leader he found in command that Kléber would hold them responsible for any hesitation in carrying out his orders.

The fight along the edge of the Matz Wood was hard going, as the Vendéens were clinging on defiantly. Tilly split his troops into two bodies, ordering Debilly to take one on the Guémené road while he led the other around the Matz Wood moving on Savenay by the Pontchâteau road.[64]

In the centre Marceau was commanding the Chasseurs-de-Cassel and 14th Chasseurs-à-Cheval in person, and Kléber was following a little to his left with the Légion-des-Francs. Weight of numbers pressed the Vendéen centre back, until their two guns stalled the republican advance. These now became the focus of a bitter struggle. Eventually the royalists were again forced to pull back, but succeeded in withdrawing these guns.

Canuel had bypassed the Touchelais Wood and passed through La Serais, detaching some men to continue along that road, while he continued on to L'Aumônerie. He detached more troops to take the Point du Jour road, then with what he had remaining he marched further south still to assault Savenay from its eastern side.[65]

It was probably around this time that Fleuriot launched a sudden cavalry charge with 2-300 men, supported by some infantry, in the direction of Bas-Matz. Cadoudal, Piron and Cady were part of this attack and succeeded in breaking through Tilly's Division and making good their escape.

The Vendéens were being forced back on Savenay and, anticipating street fighting, Marigny had deployed cannon in the Place de l'As de Carreau to fire on the republicans at point-blank range. Even after Westermann had killed a number of the gunners, Marigny managed to extract some cannon and deploy them near the church.[66]

Marigny remained with the cannon near the church as the battle moved slowly from house to house through the town. Accounts talk of blood running in the streets as the numbers of killed and wounded increased. Weight of numbers eventually told and Marigny's gunners were overpowered and the guns turned on the Vendéens.

Marigny was crying with rage, with a sword in one hand and the flag in the other, urging the men to fight on. Pushed back by those trying to escape the fight, he seems to have returned at least four times to the mêlée.[67] Practically encircled, those that remained knew they were not likely to be spared so fought ferociously.

Marigny managed to gather men near the two guns covering the Guérande road. For a while these guns continued their critical role as many refugees dispersed to seek safety across a wide area. Both Lyrot and La Roche-Saint-André seem to have succumbed when these guns were eventually overpowered. Marigny ordered the survivors to retire into the Wood of Blanche Couronne, where many would be massacred by Westermann's troops.

Several Vendéen leaders were captured, including Donnissan, Laugrenière and Des Essarts (the first two were guillotined and the latter shot). Savary wrote that 'Laugrenière retired with his troops to some houses on the left of the road, wanting to put up some resistance, but seeing that this was futile he surrendered at the invitation of a staff officer.'[68]

Marigny escaped with 300 men and managed to re-cross the Loire, and Fleuriot made good his escape to the Forest du Gâvre. Amédée de Béjarry also managed to escape, he said with 3-400 cavalry but in reality probably somewhat less. He also said he dragged away three guns which he later abandoned in the Loire. Marceau captured five abandoned cannon.[69]

Béjarry wrote that nearly 2,000 Vendéens were captured and shot but claimed that most of the victims of the battle were refugees, the sick and the wounded. He also indicated that many men escaped in small parties and more than 1,800 managed to continue the fight in Brittany, although he accepted that not all had fought at Savenay.[70]

The republicans claimed that they suffered only 30 killed and 200 wounded.

Republican columns pursued the rebels in different directions. Even Westermann, 'the Butcher of the Vendée', remarked on the extent of the massacres. Many were drowned in the Montior Marsh, others took shelter in woodland where they would be rooted out over the coming weeks. Patrols of infantry and cavalry also found rebels in surrounding villages and isolated farms and either killed them or sent them to await execution in Nantes.

Chapter 16

Charette 'King of the Vendée'

By the beginning of December small numbers of troops were trickling back across the Loire. When Pierre Cathelineau heard that the Grand Army was near Angers he marched on Les Ponts-de-Cé, but by the time he arrived they had gone. He skirmished with republican detachments on his advance from, and return to, his base at Jallais.[1]

On 7 December he completely destroyed two battalions at Chapelle-Rousselin, who were intercepted en route from Cholet to destroy Jallais.[2] Amongst those killed was the 14-year-old Joseph Barra who was turned into a martyr by the Republic and received national acclaim. Adjudant General Desmarres, who was in command of this detachment, was arrested for ineptitude and executed in January 1794.[3]

The Coastal Vendée Early December

Haxo's 4–5,000 men had gradually forced Charette towards the coast and eventually trapped his diminishing army on the Ille de Bouin, both Savin and Joly having abandoned him on the way.[4] He gained a brief respite when Haxo received orders to suspend operations and be ready to march on Nantes following developments north of the Loire. Once he was given clearance to attack Charette, he gave orders to Jordy to prepare for the assault on Bouin.

On 3 December Jordy occupied Châteauneuf and the Bois-de-Céné, and on the next day formed his men into three columns: the centre under his direct command was to march towards the La Claie Bridge, the left under Aubertin was to head for Beauvoir, and the right under Villemin was to take up position in Bourgneuf. Only Aubertin and Villemin had artillery support. Jordy selected 674 men, detached from four battalions, and Aubertin led around 1,600 men (400 from the 11th Orléans, numerous detachments including part of the 110th Line and 109th Line, and various grenadier companies); he still retained his single 4pdr. Haxo held a reserve of 300 infantry and a small detachment of cavalry, deployed between St-Gervais and Bouin.[5]

Beauvoir 5 December

On 4 December Aubertin was in Salartène and overnight marched in silence to be in position to attack Beauvoir at dawn. Beauvoir was about 3km from the coast, partially surrounded by marshland and with the Bois-de-Céné to its east. Aubertin ordered 300 men to scout these woods but to make sure they remained in sight of the main column. They were also ordered to arrive at Beauvoir at the same time as the main column.

Charette knew that the republicans were approaching and deployed some of his force to oppose them, with his left flank protected by some marshland. As usual their line was much longer than that of the republicans.

The front of the republican column left the road, to deploy in line parallel to the Vendéen left, and the rest of their army then deployed facing the rebels, supported by a small reserve. Aubertin gave orders that they open fire when only fifteen paces from the enemy, and then charge in with the bayonet. His single 4pdr fired once, but then became stuck in the soft ground and was no longer used during the engagement.

Aubertin's aim was to overpower the rebel centre. As his line advanced the Vendéens remained in position to their front, and along the republican flanks, but before either side fired a shot the rebel left flank suddenly fled in disorder back into the Bouin marshland and their centre and right headed for Beauvoir. The 300 men dispatched by Aubertin had been spotted and were probably mistaken for another republican column.[6] Charette wanted to retreat to Noirmoutier but, reaching the causeway at high tide, he had no option but to move onto the Ile de Bouin. He took the precaution of breaking several wooden bridges over the ditches and waterways as he retreated.

Aubertin followed up this withdrawal and entered Beauvoir unopposed.

Bouin 6 December

Having retreated to Bouin, Charette deployed most of his men in positions stretched from the Poirocq Bridge on the Beauvoir road, to Corbets, holding the few isolated mills and farms that stretched between the two. He had constructed three earthworks: one to his rear, and the others near windmills at La Pentecôterie and La Jaunay. His thirteen guns were deployed in these earthworks, although some may have been covering the approach roads from Beauvoir and Bois-de-Céné.

In typical fashion Charette and his men spent the night dancing and singing in a large barn, but by dawn on 6 December Couëtus guarded the approach from the Pont de la Claie with 400 men; Charette, with around 1,000 men, covered the approach from Beauvoir; and Guérin, with 250 men, was initially posted to the north of the island near the Étiers du Sud.[7]

Jordy issued orders for his three columns to be in position ready to attack at 11am. Due to the difficult terrain only his column was in place at the agreed time. He came under fire from rebel artillery on Bouin, and although under pressure he thought it better to hold his ground rather than retreat.

Aubertin had been struggling along a very difficult route from the south, and Villemin did not press his attack against Guérin, but, having considered an attack on the rebels in Pas-Opton too risky, he withdrew back to Bourgneuf without informing the others; Guérin subsequently deployed near the Pont de la Claie.

With the help of a company of sappers, and twenty wagons filled with timber, Aubertin managed to throw across about eight bridges as he advanced, all while under fire from a 16pdr naval gun deployed in a coastal battery and turned by the Vendéens to fire on his men.[8] They remained under fire until they reinstated the crossing and troops were able to advance and seize the gun.

Aubertin next found himself 'about half a league from the island', at a farm between the enemy and the sea. Nearby was a windmill, a Vendéen redoubt housing two 4pdrs, and a body of enemy troops.[9] On spotting the republicans the royalists opened fire. As it was impossible to deploy due to the nature of the terrain, or bring his single gun into action, Aubertin ordered an immediate charge, seized the redoubt, and forced the Vendéens to flee. He captured their artillery and caissons.

Aubertin stated that his column arrived in position around the same time as Jordy.[10] As he reached the island Jordy split his small command into four bodies formed from their respective detachments: the 57th on the left; 77th on the right; 10th Meurthe in the centre; and a detachment of the 109th Line in his second line. These troops advanced across a frozen canal and, lacking munitions, Guérin's men were eventually forced to withdraw. Jordy's men now advanced on the positions held by Couëtus and Charette, under bombardment from royalist cannon. As the 10th Meurthe advanced on the first entrenchment, Jordy instructed the 57th and 77th to move around the enemy flanks. The advance of the 77th Line on the left ground to a halt as they came under increasing fire. Jordy led the 10th Meurthe steadily forward with fixed bayonets while subjected to grapeshot. All three detachments had orders to fire then charge in quickly with the bayonet. They succeeded in storming and capturing the redoubt in the centre first, followed by those on the flanks.[11]

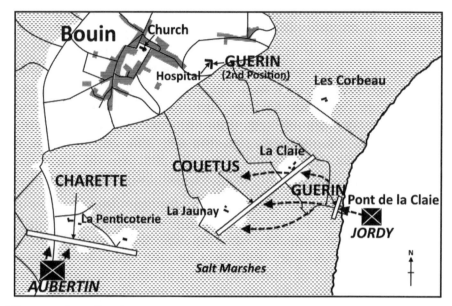

The assault on Bouin.

Couëtus fell back on Charette's position, who was putting up more resistance. With Aubertin and Jordy now marching in a curved line towards each other, with Charette between the two, he was forced to fall back on the town to avoid being trapped.[12]

Guérin had meanwhile been resupplied with ammunition and was holding out at the hospital in La Casse until numbers forced him to pull back. Charette, Couëtus and Guérin now managed to rally around 800 men in the heart of Bouin, and with this column planned to make a last desperate charge through the enemy ranks. La Championnière recalled how they were in despair until a local alerted them to a possible escape route across the salt marshes. They abandoned their horses, the wounded, and many refugees, and using fusils and poles (called *ningles*, used to leap across the many streams and ditches), they slipped away; some even resorted to swimming through the freezing water.[13]

On entering Bouin the republicans were astonished to find it deserted. Hundreds of refugees, however, were found hidden in the church tower and sent to Nantes.

After an exhausting march, Charette's miraculous escape did not conceal the terrible losses he had sustained. They totalled around 800 men and all his cannon, powder and horses.[14] The republicans admitted to around 100 killed and wounded.[15] Charette and his beleaguered band eventually appeared at Châteauneuf towards 3pm. Here he put some order into his remaining troops and inspired his men to fight on:

> 'Comrades, we have made a remarkable escape but we are not even, there is no doubt that the enemy borders the marshes and occupy posts beyond; but they can only be in small numbers. Let's close up to each other and march in closed ranks, and we will overpower these rogues if you want to have munitions.'[16]

Remarkably Charette's diminished column came across Pajot's small army. Pajot, notorious for his cruelty, now assisted in the surprise attack and rout of Haxo, his headquarters staff, the 300 men of the Ille-et-Vilaine Battalion, and thirty cavalry. This took place between Châteauneuf and the Bois-de-Céné road on the same day as the defeat at Bouin.[17]

Brushing aside further republican posts, Charette reached Saint-Etienne-de-Mer-Morte that night, bringing with them weapons, ammunition and horses captured from the enemy. It was a remarkable escape for which Haxo must take responsibility. As poor recompense, the republicans captured Charette's horse and paraded it through Les Sables as a trophy of war.

Jordy remained in Bouin while Aubertin was ordered back to Beauvoir.

Legé 7 December

Charette was keen to link up with Savin and Joly, who were then in Les Lucs, and after only a short rest he marched in that direction. When camping in the forest at La Grollière they heard firing in the distance towards Legé. Charette gave orders to race there and found Joly fighting the 800 strong garrison under Adjudant General Guillaime.[18]

Haxo was fearful for this garrison and had ordered Aubertin to head there as quickly as possible.

As Charette's men approached, the republicans sent out a detachment of infantry and a cannon to oppose him. Charette took up position on the La Blignière Heights and soon forced the republicans to pull back to entrenchments closer to the town, from where they bombarded the royalist positions with their five cannon and howitzer.

Charette's men kept up their attack for at least an hour and a half but could make no headway.[19] Seeing some hesitation, Guillaime launched a bayonet attack with the 110th Line and a Charente battalion. Charette's men retreated in good order to the Forest of Grandlande and were not pursued.

La Championnière blamed the defeat on having attacked across the more open terrain along the Nantes road. Three hours after this engagement Aubertin's column arrived, only to return to Machecoul on the following day.[20]

Towards 6pm Charette's men reached the Forest of Grandelande where they camped overnight.

Charette's March into Haut-Poitou 8 to 20 December

On 8 December, Charette, Joly and Savin linked up at Les Grand-Lucs with 2,000 infantry and 179 cavalry.[21] They decided to march into Haut-Poitou to gather recruits from those who had not crossed the Loire, as their small numbers simply could not stand up against the number of republicans in the coastal Vendée. They marched through Rochservière and Boulogne, before reaching Les Essarts. They attacked a 2,000 strong republican garrison at Les Quatre-Chemins on 11 December, reputedly inflicting around 1,000 casualties.[22] On 12 December they reached Les Herbiers where Charette was formally elected as the new commander-in-chief of the Army of Bas-Poitou, much to the annoyance of Joly.

On 13 December the army marched east to recruit in Haut-Poitou, passing through Saint-Michel, Mallièvre and Châtillon, barely troubled by the republicans. They repelled an ambush by 2-400 republicans from the Pouzauges garrison before they occupied that town. Republican brutality was encouraging men to join his ranks and Charette's infantry now totalled 3-4,000 infantry and 322 cavalry.[23]

Haxo had not lost sight of his aim to destroy Charette. On 11 December he ordered Dutruy and Dufour to march in concert with Guillaume's 1,200 men and hunt down the rebels in the Bocage.[24] Dufour marched with 2,400 men. On 15 December Adjudant General Biot was ordered to march from Fontenay to cover La Châtaigneraie with 500 men and Dufour marched from Luçon to Les Essarts. On 16 December Guillaume marched on Montaigu while Dufour headed for Chantonnay. Bard, in Luçon, was reinforced on 15 December by 450 men moving up from La Rochelle. All the republicans, however, were in a terrible state.

Chalbos ordered Joba to take command of troops gathering at Fontenay and coordinate his march with Haxo's troops. He was at Mortagne around 16 December as Dufour was heading for Pouzauges, and planned to march on La Châtaigneraie via Boupère.

On 18 December Dufour marched on Les Herbiers, aiming to hunt down Charette in the Pouzauges and Boupère area on 20 December. However the orders to hunt down Charette were suddenly curtailed on news of the return of the Grand Army towards the Loire. Dufour was immediately ordered to Champtoceaux and Bard to St-Florent.

Joba, meanwhile, had received news that Charette was at Pouzauges with a post at Réaumur. Hearing that Dufour's 3,000 men were aiming to attack Pouzauges from Les Herbiers, he gambled on launching a strike on Charette's force and attacked on 20 December, unaware that Dufour's orders had changed.[25] Joba claimed he killed 200 rebels and if Dufour had joined him he believed they would have torn Charette's force to pieces.[26]

Charette's army now headed north for Maulévrier where they arrived later that same day. He was not pursued.

Chapter 17

The End of the 'War of Giants'

By the end of 1793 the Republic had saved France from attempts by the First Coalition to bring it down: testament to the remarkable achievement of Carnot in rallying the nation to arms. The Grand Army had also been crushed in the marshlands around Savenay.

On 21 December a young man walked into Charette's temporary headquarters in Maulévrier. It was none other than Henri de la Rochejaquelein. In company with Stofflet and a small body of men, and disguised as a peasant, he had survived a number of close encounters with the republicans since crossing the Loire. La Rochejaquelein had in fact been looking for the contingent under Pierre Cathelineau when they came across Charette's troops. La Ville-Baugé left an eye witness account of the meeting that followed.[1]

Charette was clearly jealous of La Rochejaquelein's influence and justifiably concerned that the new recruits he had gathered would switch allegiance. He failed to offer La Rochejaquelein any respect or sympathy and, although dinner was served and Charette was eating as they arrived, he did not invite them to join him. La Ville-Baugé was however quizzed about events north of the Loire.

After this brief interview La Rochejaquelein and La Ville-Baugé went to eat with their men. When they later returned to meet with Charette, La Rochejaquelein was received coldly. Charette indicated that he was considering an assault on Cholet, but when La Rochejaquelein warned him of the risks and the strength of the town's garrison, Charette cuttingly replied that as La Rochejaquelein had thought fit to leave his lands (to go north of the Loire), so Charette would leave for Mortagne, adding that if La Rochejaquelein wanted to follow him he could give him a horse. La Rochejaquelein's response was short and to the point: 'I am not accustomed to following, but to being followed.'[2] This, recalled La Ville-Baugé, is how the meeting ended and the two would never meet again. As predicted, around 800 men left Charette to follow La Rochejaquelein.

Heading back towards the coastal Vendée later that day Charette attacked and massacred Cerizay's 200 strong garrison then camped at Les Herbiers that night. Hearing that Charette was at Les Herbiers, Joba and Dufour moved in that direction and were once again closing in, Dufour from the Les Essarts side and Joba from that of St-Fulgent. Joba discovered that Charette had moved to St-Fulgent and, although bad roads meant Dufour was unable to join him in time, he attacked and inflicted more losses on the rebels.

Charette's fragile command was breaking up as both Joly and Savin left and he eventually reached the Forest of Touvois.

In the last few days of the year Charette remarkably managed to unite 6-7,000 men with which he planned to come to the rescue of Noirmoutier now that the republicans were closing in. On 31 December, as a first step in that direction, he overpowered a small garrison in Machecoul.

The end of the 'Great War' of the Vendée

January 1794 was a terrible month for the royalists. Although Charette was gaining an outstanding reputation as a guerrilla fighter, he was defeated twice at Machecoul in the first few days of the year and as a consequence was unable to come to the aid of Noirmoutier which came under large scale attack on 3 January. With its fall, D'Élbée, still too ill to face a firing squad standing, was shot seated in an armchair. Weilland, the garrison commander who had surrendered to Charette, was shot alongside him.

Both La Rochejaquelein and Stofflet had some success in January facing the many republican columns sent into the Vendée to put the region to fire and sword. On 28 January La Rochejaquelein was pursuing some republicans towards Cholet when he found himself alone with a handful of his men near to the farm of La Brissonnière, south-west of Nuaillé. Spotting a grenadier running away he approached and called on him to surrender. The grenadier appeared to cooperate, then suddenly raised his musket and fired on La Rochejaquelein at close range. The shot struck him in the head and killed him instantly. To avoid the republicans finding his body, and the news spreading too quickly, his face was deliberately rendered unrecognisable and he was quickly buried.

The atrocities being committed by Turreau's 'Infernal Columns' in early 1794 led many to join rebel ranks out of desperation. Eventually, in February 1795, the relentless campaigning led the – now more moderate – Republic to offer peace terms. Charette and Sapinaud-de-la-Rairie signed the Treaty of La Juanaye, which promised freedom of religion and exemption from military service. Stofflet eventually accepted its terms that May. Yet Charette took up arms again in June and Sapinaud in October (although Sapinaud came to terms with the Republic in January 1796). Stofflet was also back at war at the beginning of 1796, only to be captured and executed that same February.

After continually eluding the many republican columns sent to hunt him down, Charette was at long last captured in March 1796 after a relentless pursuit by General Travot, which ended with him being physically pinned to the ground by republican troops. He was escorted to Nantes and shot in the square where Cathelineau had been mortally wounded back in June 1793.

After a brief upsurge of violence in 1799 the region remained calm. Only in 1815 would it again become a serious cause for concern and undoubtedly contributed to Napoleon's fall from power during the Hundred Days Campaign. In 1815 two of La Rochejaquelein's younger brothers, Sapinaud-de-la-Rairie, and a nephew of Charette, would all play a prominent role.

The French government drew a veil over the Great War in the Vendée, undoubtedly because so many of the high ideals espoused by the French Republic were replaced by the brutal and bloody suppression of a region that had dared to defy the regime. Although ultimately unsuccessful, this war against the darker side of the French Revolution came close to toppling the Republic, and no counter-revolutionary movement endured so long or achieved so much as the peasants of the Vendée Militaire.

Appendix 1

Biographies of Vendéen and Republican Leaders

With few exceptions, only those attaining the highest ranks (or in the case of the Republic at least divisional command) are listed. All ages, where known, are given in parenthesis and are as of the end of March 1793.

Vendéens

D'Autichamp, Charles-Marie-Auguste-Joseph de Beaumont, Comte (22). Born in Angers. Captain in the Royal-Dragon aged 17, then adjudant major in the Kings' Garde-à-Cheval in 1791. He was with the Émigré Army in Coblenz and at the Tuileries on 10 August 1792. Served with Bonchamps. Captured at Le Mans but escaped execution thanks to a Republican hussar officer to whom he was related (and probably masonic connections). Later fought with Stofflet until 1796. He was involved in the risings of 1799, 1815 and 1832 and received promotions and decorations after the Restoration. He died in 1859.

Béjarry, Amédée de (23). Born in Luçon. ADC to Royrand. Commanded Army of the Centre after Royrand's death. Returned to Vendée and fought until 1796. Died 1844.

Bonchamps, Charles Melchior Arthus Marquis de (29). Former captain of Grenadiers. He served in the Indes under Suffren in the Regiment de Bailli and saw action. He was at the Tuileries on 10 August 1792. Retiring to his Château of La Baronnière, near Saint-Florent-le-Vieil, he was called to lead by local peasants on 13 March. Widely regarded as the best strategist in the army and responsible for protecting the line of the Loire, he led the most well organised and largest division. He had the misfortune to be wounded in action many times, ultimately fatally, succumbing soon after the Battle of Cholet.

Cathelineau, Jacques (35). Market trader, peddler and wagoner by profession, he was held in high esteem and was called to lead on 13 March in his village of Pin-en-Mauges. Pious and extremely brave in combat he became deeply respected and loved by his men and was known as the 'Saint of Anjou'. Divisional commander and first commander in chief of the Grand Army, he was mortally wounded at the battle of Nantes and died in July.

Charette de la Contrie, François-Athanase (29). Former naval officer and had fought in the American War of Independence. He left the navy in 1790 and went to fight with the Émigré Army. Soon disillusioned with what he saw, he was at the Tuileries in August 1792 but managed to escape and return to his home at Fontéclose. He tried his best to stay out of the troubles but was soon leading thousands of peasants in the coastal region and went on to become the most celebrated of all of the leaders in the Vendée until he was finally captured and executed in 1796.

Des Essarts, Charles Marie Michel, Chevalier (in his 24th year). Former priest and émigré who had joined the rebel army by sometime in May 1793. He commanded Lescure's former division in December, escaped after Savenay, but was captured and executed in January 1794.

Dommaigné, Jean-Baptiste-Louis-Étienne de (Comte de Brulon) (43). He had been in the Garde-de-Corps for many years and was subsequently a colonel in the National Guard and deputy at the Fête of the Fédération in 1790. With the Rising he was soon given command of the Vendéen cavalry. Distinguished at Thouars and 2nd Fontenay, he was killed leading a charge at Saumur in June.

Donnissan, Guy-Joseph marquis de (56). Maréchal-de-camp and veteran of the Seven Years War. Released with his son-in-law Lescure in May, he was known to lead troops in some battles but is better remembered for his role as governor of rebel territory and his influence in war councils. He was captured at Savenay and executed in January 1794. He was the father of Madame de la Rochejaquelein.

D'Élbée, Marquis Maurice-Joseph-Louis Gigost (41). Born in Dresden but naturalised French. Former junior officer in both the infantry and cavalry, he left the army with the rank of lieutenant in 1785, retiring to his château of La Loge near Beaupréau. He was a Deputy to the Third-Estate. Put at the head of the peasants in spite of his protests he was soon a divisional general and became commander in chief after the death of Cathelineau. D'Élbée was a capable general with flashes of exceptional skill and bravery but lacked the charisma of some of the other leaders. Dangerously wounded at Cholet, he was captured and shot with the fall of Noirmoutier in January 1794.

Fleuriot, Jacques Nicolas de (54). Former Maréchal-des-Logis in the Gardes-de-Corps, he fought with Stofflet then Bonchamps. Became commander-in-chief of the Grand Army days before Savenay, from which he managed to escape. Fought with Stofflet, Sapinaud, and finally Charette until 1796. He died in 1821.

Fleuriot, Jacques (56). Former lieutenant, page to the Queen and brother of the above. Rose up with Piron then joined Bonchamps, commanding his division on several occasions (notably Montreuil-Bellay and Saumur). Mortally wounded at Nantes.

Forestier, Henri (17). A cobbler's son. Involved in 1792 rising. Joined Cathelineau March 1793. Soon appointed second-in-command of the cavalry under Dommaigné then later Talmont. He campaigned north of the Loire, then with the Chouans before joining Stofflet. In 1795 he was in England but again fought in the Vendée in 1799. Subsequently involved in various conspiracies he was condemned to death by Napoleon. Died in London 1806 in suspicious circumstances.

Joly, Jean-Baptiste. Surgeon and former sergeant in the Royal Army, commanded in La Mothe-Achard area. Fiercely independent he often fought with others in the area, and on occasion with the Grand Army, but had a difficult relationship with Charette. He left Charette after being reproached for the loss of Challans in April 1794 and was condemned to death. Disguised as a peasant, he set out to join Stofflet but was mistakenly condemned as a spy and shot.

La Rochejaquelein, Henri du Vergier, Comte de (20). From one of the foremost families of the west of France he was born at the family château of La Durbelière. An officer in the King's Constitutional Guard he was at the defence of the Tuileries on 10 August 1792 and managed to escape back to his home territory. Divisional general, then commander in chief of the army during the campaign north of the Loire. Charismatic, recklessly brave and proved to be an exceptional tactician. He was killed in January 1794.

Laugrenière, Dominique-Alexandre Chevalier Jaudonnet de (47). Former King's musketeer, nobleman. Soon in command of the Argenton-Château Division forming part of the Grand Army and fought in a number of major engagements. He campaigned north of the Loire, was captured after Savenay, and guillotined in January 1794.

Lescure, Louis Marie de Salgues, Marquis de (26). Educated at the *École-Militaire* in Paris, Lescure was a cavalry captain by 1791 and emigrated that same year. Back in Paris in 1792 he participated in the defence of the Tuileries before returning to Poitou. Arrested in April 1793 he was released on 2 May when the rebels seized Bressuire. Known by the rebels as the 'Saint of Anjou' for his piety, he is said to have never personally killed an enemy soldier. He fought most often with La Rochejaquelein and was one of the foremost Vendéen generals. Mortally wounded on 15 October he eventually died the following month.

Lyrot de la Patouillière, Francois Jean Hervé, Chevalier (60). Veteran of the American War of Independence. This former officer led the 'Men of Loroux'. Independent but often fought with Charette and the Grand Army. Distinguished during the campaign north of the Loire and killed at Savenay.

Marigny, Augustin Étienne Gaspard de Bernard de (38). Naval Lieutenant in the American War of Independence. At the Tuileries on 10 August 1792 before returning to the west. Imprisoned then later released in May from Bressuire with Lescure. Soon in command of the Grand Army's artillery. Fought in numerous battles and campaigned north of the Loire. Escaped after Savenay and returned to fight in the Vendée in 1794 with Stofflet, Sapinaud and Charette. He was accused of betraying an agreement between the generals not to attack in isolation and was blamed for having compromised a key battle. Condemned to death by Stofflet and Charette he was captured and shot in July 1794 to widespread disgust, causing some to abandon the cause.

Piron, Dominique-Louis (32). Piron had fought in the Antilles and in the American War of Independence under Rochambeau and in the émigré army. He was a captain in the Varennes National Guard. He led parishes near the Loire. One of the most outstanding generals in the rebel army. He was either shot after Savenay or killed in 1794.

Royrand, Chevalier Charles Augustin de (Sixties). Retired colonel. Commander-in-chief of the Army of the Centre. He was a rich landowner, highly regarded in the region. Mortally wounded at Entrammes. Died December 1793.

Sapinaud-de-la-Verrie (55). Former officer in Gardes-de-Corps (for 25 years). Divisional general in the Army of the Centre, sometimes fighting with the Grand Army. Killed defending the line of the River Lay in July.

Savin, Jean-René-François (27). Rich landowner who often fought with Joly and Charette. With Charette in 1794. Captured and executed in March 1796.

Stofflet, Jean-Nicolas (40). Born in Lorraine he had served for seventeen years in the Lorraine-Infanterie-Royale Regiment. He left the army as a corporal to become his former colonel's gamekeeper and warden for the forests of Maulévrier. Active in 1792. A natural leader with a forceful, sometimes violent, personality but unquestionably brave. Divisional general and later major general and second in command of the Grand Army. He fought on until 1796 when he was captured and shot.

Talmont, Antoine-Philippe de La Trémouille, Prince de (27). Involved in the La Rouërie plot in 1792. Emigrated, returning to the west in early 1793. Joined the rebels after Saumur and commanded the cavalry with variable success, although distinguished north of the Loire. Captured near Fougères, December, guillotined January 1794.

Republicans

Aubert-Dubayet, Jean-Baptiste Anibal (35). Born in Lousiana. Fought in the American War of Independence. Divisional general commanding Army of Mayence. Dismissed as a *ci-devant* in October, imprisoned until the fall of Robespierre. He died in Constantinople in 1797 when French Ambassador.

Baudry D'Asson, Esprit (42). Born in the Vendée. Long service before the Revolution, lieutenant colonel 1792, general of brigade May 1793, with Les Sables Division from March until September. Army of the West 1794. Later commandant of Rochefort. Died 1812.

Beaufranchet D'Ayat, Louis Charles Antoine de (35). Illegitimate child of Louis XV. Captain 1782, colonel 1792 (at Valmy). Berruyer's chief of staff on the day Louis XVI guillotined, overseeing the day's proceedings. General of brigade (March 1793) and later general of division. Dismissed July 1793 as a *ci-devant*, retired in 1806, died 1812.

Beaupuy, Michel Armand de Bacharetie de (37). Joined army in 1771, lieutenant in 1789. Fought on the Rhine then Mayence where he became general of brigade. General of division after Cholet and survived the dismissals of former nobles due to his fine service. Gravely wounded at Entrammes, in Vendée until 1795, transferred to Samble-et-Meuse, and killed in action in 1796.

Berruyer, Jean Francois de (55). Joined army 1751 and fought in the Seven Years War. Colonel in 1791. In 1792 he was appointed commander of the troops in Paris and was infamously remembered for ordering a roll of drums to drown out Louis XVI's attempt to address the crowd just before being guillotined. Commander-in-chief in the Vendée, recalled 28 April, dismissed June. Later with armies in the Alps and Italy then governor of Les Invalides. Died 1804.

Berthier, Loius Alexandre (39). Later famous as Napoleon's outstanding chief of staff and marshal. Veteran of Yorktown campaign; Colonel of the Versailles National Guard (1789), then on staff of General Lafayette, before chief of staff to Marshal Lucknor in 1792. General of brigade in May 1792. He was sent with Berruyer to Angers at the end of March, reputedly as a private, but reappointed General of brigade by Biron. Dismissed after Battle of Vihiers. With Napoleon in 1795, marshal 1804, died 1815.

Duc de Biron, Armand Louis de Gontaut, Duc de Lauzan (45). Famous for Lauzan's Legion of American War of Independence fame, Biron had lived a dissolute life in the royal court. Campaigned in America, Corsica and Africa. Maréchal-de-camp by 1783; general of division early in the Revolution; commander-in-chief of the Army of Italy December 1792, then in Vendée May 1793. Dismissed in July, imprisoned and guillotined 31 December 1793.

Boulard, Henri Francois Morille (in his 57th year). Joined army in 1762, captain 1789, lieutenant colonel 1791. Under Marcé in March 1793 before commanding the Les Sables Division. Retired through ill health in July, died November 1793.

Canclaux, Jean Baptiste Camille, Marquis de (52). Maréchal-de-camp before the Revolution, general of division 1791. In Britanny in 1792; commander-in-chief of the Army of the Brest Coast in May 1793, which he commanded effectively. Dismissed as a *ci-devant* in October. After Thermidor he became commander-in-chief of the Army of the West and concluded peace treaties with many of the rebels in 1795. Crushed the émigré and Chouan army at Quiberon with Hoche. Senator 1804, Comte d'Empire 1808, died 1817.

Chalbos, Francois Alexis (57). Joined the army in 1751 and fought in the Seven Years War. Captain 1789, then chef-de-bataillon. Sent to Vendée 30 April 1793; general of brigade 6 May; general of division 22 May. Subsequently served in the Army of the West until November. Army of the Rhine (1794); Brest Coast (1795); later commanded the 20th and 25th Military Divisions before commanding the Army of Mayence (1801-3). Died 1803.

Commaire, Marc Antoine (38). Long military service on land and sea. Joined Paris National Guard as a captain. Colonel 24 May 1793. A close associate of Santerre, Rossignol and Ronsin, he was general of division on 30 September. Died from exhaustion brought on by the Vendéen War.

Coustard de St-Lo, Guy (44). Joined army 1763; captain by 1789 and general of division May 1793. After Saumur he served in the Army of the Alps, dismissed as a *ci-devant* in October and saw little further active service. Died 1825.

Duhoux, Charles Francois (57). He had long service in the Royal Army. Lieutenant colonel before 1789. With Army of the North in 1792 then lieutenant general in Army of the Interior and the Vendée. Badly wounded at Chemillé and after defeat at Pont-Barré spent ten months in prison. He participated in the Royalist Rising in Paris (13 Vendémiaire). He died in or after 1799.

Dutruy, Jacques (30). Born in Geneva, served in Swiss Regiments in French service before the Revolution. Captain, 1792; chef-du-bataillon, February 1793; general of brigade, June 1793. Replaced Mieszkowski in command of Les Sables Division. He was opposed to Turreau's orders to lay waste to the region in 1794 and suspended. Later served in Army of the West, Army of England, in San Domingo, then Dalmatia. Died in 1836.

Gauvilliers, Jean Marie Gaspard (38). Joined the army 1774. Led Angers National Guard February 1793. Defeated at Beaupréau. General of brigade (June); general of division (July), suspended end September. No further active service. Died after 1814.

Grouchy, Emmanuel Marquis de (26). Joined the army 1780. Maréchal-de-camp (September 1792). Served in the Armies of: the Centre, Alps, Cherbourg Coast then Brest Coast (15 May 1793). He distinguished himself in several actions near Nantes. Suspended October. Reintegrated in Year III of the Republic and promoted general of division, returning for further service in the West. Fought at Hohenlinden. His extensive service under Napoleon is well documented. Marshal 1815. Died 1847.

Kléber, Jean-Baptiste (40). In the army 1777 until early 1780s, then in the Austrian army before becoming an architect. Joined the National Guard (1789), lieutenant colonel (1792). Promoted chef de brigade at Mayence. General of brigade (27 August) in the Army of Mayence and fought continually until the end of 1793. Subsequently fought in the Armies of: Ardennes, Rhine, Sambre-et-Meuse, England and finally the Army of the Orient. Commander-in-chief after Napoleon left Egypt and assassinated in June 1800 by an extremist.

Labarolière, Jacques-Marguerite (50). Long service in the Royal Army, reaching the rank of colonel. General of division, 6 May 1793. Illness, and his disgust at the influence of Ronsin, led to his dismissal on 30 July. Reinstated after Thermidor and retired seven years later.

L'Échélle, Jean (in his 33rd year). Joined the army 1774. Fought at Jemappes and Neerwinden. Commander of the 12th Military Division (September 1793), then commander in chief of the Army of the West (early October). Left Kléber to determine the tactics used at Battle of Cholet and responsible for the catastrophe at Entrammes. Dismissal, then died November 1793.

Leygonier, Francois (52). Joined the army 1756. Fought in the Seven Years War. Lieutenant (1761); Commanding National Guards covering the Loire (March 1793) and interim commander-in-chief of the Army of the La Rochelle Coast (May). Imprisoned April 1794, later released and retired (1800). Died 1801.

Marcé, Louis Henry Francois, Comte de (in his 62nd year). An officer from 1744. As general of brigade led the first expedition from La Rochelle in March and was defeated at La Guérinière. Guillotined January 1794.

Marceau, Francois-Séverin Desgraviers (24). Joined the army 1784; at the fall of the Bastille (1789) and the Siege of Valenciennes. Joined the *Légion-Germanique* as a lieutenant (1792); general of brigade (October), and interim commander-in-chief of the Army of the West (November and December). In 1794 he served in the Army of Ardennes then Sambre-et-Meuse. Killed at Altenkirchen on 20 September 1796.

Menou, Jacques Francois de Boussay, Comte de (42). Joined the army in 1766; colonel by 1788. He served with the Army of the North, Reserve, then sent to the Vendée as chief of staff to the Army of the La Rochelle Coast (6 May). General of division (15 May). Wounded at Saumur and Vihiers. Subsequently without a role. Later in the Armies of the Alps and Interior. Joined Napoleon's expedition to Egypt and became commander-in-chief after Kléber's assassination. Later served as governor of Tuscany then Venice. Died 1810.

Mieszkowski, Jean Quirin (49). In the Polish army from 1761, then a French hussar regiment in 1766. He fought in Senegal then America (serving in Lauzan's Legion). Major (1789), then Biron's ADC in 1792, campaigning on the Rhine and Alps. Joined Biron in the Vendée (June 1793); led the Les Sables Division in September and dismissed in October 1793. Retired in 1795 and died in 1819.

Muller, Francois (38). Served in the Royal Army. After the Revolution, he was a dancer and comedian before joining the Paris Volunteers. Adjoint in the Army of the North by November 1792. Sent to Tours (15 June); general of brigade then general of division between 12 and 30 September. A notorious drunkard he was sacked then reinstated later in the 1790s, served in the Army of Italy under Napoleon, was internally exiled as a supporter of Moreau and died in 1808.

Quétineau, Pierre (36). Joined the army in 1772. Became an officer after the Revolution and fought with the Army of the North before returning to command the National Guards in Deux-Sèvres. Catastrophically defeated at Thouars in May 1793, he was imprisoned. Guillotined in March 1794.

Rey, Antoine Gabriel Venance (29). Joined the army in 1783. Commanding troops in Chinon (June 1793); general of brigade (July) and later general of division. Suspended October. Reinstated in 1794 and fought in the West under Hoche. Fought with the Army of Italy in 1796. Back to the west in 1799, retired 1803, later holding commands in the National Guard. Died 1836.

Ronsin, Charles Philippe (41). In the army 1768-72, then a writer in Paris. Captain, Paris National Guards (1789). Heavily involved in Hébértist politics within the Paris Commune. Commissaire of war (November 1792) then assistant to the Minister of War. Sent to the Vendée (May 1793); general of brigade 4 July but badly defeated at Coron in September. Back in Paris he became the commander of the *Armée-Revolutionnaire*. Arrested in December and guillotined March 1794.

Rossignol, Jean Antoine (33). Having been a goldsmith Rossignol joined the army in 1775. He was at the storming of the Bastille, joined the National Guard in 1791, and was lieutenant colonel in the Gendarmerie when he arrived in the Vendée. A virulent *sans-culotte* and Hébértist he soon came into conflict with Biron and Westermann. Following his arrest for inciting insubordination and looting he would be exonerated by the Jacobin Club and both Danton and Robespierre came to his support. Returning to the Vendée he would become the commander-in-chief of the Armies of the La Rochelle Coast, Brest Coast, and then Army of the West. Considered a true Republican, but terrible general, he was eventually dismissed in April 1794. With possible links to the Babeuf Conspiracy (1796) and an attempt on Napoleon's life in 1800 (the 'Infernal Machine'), he would be imprisoned and deported to the Seychelles then the Comoros Islands, where he died in 1802.

Salomon, Francois Nicolas de (53). Joined the army in 1750. Fought in the Seven Years War and Corsica. Lieutenant colonel in 1769. Sent to the Vendée as a general of brigade (April 1793); general of division (30 July); suspended (30 September). After service in the Army of the Rhine he retired. Died 1799.

Santerre, Antoine Joseph Galet de (41). A successful brewer and important figure in the Paris Commune. Officer in the National Guard (1789) he led Paris Battalions to the Vendée in late May. Although repeatedly defeated, his *sans-culotte* credentials meant he attained the rank of general of division in the Army of the La Rochelle Coast. Recalled September 1793, served a period in prison, then left the army in July 1794. Died 1809.

Tilly, Jacques Louis Francois Delaistre de (44). In the army from 1761. General of brigade in the Army of the Cherbourg Coast (April 1793). Fought at Le Mans and subsequently promoted general of division. Fought throughout the Napoleonic Wars (principally in Germany then Spain). Retired in 1815 and died 1822.

Tuncq, Augustin (46). In the army from 1767. Captain in the National Guard (1792); at the attack on the Tuileries. General of brigade (1793), replaced Sandoz at Luçon (23 June). Victorious at 2nd and 3rd battles of Luçon and promoted general of division. Blamed for the defeat of Chantonnay (September) he was imprisoned, then released after Thermidor. Subsequently fought in the west and on the Rhine. Died 1800.

Westermann, Francois Joseph (41). Joined the hussars in 1767. Very active in Paris during the Revolution. Colonel of the *Légion-du-Nord* fighting on the northern frontier then, promoted to general of brigade, he was transferred to the Vendée (June 1793). Fought with mixed success in the Vendée. Although brave he became known as the 'Butcher of the Vendée' for his merciless pursuit of the rebels and actions after Savenay. Guillotined with Danton (April 1794).

Selected details of the Republican Armies

Principal sources: Vincennes Army Returns and Correspondence of the Armies; Savary and Chassin.

Abbreviations:

NtGd: National Guard; Vol: Volunteers; Gend: Gendarmes.

AdjG: Adjudant General; CdB: Chef de Brigade; GdB: General de Brigade; GdD: General de Division; CinC: Commander-in-Chief.

i: infantry; c: cavalry; a: artillery.

Div: Division; D-B: Demi-Brigade; Bn: Battalion; Co: Company; Sq: Squadron.

Troop strengths shown in parenthesis.

MARCH

11 March – NtGd and available troops mobilised from the following divisions: 12th Military Div (HQ La Rochelle): GdD Verteuil; 13th Military Div (HQ Rennes): GdD Canclaux.

Army of the Reserve (late March)

Berruyer: South of Loire, HQ Angers (18,500); Marcé: Army of the Vendée (4,500).

APRIL

Army of the Brest Coast

Nantes: CinC GdD Canclaux (3,000). Nantes NtGd (?4,000); Beysser from 17 April (2,000i, 200c, 8 guns).

Army of the Reserve

Labourdonnaye (North of Loire) replaced by Canclaux 15 April. Berruyer dismissed late April.

Northern and Eastern Fronts:

Interim CinC Leygonier (Replaced Berruyer 28 April).

Duhoux: Angers (?4,000 possibly including Ladouce).

Ladouce: Layon (2,500).

Leygonier: Doué Division (4,000i, 89c, 5 guns; rising to 6,500i, 200c, 12 x 4pdrs).

Gauvilliers: Ancenis, Varades and Ingrandes (1,500 plus Angers NtGd).

Quétineau: Bressuire/Parthenay (3,150).

Southern Front:

GdD Beaufranchet D'Ayat.

7 April - Chalbos: Luçon (219c); Ste-Hermine (1,600i, 241c); La Châtaigneraie (1000i, 54c); Fontenay (NtGds: 400i and 400c; Gend 400c).

6 April – Boulard: Les Sables Division - 1st Div Dumas: 60th Line (52i), 110th Line (116i), 1st, 2nd, 3rd Bordeaux (1,900i), Gend (125c), 207 gunners, 2 x 8pdrs. 2nd Div Baudry: 4th Marine (65i), Chasseurs du Midi (220i), Vol. Niort (211i), Fontenay Grenadiers (104i), 8th La Rochelle (22i), Vol. Barbezieux (127i), Vol de la Liberté (691i), Vols La Mothe-Achard, Les Sables and Luçon (228i), NtGd (78c), 173 gunners, 2 x 4pdrs.

19-21 April - Troops on route to Army of Reserve included: 5th and 6th Calvados and 4th Eure (1,000), Légion-Rosenthal (300i, 400c), 8th Hussars (250c), Légion-des-Alpes (400 arrived at Niort 28 May), 4 Co's Gunners (216a), 13th Chasseurs-à-Cheval.

MAY

Army of La Rochelle Coast (created around 30 April from Army of the Reserve)

North and Eastern Front:

Leygonier: Acting-CinC 28 April to 28 May, total of forces unclear.

Doué Division (2-3,000 reinforced by 2,400).

Gauvilliers: North bank of Loire (approximately 1,500).

Duhoux/Menou: Angers (?4,000).

Ladouce: Layon (2,700).

Quétineau (See below).

Southern Front:

GdD D'Ayat. HQ Niort (numbers constantly increasing).

Chalbos: La Châtaigneraie/Fontenay (3,047: increasing to 7,500 by 25th); Sandoz (arrived 11 May): St-Maixent, Fontenay then Luçon (Rising to 2-3,000); Boulard: Les Sables D'Olonne (4,300).

Quetineau's Army at Battle of Thouars (estimates only)

NtGd Bns (2,650i); 8th Var (325i); Chasseurs-du-Midi (250i); 3rd Deux-Sèvres (200i); 2-3000 raw volunteers; NtGd and Gend (80c); dragoons, hussars and chasseurs from depots (33c); 12 guns.

8 May – 5,000 recruits arrive in Nantes.

23 May – Orléans: Bns being formed under General Hesse's instruction.

26 May – New Paris Bns ordered to Vendée without delay.

Army of the La Rochelle Coast: late May. From: 'Table of forces of the Army of the Vendée and posts occupied around the country, 15-24 May 1793'. Details prepared by Ronsin (not including troops under organisation in Saumur and Tours).

Talot: Les Ponts-de-Cé, Erigné, Meure, Grande Claye, Avrillé and Brissac (2,397i, 59c, 180a, 14 guns).

'The infantry are formed of the contingent, are dressed, but few are trained and the minority are armed with hunting fusils.' Lack 350 fusils.

Gauvilliers: St Georges, Le Poissonnière, La Pommeraye and Ingrandes (1,549i, 192c, 65a, 7 guns).

'*The infantry is partly formed of fathers of families who will need replacing by the volunteers under recruitment. The cavalry needs 60 horses and the artillery 12. The battalions are mostly armed with bad hunting fusils. They need at least 500 fusils.*'

GdD Canclaux [note: Actually part of Army of Brest Coast]: Ancenis, Varades, Oudon, Fermont, Mauver and Thouar (1,457i, 84c, 9 guns).

'*The battalions are nearly all disordered.*'

GdD Canclaux & CdB Beysser: Nantes [note: Actually part of Army of Brest Coast].

Nantes (900i); Port-St-Père (800i, 40a, 9c); Machecoul (1797i, 132a, 73c); Paimboeuf (1,000i); Pornic (200i); Bourgneuf (200i); Noirmoutier (200i). 19 guns.

'*3,600 men are moving to Nantes, not including Volontaires-à-Cheval.*'

Boulard - Les Sables Division: Challans (1,278i, 37a, 39c); La Grenache (86i, 3c); St-Gilles (340i, 10c); La Chaise (86i, 3c); Vaizé (107i, 4c); Beauvoir (37i, 3c); Ille Bouin (35i). 15 guns.

La Mothe Achard (1872i, 104a, 98c, 4 guns); Les Sables d'Olonne (796i, 18a, 72c).

'*The troops in Mothe-Achard are dressed equipped and armed and have proven their discipline and valour*'.

GdD D'Ayat, HQ Fontenay: Talmont (237i, 22c); Avrillé (250i, 11c); St Cyr (80i, 22c); Port-la-Claye (450i, 14a, 26c); Luçon (462i, 104c); Fontenay (814i, 178c). La Châtaigneraie (4,573i, 296c, 54a); Ste-Hermine (2,220i, 168c, 7 guns); Niort (1,687i, 62a 81c).

'*The troops in Talmont, Avrillé, St Cyr, Port-la-Claye, Luçon and Fontenay-le-Peuple are composed of local National Guards, they are neither organised nor dressed, very badly armed, and you cannot count on those in Ste-Hermine being in a better state.*'

'*Niort: The troops are formed from the countryside contingent and are not organised. There are nearly 600 Volunteer Cavalry that can be deployed if necessary.*'

Other Forces commanded by the Army of La Rochelle: In La Rochelle, the islands, and further south (3,682 men).

Grand Total: 28,904, 91 guns (of which 1,200 line troops, 7-8,000 Volunteers).

JUNE

Army of Brest Coast CinC Canclaux

Beysser: Nantes (5,300); Coustard-de-Massy: Nantes NtGd (4,500).

Weilland and Mourain (same as for May).

Army of La Rochelle Coast CinC Biron (from 28 May).

7 June - Leygonier replaced by Duhoux.

9 June - Acting CinC Menou; Coustard de St-Lo (4,260); Santerre (1,650); Berthier (1,800-2,100); Reserve (2-4,000).

Salomon: Thouars (4,000).

Southern Front and Coast:

1 June - Niort (17,000: 6,000 fit to fight); Sandoz: Luçon (1,245i and 90c).

Mid-June - Les Sables Division: 1st Column Boulard (3,150i, 231a, 229c, 9 guns); 2nd Column Baudry (2,896i, 84c, 3 x 4pdrs, 1 x8pdr); Talmont Garrison (345i, 25c); St-Gilles Garrison (985i, 50a, 17c).

13 June State of Forces of Army of La Rochelle Coast

'Solid troops' (5,766i, 850c) of which only 87 men (from the 84th Line) were regulars.

Volunteers or Recruits (5,664i, 485c, 52a).

Requisitioned National Guards (6,826i).

21 June Army of General Duhoux in and around Tours:

Div Labarolière - AvGd (1,783i, 1,169c); 1st Div Menou: 1st Brig Joly (2,361i), 2nd Brig Santerre (4,000i); 2nd Div Coustard: 3rd Brig [blank] (2,400i) 4th Brig Chabot (1,712i); Cavalry: GdB Beffroy (505c); 2nd Brigade Barbazan: (1,648i); Reserve Descloseaux: (2,026i, 174c).

Artillery Parks (undated return, June: not including 50 battalion guns noted on 29th): 1st Div - 3 x 12pdrs, 4 x 8pdrs; 2nd Div - 8 x 8pdrs, 12 x 12pdrs. (400a).

Battle of Nantes

GdD Canclaux: CinC Army of Brest Coast and all forces in Nantes. GdB Beysser: Commandant of Nantes and second in command. Representatives of the People: Merlin de Douai and Gillet. Former Representative still in Nantes who fought with the cavalry: Coustard-de-Massy.

Defence of Eastern Suburbs: GdB Gillibert; Defence of Southern Front: GdB Boisguyon.

Infantry (estimated strengths) – Regular Troops: The 1/34th (300i: Guin says 600i); 1/39th (400i: Guin says 649i); 1/41st (400i); 1/109th (400i). Guin adds 1/3rd. Volunteer Battalions: 3rd Orne (400i); 4th Orne (400i: Guin says 80i); 8th Seine-Inférieure (400i); 11th Seine-et-Oise (600i); 13th Seine-et-Oise (600i); 1st Mayenne (400i); 1st Côtes-du-Nord (400i); Guin adds 668 Fédérés; Chasseurs de la Charente (400i); Grenadiers Maine-et-Loire (100i). Note: The combined strength of these battalions, plus two companies of Paris Gunners (see below), were reported to be 5,388 men.

Légion-Nantaise: Formed by Coustard-de-Massy on 14 June 1793 from 2,000 men. Many reported to be unarmed on 25 June.

Nantes NtGd: Deurbroucq. There is conflicting information as to how many were present. Savary refers to 4 to 5,000 (including the Légion-Nantaise). The Nantes NtGd was theoretically formed from battalions from each of the city's 16 Quarters. Not all of the NtGd was in the city and the following are mentioned: 2 Légions (unspecified strength); Vétérans (44i); Cavalry (50c); Sailors of the NtGd (around 200); Bn élèves (students). A few hundred NtGds from beyond Nantes were also present.

Other troops: 2 cos Invalides du Château.

Other Cavalry: Gend (25-50c); Côtes-du-Nord and Ille-et-Vilaine (84c).

Artillery: Probably in excess of 60 guns. Except for the 'Great Battery' on the north front the guns were deployed in ones or twos. Most were 4pdrs deployed with their infantry or in fixed positions, although there were some 6, 12 and 18pdrs. Gunners: 4 Cos Paris (Guin: 250a); 2 Cos Seine-et-Oise (Guin: 55a).

Grand Total: 10-11,000 men.

JULY

Army of La Rochelle Coast

Salomon and Rey (possibly as per June). Rossignol (1,500).

1 July - Troops in Niort and Cantonments (including St-Maixent):

GdD Chalbos - 10 Orléans Bns (6,272i); Gren. de la Convention (181i); Vols, NtGds and Gend (6,706i);

Light Troops (2,413i); Cavalry (1,385c); 3 x 8pdrs, 12 x 4pdrs, 1 howitzer.

Of these: 2,000 in the Orléans battalions were untrained and unarmed; 2,609 others unarmed; St-Maixent and Niort Garrisons included in these figures (3,955i); being sent towards Tours (3,000), and being sent to Boulard (1,955).

Troops in garrison included:

Sandoz: Luçon (2,569i, 109c, 74a).

Camp La [?Quatre] Chemins (1,197i, 61a, 3 x 4pdrs, 1 x 8pdr).

Boulard: Les Sables (4,775).

Baudry: Vairé and St-Gilles (2,585).

Châtillon Campaign July

3 July - Westermann's Légion-du-Nord: 2 Bns Chasseurs (1,130i); 4 Sqds (365c); 1 foot and 1 horse battery (14 guns); 11th Orléans (756i); 14th Orléans (469i); 2 further battalions. Total: 2,700-3,000 men (plus 2,000 conscripts by 5 July).

18 July Vihiers

CinC Labarolière. 1st Div Menou - Brigades: Fabrefond/Dutruy, Barbazan and Gauvilliers (4,000). 18 guns. 2nd Div - 1st Brigade: Santerre: 5 Paris Bns (4,160i); 2nd Brigade: Joly (1,750i: of which 500 line troops); 3rd Brigade: Chabot (2,250i: of which 600 line troops).

Cavalry - 8th and 9th Hussars; 16th and 19th Dragoons; 24th Chasseurs; Vol Mayenne (1,600c).

Artillery Parks (400a) - 1st Div: 3 x 12pdrs, 4 x 8pdrs. 2nd Div: 8 x 8pdrs, 12 x 12pdrs.

Of these troops 1,500 were left in Saumur, and 1,500 left covering Angers.

AUGUST

Army of La Rochelle Coast

CinC Rossignol (took command 31 July, arrested 25-30 August, reinstated 1 September). Santerre acting CinC 25-30 August.

North and Eastern Front:

Troops in Saumur (11 August) - Div Santerre: AvGd (3,276i, 590c); 1st Brigade (1,800-2000i); 2nd Brigade (1914i, 60c); Château Saumur (887).

12 August - Salomon (3,400). 15 August - Rey (1,300).

Southern Front:

GdD Chalbos - HQ Niort (3,500); Boulard: Les Sables Division (3,081i, 310c, 7 x 4pdrs); Baudry (1,269i, 282c 3 x 4pdrs, 1 x 8pdr). Garrisons and Posts: St-Gilles (1,218i, 21c, 3 x 4pdrs); Le Pas Opton (90i, 1c); La Fineuotte[sic] (135i); Croix-de-Vie (60i); Les Sables (679i, 36a); Talmont (339i); Avrillé (438i, 24c); Moutiers-Des-Maufaits[sic](162i, 22c); La Chaizé (300i); Les Sables Positional Guns (181a: 3 x 36pdrs, 2 x 24pdrs, 9 x 18pdrs, 6 x 12pdrs, 8 x 8 pdrs, 4 x 6pdrs, 2 x 4pdrs).

14 August - Luçon: Tuncq (5,371i, 414c, 203a, 13 x 4pdrs, 1 x 8pdr).

Army of the Brest Coast CinC: Canclaux.

Paimboeuf (2,000i, Sqd Chasseurs-à-Cheval, several guns); Loire Estuary: 10 gunboats.

11 August - In Nantes (2,739 Volunteers, 1,090 Line, 252 cavalry, 144 gunners): Part of a force of 6-7,000 in the wider area.

25 August - AvGd Blosse: Chasseurs de la Charente; Det. 31st Line; Det. Cote-d'Or; Co. Grenadiers 9th Line; 12 Cos Grenadiers; Dragoons Ille-et-Vilaine; Chasseurs of 34th Regt; 1 gun.

Grouchy: 109th Line; 100 Chasseurs of 15th Regt; Hussards-Américains; D-B: 1/34th Line, 3rd Orne, 4th Orne; D-B: 2/77th Regt, 11th and 12th Paris; 6 x 8pdrs, 6 x 4pdrs, 2 howitzers.

SEPTEMBER

1 September - Army of the La Rochelle Coast (41,000). Tens of thousands of new levies arriving.

Forthcoming dismissals: GdDs: Rey, Salomon and Gauvilliers; GdBs: Nouvion, Cannier, Bonnavita, Mieszkowski, Beffroy and Burac.

The GdDs were to be: Chalbos, Santerre, Muller, Commaire and Garonde; GdBs: Fabrefond, Dutruy, Desclozeaux, Legros, Duval, Dembarrère,

Moulin (Snr), Kléber, Haxo, Robert, Canuel, Chambon, Danican and Vimeux.

Battle of Chantonnay (5 September):

CinC Tuncq (absent). Lecomte, Marceau. Included: Chasseurs de l'Oise; 4th Dordogne; 7th Orléans; 10th Orléans; Bn Égalité; Bn l'Union; Bn Le Vengeur; 3rd Charente-Inférieure; 6th Charente-Inférieure; Bn Calvados; 3rd Deux-Sèvres; Bn du Loiret; 2 Sqds Gend; Sqd 11th Hussars; 2 Sqds 14th Chasseurs; 11 x 4pdrs; 1 x 8pdr; Artillerie-Volante (2 light guns). Total (8,000).

Army of the La Rochelle Coast (Mid-September):

CinC Rossignol. AvGd (2,828i, ?guns); 1st Brigade: Joly (2,127i, ?guns); 2nd Brigade: ? (2,247i, 6 guns); 3rd Brigade: Chabot (?i, 8 guns); Cavalry (656c); Saumur château (998i).

Southern Front:

Chalbos (11,000); Les Sables/Luçon area (4,000).

Army of Mayence Aubert-Dubayet (placed under Canclaux's command):

AvGd: Kléber; 1st Brigade: Vimeux; 2nd Brigade: Beaupuy; Reserve: Haxo. End August: 9,075 fit to fight. 24 guns.

Army of Brest Coast CinC Canclaux:

Nantes area (6,270); Nantes NtGd (3,000); (other garrisons as for August).

Mid-September - Grouchy (2,821): 1,160 from Army of Mayence (600 needed new fusils); 1,200 grenadiers forming AvGd of Army of Brest Coast; 21 *Cavalarie-Nantais*; 2 x 12pdrs, 2 x 8pds, 3 x 4pdrs, 1 howitzer.

OCTOBER

Army of Mayence - 8 October: including some troops integrated from Army of Brest Coast.

Briefly in command - GdB Kléber. AvGd - GdB Beaupuy: 3rd D-B - Légion-des-Francs (349i, 37c); Chasseurs-de-Cassel (434i); Chass Côtes-d'Or (86i); Chasse Charente (100i); 7th Light (52i). 6th D-B - 1st Bn Grenadiers (563i); 2nd Grenadiers (726i); Bn 2nd Jura & 13th Nièvre (432i); 4th Haut-Rhin (372i); 7th &11th Vosges (337i); Artillery (44a, 4 guns). 1st Division - GdB

Vimeux: 1st Brigade - 82nd Regt (217i); Grenadiers of 37th, 60th ,84th, 88th Regts (149i); 8th Vosges (153i); 9th Jura (426i); 62nd Regt (337i); 6th Calvados (245i); 4th Calvados (244i); 5th Eure (370i).[2nd] Brigade - 2nd Seine-et-Oise (238i); 1st République (143i); 1st Fédérés-Nationaux (205i); 2nd Amis de la République (237i); Chasseurs de Saône-et-Loire (144i); Artillery (45a, 5 guns); Artillery Park (161a, 3 guns); Artillerie-Volante (49a, 4 guns); Chasseurs-à-Cheval (263c).

2nd Division - AdjG Scherb: CdB Saint-Sauveur - 32nd Regt (242i); Det 13th Regt (47i); 2nd Haute-Saône (255i); 9th Haute-Saône (378i); 10th Haute-Saône (183i); Det 4th Haute-Saône(14i); 11th Haute-Saône (230i); 12th Haute-Saône (278i); Artillery (26a), 3 guns.

Reserve - GdB Haxo: CdB Jordy - 2nd Ain (373i); 2/57th Regt (257i); 1st Meurthe (104i); 3rd Vosges (353i); 1/57th Regt (263i); 6 co's Grenadiers-Réunis (155i); Artillery (82a, 5 guns).

Grand Total: 10,394 and 24 guns (An additional 4,498 were in hospital).

Army of the West (formed 8-14 October) CinC L'Échélle:

1st Division GdD Kléber - Beaupuy: AvGd (3,400); Vimeux: 1st Brig (3,000); Scherb: 2nd Brig (1,600); Haxo: Res (2,000). 2nd Division Chalbos - GdD Muller, GdB Lecomte, Chabot, Legros, Canuel and Westermann (11,000).

Bard: Luçon troops (3,500).

Dutruy: Les Sables (3,500).

NOVEMBER: Campaign North of the Loire

Details poor due to frequent reorganisation.

10 November - Army of Brest Coast: Rennes Garrison (7,863: including 2,081 unusable raw levies).

11 November - Rennes Garrison and Army of the West: Rossignol (24,000 including most of above).

Army of Cherbourg Coast: Sepher (6-8,000).

Army of Brest Coast (part) GdD Tribout (4,400).

Siege of Granville

1st/31st Regt 'Aunis' (500i); 6th Somme; 6th and 11th Manche; elements of the 9th Marche, Réunion, 19th Chasseurs, Côtes-d'Or, 6th Calvados; 4 Co's. St-Lô Volunteers; Co. Evreux Chasseurs; Granville NtGd (600i); Levies and Volunteers from Carentan, Coutances, Cherbourg and Valognes; Le Manche Gends (46c); Hussars (25c); 3 Co's. Paris Gunners and 1 of NtGds; 68 Guns: 2 x 48pdrs, 5 x 36 pdrs, 36 x 24 pdrs, 7 x18pdrs and 6 x 8pdrs, 8 mortars: the rest probably 4pdrs . Total: 5,335 (3,183 of which armed).

Republican Troops at the Battles of Dol-Antrain 20-23 November (estimates only)

Army of the West: CinC Rossignol.

1st Division GdD Kléber - LtAvGd: GdB Marigny (1,600i, 100c); AvGd: GdB Marceau (3,000 including 200c); GdB Westermann (1,500 including 100c); Foot Artillery: 1x8pdr; Horse Artillery: 2x4pdrs, 1x howitzer; Reserve: AdjG Klinger(1,500); 2nd Division GdD Muller - GdB Legros (3,000); GdB ? (3,000).

Army of the Brest Coast - AvGd: GdB Chambertin (1,800); GdB Canuel (3,000); CdB Amey (1,800); GdB Boucret (2,200). Grand Total: approximately 21,000.

27 November - Field Armies of the West, Brest (part) and Cherbourg (part) - 25-30,000 men: Including: Rennes 10,000; Avranches 9-10,000 and Laval 3-4,000.

Selected Garrisons near and south of the Loire:

1 November - Div Les Sables: Dutruy - 60th Line (47i); 110th Line (168i); 1st Bn des Illes (504i); 4th Marine (64i); 5th Marne (954i); 24th Charente (741i); 10th Gironde (358i); Co.Franches (323i); Inhabitants of Les Sables (117i); Gend (65c); Cav Nat (11c). Artillery (140a).

15 November - Nantes (11,169i/a, 852c).

Early November - Saumur (3028i, 577a, 116c); Cholet (3,701i, 261c); Thouars (1,902i); Doué (610).

DECEMBER

<u>Le Mans</u>

Army of West contingent – CinC Marceau:

GdD Kléber – Delaage/Decaen (LtAvGd); Canuel (Brigade); Scherb (Brigade); Westermann (Cavalry). GdD Muller – Carpentier (Brigade); Legros (Brigade).

Army of Cherbourg Coast contingent – GdD Tilly:

Vachot – AvGd: 9th Hussars (50c); 19th Chasseurs (200i); Reg't d'Armagnac (Grenadiers and Fusiliers (100i)); Det.Regt d'Aunis (100i). Vial – 1st Brigade: ½ Bn 6th Line; Bn Dordogne; Gend (200i); Bn 1st Paris. 2nd Brigade (d'Alancourt): Bn d'Aunis; Bn l'Aude; Gend (200i); Bn 2nd Paris.

Appendix 3

Selected details of the Royalist Armies

M ost of the information on the development of the armies is covered within this book. Principal sources: P.Doré-Graslin, Bittard-des-Portes, Poirier-de-Beauvais, D'Obenheim, Savary, RSV (various).

March to May

In the coastal region there were at least a dozen who retained an important role throughout 1793, the most significant being Charette, Joly and La Cathelinière.

In the Mauges, Cathelineau, D'Élbée, Bonchamps and Stofflet (the latter around Maulévrier) were the most important leaders by April and in Upper Poitou La Rochejaquelein and Lescure came to the fore by early May. Royrand, Sapinaud-de-la-Verrie and Sapinaud-de-la-Rairie were soon commanding in the Bocage.

In the Mauges the peasants entitled themselves the *Armée-Chrétien* or *Armée Catholique-et-Royale* by end March. Other names included *Armée d'Anjou* and *Armée de Poitou* (or *Haut-Poitou*) for their respective areas. In the coastal Vendée names included the *Armée du Bas-Poitou* (i.e. Lower Poitou to distinguish it from *Haut-Poitou*) and the *Armée de Pays-de-Retz*. The *Armée-du-Centre* formed on 4 April.

Organisation Late May

The Grand Army Catholic and Royal of Anjou and Haut-Poitou

Headquarters: Cholet.

Divisional Generals - Lescure: Bressuire; Cathelineau: Pin-en-Mauges and environs; Bonchamps: Area south of Loire centred on St-Florent; Stofflet: Maulévrier and Vihiers; D'Élbée: Beaupréau and Cholet; La Rochejaquelein: Les Aubiers and Châtillon; Laugrenière: Argenton.

The Catholic and Royal Army of the Centre

CinC Royrand. Headquarters: Les Herbiers.

Principal Divisions – Royrand: Montaigu; Sapinaud-de-la-Verrie: Mortagne. Baudry D'Asson may also have commanded a division in the La Châtaigneraie area.

The Army of the Pays-de-Retz and Bas-Poitou

Comprised a number of semi-independent bands. Principal emerged as (later numbered 1 to 4):

1st Division – Joly: La Mothe-Achard and Les Sables; 2nd Division – Lyrot: Loroux and approaches to Nantes; 3rd Division – Charette: Legé and Machecoul; 4th Division – La Cathelinière: Pays-de-Retz.

Numerous semi-independent bands: La Robrie (St-Philibert); Vrignault (Vieillevigne); Pajot (Bouin); Savin (Palluau); St-Pal (Mareuil area), Couëtus (St-Philbert-de-Grand-Lieu), Guérin (Bourgneuf), Bulkeley (La Roche-sur-Yon area); Guerry-du-Cloudy (near St-Gilles); Du Chaffault (south of La Mothe-Achard); Championnière (Pellerin/Brains area). This is not an exhaustive list and some leaders changed during the war.

By the summer Charette had virtually established himself as overall commander although personally fielded no more than 5,000. Lyrot fought with both the Grand Army and Charette.

Organisation determined after capture of Saumur (9-10 June)

CinC Jacques Cathelineau. Headquarters: Cholet.

The Grand Army of Anjou and Haut-Poitou

Lescure – 1st Division: Bressuire, Châtillon and Thouars; Cathelineau – 2nd Division: Saint-Florent, Beaupréau and Les Mauges; Bonchamps – 3rd Division: Banks of the Loire; Stofflet – 4th Division: Vihiers and Maulévrier; D'Élbée – 5th Division: Cholet and Chemillé; Laugrenière – 6th Division: Thouars to Argenton; La Rochejaquelein: 7th Division – Châtillon; Talmont: Cavalry; Marigny: Artillery.

This Army formed up to 40,000 men. There were other commanders who occasionally fought independently, notably Duhoux, Piron and Cady.

Army of the Centre

CinC Royrand. Headquarters: Les Herbiers.

Principal Divisions – Royrand: 1st Division - Montaigu; Sapinaud-de-la-Verrie: 2nd Division - Mortagne.

This army could field 10,000 troops. There were several smaller forces in their area that drifted between the three main armies.

D'Élbée became commander-in-chief in mid-July, Stofflet was appointed major general. Four were appointed to more senior command: Bonchamps (Anjou), Lescure (Haut-Poitou), Royrand (Centre) and Donnissan (Bas-Poitou and Pays-de-Retz).

Orders of Battle are difficult to establish. As an example, one of the more detailed is as follows:

Battle of Nantes 29-30 June

The Grand Army Catholic and Royal of Anjou and Haut-Poitou

CinC Cathelineau.

Northern Front (14-15,000) - Divisions under Cathelineau and D'Élbée; Talmont (500 cavalry); 14 cannon.

Eastern Front_(7-8,000) - Division Bonchamps: Fleuriot (AvGd) and D'Autichamp.

North or East Front - Division Stofflet and part of the Divisions of Argenton and Bressuire (most, however, remained with La Rochejaquelein and Lescure in Haut-Poitou).

Southern Front

Legé-et-Machecoul (5,000 including 100 cavalry) - CinC Charette. Contingents: Couëtus, Eriau, Leblanc, La Robrie, Goulaine and Vrignault. Cavalry: Prudent de la Robrie. Artillery: Leblanc. Approximately 12 cannon.

Pays-de-Retz (5,000) - CinC La Cathelinière.

Loroux (5,000) - CinC Lyrot. D'Esigny (AvGd). Artillery: A few small cannon.

Campaign north of the Loire: November

CinC: La Rochejaquelein; Second-in-command: Major General Stofflet; Adjudant General: De Hargues; Adjudant-en-Second: Duhoux; Governor General and President of the Council of War: Donnissan; Chief Engineer: D'Obenheim.

Grand Army (25-30,000).

Division Poitou: Des Essarts; Division Banks of Loire: Fleuriot; Division Anjou: Villeneuve de Cazeau.

(D'Élbée's division: had merged with others).

Army of the Centre (3-4,000 men): Amédée de Béjarry.

Loroux Contingent (1-2,000 men): Lyrot and D'Ésigny.

La Petite-Vendée (Approximately 4,000 men): Talmont leading two corps under Jean Chouan and Besnier-de-Chambray.

Cavalry (1,200): Talmont.

Artillery Marigny: 1 x 12pdr, 4 x 8pdrs, about 40 x 4pdrs, 30 caissons, 2 mobile forges. (Numbers fluctuated).

Refugees (10-15,000) 2-3,000 were on horseback and over 200 carriages accompanied them.

December 20-21

Grand Army - CinC Fleuriot. Other senior officers: Piron, Forestier, Lyrot, Marigny, Des Essarts, Laugrenière, Duhoux d'Hauterive and Amédée de Béjarry.

Endnotes

Introduction

1. J.Hussenet (ed), *Détruisez la Vendée!* (CVRH:2007), p.15.

Chapter 1: Fighting the Revolution, a Brief Background to the Vendée Rising

1. C.L.Chassin, *La Preparation de la Guerre de la Vendée.* Vol.P3. (Paris:1892), p.289 (hereafter the volumes by C.L.Chassin entitled *La Preparation de la Guerre de la Vendée* are referred to as Vol.P1 to P3).
2. R.Secher, *La Véndee-Vengé,* (Perrin:2006), p.109.
3. C.L.Chassin, *op.cit.* Vol.P3, p.271.
4. J.Hussenet, *op-cit.* pp.583–618, provides detailed statistics for the settlements.
5. *Ibid.* p.621.
6. H.Coutau-Bégarre and C.Doré-Graslin(eds), *Histoire Militiare des Guerres de Vendée,* (Paris:2010), pp.97-114.

Chapter 2: 'Patriots, Robbers and Cowards': The Republican Armies in the Vendée

1. C.Rousset, *Les Volontaires 1791-1794* (Paris:1894), p.3, and J.A.Lynn, *The Bayonets of the Republic: Motivation and Tactics in the Army of Revolutionary France 1791-4* (Westview:1996), p.62.
2. C.Rousset, *op.cit.* p.4.
3. *Ibid.* p.107.
4. A.Crépin, *Révolution et Armée nouvelle en Seine-et-Marne 1791-1797,* (CTHS:2008).
5. SHD-B5/3-30:30th March.
6. SHD-B5/125-6:25th-26th August.
7. SHD-B5/5-47:18th June.
8. SHD-B5/5-50:20th June.
9. SHD-B5/4-81:27th May; SHD-B5/5-20:7th June.
10. SHD-B5/15-7:5th June.

11. C.H.Carrier, *Correspondence of Jean-Baptiste Carrier,* (London:1920), pp.102-4.

12. A.Soboul, *Dictionnaire historique de la révolution francaise* (Paris:1989), p.490.

13. R.Bittard-des-Portes, *Charette et la Guerre de la Vendée 1763-1796,* (Paris:1902), p.71.

14. This can cause confusion: the 8th Hussars became the 9th Hussars (February 1793), being renamed the 8th (June 1793). The 9th Hussars had been the 10th (March-June 1793) then renamed the 9th. The 7th Hussars served under Labarolière.

15. *Le Général Beysser et le 15e Chasseurs: Carnet de la Sabertache (1896),* pp.637-41.

16. For useful detail on the légions: Didier Davin, *Corps Francs, Légions et Compagnies Franches de la Revolution 1792-4.* https://sehrileblog.wordpress.com/tag/legions/

17. C.L.Chassin, *La Vendée Patriote,* Vol.V1, pp.493-5, and V.2, p.53 (hereafter the volumes by C.L.Chassin entitled *La Vendée Patriote* are referred to as Vol.V1 to V4).

18. *Ibid.* p.495.

19. *Ibid.* p.492.

20. SHD-B5/5-100:15th July; SHD-B5/6-29:19th August.

21. SHD-B5/6-60:10th September.

22. C.L.Chassin, *op-cit.* Vol.V2, p.179 and p.183.

23. SHD-B5/6-98:27th September.

24. C.L.Chassin, *op-cit.* Vol.V1, p.497.

25. SHD-B5/4-22:7th May.

26. SHD-B5/5-62:25th June.

27. S.Calvert, *Cambronne: La Legende de Waterloo,* (Vendémiarie:2016), p.54.

28. SHD-B5/3-67:19th April.

29. SHD-B 5/14-44:6th July.

30. Sent to Tours late April, with *Hussards d'Égalité* (SHD-B5/3-72).

31. SHD-B5/4-9:6th May.

32. C.H.Carrier, *op-cit.* p.110.

Chapter 3: 'For God and the King': The Catholic and Royal Armies

1. A.Billaud and J.d'Herbauges, *1793 La Guerre au Bocage Vendéen* (Choletais:1993), pp.171-4.

2. J.J.Savary, *Guerres des Vendéens et des Chouans contre le République* Française. Vol.4, (1827), pp.77-92.

3. R.Blanchez, *Bonchamps et l'Insurrection Vendéene 1760-1793*, (Paris:1902), pp.180-1.

4. P.Gréau, *La Virée de Galerne*, (Cholet:2012), p.65.

5. RSV:No.225 Dec.2003. *Le Journal du Capitaine de Fay.*

6. RSV:No.231. Article by Michel Chatry.

7. J.M.Crosefinte, *Les Guerres de l'Ouest 1793-1796. Le Costume du Combattants Vendéen* (Niort:1986), p.291.

8. R.Bittard-des-Portes, *op-cit.* p.159.

9. *Ibid.* p.168.

10. F.Deniau, *op-cit.* Vol.3, p.172.

11. C.L.Chassin, *op-cit.* Vol.V1, pp.438-9.

12. R.Bittard-des-Portes, *op-cit.* p.151.

13. P.Dore-Graslin, *Journal de la Guerre de Géants 1793-1801* (Cholet:1992), p.35

14. L. de la Championnière, *Mémoires d'un Officer Vendéen 1793-1796* (Reprint Cholet:1994), p.37.

15. *Collinet, Manuscrit de, 1778-1804. Les Sables et la Guerre de Vendée* (La Roche-sur-Yon:2003), p.110.

16. J.M.Crosfinte, *op-cit.* (1986), p.38.

17. *Ibid.* p.77: quoting Boutellier-de-Saint-Andre and Mme-de-la-Bouëre.

18. *Ibid.* p.290.

19. *Ibid.* p.291.

20. R.Bittard-des-Portes, *op-cit.* Footnote:p.168.

21. For details of Vendéen dress see J.M.Crosfinte, *op-cit.* (1986): http://guerre. Vendée.free.fr/

22. A.Perracheau, *Jean-Baptiste Joly* (Le Circle d'Or:1986), p.147.

23. R.Bittard-des-Portes, *op-cit.* pp.152-3.

24. SHD-B5/7-77:15th December.

25. J.M.Crosefinte, *op-cit.* (1986), p.65.

26. J.M.Crosefinte, *Les Guerres de L'Ouest 1793-1796. Les Drapeaux Vendéens* (Niort:1988).

27. *Ibid.* p.79.

28. General Turreau, *Mémoires pour server a l'histoire de la guerre de la Vendée* (Paris:1824), p.29.

29. SHD-1.M-489: Général Damas, *Copie d'un journal de d'Obenheim, officier du genie.*

30. J.J.Savary, *op-cit.* Vol 2. p.341.

31. *Ibid.* p.340.

32. SHD-B5/3-89:28th April.

33. SHD-B5/15-29:22nd September.

34. H.Baguenier-Desormeaux, *Kléber en Vendée 1793-1794* (Paris:1907), pp.477-84.

Chapter 4: 'Running like a Trail of Gunpowder': The Rising Takes Hold

1. F.Deniau, *Histoire de la Guerre de la Vendée.*Vol.1, (1878. Reprint Cholet:2004), p.407.
2. *Ibid.* pp.403-5.
3. *Ibid.* p.424.
4. *Ibid.* p.423.
5. L.Rostu, *Histoire extérieure et maritime des Guerres de Vendée,* (Le Circle d'Or:1987), p.27.
6. J.Bourgeon and P.Hammon(eds), *L'insurrection de Mars 1793 en Loire-Inferieure* (Association Nantes Histoire 1993), pp.64-5 and p.81.
7. J.J.Savary, *op-cit.* Vol.1, p.68.
8. *Ibid.* p.69.
9. F.Deniau, *Histoire de la Guerre de la Vendée.*Vol.1, p.423.
10. F.Deniau suggests 4,000 (probably an exaggeration). *Ibid.* p.429.
11. J.J.Savary, *op-cit.* Vol.1, p.69.
12. F.Deniau, *op-cit.* Vol.1, p.442, 100 to Chalonnes; detachments to May and St-Macaire.
13. E.Gabory, *op-cit.* p.102.
14. F.Deniau *op-cit.*Vol.1. p.443.
15. E.Gabory, *op-cit.* footnote:p.103. F.Deniau, *Ibid.* p.444, suggests 2,000. Sources vary wildly.
16. J.J.Savary, *op-cit.*Vol.1, p.70. States 3 culverins.
17. F.Deniau, *op-cit.* Vol 1, p.445.
18. E.Gabory, *op-cit.* p.103.
19. C.Coubard, *La Guerre de la Vendée: Cholet 1793-4* (Choletais:1992), pp.27-8, indicates 8-900 National Guards, 100 from 19th Dragoons, 4 light guns.
20. P.Doré-Graslin, *Journal de la Guerre des Géants 1793-1801* (Cholet:1992), p.51, indicates 15-18,000.
21. E.Gabory, *op-cit.* p.104. The Royalists exaggerated their strength at 30,000.
22. C.Coubard, *op-cit.* p.30.
23. E.Gabory, *op-cit.* p.105.
24. *Ibid.* p.115. Nearly all National Guards plus 66 cavalry.
25. F.Deniau, *op-cit.* p.480.
26. *Ibid.* p.481.

27. J.J.Savary, *op-cit*. pp.89-90.
28. *Ibid*. pp.89-90.
29. *Ibid*. pp.99-100.
30. J.Bourgeon and P.Hammon(eds), *op-cit*. p.67. Those from Clisson enduring 'a 12 hour march and 9 combats'.
31. F.Deniau, *op-cit*. p.517.
32. *Ibid*. p.516.
33. *Ibid*. p.512.
34. *Ibid*. pp.534-535.
35. Doré-Graslin, *op-cit*. p.53.
36. C.L.Chassin, *op-cit*. Vol.P3, p.468.
37. H.Coutau-Bégarie and C.Doré-Graslin(eds), *op-cit*. p.180: The leaders were Royrand; Royrand's brother; Sapinaud-de-la-Verrie, Sapinaud-de-la-Rairie; Gabriel Baudry d'Asson; Amédée and Auguste Béjarry; Jacques-Louis Verteuil, Mathieu Verteuil, William Bulkeley and De Chouppes.
38. See C.L.Chassin, *op-cit*. Vol.P3. pp.454-522.
39. J.J.Savary, *op-cit*. Vol.1, p.117.
40. A.Billaud and J.d'Herbauges, *1793 La Guerre au Bocage Vendéen* (Cholet:1993), pp.101-2.
41. 800 National Guards from Rochefort and La Rochelle formed part of this flank.
42. A.Billaud and J.d'Herbauges, *op-cit*. p.103.
43. *Ibid*. p.103.
44. *Ibid*. p.104.
45. P.Doré-Graslin, *op-cit*. p.49.
46. J.Bourgeon and P.Hammon(eds), *op-cit*. p.93-94.
47. R.Bittard-des-Portes, *op-cit*. Footnote:p.15.
48. *Ibid*. p.18, indicates a quarter were armed.
49. *Ibid*. p.19, and J.Bourgeon/P.Hammon(eds), *op-cit*. p.97.
50. Collinet, *op-cit*. pp.94-104 for build-up of troops; F.Deniau, *op-cit*. Vol.1. p.562 suggests 1,500 were defending Les Sables so perhaps others dispersed? They comprised 3,000 infantry, 300 sailors and 200 cavalry.
51. C.L.Chassin, *op-cit*. Vol.V1, p.6.
52. Collinet, *op-cit*. p.104.
53. *Ibid*. p.107.
54. *Ibid*. p.108. C.L.Chassin, *op-cit*. Vol.V1. p.17 suggests 8-9,000 rebels.
55. Collinet, *op-cit*. p.104.
56. Chassin, *op-cit*. Vol.V1, p.16.
57. Collinet, *op-cit*. p.109.

58. Chassin, *op-cit.* Vol.V1, p.16.

59. Collinet, *op-cit.* p.104.

60. *Ibid.* p.104-5.

61. RSV:No.267, p.22.

62. Collinet, *op-cit.* p.107 and 110.

63. *Ibid.* p.110.

64. *Ibid.* p.111.

65. RSV:No.267, p.23.

66. Collinet, *op-cit.* p.113.

67. *Ibid.* p.113.

68. *Ibid.* p.114.

69. *Ibid.* p.115.

Chapter 5: 'In Less than a Month the Troubles in the Vendée will be at an End'

1. F.Deniau, *op-cit.* Vol.1, p.593.

2. *Ibid.* p.594.

3. C.L.Chassin, *op-cit.* Vol.V1, pp.100-101.

4. F.Deniau, *op-cit.* Vol.1, p.661.

5. *Ibid.* p.608.

6. *Ibid.* p.610.

7. J.Crétineau-Joly, *Histoire de la Vendée Militaire.* Vol.1. (1895, Reprinted Cholet:1994), pp.69-70.

8. F.Deniau, *op-cit.* Vol.1, p.632.

9. A. Gérard & T.Heckmann, *Les oubliés de la guerre de Vendée,* (Société d'Emulation de la Vendée:1992), pp.214-5.

10. F.Deniau, *op-cit.* Vol.1, p.633.

11. *Ibid.* p.633.

12. J.J.Savary, *op-cit.* Vol.1, p.162.

13. Madame de la Rochejaquelein, *Mémoires* (Edition of 1877, Cholet:1994), p.117 (hereafter Mme Rochejaquelein).

14. C.Coubard, *op-cit.* p.14.

15. F.Deniau, *op-cit.* Vol.1, p.647 suggests half this figure as many peasants returned home after initial conflicts.

16. *Ibid.* p.647.

17. *Ibid.* p.648.

18. T.Muret, *Vie Populaire de Cathelineau,* (Paris:1845), p.17.

19. C.L.Chassin, *op-cit.* Vol.V1, p.104.

20. F.Deniau, *op-cit.* Vol.1, p.656.

21. *Ibid.* Vol.1, p.657.
22. *Ibid.* Vol.1, p. 655, reporting on meeting of the Convention 27th April.
23. C.L.Chassin, *op-cit.* Vol.P1, pp.186-8.
24. *Ibid.* pp.186-8.
25. *Ibid.* pp.188-9.
26. F.Deniau, *op-cit.* Vol.1, p.662.
27. C.L.Chassin, *op-cit.* Vol.P1, p.177.
28. Collinet, *op-cit.* p.118.
29. *Ibid.* p.118-9.
30. C.L.Chassin, *op-cit.* Vol.P1, p.177.
31. *Ibid.* p.219.
32. *Ibid.* p.219.
33. F.Deniau, *op-cit.* Vol.1, p.666.
34. R.Bittard-des-Portes, *op-cit.* p.31.
35. C.L.Chassin, *op-cit.* Vol.P1, p.219.
36. *Ibid.* p.178.
37. *Ibid.* p.178, suggests this was the 9th.
38. *Ibid.* pp.180-1.
39. *Ibid.* pp.178-9. Niou had put these ships at Boulard's disposal to assist with recapturing Noirmoutier.
40. *Ibid.* p.220.
41. R. Bittard-des-Portes, *op-cit.* p.32.
42. C.L.Chassin, *op-cit.* Vol.P1, p.190.
43. *Ibid.* p.220.
44. F.Deniau, *op-cit.* Vol.1, p.668.
45. C.L.Chassin, *op-cit.* Vol.P1, p.190.
46. *Ibid.* p.220.
47. F.Deniau, *op-cit.* Vol.1, p.669.
48. R. Bittard-des-Portes, *op-cit.* p.34.
49. C.L.Chassin, *op-cit.* Vol.P1, p.220.
50. *Ibid.* p.220 and Collinet, *op-cit.* p.122.
51. F.Deniau, *op-cit.* Vol.1, p.670.
52. *Ibid.* p.671.
53. C.L.Chassin, *op-cit.* Vol.P1, p.220.
54. *Ibid.* p.191.
55. R. Bittard-des-Portes, *op-cit.* pp.36-7 and L.Dumarcet, *Charette, Une Histoire Veritable* (Paris:1997), p.198.
56. *Ibid.* (L.Dumarcet, p.200).
57. C.L.Chassin, *op-cit.* Vol.P1, p.192 and p.221.

58. R. Bittard-des-Portes, *op-cit*. p.38.
59. C.L.Chassin, *op-cit*. Vol.P1, p.198.
60. R. Bittard-des-Portes, *op-cit*. p.39.
61. F.Deniau, *op-cit*. Vol.1, p.673.
62. C.L.Chassin, *op-cit*. Vol.P.I, pp.214-218.
63. J.J.Savary, *op-cit*. Vol.1, p.172.
64. C.L.Chassin, *op-cit*. Vol.V1, p.227: 4th Line (200 men), Volunteers Charente and Loire-Inférieure (400 men) and some grenadiers.
65. *Ibid*. Vol.V1, p.227.
66. R. Bittard-des-Portes, *op-cit*. p.43.
67. C.L.Chassin, *op-cit*. Vol.V1, pp.228-229.
68. R. Bittard-des-Portes, *op-cit*. p.43.
69. J.J.Savary *op-cit*. Vol.1, p173.
70. F.Deniau, *op-cit*. Vol.1, p.681.
71. *Ibid*. p.682.
72. R. Bittard-des-Portes, *op-cit*. p.48; H.Coutau-Bégarie and C.Doré-Graslin(eds), *op-cit*. p.212: Chantreau places this event after 30th April with Charette back in Legé 5th May.
73. C.L.Chassin, *op-cit*. Vol.V1, p.229.
74. J.J.Savary *op-cit*. Vol.1, p.176.
75. *Ibid*. p.177.
76. F.Deniau, *op-cit*. Vol.1, p.686. A number of his men were dispersed garrisoning the area.
77. L.Rostu, *op-cit*. p.46.
78. C.L.Chassin, *op-cit*. Vol.V1, p.231 and R. Bittard-des-Portes, *op-cit*. p.51.
79. F.Deniau, *op-cit*. pp.692-3.
80. R. Bittard-des-Portes, *op-cit*. p.52.
81. F.Deniau, *op-cit*. Vol.1, Footnote:p.693.
82. *Ibid*. pp.692-3
83. *Ibid*. pp.692-3.

Chapter 6: The Rise of the Grand Army

1. C.L.Chassin *op-cit*. Vol.V1, p.255.
2. *Ibid*. p.256.
3. SHD-B5/4-8.
4. C.L.Chassin, *op-cit*. Vol.V1, p.257.
5. F.Deniau, *op-cit*. Vol.2, p.9.
6. *Ibid*. p.10.
7. *Ibid*. p.12.

8. *Ibid.* p.13.
9. J.J.Savary, *op.cit.* Vol.1, pp.206-7.
10. These troops played little part in the fighting.
11. Deniau *op-cit.* Vol.2, p.30.
12. H.Coutau-Bégarie and C.Doré-Graslin(eds), *op-cit.* p.240.
13. J.J.Savary *op.cit.* Vol.1, p.219.
14. SHD-B5/4-45.
15. A.Billard and J.d'Herbauges, *op-cit.* pp.156-7.
16. SHD-B5/4-45.
17. Poirier-de-Beauvais, *op-cit.* p.46: Indicates 200 dead, 300 prisoners.
18. F.Deniau, *op-cit.* Vol.2, p.60.
19. A.Billard and J.d'Herbauges, *op-cit.* pp.156-7.
20. Mme.Rochejacquelein, *op-cit.* pp.153-4.
21. J.J.Savary, *op-cit.* Vol.1, p.219.
22. C.L.Chassin, *op-cit.* Vol.V1 , pp.322-323.
23. *Ibid.* p.346-7.
24. *Ibid.* p.316 and 347.
25. *Ibid.* p.350-1.
26. J.Artarit, *Fontenay-le-Comte sous la Revolution (CVRH)*, p.140; Municipal Register indicates 6,000.
27. C.L.Chassin, *op-cit.* Vol.V1, p.400.
28. *Ibid.* p.346.
29. J.J.Savary, *op-cit.* p.221, possibly including D'Ayat's troops on his left wing.
30. C.L.Chassin, *op-cit.* Vol.V1, p 400.
31. SHD-B5/4-53.
32. S.Hilard, *Marigny et mémoire assassinée* (Choletais:1998), pp.54-6.
33. J.Crétineau-Joly, *op-cit.* p.140
34. S.Hilard, *op-cit.* pp.54-6.
35. Mme.Rochejacquelein, *op-cit.* pp.154-5.
36. CL.Chassin, *op-cit.* Vol.V1, p.400 and SHD-B5/4-53.
37. Mme. Rochejacquelein, *op-cit.* pp.154-155.
38. SHD-B5/4-61; J.Artarit, *op-cit.* p.142, Municipal Register indicates 7,400.
39. C.L.Chassin, *op-cit.* Vol.V1, p.396.
40. Mme Rochejaquelein, *op-cit.* p.159 suggests 40,000; A.Béjarry, *op-cit.* p.94-5 states 4,000 from Army of the Centre; S.Hilard, *op-cit.* pp.56-8 indicated this should be added to at least 20,000 for the Grand Army; C.L.Chassin, *op-cit.* Vol.V1, p.400: Principal Agent of Niort indicates 30,000.
41. Figures from J.J.Savary Vol.1, p.227; P.Doré-Graslin p.70; Poirier-de-Beauvais pp.48-50, S.Hilard p.58-60. Most artillery probably 4pdrs.

42. Mercier-de-Rocher in C.L.Chassin, *op-cit.*, Vol.V1, p.398.

43. *Ibid.* p.398.

44. A. de Beauchamps: *Histoire de la Guerre de Vendée et des Chouans:* Vol.1 (Paris:1807), p.174, suggests the right under Bonchamps, centre Lescure and left La Rochejaquelein.

45. J.Crétineau-Joly, *op-cit.* p.144.

46. Mme Rochejaquelein, *op-cit.* p.160, placed him with the cavalry. (See also P.Dore-Graslin p.70, E.Gabory p.63-4, Poirier-de-Beauvais p.48-50).

47. C.L.Chassin, *op-cit.* Vol.V1, pp.401-2.

48. *Ibid.*,p.398.

49. S.Hilard, *op-cit.* pp.58-60.

50. Mme Rochejaquelein, *op-cit.* p.160.

51. C.L.Chassin, *op-cit.*Vol.V1, p.430.

52. *Ibid.* pp.400-1.

53. *Ibid.* p.406.

54. Poirier-de-Beauvais, *op-cit.* p.49.

55. C.L.Chassin, *op-cit.* Vol.V1, p.399.

56. *Ibid.* p.399.

57. *Ibid.* p.400.

58. Mme Rochejaquelein, *op-cit.* p.161.

59. Chassin, *op-cit.* Vol.V1, p.408.

60. A.Béjarry, *op-cit.* pp.94-5.

61. *Ibid.* pp.94-5.

62. C.L.Chassin, *op-cit.* Vol.V1, p.400.

63. *Ibid.* p.408, 412, 435 and 453 (differing sources) states figures of 3,250, 2,800, 4-5,000 and 3,400-3,500; J.Crétineau-Joly, *op-cit.* p.150 states 3,000; Mme Rochejaquelein, *op-cit.* p.15 states 700 killed and 3-4,000 captured, pp.163-4.

64. Mercier-de-Rocher in C.L.Chassin, *op-cit.* Vol.V1, p.399.

65. S.Hilard, *op-cit.* pp.58-60.

66. Mme Rochejaquelein, *op-cit.* pp.161-2.

67. C.L.Chassin, *op-cit.* Vo.V1, p.405.

68. RSV: No.203. June 1998: See article pp.6-21.

69. Bittard-des-Portes, *op-cit.* Footnote:p.57.

70. *Ibid.* p.58.

71. *Ibid.* p.59.

72. *Ibid.* pp.63-6.

73. This account from J.J.Savary, *op-cit.* Vol.1, p.185 and H.Coutau-Bégarie/C. Doré-Graslin(eds), *op-cit.* pp.213-4.

74. Bittard-des -Portes, *op-cit.* p.62: He led 400 infantry, 50 cavalry and 2 guns.

75. L.Dumarcet, *op-cit.* p.218 quotes Labory having 300-320 men.
76. *Ibid.* pp.218-9.
77. H.Coutau-Bégarie and C.Doré-Graslin(eds), *op-cit.* p.215: Indicates 274 of 72nd Line deserted.
78. C.L.Chassin, *op-cit.* Vol.V1, pp.360-379.
79. Bittard-des-Portes, *op-cit.* p.79.
80. *Ibid.* p.79.
81. C.L.Chassin, *op-cit.* Vol.V1, p.361.
82. Bittard-des-Portes, *op-cit.* p.80.
83. *Ibid.* p.80.
84. *Ibid.* p.81.
85. C.L.Chassin, *op-cit.* Vol.V1, pp.361-2.
86. *Ibid.* pp. 361-2.
87. Collinet, *op-cit.* p.140; Bittard-des-Portes, *op-cit.* p.90.
88. Bittards-des-Portes, Footnote:p.84.
89. Collinet, *op-cit.* p.140.
90. *Ibid.* p.142.

Chapter 7: The Republic in Crisis

1. A.Soboul, *op-cit.* p.259.
2. J.J.Savary, *op-cit.* Vol.1, p.242.
3. *Ibid.* p.249.
4. *Ibid.* p.250.
5. F.Deniau , *op-cit.* Vol.2, pp.155-6.
6. *Ibid.* pp.156-7.
7. *Ibid.* p.157.
8. *Ibid.* p.158, indicates 800 infantry and a platoon of the 8th Hussars who had been at Montilliers when informed the rebels were in Vihiers. Mme Rochejaquelein says 2,000; SHD-1 M 488 - Joseph Dupont, lieutenant *Relation de la bataille de Saumur livrée le 9 juin 1793* (1829).
9. F.Deniau, *op-cit.* Vol.2, p.158.
10. *Ibid.* p.159.
11. *Ibid.* p.171.
12. F.Deniau, op-cit. Vol.2, p.159.
13. J.Crétineau-Joly, *op-cit.* p.167.
14. Mme Rochejaquelein, *op-cit.* pp.171-2; J.J.Savary, *op-cit.* Vol.1, p.248.
15. SHD B 5/5-25 & 5-25: 10th June; F.Deniau suggests about 6,000 (Vol.2, p.162); Dupont suggests 8,348 men, but his figures are largely based on optimistic assumptions of unit strengths.

16. F.Deniau, *op-cit*. Vol.2, p.163. for number of cannon, Dupont for infantry and cavalry.

17. SHD-B5/5-21:8th June.

18. F.Deniau, *op-cit*. Vol.2, p.164.

19. J.Cretineau-Joly, *op-cit*. p.167.

20. SHD-B5/5-23:9th June.

21. See SHD-B5/5-23 to 5-25.

22. F.Deniau, *op-cit*. Vol.2, p.165.

23. SHD-B5/5-21:8th June.

24. *Ibid.*

25. *Ibid.*

26. J.J.Savary, *op-cit*. Vol.1, p.251 notes 5th Calvados, 640 men; 6th Calvados, 629 men; 14th Paris, 400 men; 1st Chinon, 960 men; Légion de Rosenthal, 200 men; 35th Gendarmerie under Rossignol,500 men; 100 gunners with 6x4pdr guns; detachment of lancers from *Légion-de-la-Fraternité*, 50 men. In C.L.Chassin, *op-cit*. Vol.V2, p.45. An eye witness indicates: 2 Orléans battalions; 1 Calvados battalion; a company of foot chasseurs; the *Légion-de-Rosenthal*; 35th Gendarmerie; a detachment from *Legion-de-la-Fraternité*; total: 3,600 men). His cavalry was 500 strong.

27. C.L.Chassin, *op-cit*. Vol.V2, pp.44-5.

28. Poirier-de-Beauvais, *op-cit*. pp.51-2.

29. Mme Rochejaquelein, *op-cit*. p.173.

30. *Ibid.*

31. E.Gabory, *op-cit*. pp.171-2.

32. C.L.Chassin, *op-cit*. Vol.V.2, footnote: p.48. Fleuriot, Donnissan and Beauvolliers commanded around 8,000. Cathelineau, Lescure and Desessarts may have contributed.

33. E.Gabory, *op-cit*. pp.171-2.

34. C.L.Chassin, *op-cit*. Vol.V.2, p.41 and 48.

35. SHD-B5/5-29:12th June.

36. F.Deniau, *op-cit*. Vol.2, p.171.

37. F.Favier, *Berthier L'Ombre de Napoléon*, (Perrin:2015) p.63.

38. Dupont indicates 72 cannon (many 4pdrs). They placed 30 guns in an artillery park within Saumur, suggesting they lacked gunners.

39. Dupont: 13,000; J.J.Savary Vol.1, p.257: 7-8,000 of which 400 were line troops; C.L.Chassin, Vol.V2, p.258 states less than 8,000; F.Deniau states 8-9,000 (Footnote:Vol.2, p.173).

40. J.J.Savary, *op-cit*. Vol.1, p.258.

41. SHD-B5/5-24 and 5-25.

42. J.J.Savary, *op-cit.* Vol.1, p.258.
43. H.Coutau-Bégarie and C.Doré-Graslin(eds), *op-cit.* p.259.
44. *Ibid.* pp.252-3.
45. J.J.Savary, *op-cit.* Vol.1, p.259, suggests 400 men of the 35th Division Gendarmerie fell under his command, but might be mistaken as these were with Salomon.
46. Other troops present included: 3rd and 5th Paris; detachment *Légion-de-Rosenthal*; two more Orléans battalions; a *Co-Franche des Pyrénées*; detachment 72nd Line; detachments from 8th Hussars, 10th, 13th and 19th Dragoons.
47. F.Deniau, *op-cit.* Vol.2, p.179.
48. Mme Rochejaquelein, *op-cit.* p.175; H.Coutau-Bégarie/C.Dore-Graslin(eds), *op-cit.* p. 260, indicates this cavalry was 200 strong.
49. C.L.Chassin, *op-cit.* Vol.V2, p.49, indicates they placed him at the mouth of a cannon. The exact timing of this second attack is unclear, some placing it towards 8pm.
50. F.Deniau, *op-cit.* Vol.2, p.175. and J.J.Savary, *op-cit.* Vol.1, p.260 reflect the different accounts.
51. C.L.Chassin, *op-cit.* Vol.V2, p. 50.
52. F.Deniau, *op-cit.* Vol.2, p.179. The cuirassiers possibly charged more than once during the day and the accounts may have become blurred. There were 122 cuirassiers at Saumur and only 34 came out of the battle unscathed (C.L.Chassin, *op-cit.* Vol.V.2, p.53).
53. J.J.Savary, *op-cit.* Vol.1, p.260.
54. Mme Rochejaquelein, *op-cit.* p.470.
55. H.Coutau-Bégarie and C.Dore-Graslin(eds), *op-cit.* p.262.
56. *Ibid.* p.262.
57. *Ibid.* p.266.
58. *Ibid.* p.262
59. Mme. Rochejacquelein, *op-cit.* p.470.
60. Deniau, *op-cit.* Vol.2 pp.180-1.
61. *Ibid.* p.181.
62. H.Coutau-Bégarie and C.Dore-Graslin(eds), *op-cit.* p.264.
63. *Ibid.* p.263
64. *Ibid.* p.264.
65. F.Deniau, *op-cit.* Vol.2, p.182.
66. *Ibid.* p.179.
67. Mme. Rochejacquelein, *op-cit.* p.176.
68. F.Deniau, *op-cit.*, Vol.2, p.186.

69. C.L.Chassin, *op-cit.*, Vol.V2, pp.49-50.

70. SHD-B5/5-31:13th June.

71. This is an exaggeration. Sources vary for Republican losses: 80 guns, 100,000 fusils, 11,000 prisoners (J.Cretineau-Joly, *op-cit.*,p.173); Mme Rochejaquelein: 4,000 killed and wounded and 6,000 captured between 3 and 10 June; Blordier-Langlois: 3,000 Republican to 2,000 Vendéen casualties (F.Deniau, *op-cit.* Vol.2, Footnote: p.193). A report from August 1794 stated 45 guns lost and entire Paris battalions threw away their fusils without firing a shot (CL. Chassin, *op-cit.* Vol.1. p.482).

72. Mme Rochejaquelein, *op-cit.* pp.177.

73. *Ibid.* p.177, indicates 60 killed, 400 wounded.

74. J.J.Savary , *op-cit.* pp.263-4.

75. F.Deniau, *op-cit.* Vol.2, p.195.

76. SHD-B5/5-32:13th June.

77. SHD-B5/5-31:13th June.

78. F.Deniau, *op-cit.* Vol.2, p.201.

79. H.Coutau-Bégarie and C.Dore-Graslin(eds), *op-cit.* p.273.

80. F.Deniau, *op-cit.* Vol.2, p.210.

81. E.Stofflet, *Stofflet et La Vendée* 1753-1796 (Pont-a-Mousson:1868), pp.100-101.

82. SHD-B5/5-26:11th June.

83. SHD-B5/5-32. They had 25 wagons but needed 300.

84. H.Coutau-Bégarie and C.Dore-Graslin(eds), *op-cit.* p.274.

85. *Ibid.* p.275.

86. *Ibid.* p.277.

87. J.J.Savary., *op-cit.* Vol.1, p.309.

88. *Ibid.* p.311.

89. *Ibid.* p.311.

90. *Ibid.* pp.329-30.

91. R.Bittard-des-Portes, *op-cit.* pp.94-100.

92. *Ibid.* Footnote: p.103.

93. *Ibid.* p.105.

94. *Ibid.* Footnote: pp.105-6.

95. F.Deniau, *op-cit.* Vol.2, p.226.

96. H.Coutau-Bégarie and C.Dore-Graslin(eds), *op-cit.* p.249.

97. F.Deniau, *op-cit.* Vol.2, p.227.

98. C.L.Chassin, *op-cit.* Vol.P2, p.95.

99. F.Deniau , *op-cit.* Vol.2, p.240.

100. F.Deniau, *op-cit.* Vol.2, p.253.
101. Mme Rochejaquelein, *op-cit.* p.196.
102. R.Bittards-des-Portes, *op-cit.* pp.111-12.
103. Y.Guin, *La Bataille de Nantes, 29 Juin 1793* (Laval:1993), p.89, indicates 600 men: 3rd Loire-Inférieure, National Guards from Nort and Châteaubriant.
104. C.L.Chassin, *op-cit.* V.2, p.240.
105. Y.Guin *op-cit.* p.104.
106. *Ibid.* p.101.
107. R.Bittard-des-Portes *op-cit.* p.112.
108. *Ibid.* p.112.
109. *Ibid.* p.113.
110. C.L.Chassin *op-cit.* Vol.V2, p.241.
111. P.Doré-Graslin, *op-cit.* p.77.
112. J.Cretineau-Joly, *op-cit.* p.196.
113. C.L.Chassin *op-cit.* Vol.V2, p.248.
114. Y.Guin *op-cit.* p.106.
115. *Ibid.* p.110.
116. *Ibid.* p.111.
117. *Ibid.* p.112. The shot came from the Hotel de la Tête-Noire (top of Rue des Hauts-Pavés).
118. *Ibid.* p.110.
119. C.L.Chassin *op-cit.* Vol.V.2, p.255.
120. *Ibid.* p.252.
121. R.Bittard des Portes *op-cit.* p.118.
122. *Ibid.* p.119.
123. Y.Guin, *op-cit.* pp.117-18.
124. The *Légion-du-Nord* comprised 1,200 infantry, 400 cavalry and 8 guns: Chassin *op-cit.* Vol.V2, p.183.
125. Rebel numbers are unclear, Westermann exaggerates their strength as 8-10,000 (Chassin, *op-cit.* Vol.V2, p.183).
126. *Ibid.* p.183.
127. This account is extracted from Mme Rochejaquelein, *op-cit.* pp.192-3 and SHD-B5/5-62: Report by Westermann 25th June.
128. H. Coutau-Bégarie and C.Doré-Graslin(eds), *op-cit.* pp.222-3.
129. C.L.Chassin, *op-cit.* Vol.V2, pp.216-22. Gautron (in H. Coutau-Bégarie/C. Doré-Graslin(eds), *op-cit.* p.224), suggests he had 700 infantry and 1,300 cavalry.
130. Collinet, *op-cit.* p.146.
131. *Ibid.* pp.144-5.
132. *Ibid.* p.147.

Chapter 8: The *Sans-Culotte* Army

1. C.L.Chassin, *op-cit.* Vol.2, p.471.
2. *Ibid.* p.413.
3. J.Cretineau-Joly, *op-cit.* Vol.1 pp.200-203.
4. C.L.Chassin, *op-cit.* V.2, 287.
5. Known today as Pont-Paillet.
6. L.Fuchard, *Les Quatre Guerres à Chatillon-sur-Sèvre* (Choletais:1992) p.107. The Vendéens had 3,000.
7. C.L.Chassin, *op-cit.* V.2, p.287.
8. J.J.Savary, *op-cit.* Vol.1, p.354.
9. L.Fuchard, *op-cit.* p.107 suggests 3,000 at St-Jouin, but this seems very high; Aubertin, Adj-Gen, *Mémoires inédits sur la Guerre de la Vendée 1793-4*, in *Mémoires du General Hugo* (Paris:1823) p.24.
10. A.Béjarry, *op-cit.* p.97-100.
11. Poirier-de-Beauvais, *op-cit.* pp.68-9.
12. *Ibid.* p.68.
13. S.Hilard, *Marigny et la memoire assassinée* (Choletais:1998), pp.80-82.
14. Aubertin, *op-cit.* p.25.
15. Poirier-de-Beauvais, *op-cit.* pp.69.
16. C.L.Chassin, *op-cit.* Vol.V2, p.289.
17. Mercier-de-Rocher in C.L.Chassin, *op-cit.* Vol.V2 p. 288.
18. L.Fruchard, *op-cit.* p.111.
19. R.S.V: June 1998 pp.41-3.
20. C.L.Chassin, *op-cit.* Vol.V.2, p.289.
21. Quoted in C.L.Chassin, *op-cit.* V.2, p.290.
22. R.S.V: June 1998, pp.41-3.
23. L.Fruchard, *op-cit.* p.112.
24. Hilard, *op-cit.* pp.80-2.
25. R.S.V: June 1998, pp.41-3.
26. Béjarry, *op-cit.* p.99.
27. Poirier-de-Beauvais, *op-cit.* pp.68.
28. This was one of the Orléans battalions: starting 470 strong and ending with 17. Béjarry, *op-cit.* p.100.
29. S.Hilard, *op-cit.* pp.80-2.
30. Mme Rochejaquelein, *op-cit.* pp.202-3.
31. Aubertin, *op-cit.* p.25.
32. *Ibid.* p.26.
33. Poirier-de-Beauvais, *op-cit.* p.69.

34. *Ibid.* p.70.
35. *Ibid.* p.72.
36. J.J.Savary, *op-cit.* Vol.1, p.360.
37. A.Béjarry, *op-cit.* p.100.
38. J.J.Savary, *op-cit.* Vol.1, p.363.
39. *Ibid.* p.365.
40. *Ibid.* p.356 (i.e. troops in Coulanges, 5,000 with Westermann and 7,000 with Biron)
41. *Ibid.* p.367.
42. *Ibid.* p.367.
43. *Ibid.* p.368.
44. *Ibid.* p.369.
45. *Ibid.* pp.369-70.
46. *Ibid.* p.375.
47. *Ibid.* pp.372-73.
48. *Ibid.* p.373.
49. *Ibid.* p.375.
50. *Ibid.* p.377.
51. R.Blachez , *Bonchamps et l'Insurrection Vendéene 1760-1793* (Paris:1902) p.221.
52. S.Hilard , *op-cit.* pp.83-5.
53. Mme Rochejaquelein, *op-cit.* p.227.
54. R.Blachez, *op-cit.* p.222, suggests this detour was pointless as the river was fordable in numerous places.
55. Poirier-de-Beauvais, *op-cit.* p.73.
56. R.Blachez, *op-cit.* p.222.
57. Poirier-de-Beauvais, *op-cit.* p.73.
58. R.Blachez, *op-cit.* p.223.
59. *Ibid.* p.224.
60. Poirier-de-Beauvais, *op-cit.* p.74.
61. S.Hilard, *op-cit.* pp.83-5.
62. R.Blachez, *op-cit.* p.225.
63. Mme Rochejaquelein, *op-cit.* pp.228-9.
64. Poirier-de-Beauvais, *op-cit.* p.75.
65. J.J.Savary, *op-cit.* Vol.1, p.377.
66. RSV: No.202. March-April 1998, pp.25-6.
67. These were probably Chabot and Joly's troops. Loidreau suggests they placed forty guns near Jusalem Farm but gives no source (RSV:No.202). P.Mercier, *Piron de la Varenne* (Paris:1938), p.52, notes forty guns dispersed amongst the army, saying many were fresh from foundries.

68. Royalist account of the battle suggests 15,000 with 30 guns; Loidereau: 7-8,000 with little artillery; Mercier-de-Rocher: 10-12,000; P.Doré-Graslin: 10,000.

69. Mercier-de-Rocher, *op-cit*. p.53.

70. J.J.Savary, *op-cit.*, Vol.1, p.397.

71. *Ibid.*

72. R.S.V: No.202.

73. J.J.Savary, *op-cit.* Vol.1, p.387.

74. *Ibid.* p.387.

75. J.G.Gallaher, *The Iron Marshal* (Greenhill:2000) pp.21-23.

76. J.J.Savary, *op-cit.* pp.392-3.

77. *Ibid.* pp.393-4.

78. *Ibid.* pp.421-2.

79. *Ibid.* p.418.

80. Ibid. pp.419-24.

81. P.Doré-Graslin, *op-cit.* pp.82-3.

82. F.L'Hostis, *Les-Ponts-de-Cé, une ville à feu et a sang 1793-6* (Choletais:1995), pp.50-1.

83. J.J.Savary, *op-cit.* Vol.1, p.420.

84. F.L'Hostis, *op-cit.* pp.51 and 55.

85. *Ibid.* p.424 suggests detachments from the Sarthe and Jemappes battalions and Angers National Guard involved in this assault.

86. J.J.Savary, *op-cit.* Vol.1, p.394.

87. *Ibid.* p.395.

88. *Ibid.* pp.402-3. Reported by Tuncq.

89. F.Deniau, *op-cit.* Vol.2, Footnote: p.410.

90. *Ibid.* p.410

91. P.Doré-Graslin, *op-cit.* p.82.

92. A.Béjarry, *op-cit.* pp.102-3.

93. F.Deniau, *op-cit.* Vol,2, p.411

94. A.Billaud and J.d'Herbauges, *op-cit.* p.223.

95. F.Deniau, *op-cit.* Vol.2, p.412.

96. R.Bittard-des-Portes, *op-cit.* p.128.

97. P.Doré-Graslin, *op-cit.* p.83.

98. T.Rouchette, *André Mercier de Rocher, Memoires pour server a l'histoire de la guerre de Vendée* (Loudéac:1989) p.208 suggests Tuncq led 3,600 men.

99. Rebel numbers are unclear. Some Royalist accounts talk of 25-30,000 men but Republican accounts, normally the ones to exaggerate rebel strength, indicate 8-9,000 (C.L. Chassin, *op-cit.* Vol.V2, pp.181 and 259).

100. The 11th Hussars formed 26th June from *Légion-de-la-Fraternité* and *Hussards-de-la-Liberté*. Chalbos sent them to support Tuncq.

101. Poirier-de-Beauvais, *op-cit.* pp.91-2.

102. *Ibid.* pp.91-2. A messenger reported to the Republicans in Les Sables that 3–4,000 rebels had been repulsed with the loss of 160 men: Collinet, *op-cit.* p.148.

103. Collinet, *op-cit.* p.149.

104. *Ibid.* pp.154-5.

105. J.J.Savary, *op-cit.* Vol.1, p.426.

106. *Ibid.* p.428.

Chapter 9: 'Destroy the Vendée!'

1. J.J.Savary, *op-cit.* Vol.1, pp.429-31.

2. J.J.Savary, *op-cit.* Vol 2, pp.18-22.

3. C.L.Chassin, *op-cit.* Vol.V2, p.437.

4. J.J.Savary, *op-cit.* Vol 2, p.11.

5. Grouchy, Marquis de, *Mémoires du Maréchal de Grouchy*.Vol.1 (Paris:1873), p.37.

6. *Ibid.* p.37. Comprising 2,739 volunteers, 1,090 line troops, 252 cavalry and 144 gunners.

7. J.J.Savary, *op-cit.* Vol.2, p.13.

8. *Ibid.* p.24-5.

9. *Ibid.* p.16.

10. *Ibid.* p.23.

11. F.Deniau, *op-cit.* Vol.2, pp.439-40.

12. J.J.Savary, *op-cit.* Vol.2, p.23.

13. *Ibid.* p.12.

14. Mme Rochejaquelein, *op-cit.* pp.219-20.

15. *Ibid.* pp.219-20.

16. Poirier-de-Beauvais, *op-cit.* p.95.

17. Mme Rochejaquelein, *op-cit.* pp.219-20.

18. A.Béjarry, *op-cit.* pp.106-7; Mme Rochejaquelein, *op-cit.* pp.219-20.

19. Poirier-de-Beauvais, *op-cit.* pp.94-5.

20. *Ibid.* p.96.

21. *Ibid.* p.95.

22. Mme Rochejaquelein, *op-cit.* pp.219-20.

23. A.Béjarry, *op-cit.* p.109.

24. Poirier-de-Beauvais, *op-cit.* pp.101-2.

25. The Republicans claimed 2x12 pdrs, 4x8 pdrs, 10x4pdrs and 6 caissons (C.L.Chassin, *op-cit.* Vol.V2, p.463-4); Beauvais estimated their loss at 1,200 (800 from Charette's troops).

26. Collinet, *op-cit*. p.161.
27. *Ibid*. p.162.
28. R.Bittard-des-Portes, *op-cit*. p.154-5.
29. F.Deniau, *op-cit*. Vol.2, p.484.
30. Collinet, *op-cit*. p.163.
31. J.J.Savary, *op-cit*. Vol.2, p.71-2.
32. R.Bittard-des-Portes, *op-cit*. p.156.
33. C.L.Chassin, *op-cit*. Vol.V2, p.557.

Chapter 10: 'The Promenade of the Sovereign People'

1. Grouchy, *op-cit*. pp.46-7.
2. C.L.Chassin, *op-cit*. Vol.V3, pp.17-18.
3. *Ibid*. p.19. Sybarites better translate today as hedonists.
4. *Ibid*. p.20.
5. *Ibid*. pp.20-2.
6. *Ibid*. p.25.
7. *Ibid*. Vol.V.2, p.557.
8. R.Bittard-des-Portes, *op-cit*. pp.161-2.
9. *Ibid*. p.162.
10. C.L.Chassin, *op-cit*. Vol.V2, pp.557-8.
11. R.Bittard-des-Portes, *op-cit*. p.163.
12. C.L.Chassin, *op-cit*. Vol.V2, p.558. Grouchy claimed 10,000 rebels attacked.
13. R.Bittard-des-Portes, *op-cit*. p.163.
14. F.Deniau, *op-cit*. Vol.2, p.501.
15. *Ibid*. p.501.
16. J.Crétineau-Joly, *op-cit*. Vol.1, p.253.
17. Poirier-de-Beauvais, *op-cit*. pp.103-4.
18. J.J.Savary, *op-cit*. Vol.2, p.120: Lecomte reported 200 to Chalbos (8th September); A.Billaud & J.d'Herbauges, *op-cit*. pp.229-30, suggests 3,000; H.Servien, *Petite Histoire des Guerres de Vendée* (Chiré 1981), p.66, cites 3,000 killed, hundreds captured, with the Vendéens losses at 1,500.
19. J.J.Savary, *Ibid*. p.121.
20. 4th, 5th,15th Orléans, 8th Hussars, 26th Div-Gendarmerie.
21. C.L.Chassin, *op-cit*. Vol.V3, pp.40-1.
22. *Ibid*. p.59.
23. E.Gabory, *op-cit*. p.262.
24. *Ibid*. p.262.
25. J.J.Savary., *op-cit*. Vol.2, p.157.

26. C.L.Chassin, *op-cit.* Vol.V3, p.44.
27. D'Autichamp commanded in place of the wounded Bonchamps.
28. Detachments from Sarthe, Jemappes, 6th and 8th Paris (J.J.Savary, *op-cit.* Vol2, pp.127-8).
29. F.L'Hostis, *Les-Ponts-de-Cé, une ville à feu et à sang 1793-6* (Choletais:1995), p.62.
30. J.J.Savary, *op-cit.* Vol.2, p.129.
31. H.Coutau-Begarie and C.Dore-Graslin, *op-cit.* p.464.
32. Mme Rochejaquelein, op-cit. p.234. Imbert suggests the reinforcements comprised 20,000 levies.
33. Hugues Imbert: *Petite Histoire de Thouars* (PRNG:2015), p.233.
34. Mme Rochejaquelein, *op-cit.* pp.234-5, indicated Lescure was adored by the soldiers because he was always ready to help carry stretchers and evacuate the wounded.
35. Poirier-de-Beauvais, *op-cit.*,pp.110-11. Casualties on both sides were light.
36. J.Crétineau-Joly, *op-cit.* Vol.1, p.262.
37. Poirier-de-Beauvais, *op-cit.* p.109.
38. J.J.Savary, *op-cit.* Vol.2, p.162.
39. J.Crétineau-Joly, *op-cit.* p.268-9.
40. C.L.Chassin, *op-cit.* Vol.V3, p.90.
41. J.J.Savary, *op-cit.* Vol.2, p.166.
42. H.Coutau-Begarie and C.Dore-Graslin (eds), *op-cit,* p.464: Sarazin suggests 9,000 levies formed around his existing 6,000 men. Rossignol indicates 8,000 levies and 3,000 existing troops.
43. F.Deniau, *op-cit.* Vol.2, pp.578-9.
44. H.Coutau-Begarie and C.Dore-Graslin(eds), *op-cit.* p.467 and C.L.Chassin, op-cit. Vol.V3, p.88-9.
45. P.Doré-Graslin, *op-cit.* p.94.
46. H.Coutau-Begarie and C.Dore-Graslin(eds), *op-cit.* p.467.
47. *Ibid.* p.468.
48. Poirier-de-Beauvais, *op-cit.* pp.262-3.
49. J.J.Savary, *op-cit.* Vol.2, p.167.
50. H.Coutau-Begarie and C.Dore-Graslin(eds), *op-cit.* p.468.
51. E.Gabory, *op-cit.* pp.262-3.
52. R.Bittard-des-Portes, *op-cit.* p.169.
53. Kléber indicates these companies were marching through partially covered terrain, which accounts for the deployment. R.Nougaret, *op-cit.* pp.92-3.
54. *Ibid.* p.94.
55. R.Bittard-des-Portes, *op-cit.* p.182.

56. Accounts vary: 12-15,000 (R.Bittard-des-Portes, *op-cit.* Footnote: p.190); 20,000 (R.Blanchez, *op-cit.* p.346); overestimated 40,000 (Mme Rochejaquelein, *op-cit.* p.242); D'Élbée had 6,000 Angevins, 900 cavalry, and 30 guns (F.Charpentier, *D'Élbée 1752-1794 Generalissime des Armées Vendéenes* (1905; Cholet:2006), p.177). Around 25-30,000 seems most likely: Charette and bands of Coastal Vendée: 4-5,000; Bonchamps: 7-8,000; Royrand: 5-6,000; Lescure: 7-8,000 (including 2-3,000 from La Rochejaquelein's division).

57. J.J.Savary, *op-cit.* Vol.2, p.172.

58. *Ibid.* p.170.

59. Lucas de la Championnière, *op-cit.* p.47.

60. R.Bittard-des-Portes, *op-cit.* p.183.

61. H.Servien, *op-cit.* p.69.

62. Mme Rochejaquelein, *op-cit.* pp.240-2.

63. F.Charpentier, *op-cit.* pp.179-80.

64. Poirier-de-Beauvais, *op-cit.* p.119.

65. J.J.Savary, *op-cit.* Vol.2. p.170.

66. Poirier-de-Beauvais, *op-cit.* p.119.

67. R.Bittard-des-Portes, *op-cit.* p.184, quoting Beauchamp.

68. *Ibid.* p.185, quoting Muret.

69. J.J.Savary, *op-cit.* Vol.2, pp.170-1.

70. L de la Championnière, *op-cit.* p.47.

71. *Ibid.* p.47.

72. The story of Chevardin's last stand at the bridge has recently been disputed, Kléber only states that he was killed covering the retreat. See http://www.Vendéensetchouans.com/archives/2015/07/05/32316690.html

73. R.Nougaret, *op-cit.* p.242.

74. Mme Rochejaquelein, *op-cit.* p.242.

75. Poirier-de-Beauvais, *op-cit.* p.120.

76. C.L.Chassin, *op-cit.* Vol.V3, p.99.

77. *Ibid.* p.99.

78. R.Bittard-des-Portes, *op-cit.* p.190.

79. J.J.Savary, *op-cit.* Vol.2, p.174.

80. F.Charpentier, *op-cit.* p.183.

81. A.Béjarry, *op-cit.* p.115, indicates that he had 3,000 infantry and 100 cavalry at Torfou.

82. J.J.Savary, *op-cit.* Vol 2, p.176.

83. *Ibid.* p.180.

84. R.Bittard-des-Portes, *op-cit.* p.193.

85. *Ibid.* pp.193-4.
86. Poirier-de-Beauvais, *op-cit.* p.121.
87. R.Bittard-des-Portes, *op-cit.* pp.194-5.
88. Poirier-de-Beauvais, *op-cit.* p.121.
89. R.Bittard-des-Portes, *op-cit.* pp.195.
90. Poirier-de-Beauvais, *op-cit.* p.122.
91. *Ibid.* p.123.
92. R.Bittard-des-Portes, *op-cit.* pp.197.
93. C.L.Chassin, *op-cit.* Vol.V3, pp.103-5.
94. *Ibid.* p.107.
95. R.Bittard-des-Portes, *op-cit.* p.198.
96. C.L.Chassin, *op-cit.* Vol.V3, p.105. Joly was probably responsible.
97. *Ibid.* p.104.
98. A.Béjarry, *op-cit.* p.117.
99. R.Nougaret, *op-cit.* p.111.
100. *Ibid.* p.112.
101. F.Deniau, *op-cit.* Vol.2, p.610.
102. R.Nougaret, *op-cit.* p.112.
103. *Ibid.* p.113.
104. R.Nougaret, *op-cit.* p.114.
105. Mme Rochejaquelein, *op-cit.* p.243-4.
106. R.Nougaret, *op-cit.* p.114.
107. Poirier-de-Beauvais, *op-cit.* p.125.
108. C.L.Chassin, op-cit. Vol.V3, pp.71-2.
109. *Ibid.* p.79.
110. R.Bittard-des-Portes, *op-cit.* p.202.
111. E.Gabory, *op-cit.* p.266, and Poirier de Beauvais, *op-cit.* p.126.
112. C.L.Chassin, *op-cit.* Vol.V3, p.110.
113. R.Bittard-des-Portes, *op-cit.* p.201.
114. L de la Championnière, *op-cit.* p.52.
115. Poirier-de-Beauvais, *op-cit.* p.126.
116. R.Bittard-des-Portes, *op-cit.* p.202.
117. *Ibid.* Footnote: p.203.
118. Poirier-de-Beauvais, *op-cit.* Footonote: pp.126-7.
119. *Ibid.* p.126.
120. C.L.Chassin, *op-cit.* Vol.V3 pp.113 and 116.
121. R.Bittard-des-Portes, *op-cit.* p.208.
122. *Ibid.* p.212.
123. *Ibid.* p.213.

Chapter 11: 'The Rebels Fought like Tigers and our Soldiers like Lions'

1. J.J.Savary, *op-cit.* Vol.2, pp.191-2.
2. *Ibid.* p.195.
3. *Ibid.* pp.196-7.
4. 350 men of the *Légion-du-Nord* were commanded by Joba on 11 September. This légion was composed of part of Westermann's cavalry, reinforced by others. C.L.Chassin, *op-cit.* Vol.V3, p.78.
5. *Ibid.* pp.147-8.
6. J.J.Savary, *op-cit.* Vol.2, pp.198-9.
7. *Ibid.* p.205.
8. *Ibid.* p.207.
9. R.Nougaret, *op-cit.* p.119.
10. Poirier-de-Beauvais, *op-cit.* pp.131-3.
11. R.Nougaret, *op-cit.* p.121.
12. *Ibid.* p.121.
13. *Ibid.* p.122.
14. Poirier-de-Beauvais, *op-cit.* p.132.
15. R.Nougaret, *op-cit.* p.123.
16. *Ibid.* p.124.
17. *Ibid.* p.128.
18. *Ibid.* p.129.
19. Mme Rochejaquelein, *op-cit.* pp.248-53, Lescure and La Rochejacquelein: 6,000. After Bois-aux-Chèvres they were joined by 2,000 more under the Chevalier-de-la-Sorinière.
20. Aubertin, *op-cit.* p.30. Aubertin had joined Chalbos' staff.
21. C.L.Chassin, *op-cit.* Vol.V3, p.195.
22. Aubertin, *op-cit.* pp.31-2.
23. According to Aubertin (p.32) this was generally the case in the Vendée.
24. Aubertin (p.32) noted that he had just arrived at Bressuire, having been promoted from lieutenant of chasseurs to general of brigade and was in an army that was totally new to him. He considered him useless.
25. *Ibid.* p.32.
26. E.Stofflet, *op-cit.* p.112. J.Crétineau-Joly, *op-cit.* p.290, indicates 2-300 cavalry under Beaurepaire.
27. Aubertin, *op-cit.* p.33.
28. *Ibid.* p.34.
29. *Ibid.* p.35.

30. *Ibid.* pp.34-6.
31. *Ibid.* p.36.
32. *Ibid.* p.36.
33. *Ibid.* p.36.
34. *Ibid.* pp.36-7.
35. E.Stofflet, *op-cit.* p.112.
36. Aubertin, *op-cit.* p.38.
37. *Ibid.* p.38.
38. L.Fruchard, *op-cit.* pp.138.
39. J.Crétineau-Joly, *op-cit.* p.290.
40. Sources differ between 500 and 2,000 men with him (L.Fruchard, *op-cit.* pp.137-42). Savary states he had fifty cavalry and two guns.
41. Poirier-de-Beauvais, *op-cit.* p.128.
42. Aubertin, *op-cit.* p.40.
43. *Ibid.* pp.40-1.
44. Poirier-de-Beauvais, *op-cit.* p.128.
45. *Ibid.* p.128.
46. Aubertin, *op-cit.* p.41.
47. Poirier-de-Beauvais, *op-cit.* pp.128-9.
48. *Ibid.* p.129.
49. Aubertin, *op-cit.* p.43.
50. *Ibid.* p.44.
51. *Ibid.* p.44.
52. Chalbos says 6-700 infantry and 60 cavalry were used in the counter-attack (J.J.Savary, *op-cit.* Vol.2, p.243).
53. Poirier-de-Beauvais, *op-cit.* p.129-30.
54. Mme Rochejaquelein, *op-cit.* p.257.
55. Aubertin, *op-cit.* p.45.
56. *Ibid.* p.45.
57. J.J.Savary, *op-cit.* Vol.2, pp.252-3.
58. Mme Rochejaquelein, *op-cit.* p.260.
59. C.Coubard, *op-cit.* p.57.
60. *Ibid.* pp.57-8.
61. J.J.Savary, *op-cit.* Vol.2, p.256. Beaupuy had four guns.
62. J.J.Savary, *op-cit.* pp.256-7.
63. *Ibid.* p.257.
64. Mme Rochejaquelein, *op-cit.* pp.260-1.
65. Poirier-de-Beauvais, *op-cit.* p.140.
66. Mme Rochejaquelein, *op-cit.* pp.259-60.

67. Poirier-de-Beauvais, *op-cit.*, p.141-2.

68. J.J.Savary, *op-cit.* p.258.

69. *Ibid.* p.142.

70. F.Deniau, *op-cit.* Vol.2, p.30.

71. F.Deniau, *op-cit.* Vol.3, p.27 notes the following sources: Muret: 40,000 and 1,500 cavalry; Bourniseaux: 38,000 infantry, 1,500 cavalry and 18 guns; Savary and Mme Rochejaquelein: 40,000; Léchelle: 30,000. From this should be extracted troops sent to secure the Loire.

72. *Ibid.* p.27. Kléber: 9,737, Marceau: 3,000, Chalbos: 10,000; total: 22,737.

73. C.Coubard, *op-cit.* p.75.

74. *Ibid.* p.75.

75. J.J.Savary, *op-cit.* Vol.2, p.269.

76. C.Coubard, op-cit., p.77.

77. J.J.Savary, *op-cit.* pp.268-9.

78. C.Coubard, *op-cit.* p.76.

79. Around the northern ends of the present Joffre and Faidherbe Boulevards (Souvenir Vendéen, *La Bataille de Cholet* (Cholet:2014), p.19).

80. F.Deniau, *op-cit.* Vol.3, p.40.

81. C.Coubard, *op-cit.* p.77.

82. *Ibid.* p.76-7.

83. F.Deniau, *op-cit.* Vol.3. p.41.

84. Souvenir Vendéen, *La Bataille de Cholet* (Cholet:2014), p.17.

85. C.Coubard, *op-cit.* p.78.

86. *Ibid.* p.79.

87. R.Nougaret, *op-cit.* p.146.

88. *Ibid.* p.147.

89. They probably salvaged around 45 guns. Mme Rochejaquelein (*op-cit.* p.275) indicates they abandoned the rest or pushed them into the Loire.

90. P.Gréau, *op-cit.* (2012) p.96.

91. Mme Rochejaquelein, *op-cit.* p.274, indicates 40-50,000 fighters of 60,000 men in total, including many wounded or who had never fought, followed by 15-20,000 civilians. H.Coutau-Bégarie/C.Doré-Graslin(eds), *op-cit.* p.293, cites republican claims varying from 40-80,000.

Chapter 12: The Coastal Vendée stands Alone: October and November

1. R.Bittard-des-Portes, *op-cit.* p.217.

2. *Ibid.* p.219.

3. *Ibid.* p.221.

4. F.Deniau, *op-cit.* Vol.4, pp.10-11.
5. Comtesse de la Bouëre, *La Vendée Angevine 1793-6. Souvenirs de la Guerre de la Vendée* (Paris:1890) p.93.
6. *Ibid.* p.99.
7. C.L.Chassin, *op-cit.* Vol.V3, p.381.
8. Collinet, *op-cit.* p179.
9. *Ibid.* p.176.
10. *Ibid.* p.191.
11. *Ibid* . pp.191-2.
12. *Ibid.* pp.192-3.
13. *Ibid.* pp.180-1 and p.185.
14. R.Bittard-des-Portes, *op-cit.* pp.231.
15. C.L.Chassin, *op-cit.* Vol.V3, p.384.
16. Collinet, *op-cit.* p.184.
17. R.Bittard-des-Portes, *op-cit.* p.231.
18. Aubertin, *op-cit.* p.73.
19. R.Bittard-des-Portes, *op-cit.* p.232 suggests Charette was repulsed.
20. C.L.Chassin, *op-cit.* Vol.V3, pp.386-7.

Chapter 13: The March on Granville

1. E.Gabory, *op-cit.* p.1119.
2. *Ibid.* p.1116.
3. F.Deniau, *op-cit.* Vol.3, p.116. (E.Gabory, *op-cit.* p.287, suggest 3,000.)
4. *Ibid.* p.117 notes that Esnue-Lavallée, who led the troops to Craon, may have retreated before the battle. P.Gréau, *op-cit.* p.104.
5. *Ibid.* p.117.
6. Poirier-de-Beauvais, *op-cit.* pp.157-8.
7. Mme Rochejaquelein, *op-cit.* p.288.
8. RSV:No.220, Sept 2002 pp.14-33.
9. J.J.Savary, *op-cit.* Vol.2, p.280.
10. *Ibid.* p.293. He suggests Olagnier did not receive these orders.
11. F.Deniau, *op-cit.* Vol.3, p.124.
12. *Ibid.* p.125.
13. *Ibid.* p.125.
14. *Ibid.* p.125.
15. F.Deniau, *op-cit.* pp.126-7, and J.J.Savary, *op-cit.* Vol.2, pp.298-9.
16. P.Gréau, *26 Octobre 1793. La Bataille d'Entrammes* (Laval:2007), p.52.
17. Mme Rochejaquelein, *op-cit.* Footnote: p.291.
18. F.Deniau, *op-cit.* Vol.3, pp.130-1.

19. *Ibid.* p.130 and P.Gréau, *op-cit.*(2007), p.55.

20. *Ibid.* (P.Gréau, p.52). He places Royrand's wounding in the initial fighting north of the Jouanne.

21. *Ibid.* p.55.

22. F.Deniau, *op-cit.* p.133.

23. J.J.Savary., *op-cit.* Vol.2, p.302. Muller may have been leading Chalbos' column as Savary suggests he halted there rather than advance further.

24. C.L.Chassin, *op-cit.* Vol.V3, p.245.

25. *Ibid.* p.245.

26. Poirier-de-Beauvais, *op-cit.* p.160.

27. F.Deniau, *op-cit.* Vol.3, p.135.

28. *Ibid.* p.135.

29. P.Gréau, *op-cit.* p.60.

30. R.Nougaret, *op-cit.* pp.164-5.

31. F.Deniau, *op-cit.* Vol.3, p.136.

32. P.Gréau, *op-cit.* (2007), p.60, indicates that these rebels crossed the Mayenne at Villiers and entered the town by the Craon road.

33. F.Deniau, *op-cit.* Vol.3, p.139.

34. *Ibid.* p.140.

35. *Ibid.* pp.146-7.

36. *Ibid.* pp.145-6.

37. E.Gabory, *op-cit.* p.1121.

38. T.Lemas, *Le District de Fougères pendant les Guerres de l'Ouest et de la Chouannerie 1793-1800* (Rennes:1994), p.55.

39. J.Crétineau-Joly, op-cit. p.367.

40. Poirier de Beauvais, *op-cit.* p.164.

41. F.Deniau, *op-cit.* Vol.3, p.149.

42. J.J.Savary, *op-cit.* Vol.2, p.325.

43. Poirier-de-Beauvais, *op-cit.* pp.167-9.

44. Gréau states this was at Charné p.124

45. J.J.Savary, *op-cit.* Vol.2, pp.336-7.

46. *Ibid.* p.337.

47. T.Lemas, *op-cit.* p.59.

48. J.J.Savary, *op-cit.* Vol.2, p.338.

49. Poirier-de-Beauvais, *op-cit.* pp.169-70.

50. *Ibid.* p.170.

51. J.J.Savary , *op-cit.* Vol.2, pp.330-1.

52. R.Nougaret, *op-cit.* p.174.

53. Mme Rochejaquelein, *op-cit.* pp.307-9.

54. See SHD-1 M489: *Mémoire d'Obenheim sur la Virée de Galerne.*
55. T.Lemas, *op-cit.* p.81.
56. E.Gabory, *op-cit.* pp.1122-3.
57. C.L.Chassin, *op-cit.* Vol.3, p.283.
58. *Le Goulu, L'Anonyme* and *Râfleur*, although Peyre mentions only two.
59. SHD-B5/20-9: 11th November.
60. A.Béjarry, *op-cit.* p.137.
61. R.Sinsoilliez, *La Siege de Granville* (L'Ancre de Marine:2004), pp.113-14.
62. Poirier-de-Beauvais, *op-cit.* pp.178-9.
63. R.Sinsoilliez, *op-cit.* p.84.
64. Poirier-de-Beauvais, *op-cit.* p.179.
65. R.Sinsoilliez, *op-cit.* p.87.
66. Poirier-de-Beauvais, *op-cit.* pp.179-80.
67. R.Sinsoilliez, *op-cit.* pp.88-9.
68. C.L.Chassin, *op-cit.*,. Vol.V3, p.290.
69. R.Sinsoilliez, *op-cit.* p. 90.
70. Poirier-de-Beauvais, *op-cit.* pp.180-1.
71. *LE DIDAC'DOC.Service éducatif des archives départementales de la Manche* (November 2011), p.51.
72. C.L.Chassin , *op-cit.* Vol.V3, p.301.
73. J.J.Savary, *op-cit.* Vol.2, pp.352-3.
74. R.Sinsoilliez, *op-cit.* p.92.
75. C.L.Chassin, *op-cit.* Vol.V3, p.301, quoting *The Register of the General Council of the Granville Commune*, written that evening.
76. J.J.Savary, *op-cit.* pp.352-3.
77. Beauvais does not mention the one north of the Boscq, but does indicate a third in a field, right of the battery west of Grande-Houle, and possibly meant this one further north.
78. A low rampart allowing guns to fire over the parapet.
79. R.Sinsoilliez, *op-cit.* p.101-2.
80. *Ibid.* p.104.
81. *Ibid.* p.106.
82. Poirier-de-Beauvais, *op-cit.* p.182.
83. A.Béjarry, *op-cit.* pp.138-9.
84. Poirier-de-Beauvais, *op-cit.* p.182.
85. It was from here that Beauvais had organised the firing of red hot shot, but it passed uselessly over the town as the men serving the guns were inebriated, unlike a Republican battery that was scoring some success in counter-fire.
86. *Ibid.* p.185.

87. R.Sinsoilliez, *op-cit.* p.122.
88. Vendéens: Hundreds killed, 800 stragglers over following days (E.Gabory, *op-cit.* p.298); 600 (F.Deniau, *op-cit.* Vol.3, p.212). Republicans: 343 dead, 60 wounded (SHD-B5/16-20).
89. Army Historical Research Vol.29, No.120 (1951): *The Campaign in Flanders of 1793-5. Journal of Lt Charles Stewart 28th Foot.*
90. Jersey Record Office Ref:L/F/08/A/24.
91. Jersey Record Office Ref:L/F/08/A/16. Balcarres to Moira 8th December. Pierre-Nicolas Gilbert, Chevalier de Solérac, joined the Vendéens in mid-August and established links to agents in Jersey. He was not considered a significant figure amongst the Vendéens but had the ear of the Military Council. He escaped to Jersey in late November (RSV:No.223, June 2003).
92. RSV: No.223, June 2003, p.17.
93. *Ibid.* p.17.
94. RSV: No.224 September 2003, p.7.

Chapter 14: The Race to the Loire

1. R.Nougaret, *op-cit.* p.176.
2. J.J.Savary, *op-cit.* Vol.2, p.357.
3. C.L.Chassin, *op-cit.* Vol.V3, p.312, states they had twelve guns.
4. F.Deniau, *op-cit.* Vol.3, p.221.
5. *Ibid.* p.221.
6. *Ibid.* p.221.
7. See RSV:No.206, June 2001, article by Paul Liguine.
8. *Ibid.* Benaben reported that 600 troops from the 77th Line reached Antrain around midnight (half being wounded).
9. Mme Rochejaquelein, *op-cit.* p.317; Liguine notes Republicans losses of 1,000-1,200 men (RSV:No.206, June2001).
10. C.L.Chassin, *op-cit.* Vol.V3, p.312.
11. F.Deniau, *op-cit.* Vol.3, p.226.
12. C.L.Chassin, *op-cit.* Vol.V3, p.312.
13. F.Deniau, *op-cit.* Vol.3, p.227.
14. J.J.Savary, *op-cit.* Vol.2, pp.368-9.
15. A.Jamaux, *Les Batailles de Dol, de Pontorson a Antrain Novembre 1793,* (self-published), p.46.
16. *Ibid.* pp.49-50.
17. *Ibid.* p.51.
18. *Ibid.*, pp.55-6.
19. *Ibid.*, pp.56-7.

20. *Ibid.*, p.61.
21. *Ibid.*, p.67.
22. R.Nougaret, *op-cit.* p.200.
23. J.J.Savary, *op-cit.* Vol.2, p.389.
24. R.Nougaret, *op-cit.* p.207.
25. J.J.Savary, *op-cit.* Vol.2, p.406.
26. P.Gréau, *op-cit.* (2012), p.170.
27. A.Danican, *Les Brigands démasqués* (London:1796), p.173.
28. F.Deniau, *op-cit.* Vol.3, pp.291-6, details the defences.
29. J.J.Savary, *op-cit.* Vol.2, p.410.
30. *Ibid.* p.410.
31. S.Hilard, *Marigny et la Mémoire assassinée* (Choletais:1998), pp.125-6.
32. C.L.Chassin, *op-cit.* Vol.V3, p.344.
33. F.Deniau, *op-cit.* Vol.3, pp.296-7.
34. C.L.Chassin, *op-cit.* Vol.V3, p.344.
35. F.Deniau, *op-cit.* Vol.3, p.298.
36. Poirier-de-Beauvais, *op-cit.* p.208.
37. *Ibid.* 210.
38. J.J.Savary, *op-cit.* Vol.2, p.410.
39. C.L.Chassin, *op-cit.* Vol.V3, p.345.
40. J.J.Savary, *op-cit.* Vol.2, p.410.
41. C.L.Chassin, *op-cit.* Vol.V3, p.345.
42. F.Deniau, *op-cit.* Vol.3, p.302.
43. C.L.Chassin, *op-cit.* Vol.V3, p.346.
44. *Ibid.* p.351.
45. *Ibid.* p.345.
46. Mme Rochejaquelein, *op-cit.* p.340; F.Deniau, *op-cit.* Vol.3, p.303.
47. F.Deniau, *op-cit.* Vol.3, pp.302-3.
48. *Ibid.* p.306.
49. F.Deniau, *op-cit.* Vol.3, p.308.
50. *Ibid.* p.307.
51. *Ibid.* p.307.
52. J.J.Savary, *op-cit.* Vol.2, p.409.
53. F.Deniau, *op-cit.* Vol.3, p.308. They tracked La Rochejaquelein's cavalry back to Angers.
54. J.J.Savary, *op-cit.* Vol.2, pp.409-10.
55. *Ibid.* p.411.
56. F.Deniau, *op-cit.* p.313, quoting Grille; J.J.Savary, *op-cit.* Vol.2, p.411, mentions the cannons.

57. F.Deniau, *op-cit*. Vol.3, p.302.
58. J.J.Savary, *op-cit*. Vol.2, p.415.

Chapter 15: The Death of an Army

1. F.Deniau, *op-cit*. Vol.3, p.315.
2. J.J.Savary, *op-cit*. Vol.2, pp.414-5.
3. J.J.Savary, *op-cit*. Vol.2, p.420.
4. RSV: No.201, Dec 1997, p.49.
5. *Ibid*. pp.49-50.
6. Mme Rochejaquelein, *op-cit*. pp.346-7.
7. *Ibid*. p.346.
8. J.J.Savary, *op-cit*. Vol.2, p.421.
9. *Ibid*. p.422.
10. *Ibid*. p.422.
11. Mme Rochejaquelein, *op-cit*. p.347.
12. *Ibid*. p.348, and H.Chardon, *Les Vendéens dans la Sarthe* (Le Mans:1869), Vol.1, p.336.
13. E.Gabory, *op-cit*. p.312.
14. Most details from C.L.Chassin, *op-cit*. Vol.V3, pp.409-11 and H.Chardon, *op.cit*.
15. H.Chardon, *op-cit*. Vol.1, p.347 (probably the l'Epau Wood).
16. *Ibid*. p.348.
17. G.Pontavice, *Les Armées Catholique et Royale au Nord de la Loire* (Yves Salmon:1989), p.83.
18. A.Lévy, *Les Batailles du Mans* (Bordessoules:1993), p.8.
19. Westermann claimed this battle lasted three hours but this does not fit with the timing of the following events. H.Chardon, *op-cit*. Vol.2, p.18.
20. *Ibid*. p.9.
21. *Ibid*. p.10.
22. Mme Rochejaquelein, *op-cit*. p.349 and H.Chardon, *op-cit*. Vol.2, p.11.
23. H.Chardon, *Ibid*. Vol.2, p.15.
24. *Ibid*. p.15.
25. *Ibid*. p.40.
26. *Ibid*. pp.39-40.
27. Mme Rochejaquelein, *op-cit*. pp.349-50.
28. H.Chardon, *op-cit*. Vol.2, p.41.
29. A.Lévy, *op-cit*. p.20.
30. H.Chardon, *op-cit*. Vol.2, p.29.
31. *Ibid*. p.34.

32. *Ibid.* p.47.

33. *Ibid.* p.42 states it was where the Rue-Basse split into several roads which led to the Place des Halles.

34. *Ibid.* Footnote: p.42.

35. *Ibid.* pp.42 and 46.

36. *Ibid.* p.46.

37. *Ibid.* p.47.

38. *Ibid.* p.50.

39. *Ibid.* p.63.

40. *Ibid.* p.61.

41. *Ibid.* p.65.

42. *Ibid.* p.78.

43. C.L.Chassin, *op-cit.* Vol.V3, p.355.

44. P.Gréau, *op-cit*(2017), p.198.

45. http://www.didac.ehu.es/antropo/27/27-3/Cabot.htm

46. P.Gréau, *op-cit.* (2017), p.199.

47. Maignon (C.L.Chassin, *op-cit.* Vol.V3, p.417). Chassin indicates the Vendéens retained around fifteen guns including one 12pdr when at Laval (*Ibid.* p.425).

48. *Ibid.* p.417.

49. P.Gréau, *op-cit.* (2017) p.206.

50. F.Deniau, *op-cit.* Vol.4, p.89.

51. H.Coutau-Bégarie and C.Doré-Graslin(eds), *op-cit.* p.298. Loidreau implies a similar number of unarmed men. A.Béjarry said they had 6-7,000 men and a further 4,000 refugees (p.158). It seems only seven guns were used at Savenay, so some may have been abandoned en route.

52. These were 600 grenadiers under Cambray, who retreated towards Croisic (F.Gueriff, *La Bataille de Savenay dans la Revolution* (J.M.Pierre:1988), p.126).

53. H.Coutau-Bégarie and C.Doré-Graslin(eds), *op-cit.* p.307.

54. F.Deniau, *op-cit.* Vol.3, p.429.

55. *Ibid.* p.430.

56. H.Coutau-Bégarie and C.Doré-Graslin(eds), *op-cit.* p.302.

57. J.J.Savary, *op-cit.* Vol.2, p.455.

58. H.Coutau-Bégarie and C.Doré-Graslin(eds), *op-cit.* p.302.

59. R,Nougaret, *op-cit.* p.277.

60. Mme Rochejaquelein, *op-cit.* p.365.

61. A,Béjarry, *op-cit.* pp.158-60

62. S.Hilard, *op–cit.* p.137.
63. F.Deniau, *op–cit.* Vol.3, p.435.
64. H.Coutau-Bégarie and C.Doré-Graslin, *op–cit.* p.309: The Armagnac Regiment was on the Guérande road and marched via the Vignes Hill.
65. *Ibid.* pp.308-9.
66. *Ibid.* p.310.
67. *Ibid.* p.310 and J.J.Savary, *op–cit.* Vol.2, p.457.
68. *Ibid.* p.456.
69. A.Béjarry, *op–cit.* p.160.
70. *Ibid.*

Chapter 16: Charette 'King of the Vendée'

1. La Bouëre, *op–cit.*, pp.112-4.
2. F.Deniau, *op–cit.* Vol.4, p.20.
3. La Bouëre, *op–cit.* p.100.
4. F.Deniau, *op–cit.* Vol.4, p.55.
5. Lucas de la Championnière, *op–cit.* p.60
6. Aubertin, *op–cit.* p.66
7. F.Deniau, *op–cit.* Vol.4, 59.
8. Aubertin, *op–cit.* p.70. These ditches were each about 9 feet wide.
9. Unless Aubertin is mistaken, this suggests a further rebel redoubt south on the Beauvoir road.
10. Guérin is sometimes placed covering Charette's left so may have left a detachment to the north of the island.
11. C.L.Chassin, *op–cit.* Vol.V.3, p.388.
12. Deniau, *op–cit.* Vol.4, p.60.
13. L. de la Championnière, *op–cit.* p.60.
14. R.Bittard-des-Portes, *op–cit.* p.242.
15. C.L.Chassin, *op–cit.* Vol.V.3 p.388.
16. R.Bittard-des-Portes, *op–cit.* p.242.
17. *Ibid.* p.243.
18. Aubertin suggest there were 1,200. p.77.
19. L. de la Championnière, *op–cit.* pp.62-3.
20. Aubertin, *op–cit.* p.77.
21. F.Deniau, *op–cit.* Vol.4, p.68.
22. L. de la Championnière, *op–cit.* p.65; R.Bittard-des-Portes, *op–cit.* pp.248-250; Chassin Vol.V3, p.389.
23. F.Deniau, *op–cit.* Vol.4, p.79 quoting Le Bouvier-Desmortiers.

24. C.L.Chassin, *op-cit.* Vol.V.3, p.395 details these moves.
25. *Ibid.* 391.
26. *Ibid.* pp.398-9.

Chapter 17: The End of the 'War of Giants'

1. F.Deniau, *op-cit.* pp.83-4; Bittard-des-Portes, *op-cit.* pp.257-7 and Mme Rochejaquelein, *op-cit.* pp.433-4.
2. *Ibid.* (Deniau pp.83-4).

Bibliography

Archives

Archives Militaires de la Guerre de la Vendée conserves au Service Historique de la Defense (Vincennes):

-Etats de situation (army situation reports) Series B5/125 Army of the La Rochelle Coast; B5/119-125 Army of the West; B5/125 Army of the Brest Coast; B5/124-125 Combined armies of La Rochelle, West, Brest and Cherbourg.

-Registres Correspondence (Register of Correspondence) for the Armies of the Interior, Reserve, La Rochelle Coast, Brest Coast and Cherbourg: Series B5/3; B5/4-6; B5/14-16 and B5/20.

-Commission et Tribunaux militaires, series B1/329, B1/335, B1/336 and B1/337 to 339

-SHD 1 M 488 - Joseph Dupont, Lieutenant, *Relation de la bataille de Saumur livrée le 9 juin 1793* (1829).

-SHD 1 M 489 *Mémoire du capitaine d'Obenheim sur la Virée de Galerne*, 1815.

-SHD 1 M 491 *Observations sur la guerre de Vendée* par le général Danican.

Archives de la Guerre de la Vendée service aux Archives Nationales:

-Correspondance of the Committee of Public Safety, Representatives of the People (Series AFII).

-Revolutionary Tribunal W7, W27, W121, W285, W305b, W316, W338, W345.

Departmental Archives for the Vendée, Deux-Sevrès, Maine-et-Loire, Loire-Atlantique, Mayenne, Sarthe, Ille-et-Vilaine and Manche.

Published sources

Andress, D: *The Terror, Civil War in the French Revolution* (London:2012).

Artrait, J: *Fontenay-le-Comte sous la Revolution* (CVRH).

Aubertin, Adj-Gen: *Mémoires inédit sur la Guerre de la Vendée 1793-4* (in *Mémoires du Général Hugo* (Paris:1823)).

Augris, F: *Vendéens et Républicains dans la Guerre de Vendée 1793-6* (2 volumes) (Choletais:1993).

Baguenier-Desmoreaux, H: *Kléber en Vendée 1793-1794* (Paris:1907).

Bamfield, V: *Victory of the Vanquished* (Shrewsbury:1990).

Barrucand, V: *La vie veritable de citoyen Jean Rossignol* (Paris:1896).

Beauchamp, A de: *Histoire de la Guerre de Vendée et des Chouans* (3 volumes) (Paris:1806).

Béjarry, A de: *Souvenir Vendéens* (1884 edition, reprinted Yves Salmon 1981).

Billaud, A and d'Herbauges, J: *1793 La Guerre au Bocage Vendéen* (Choletais:1993).

Bittard des Portes, R: *Charette et la Guerre de la Vendée 1763-1796* (Paris:1902).

Blanchez, R: *Bonchamps et l'Insurrection Vendéene 1760-1793* (Paris:1902).

Bouëre, Comtesse de la: *La Vendée Angevine 1793-6 Souvenirs de la Guerre de la Vendée* (Paris:1890).

Boutillier de la Saint-André: *Memoires d'un Père a ses enfants 1793-96* (Paris:1896).

Brégeon, J.J: *Carrier et la Terreur Nantaise* (Perrin:2016).

Brégeon, J.J. and Guicheteau, G: *Nouvelle histoire des guerres de Vendée* (Perrin:2017).

Bruneau, J and Pageot, J: *Vendée Militaire 1793-1796* (Pierre Gauthier:1980).

Calvet, S: Cambronne: *La Légende de Waterloo* (Vendémiaire:2016).

Carrier, C.H: *Correspondance of Jean-Baptiste Carrier* (London:1920).

Chabot, F: *Henri de la Rochejaquelein Generalissime des Armées Catholique et Royale 1772-1794* (1889).

Chabot, F: *Un Canton du Bocage Vendéen. Souvenirs de la Grande Guerre* (Melle:1891).

Championnière, Lucas de la: *Mémoires d'un officer Vendéen 1793-96* (Reprint Cholet).

Chardon, H: *Les Vendéens dans la Sarthe* (3 Vols) (Le Mans:1869).

Charpentier, F: *D'Elbée 1752-1794 Généralissime des Armées Vendéenes* (1905, Cholet:2006).

Chassin, C.L: *La Preparation de la Guerre de Vendée; La Vendée Patriote; Les Pacification de l'Ouest 1794-1815* (Mayenne:1973).

Chiappe, J-F: *La Vendée en Armes. Les Chouans* (Perrin:1982).

Coubard, C: *La Guerre de la Vendée. Cholet 1793-4* (Choletais:1992).

Coutau-Bégarie, H & Doré-Graslin, C (editors): *Histoire Militaire des Guerres de Vendée* (Paris:2010).

Crépin, A: *Révolution et Armée nouvelle en Seine-et-Marne 1791-1797* (CTHS:2008).

Crétineau-Joly, J: *Histoire de la Vendée Militaire* (5 volumes) (1895).

Crossfinte, J.M, *Les Guerres de l'Ouest 1793-6: Le Costume du Combatants Vendéen* (Niort:1986), and *Les Drapeau Vendéen* (Niort:1988).

Danican, A: *Les brigands démasqués* (London:1796).

Deniau, F: *Histoire de la Guerre de la Vendée* (6 volumes) (1878: Reprint Cholet:2004).

Detaille, E: *L'Armée Française. An illustrated History of the French Army 1790-1885* (Waxtel & Hasenauer:1992).

Doré-Graslin, P: *Journal de la Guerre des Géants 1793-1801* (Cholet:1992).

Doyle, W: *The Oxford History of the French Revolution* (Oxford:1989).

Dumarcet, L: *Francoise Athanase Charette de la Contrie Une histoire veritable* (Paris:1977).

Elting, J.R: *Napoleonic Uniforms Volume 1* (Greenhill:2007).

Favier, F: *Berthier l'ombre de Napoléon* (Perrin:2015).

Fillon, B: *Les Vendéens à Fontenay* (Fontenay:1847).

Fruchard, L: *Les Quatre Guerres à Chatillon-sur-Sèvre* (Choletais:1992).

Funcken, L and F: *Uniformes et Armes, les Soldats de la Revolution Française* (Casterman:1988).

Gabory, E: *Les Guerres de Vendée* (R. Laffort edition:1989)

Gallaher, J.G: *The Iron Marshal: A Biography of Louis N. Davout* (London Greenhill Books:2000)

Genlis, La Comtesse de (ed): *Mémoires de Madame la Marquise de Bonchamps sur la Vendée* (Paris:1823).

Gérard, A: *'Par principle d'humanité' La Terreur et la Vendée* (Fayard:1999).

Gérard, A and Heckmann, T: *Les oubliés de la guerre de Vendée* (Soc d'Emulation de la Vendée:1992).

Grall, J: *Girondins et Montagnards les dessous d'une insurrection 1793* (Soc. FeniXX:2015)

Gréau, P: *La marche sanglante des Vendéens, La Virée de Galerne* (Cholet:2012).

Gréau, P: *26 Octobre 1793. La Bataille d'Entrammes* (Laval:2007).

Grouchy, Marquis de: *Mémoires du Maréchal de Grouchy*. Volume 1 (Paris:1873).

Gueriff, F: *La Bataille de Savenay dans la Révolution* (J.M. Pierre:1988).

Guézengar, A: 1793 *Saint-Florent-le Vieil* (St-Florent:1993).

Guin, Y: *La Bataille de Nantes 29 Juin 1793* (Laval:1993).

Haythornthwaite, P: *Uniforms of the French Revolutionary Wars 1789-1802* (Blandford:1981).

Hilard, S: *Marigny et la mémoire assassinée* (Choletais:1998).

Hussenet, J (editor): *Détruisez la Vendée!* (CVRH:2007).

Jamaux, A: *Les Batailles de Dol, de Pontorson à Antrain Nov 1793* (self-published).

Jouineau, A & Mongin, J.M: *French Hussars Volume 1 Ancien Régime à l'Empire* (Histoire et Collections).

Lefebvre, G: *The French Revolution 1793-1799* (London:1964).

Lemas, T: *Le District de Fougères pendant les Guerres de l'Ouest et de la Chouannerie 1793-1800* (Rennes:1994).

Le Menuet de la Jugannière, P: *Campaign d'Outre-Loire de l'Armée Vendéene 1793* (1900).

Letrin, L and Mongin, J.M: *Officers and Soldiers de l'Artillerie, Le System Grèbeauval. Volumes 1 to 3 1786-1815; Chasseurs à Cheval Volume 1: 1779-1800; Dragoons* (Histoire et Collections).

Lévy, A: *Les Batailles du Mans* (Bordessoules:1993).

L'Hostis, F: *Les-Ponts-de-Cé, une ville à feu et à sang 1793-6* (Choletais:1995).

Lynn, J.A: *The Bayonets of the Republic. Motivation and Tactics in the Army of Revolutionary France, 1791-4* (Westview:1996).

Madame de la Rochejaquelein. *Mémoires* (1877)

Manuscrits de Collinet 1788-1804. Les Sables et la Guerre de Vendée (La Roche-sur-Yon:2003)

Mercier, P: *Piron de la Varenne* (Paris:1938).

Mercier du Rocher, A: *Memoires pour server a l'histoire de la Guerre de Vendée* (Yves Salmon:1989).

Ministère de la Guerre. *Histoire des Corps de Troupe de l'Armée Françoise 1569-1900* (Paris:1900).

Muret, T: *Vie Populaire de Cathelineau* (Paris:1845).

Nougaret, R: *Kléber: Memoires politique et militaires 1793-1794.* (Tallandier:1989).

Perracheau, A: *Jean-Baptiste Joly* (Le Circle d'Or:1986).

Pigeard, A: *Les Étoiles de Napoléon. Maréchaux, Amiraux, Géneraux 1792-1815* (Quatuor:1996).

Poirier-de-Beauvais. *Mémoires sur la Guerre de la Vendée* (March:1893).

Pontavice, G du: *Les Armées Catholique et Royale au Nord de la Loire* (Yves Salmon:1989).

Revue de Souvenir Vendéen (various).

Rostu, L du: *Histoire extérieure et maritime des Guerres de Vendée* (Le Circle d'Or:1987).

Rousset, C: *Les Volontaires 1791-1794* (Paris:1874).

Saint-Pierre, M de: *Memoires de Charette, Chevalier du Roi* (Paris:1977).

Sapinaud de Bois-Huguet, M: *Mémoires de Madame de Sapinaud sur la Vendée* (Paris:1824).

Savary, J.J: *Guerres des Vendéens et des Chouans contre le République Française.* Volumes 1-4 (1827).

Secher, R: *La Vendée-Vengé. La genocide franco-français* (Perrin:2006).

Servian, H: *Petite Histoire des Guerres de Vendée* (Chiré:1981).

Sinsoilliez, R: *La Siège de Granville* (L'Ancre de Marine:2004).

Soboul, A: *Dictionnaire historique de la Révolution Française* (Paris:1989).

Soboul, A: *The French Revolution 1787-1799* (New York:1975).

Souvenir Vendéen: *La Bataille de Cholet* (Cholet:2014).

Stofflet, E: *Stofflet et la Vendée 1753-1796* (Cholet reprint).

Taylor, I.A: *The Tragedy of an Army: The Vendée in 1793* (London:1913).

Thompson, J.M: *The French Revolution* (Oxford:1966).

Tulard, J (editor): *La Contre-Revolution* (Perrin:1990).

Turreau, Général: *Mémoires pour server a l'histoire de la Guerre de la Vendée* (Paris:1824).

Valin, C: *Le Rochelle-La Vendée 1793* (Paris:1997).

Ventaron, J.S. de: *Jacques Cathelineau* (Lenore-Sorlot:1988).

Williaume, R: *Luçon dans le Guerre de Vendée* (CVRH:2009).

Index

Note for index: Vendéen or Republican officers are references as (Ven) or (Rep) after their respective entries.